★★★★ Praise For Previous Editions ★★★★

"AN EXCELLENT, NO-NONSENSE HANDBOOK . . . This timely and comprehensive career guide offers predictions on job and economic trends for the next decade—and how to act on them . . . An excellent, no-nonsense handbook that presents information in an accessible fashion"

—ALA Booklist

"A TRULY IMPRESSIVE BOOK . . . filled with advice on how to spot jobs of tomorrow, how to best determine your capabilities, how to communicate your qualifications, and even has an unusual section on how to evaluate the kinds of communities in which you might most like to live."

—Career Opportunities News

"THE BOOK IS OUTSTANDING . . . a thorough treatment of the U.S. economy and its trends and employment . . . Areas that have been covered in many other books are covered in this one with characteristic thoroughness."

—Small Press Book Review

"THE PERFECT CHOICE . . . is future-oriented in its approach; dedicated to helping individuals prosper in transitional job environments . . . the real value lies in discussions of future job situations which may demand new skills and even relocation. Readers anticipating change will find this goes beyond the more casual job search titles."

—The Midwest Book Review

"AN EXTRAORDINARY BOOK . . . one of the most comprehensive and thorough books available."

—The Search Bulletin

"ONE OF THE VERY BEST all purpose tool kits available for job search and career management."

—CAREERPLUS

Change Your Job, Change Your Life

Books and CD-ROMs by Ronald L. Krannich

101 Dynamite Answers to Interview Questions
201 Dynamite Job Search Letters
The Almanac of International Jobs and Careers
Best Jobs For the 1990s and Into the 21st Century
Change Your Job, Change Your Life
The Complete Guide to International Jobs and Careers
The Complete Guide to Public Employment
The Directory of Federal Jobs and Employers
Discover the Best Jobs For You!
Dynamite Cover Letters
Dynamite Networking For Dynamite Jobs
Dynamite Resumes
Dynamite Salary Negotiations
Dynamite Tele-Search
The Educator's Guide to Alternative Jobs and Careers
Find a Federal Job Fast!
From Air Force Blue to Corporate Gray
From Army Green to Corporate Gray
From Navy Blue to Corporate Gray
High Impact Resumes and Letters
Interview For Success
Job-Power Source CD-ROM
Jobs and Careers With Nonprofit Organizations
Jobs for People Who Love Travel
Mayors and Managers
Moving Out of Education
Moving Out of Government
The Politics of Family Planning Policy
Re-Careering in Turbulent Times
Resumes and Cover Letters For Transitioning Military Personnel
Shopping and Traveling in Exotic Asia
Shopping in Exotic Places
Shopping the Exotic South Pacific
Treasures and Pleasures of Australia
Treasures and Pleasures of China
Treasures and Pleasures of Hong Kong
Treasures and Pleasures of India
Treasures and Pleasures of Indonesia
Treasures and Pleasures of Italy
Treasures and Pleasures of Morocco
Treasures and Pleasures of Paris and the French Riviera
Treasures and Pleasures of Singapore and Malaysia
Treasures and Pleasures of Thailand
Treasures and Pleasures of the Philippines
Ultimate Job Source CD-ROM

CHANGE YOUR JOB, CHANGE YOUR LIFE

High Impact Strategies For Finding Great Jobs Into the 21st Century

Sixth Edition

Ronald L.Krannich, Ph.D.

IMPACT PUBLICATIONS
Manassas Park, VA

❖ CHANGE YOUR JOB, CHANGE YOUR LIFE ❖
**High Impact Strategies For Finding Great
Jobs Into the 21st Century**

Sixth Edition

Copyright © 1989, 1991, 1993, 1994, 1995, 1997 by Ronald L. Krannich

Library of Congress Cataloging-in-Publication Data

Krannich, Ronald L.
     Change your job, change your life: high impact strategies for finding great jobs into the 21st century / Ronald L. Krannich.—6th ed.
          p. cm.
     Rev. ed. of: Careering and re-careering for the 1990's. 3rd ed. c1993.
     Includes bibliographical references and index.
     ISBN 1-57023-066-8 (alk. paper)
     1. Vocational guidance—United States. 2. Career development—United States. 3. Career changes—United States. I. Krannich, Ronald L. Careering and re-careering for the 1990's. III. Title.
HF5382.5.U5K69   1997
650.14—dc20   96-36772
                                                                              CIP

For information on distribution or quantity discount rates, call 703/361-7300 or write to: Sales Department, IMPACT PUBLICATIONS, 9104-N Manassas Drive, Manassas Park, VA 20111-2366, Tel. 703/361-7300, Fax 703/335-9486 or e-mail: impactp@impactpublications.com. Distributed to the trade by National Book Network, 4720 Boston Way, Suite A, Lanham, MD 20706, Tel. 301/459-8696.

Contents

Preface xi

CHAPTER 1: Take Charge of Your Career and Your Life 1

- The Power of Choice, the Promise of Persistence 1
- Welcome to the Rest of Your Life 1
- Shape Your Future 2
- Beyond "Getting" 2
- Examine the Evidence 3
- Empower Yourself 4
- Organize and Discipline Your Thinking 5
- Select the Right Resources 6
- Redirect Your Life 7

Part I
PREPARE FOR TURBULENCE AND NEW OPPORTUNITIES

CHAPTER 2: Get Ready For the Future 11

- Work and Meaningful Lifestyles 11
- Prepare for Life in a Boom and Bust Economy 12
- Understand Employment Dynamics in a Dual Society 15
- Face Increased Structural Unemployment 18
- Take Initiative in a Fundamentally Flawed System 19
- Predict and Prepare For an Uncertain Future 20
- Beware of Incomplete Approaches 23
- Career and Re-Career For Today and Tomorrow 26
- Approach the Subject Differently 27
- Achieve Results 27

CHAPTER 3: Prepare For New Career Challenges 29

- Images of the Future 29
- Turn Turbulence Into New Opportunities 29
- Face New Demographics 30
- Experience the Impact of New Technologies 34
- Prepare For 33 Coming Changes 37
- Be Realistic 51

CHAPTER 4: Identify the Jobs of Tomorrow 53

- Beware of Changing Occupational Profiles 53
- Expect Job Growth in Most Occupations
  and For Most Groups 55
- Examine Growing and Declining Occupations 60
- Determine "The Best" Job For You 63
- Look For Exciting New Occupations in the 21st Century 65
- Consider the Implications of Future Trends For You 66

CHAPTER 5: Acquire Skills Appropriate For Today's Economy 68

- Skills Imbalance 68
- On Your Own in a Sea of Good Intentions 69
- Train and Retrain For an Uncertain Future 71
- Question Public Education Performance 72
- Learn More About Private Efforts 73
- Become a Generalist-Specialist 74
- Identify Your Major Training Options 75
- Become an Informed Consumer 79
- Know How to Finance Your Future 82
- Compare Costs and Performance Options 83
- Beware of Myths 84

CHAPTER 6: Myths, Realities, and Planning Your Success 85

- Identify the Prerequisites to Success 85
- Understand Key Myths and Realities 86
- Find Jobs and Change Careers 99
- Understand the Career Development Process 100
- Organize and Sequence Your Job Search 103
- Test Your Careering Competencies 104

- Seek Professional Assistance When Necessary 107
- Options 107
- Alternative Services 108
- Choose the Best 113
- When in Doubt, Take Action 113
- Use Time Wisely 114
- Plan to Take Action 118
- Strategies For Success 118
- Take Risks and Handle Rejections 122
- Form a Support Group 123

Part II
DEVELOP POWERFUL CAREERING
AND RE-CAREERING SKILLS

CHAPTER 7: Identify Your Skills and Abilities 129

- Identify Your Skills 129
- Types of Skills 130
- Your Strengths 131
- Ask the Right Questions 131
- Functional/Transferable Skills 132
- Identify Your Skills 135
- Checklist Method 136
- Skills Map 136
- Autobiography of Accomplishments 136
- Computerized Assessment Systems 137

CHAPTER 8: Specify Your Interests and Values 138

- Vocational Interests 138
- Work Values 143
- Computerized Systems 148
- Your Future as Objectives 148

CHAPTER 9: Know Your Motivated Skills and Abilities (MAS) 149

- What's Your MAS? 149
- The Skills Map 150
- Autobiography of Accomplishments 151
- Motivated Skills Exercise 151
- Other Alternatives 156

- Benefit From Redundancy 158
- Bridging Your Past and Future 158

CHAPTER 10: Develop a Realistic Objective 160

- Goals and Objectives 160
- Examine Your Past, Present, and Future 161
- Orient Yourself to Employers' Needs 161
- Be Purposeful and Realistic 162
- Project Yourself Into the Future 163
- State a Functional Objective 177

CHAPTER 11: Produce Effective Resumes and Letters 181

- Communicating Positive Images 181
- Writing Resumes 181
- Ineffective Resumes 182
- Types of Resumes 183
- Structuring Resume Content 184
- Producing Drafts 185
- Evaluating the Final Product 186
- Final Production 187
- Job Search Letters 188
- Basic Preparation Rules 189
- Types of Letters 190
- Distribution and Management 191
- Responding to Classified Ads 192
- Self-Initiated Methods 193
- Electronic Resume Databases 193
- Recordkeeping 194

CHAPTER 12: Research Alternative Jobs and Communities 209

- Research Purposes 209
- Investigate Alternative Jobs and Careers 210
- Target Organizations 214
- Contact Individuals 215
- Ask the Right Questions 216
- Identify the Right Community 218
- Know What's Important 221

CHAPTER 13: Network For Information, Advice, and Referrals .. 222

- Focus on Getting Interviews 222
- Prospecting and Networking 222
- Communicate Your Qualifications 223
- Develop Networks 225
- Prospect For Leads 227
- Handle and Minimize Rejections 228
- Be Honest and Sincere 229
- Practice the 5R's of Informational Interviewing 229
- Approach Key People 230
- Conduct the Interview Well 232
- Telephone For Job Leads 234
- Use Job Clubs and Support Groups 236
- Explore Electronic Networking 237

CHAPTER 14: Interview For Job Offers 239

- Interviewing For the Job 239
- Communication 240
- Answering Questions 240
- Handle Objections and Negatives With Ease 243
- Encountering Behavior-Based Interviews and Questions 247
- Illegal Questions 249
- Asking Questions 250
- Dress Appropriately 251
- Appear Likable 255
- Close the Interview 256
- Remember to Follow-Up 257

CHAPTER 15: Negotiate Salary, Benefits, and Your Future 258

- Approach Salaries as Negotiable 258
- Look to Your Financial Future 259
- Prepare for the Salary Question 259
- Keep Salary Issues to the Very End 259
- Handle the Salary Question With Tact 260
- Reach Common Ground and Agreement 262
- Treat Benefits as Standard 263
- Offer a Renegotiation Option 264
- Take Time Before Accepting 264
- Translate Your Value Into Productivity For Others 266

Part III
CREATE YOUR OWN OPPORTUNITIES

CHAPTER 16: Advance Your Career 269

- Take More Positive Actions 269
- Be Alert to Changing Job Requirements 270
- Beware of Office Politics 270
- Conduct an Annual Career Check-Up 271
- Use Job-Keeping and Advancement Strategies 272
- Assess and Change When Necessary 274
- Revitalize Your Job 275
- Prepare For Change 276

CHAPTER 17: Find Your Ideal Place to Live and Work 277

- Relocate to Career and Re-Career 277
- Target Communities 278
- Know the Growing States and Communities 280
- Consider the Best Places to Work 291
- Find the Best Place to Live 292
- Seek Out the Best Employers 294
- Look For Solid Metro Areas 297
- Select a Location Properly 299
- Consider Your Financial Costs 300
- Conduct a Long-Distance Job Search 303
- Penetrate the Local Job Market 305
- Identify Opportunity Structures 307

CHAPTER 18: Start Your Own Business 311

- Consider Your Alternatives 311
- Examine Risks and Motivations 312
- Possess the Right Strengths For Success 314
- Know Yourself 314
- Look For New Opportunities 316
- Prepare the Basics 316
- Get Useful Advice 318
- Continue Your Success 319

Part IV
GET STARTED IN THE RIGHT DIRECTION

CHAPTER 19: Take Action to Implement Your Goals 323

- Welcome Rejections as Learning Opportunities 324
- Get Motivated and Work Hard 324
- Find Time 325
- Commit Yourself in Writing 325
- Career and Re-Career For Your Future 328

CHAPTER 20: Use the Right Resources 330

- Types of Resources 330
- Choose What's Best For You 331
- What You Get 331
- Process and Strategy Skills 332
- Specific Employment Fields 336
- Specialized Career Groups 337
- Bibliography 338

CHAPTER 21: Join the Electronic Revolution 347

- Creating "Software Sensitive" Resumes 347
- New Resume Initiatives 348
- Where Is the Revolution? 351
- Job Hunting That Never Stops 352
- Who Are the New Revolutionaries? 353
- Resume Databases 354
- Online Services 356
- The Internet's World Wide Web 358
- Other Electronic Networks 360
- Key Electronic Job Search Resources 361
- Beware of the Lazy Way to Job Search Success 362
- Conduct a Dynamite Job Search 363

The Author **364**

Index **365**

Career Resources **371**

Preface

Forget all the trendy theories about the end of inflation, unemployment, and jobs. Let's deal with reality. Since jobs change, so must you. Today's economy continues to transform the nature of work and the workplace with lightning speed. The skills you acquired recently may soon become obsolete. Not surprising, the job you hold today may disappear tomorrow. One thing is certain: we live in a highly volatile economy where jobs are constantly created and destroyed in response to the changing nature of the economy. If left to the winds of change, your future will be very uncertain. The job you possess today will not be the one you possess five years from now. And the job you'll have in five years may pay less than the one you have today.

What, then, should you do in the face of such an uncertain job future? Are you prepared to take fundamental control of your life?

It's okay to do it—change your job. However, you'll need some practice for handling the challenging job markets of the 21st century.

If you feel your job is a life sentence, if you dread going to work, if you think you're inadequately compensated, or if you're not doing what you really love to do, consider changing your job—and your life. You'll never regret having taken a risk to create a better life for you and those around you.

I know, because I and millions of others have successfully careered and re-careered. Thousands of others do so each year. We've discovered the secrets to changing our lives by changing our jobs.

Where are you going with the rest of your life? Do you have the power to shape your future and change your life, or do you feel powerless—a passive recipient of changes initiated by others?

If you want to change your life, you first must possess the power to change your job and your career direction. For the power to change jobs and chart new careers is also the power to potentially change your life.

Whether you are starting your first job or changing jobs or careers, you're joining millions of other people who redefine their lives by changing what they do. Possessing this power to change is one of the most important assets for determining what you will do with the rest of your life.

Change your job and you'll probably change your life too! Never has this dictum been truer than in today's economy. The job you occupy today will most likely be radically different from the one you will perform ten or twenty years from now. Like it or not, you *will* pursue careers that never existed ten or twenty years ago. You will probably seek jobs and careers that are most comparable with your worklife goals. When given the choice, you will change jobs because you want to change your life. If you're smart about your future, you will pursue jobs fit for you rather than try to fit your interests and skills into existing jobs.

While many successful people acknowledge a mixture of serendipity, excellent connections, sound planning, and smart decisions for their career fortunes, few people are lucky enough to see their career and lifestyle dreams come true. Buffeted by the winds of change, many people feel they lack the power to shape their lives. Indeed, most people fall into jobs by chance, fail to examine many job and career alternatives suitable for their interests and skills, and pursue careers that are less than fully rewarding. After a few years of work experience, they wish they had better planned their careers as well as their lives. But by then many feel it is too late to make fundamental changes in their career direction. Their jobs lock them into particular lifestyles which appear increasingly difficult to change. Facing the realities of family, home ownership, mortgages, and the high cost of daily living, they either don't dream or they feel limited in their ability to make their dreams come true by taking the risks necessary for changing jobs and careers. Like millions of others, they feel stuck in what appears to be a career rut. Only if they lost their present job would they be forced into making some major changes in how they approach the world of work and their lives.

If you are not doing what you really love to do, if you're unsure what you might do better, if you are interested in exploring new career possibilities, or if you are interested in creating a worklife that is compatible with a desirable lifestyle, then this book is for you. If followed closely, it will help you give renewed direction to your career as well as chart a clear course for doing what you really want to do with the rest of your life.

This book is all about how to better experience serendipity, plan your career, and make intelligent job moves in the challenging economy and job markets of the 1990s and beyond. It's a very different book for individuals interested in finding jobs and planning their futures. Unlike other career books, this one focuses on the *processes* of careering and re-careering within the *context* of an economy and society undergoing fundamental restructuring. Given this context, job search skills alone are not enough for long-term job and career success. Individuals must learn to career and re-career several times during their work lives. This means continuously acquiring new work-content skills, making strategic career moves, and relocating to communities which offer better job and career opportunities.

With vision, determination, and a well organized plan of action, you should do well in finding rewarding jobs and careers in the 1990s and beyond. But if you lack the necessary knowledge, skills, and motivation, you could well repeat past patterns as well as find yourself in a deadend job which offers few rewards and a less than promising future.

This new edition reflects several changes taking place in the job market during the second half of the 1990s. While we expect the next few years to be another boom and bust period for the American economy and thus the job market, the first half of the 1990s has been a tough time for millions of Americans. Although unemployment dropped to a low of 5.4 percent at the beginning of 1995 (down from 6.5 percent in 1994) and continued to fall to 5.2 percent at the beginning of 1997, income and wage growth remained very low. Indeed, with nearly 7 million people unemployed and with millions of others experiencing income and wage declines, careering and re-careering are even more important today than ever before.

If you are unemployed or about to experience a major career transition, this may be the best time to seriously consider acquiring new skills and relocating to communities offering more promising job and career opportunities. For what will certainly emerge in the decade ahead is a restructured job market in which the best jobs go to those who have the requisite education, training, and retraining capabilities demanded by employers in the new and rapidly changing job market. The worst jobs— those offering limited opportunities for career advancement and few financial

> **No one is responsible for giving you a job nor keeping you on the job indefinitely.**

rewards—will go to those who fail to take initiative to acquire the necessary education, training, and retraining to get ahead in this job market.

One thing has not changed in this new edition—my underlying philosophy in writing this book. It's very simple, real, and achievable: you are responsible for your own employment fate in a capitalistic and entrepreneurial economy. And you must become even more responsible for your employment in the decade ahead, a revolutionary period of major economic restructuring both at home and abroad. No one is responsible for giving you a job nor keeping you on the job indefinitely. While the government operates many different employment programs, these are primarily designed for the poor and hard core unemployed who lack basic work skills. They help train people for an uncertain and unpredictable job market affected by a larger, yet equally uncertain and unpredictable, economy which is responsible for both creating and destroying jobs. On the other hand, employers spend over $200 billion each year on training and retraining programs for ensuring a competent and competitive work force.

You should put your employment fate in your own hands by learning how to operate in the job markets of today and tomorrow. In other words, my philosophy is one of individual responsibility, decentralization, and empowerment—empower yourself to make things happen your way rather than in response to the wishes and whims of others as well as the boom and bust cycles of the economy. Today's 7 million unemployed merely testify to the validity of this philosophy. Many wish they had taken better care of their jobs and careers prior to receiving the shocking news that they were dismissed. And millions of others seek better paying jobs.

While I focus primarily on the individual, I'm also keenly aware of the importance of other forces and actors affecting jobs and careers. Consequently, the first part of this book places the individual within the larger context of today's changing economy. There I analyze the present economy and employment situation as well as identify trends and make predictions for the future that have particular relevance for individuals. For the remaining 80 percent of the book, I return to you, the individual, who must operate within this larger organizational and societal context.

I again wish to thank my many readers, from book reviewers and career counselors to students, professionals, and job seekers, who found the first five editions of this book well organized, enlightening, realistic, practical, and both useful and usable. Their many letters and phone calls have helped further strengthen this present edition.

Special thanks goes to Caryl Rae Krannich, who encouraged me to take on the subject, provided invaluable suggestions, wrote most of the section on interviewing, and spent numerous hours editing the manuscript. Her sense of form, style, and quality are found throughout the book. My frequent reference to "we" indicates our joint effort and ongoing partnership.

We wish you well as you navigate your career through this exciting and challenging decade. If you put into practice much of the advice found in the following chapters, you will begin reshaping your career—and your life—in the direction of your major interests, skills, and goals. Most important, you will be able to make critical job and career changes when necessary, despite the state of the economy or what others may tell you to the contrary. You will be able to do what we hope you will now do best—take charge of your own future. You can change your life because you have the power to change your job!

Ronald L. Krannich

Change Your Job, Change Your Life

1

Take Charge of Your Career
... and Your Life

Where do you want to go with the rest of your life? Is your career or job the center of your life, or do you work so you can have a fulfilling life? Are you doing what you really love to do or are there other things you would rather be doing with your life?

A job should not become a life sentence. It should give you the freedom to do what you do well and enjoy doing. It should fit right. A job that doesn't fit right can be miserable. It can make life more difficult than it need be—unless you take action. Changing that job may forever change your life. But you must first acquire the power to make the necessary changes. That's what this book is all about—acquiring the power to change your job, and your life!

The Power of Choice, The Promise of Persistence

Jobs and life need not be difficult if you possess the power of choice and persist in pursuing your goals. Your job should make life easier for you and those around you. You will know if your job is a good fit: it will feel good and be a rewarding experience. You'll enjoy going to work where you can fully use your knowledge, skills, and abilities and be rewarded accordingly.

Since you're reading this book, we assume you're sufficiently motivated to do something about your job and your life. If not, the following pages may help motivate you to take the necessary actions for changing your life.

Welcome to the Rest of Your Life

So you're thinking of taking a major risk—seeking a job or pursuing a new career that may put you on the road to renewed success in the decade ahead.

But what exactly do you want to do with the rest of your life? How will you go about turning your dreams into realities over the next few weeks or

1

months? Do you have goals and hidden talents that could be best directed elsewhere than in your present job or career?

Let's examine these and many other important questions for taking charge of your career today, tomorrow, and into the 21st century. For in answering these questions, you will begin acquiring key skills and using effective strategies for shaping your future in the direction of your dreams.

Shape Your Future

Charting your career future through the power of choice and the promise of persistence is the subject of this book. Not everyone has the luxury of choice. Many people lose their jobs to the winds of economic change or to the whims of organizational politics. Recessions, lay offs, failed businesses, organizational changes, and on-the-job conflicts daily force thousands of people into unemployment lines. Indeed, millions of Americans lose their jobs

> **The future may not be predictable but it is something you can shape for yourself.**

each year. And millions of others quit their jobs for opportunities elsewhere.

Whatever your situation—forced or shaped by choice—the most important decision is how and what you choose to do *now* with your life. If you focus on your future in a disciplined and thoughtful manner—rather than dwell on past negatives or adopt a "can't do" attitude—you will begin turning your dreams into new realities.

The future is something we all would like to better know and control. Most people prefer to plan their future rather than wait to see what tomorrow will bring. But how do you better plan for tomorrow when much of life seems to be beyond one's control?

While the future may not be predictable, it is something you can and should shape for yourself. To do so requires vision, determination, and a well organized plan of action. You must first know where you are at present and then develop a clear vision of where you want to go in the future. But most important of all, you should develop and implement a plan of action for making your dreams come true.

Without an analysis of your present, a vision of the future, and a plan of action, your future will most likely be a repeat performance of your past patterns of behavior. You will be blown by the winds of change and whims of chance rather than direct and control your own destiny.

Beyond "Getting"

This book is all about taking better charge of your future in one of the most important areas of your life—your career. Few people actually plan their lives. Instead, they seem to be buffeted by forces beyond their control.

Usually on the receiving end of life, they are great "getters": they get an education; they get married and get a family; they get a house; they get a job; they get taxed; and they get buried. If they are lucky—as Andy Worhol would have us remember—they may even get famous for 15 minutes sometime during their lives. In the highly speculative 1990s, some even get rich for 15 minutes! While they may plan for some major events in their lives, few people consciously shape their future through deliberate action on an on-going basis.

A career is something you *can* shape if you plan properly and have the requisite motivation and skills and use effective strategies to make it happen. However, the popular notion that all you need to do is get a good education that will lead to a good job and career, after which you live happily ever after, has been eroded in a society that has undergone rapid change in education, training, occupations, and the work place. The *"one job, one career, one work life"* phenomenon has all but ended for most occupations. The *"15 jobs, 5 careers, 10 geographic moves, and many work lives"* phenomenon is now upon us in a new careering and re-careering era. In this era the future becomes synonymous with change. Therefore, you are well advised to anticipate, plan, and manage changes to your advantage.

> The *"one job, one career, one work life"* phenomenon has all but ended for most occupations.

Examine the Evidence

The 1980s was an extremely turbulent and rewarding decade for many American workers. Millions of individuals first entered the rapidly expanding work force. At the same time, millions of these and other workers experienced unemployment brought on by larger structural changes taking place in both the international and domestic economies. Rapid technological changes made many skills increasingly obsolete for the jobs of today and tomorrow. While many of the unemployed expected to return to work once the economy improved, many would not because their skills were no longer appropriate for the job market. Unfortunately, they were not likely to acquire the necessary skills because they failed to take initiative, and neither the public nor private sectors were preparing them for new jobs. In the meantime, high unemployment existed in the midst of major labor shortages.

We are in the midst of a profoundly revolutionary period which will require individuals to career and re-career several times during their work lives. Knowing job search skills alone will be insufficient to function effectively in the rapidly changing job markets of the 1990s and into the 21st century. Job search skills must accompany concrete work-content skills. Individuals must continuously update present skills as well as acquire new skills in order to adjust to changing job market realities.

Empower Yourself

So why write another book on jobs and careers? Because there is a need for an approach to employment that also focuses on the future. Previous approaches have not prepared individuals well for the coming changes in American society. Educational institutions, for example, primarily exist to provide employment for self-actualizing educators rather than to train their clientele—paying students—for specific jobs and careers. Governments mainly provide training programs for the hardcore unemployed—the ones least likely to be trainable or benefit from training. Businesses continue to maximize short-run profits; start-up with venture capital and a vision of reaping huge profits from quickly going public; restructure through mergers rather than innovation; and view training as a luxury or perk to be given primarily to supervisors and managers. And many career advisors still preach an outdated job search doctrine: *"Anyone can find a job if they only know how to find a job."* They train people to develop and use *job search skills* regardless of whether they have marketable *job performance skills*; few provide useful guidance on job relocation.

This book is all about empowerment—better develop your ability to take charge of your future. It is designed to fill the need for an expanded perspective on jobs and careers for the decade ahead. For the problem of jobs, careers, and employment needs to be addressed with the larger future in mind. Many so-called experts tend to "stand where they sit" as well as "major in their own problems." Educators, for example, believe people need to come to them and their institutions for training when, in fact, educational institutions are more often part of the problem rather than the solution, and educators continue to face important employment problems themselves. Politicians and bureaucrats tend to do what they do best—think in narrow policy terms: create another magical government program which they hope "this time" will produce results. Today, they propose "jobs training" and "workfare" programs for the hardcore unemployed and a few displaced workers. Preferring to be at the creation of new policies (photo opps) rather than face the practical problems of translating policies and programs into action, few know how to implement policies and programs at the local level where job creation and training must take place. Tomorrow, they will probably suggest another trickle-down "tax credit incentive program" for the middle and upper classes. And career counselors and futurists seem unprepared to provide practical guidance, especially on relocation, to unemployed workers in the struggling economies of West Virginia, Louisiana, Alaska, New Mexico, California, South Carolina, and Puerto Rico which simply lack enough jobs to go around.

The perspective presented in this book synthesizes important skills training and job search approaches in relation to a society undergoing major social, economic, and political restructuring. This is a "no excuses" book that stresses the importance of individual choices relating to goals, organization, discipline, and sheer tenacity. It places full responsibility for employment on the shoulders of the individual. No one owes anyone a job or career, and few people have valid excuses for not acquiring the education and training necessary to function effectively in today's job market. Therefore, you must be responsible for your own employment fate. You shape your own future by the decisions you made yesterday and make today as well as by those you will make tomorrow. This book is designed to prepare you for turbulent times by providing you with the necessary knowledge to make informed choices about your future.

Organize and Discipline Your Thinking

This book should become a flexible guide to your future which you can use over and over again in the coming years. The twenty chapters that follow move from description and explanation to prediction and prescription. Since chapters are related to one another, it's best to read each section and chapter in sequence. However, you may wish to read them in a different order, or go directly to a few chapters that are of greatest interest to you.

> **No one owes anyone a job or career, and few people have valid excuses for not acquiring the education and training necessary for functioning in today's job market.**

If, for example, you are interested in moving to another community, go directly to Chapter 17 for tips on how to relocate and conduct a long-distance job search. If you are scheduled for a job interview in a few days, examine Chapter 14 on how to conduct an effective interview. And if you are curious about the future, browse through Chapter 3 which examines 33 important changes in the decade ahead.

The book is purposefully designed to be a comprehensive, flexible, and usable guide for readers with different interests and goals. Each part, as well as most chapters, can stand alone in addressing important issues of concern to millions of individuals.

Part I sketches the larger context for individual careering and re-careering skills and strategies in the coming decade. It sets the stage for subsequent how-to chapters by analyzing industries and occupations, explaining the educational and job markets, and predicting future changes in occupations and employment. Taken together, these chapters develop a vision of what the future looks like for careering and re-careering efforts. If read in sequence, this section will help you better understand the how-to strategies and tactics outlined in Parts II and III. But if such contextual descriptions, explanations, analyses, and predictions are of peripheral interest to you, feel free to skip this section and proceed to the remaining chapters that offer practical how-to careering and re-careering advice.

If you are mainly interested in prescriptions for finding a job, then go directly to Chapter 6. This chapter provides an important introduction and transition to the seven how-to chapters in Part II. These practical chapters focus on how to develop and implement an effective job search, from specifying a job objective to writing resumes, networking, conducting research, interviewing, and negotiating salaries.

Part III addresses important careering and re-careering opportunities you can create for yourself, from advancing on the job to relocating to another community or starting your own business. Many readers have found this section most instructive because it includes important career and lifestyle issues normally absent in other career planning and job search books.

Part IV addresses the key issue of implementation. In addition to presenting practical exercises for putting this book into practice, it includes two chapters on the best career resources—from books to electronic job search services—available today. The three chapters in this section function as a bridge between this book and several other useful resources available for assisting you in your careering and re-careering efforts.

Select the Right Resources

We wish you well as you take this journey into an exciting and sometimes confusing world of self-discovery and action. We are primarily concerned with relating key job and career issues to your situations—from understanding the nature of the job market to developing job search skills, acquiring work-content skills, relocating to other communities, and translating this book into action. Many of these issues, which also are job search steps, are outlined in our other books: *Discover the Best Jobs For You!, High Impact Resumes and Letters, Dynamite Resumes, Dynamite Cover Letters, Dynamite Tele-Search, 201 Dynamite Job Search Letters, Interview For Success, 101 Dynamite Answers to Interview Questions, Dynamite Networking For Dynamite Jobs*, and *Dynamite Salary Negotiations*. We also address particular jobs and career fields in the following books: *The Best Jobs For the 1990s and Into the 21st Century, The Complete Guide to Public Employment, The Directory of Federal Jobs and Employers, Find a Federal Job Fast, The Complete Guide to International Jobs and Careers, The Almanac of International Jobs and Careers, Jobs and Careers With Nonprofit Organizations, Jobs For People Who Love Travel*, and *The Educator's Guide to Alternative Jobs and Careers*. While available in many bookstores and libraries, these and many other job search books also are available directly from Impact Publications. For your convenience, you can order them by completing the order form at the end of this book.

Impact Publications also publishes a brochure of additional job and career resources. To receive a free copy of this listing, send a self-addressed stamped envelope (#10 business size) to:

IMPACT PUBLICATIONS
ATTN: Free Resource Listing
9104-N Manassas Drive
Manassas Park, VA 20111-2366

You also may want to visit their World Wide Web site for a complete listing of career resources:

http://www.impactpublications.com.

Their site contains some of the most important career and job finding resources available today, including many titles that are difficult, if not impossible, to find in bookstores and libraries. You will find everything from books on self-assessment, resumes, and cover letters to books on networking, interviewing, government and international jobs, military, women, minorities, entrepreneurs as well as CD-ROM programs, software, and videos. This is

> **This is all about empowerment—you have within you the power to shape your own destiny.**

an excellent resource for keeping in touch with the major resources that can assist you with every stage of your job search and with your future career development plans.

Redirect Your Life

The processes I call careering and re-careering emphasize the need to prepare for an uncertain employment future. It requires linking work-content skills to job search skills and relocation issues within the context of a rapidly changing economy characterized by periodic boom and bust cycles. These economic cycles often witness the fundamental restructuring of businesses, jobs, and the job market.

The chapters that follow are all about empowerment—you have within you the power to shape your own destiny. As such, the remaining twenty chapters reveal how you can redirect your life through new and exciting opportunities in the world of work.

Let me take you on a powerful journey where you will discover how to best turn your dreams into new realities. It's an exciting and challenging journey you won't want to miss!

Part I

PREPARE FOR TURBULENCE AND NEW OPPORTUNITIES

Get Ready For the Future

L et's examine your future to better understand where you are going with your career and your life. You've come a long way, but you still have many years ahead. What exactly are your goals? What do you want to do with the rest of your life? Where do you see your career and lifestyle 5, 10, or 20 years from now? Are your goals realistic given your interests, skills, motivations, and image of the future? What types of jobs and careers will you choose? Will these choices be the right ones for you? How will they affect your lifestyle? How much control do you want over your life? What are you willing to risk in the decade ahead?

Work and Meaningful Lifestyles

The beginnings and ends of decades are times for reflection, assessment, and redirection. The past decade and a half has been a turbulent period for jobs, careers, and lifestyles. The best laid plans were subjected to unprecedented changes as millions of Americans first entered the job market, experienced unemployment, or changed jobs and careers several times. Many people attempted to develop lifestyles in the face of a turbulent economic world where jobs and careers were as unpredictable as the economy.

The first half of the 1990s were equally turbulent. A highly predictable recession took a major toll on businesses and employees alike as more than 12 million Americans joined the unemployment rolls. Millions of others became discouraged and abandoned their job search altogether. A deficit ridden and anemic economy gradually turned around, but it would be a long time before it returned, if ever, to the go-go boom years of the 1980s. In the meantime, millions of jobs were lost forever as the economy underwent major restructuring. Accordingly, millions of individuals were learning to play a new employment game—they would need to career and re-career throughout the 1990s and into the 21st century.

Prepare For Life in a Boom and Bust Economy

The 1980s began with serious economic problems and ended with few promises of improved future performance. These were the best and worst of times, depending on where and how you lived. Unemployment soared to nearly 11% in 1982—the worst since the Great Depression. Yet it fell to less the 6% in 1988, the lowest in 15 years, settled in at a relatively persistent 7.7% in 1992, gradually leveled off to a nagging 6.8% in 1993, and further dipped to 5.2 percent by the beginning of 1997. Trendy theories about the end of inflation, recessions, and boom/bust cycles and the rise of full employment—reminiscent of 1965—began appearing in 1996.

Economic problems in the 1980s baffled the best of minds as the economy underwent major restructuring, millions of individuals experienced unemployment, and the education and political systems remained inert. Inflation and high unemployment during the first half of the 1980s was blamed on a variety of evils, including excessive public spending, the Vietnam War, Wall Street, irresponsible labor unions and corporations, the rich and the poor, liberals, conservatives, Democrats, Republicans, FDR, and the Japanese. Huge deficit spending and major trade imbalances during the 1980s were blamed on similar culprits as trade protectionist sentiments misdiagnosed the long-term nature of America's economic and employment problems. The key problems were *productivity* and *investment in the future* —or the lack thereof—rather than the need to artificially limit competition in order to protect obsolete and inefficient jobs at home.

Although some thinking about employment began to change, most continued to be based upon outmoded theories, short-term approaches, and trendy thinking to stimulate the economy, create jobs, and find employment. A relatively uninnovative educational system, lagging a decade behind the times, remained mired in irrelevant debates about educational theories and approaches. It failed to provide individuals with the skills necessary to function in an emerging 21st century economy. The unemployment insurance system continued to provide short-term income support rather than to invest in the long-term employment future of the unemployed by providing support for relocation, retraining, and job search activities. An antiquated, nonportable insurance-based health care system was responsible for creating "job lock" amongst at least 20% of the workforce; over 25 million workers could not risk changing jobs because they would automatically lose their health benefits. Limited changes to this archaic system finally started in 1996. But the tax code continued to provide few incentives for employers to provide, or workers to seek, retraining. And relatively nonportable pension plans discouraged workers from relocating.

Unfortunately, the public policy system created many of the very evils it was supposed to correct. How could it encourage training, retraining, and job mobility when the education, unemployment compensation, tax, health care, and pension systems were designed for other purposes? No one seemed to understand how such policies continued to work against everyone's best interests except those who operated the current systems, especially educators and insurance companies. Low productivity, disinvestment in the workplace, and limited job mobility would most likely continue until major changes take place in these systems. In the end, many concerned people wondered how could so many smart people create such a dumb system and then blame the evils on others?

The public policy failures of America's checkerboard political system in the 1980s were enormous, and they would most likely continue to plague the economy and employment picture throughout the 1990s and into the 21st century. No one had the political will to substantially slash defense spending, restructure education and training programs, nor cut the great middle and upper-class subsidies, primarily affecting the elderly, that continued to bleed the federal budget—

> **How could so many smart people create such a dumb system and then blame the evils on others?**

Social Security and Medicare entitlement programs. Rather than invest in building human capital, the government continued to cater to special interests and engage in politically symbolic, and safe, reforms—restructure welfare, dismantle affirmative action, and downsize the federal bureaucracy. Its "jobs" rhetoric would not be matched by new and costly policy initiatives for investing in the future.

Despite a great deal of tough public talk, leadership in the 1980s and 1990s failed to develop effective education and training programs to produce long-term employment results. In the meantime, educators continued to manage an education system of questionable quality. Others reconfirmed what they do best—debate educational theories and approaches in meaningless jargon. At the same time, politicians advanced another trendy theory and middle class subsidy—privatizing public education—and developed highly visible policies for the poor with few program successes. Somehow America's relatively nondirected, fragmented, and decentralized economic and political systems were supposed to simultaneously resolve education, employment, and economic problems. The results were otherwise: they wasted human capital rather than invest it for the future.

The end of the 1980s began to close with a booming economy experiencing unprecedented levels of employment. The economy had generated the largest number of new jobs ever in the history of the United States. Indeed, nearly 3 million new jobs were created each year. However, in 1990 it became increasingly evident that the boom of the 1980s was largely built on a highly volatile house of cards—junk bonds; massive government, corporate, and individual debt; and a highly inflated, nonproductive, and speculative real estate market. Accompanying this temporary flight into prosperity was the cumulative yearly litany of millions of unemployed, thousands of business failures, an incredible national deficit hobbled by expensive and nonproductive entitlement programs, and major international dislocations—all threatening to restructure the economic and employment pictures of the 1990s in the direction of the early 1980s, or even worse.

The 1990s began with the unexpected collapse of the Russian Empire, the crumbling of communist regimes and nation-states in Eastern Europe, the ending of the Cold War, the emergence of new armed conflicts in the Middle East, and preparation for an economically unified Europe as the largest consumer market in the world. These changes promised a newly restructured political and economic world order where the U.S. would become the major force shaping the new post-Cold War international political and economic order. How-ever, chaos rather than predictable change and prosperity reigned as the ex-communist states became economic basket cases, new armed conflicts centering on traditional ethnic rivalries emerged in Eastern Europe and Africa, and the economies of the Pacific Rim experienced the greatest growth and promise for the future. European econ-omies within the much hyped new European Union—many with unem-ployment rates exceeding 11 percent—continued to be some of the world's most anemic. The U.S. economy became increasingly internationalized and job growth more dependent on U.S. exports to Asia. In fact, what economic growth took place in the U.S. in the 1990s was largely due to the export of U.S. products and services in a world where the U.S. dollar continued to be eroded in relation to the Japanese yen and the German mark. However, unexpected problems in the Middle East threatened the newly emerging world economic and political order. The U.S. and United Nations' response to continuing crises, coupled with a mounting national debt and the collapse of major financial institutions, helped trigger a recession and a new cycle of unemployment to mark the beginning of the decade. These "unique events" tested important institutions and relationships that would help shape the employment situation throughout the 1990s.

> The public policy failures of America's checkerboard political system in the 1980s and 1990s were enormous, and they would most likely continue to plague the economy and employment picture in the decade ahead.

For many Americans, the 1990s were best approached as another turbulent decade punctuated by boom and bust cycles and a repeat per-formance of public policy failures in education and employment. But by 1997 some economists concluded, based on three years of low inflation and high employment, that the traditional boom/bust economy and its attendant recessions and unemployment cycles were over; the economy had now reached a new steady-state of growth characterized by full employment. However, only the naive and inexperienced could swallow such a theory. Recent experience with a turbulent international environment and "unique events" seemed to be a better guide to the future than this new trendy low inflation theory. Boom and bust seemed to be well and alive and shaping an uncertain future. Indeed, 1997 began with an extremely over-valued stock market that seemed to be on the verge of a major correction, if not a collapse. The 1994-1996 period had witnessed unprecedented speculation in the stock market; a major infusion of venture capital into start-up companies of marginal performance but which managed to quickly go public; and a great deal of hype about high tech industries and elusive business opportunities on the Internet. The bust side of another boom/bust cycle was fast approaching. Economists would soon have to compare this period with similar excesses of the 1980s and early 1990s, when real estate and junk bond speculation drove the memorable boom/bust cycles.

As we move into the 21st century, unemployment over the next decade is likely to fluctuate between five and nine percent. Millions of Americans will enter the job market for the first time; millions of others will experience unemployment; and millions more will change jobs and careers. Assuming continuing inertia in the public sector and political and economic turmoil in an international arena, individuals will face an uncertain future requiring greater initiative to regularly acquire new skills, change jobs and careers, develop greater financial security, and relocate to growing communities.

Public opinion polls toward the end of 1996 noted disturbing new perceptions arising during this decade of change and uncertainty: while unemployment is at an all-time low (5.2 percent) and job changing has not significantly increased during the past decade, perceptions of unemployment and individual job insecurity are at an all-time high. Indeed, millions of Americans actually perceive unemployment to be closer to 25 percent and believe they are very vulnerable to job loss. This gap between objective and subjective reality for individuals has continued to grow throughout the turbulent 1990s. It will likely continue in the decade ahead.

Perceptions are reality for most people. If Americans learned anything about economics and employment in the during the past decade, it was this:

> We live in a highly complex society with an unpredictable and risky market place where even the best laid plans go awry due to numerous changes beyond one's control. Since economic and employment futures are unpredictable, one is well advised to develop flexible job and career strategies for dealing with uncertainty.

At the very least these strategies must address the issues of skills, lifestyles, opportunities, and risk-taking at the most significant level in society—the individual. In other words, you are on your own in a sea of change, so you had better take initiative in shaping and securing your own economic and employment future. No one else, nor trendy theory, will do this for you.

Understand Employment Dynamics in a Dual Society

Employment in the United States is closely tied to an economic restructuring process taking place at the international, national, and local levels.

During the past two decades the United States rapidly moved from a primarily industrial and technological society to one based on high technology, energy, services, and export-oriented manufacturing. It also moved from a credit nation to a debtor nation—fueling the international economy with its high level of spending and consumption but positioning itself for even more vulnerable economic times ahead.

The signs of an economy and job market undergoing major restructuring are especially apparent when examining the paradoxical unemployment/labor shortage problem: high unemployment persists at the same time major labor shortages exist. As millions of Americans become unemployed, millions of jobs also go unfilled at the two extreme ends of the job market: those requiring high level skills and those requiring low level skills. Many unemployed individuals lack the necessary skills to function in a newly emerging post-industrial, high-tech society; refuse to take low-paying service jobs; or do not know how to find a job appropriate for their level of skills and experience. Like the dual societies of Third World countries—one rural/agricultural and another urban/industrial—America is a dual society of a different type.

The dual society in America consists of two sectors. The first and most traditional sector is located mainly in the older urban centers of the Northeast and North Central regions. Known as America's "rust belt" and based largely on manufacturing and related service industries, this sector was characterized by stagnation, decline, and high levels of unemployment and underemployment in the early 1980s. A disproportionate number of poor, unskilled, and displaced people live in these aging communities which also have serious problems with deteriorating infrastructure, excessive welfare burdens, and high costs of living. The state of Michigan led this sector in 1983 with a depressing 18% unemployment rate. Ohio, Illinois, West Virginia, Indiana, and Pennsylvania were not far beyond.

The latter half of the 1980s witnessed a resurgent economy as some of the highest unemployment rates since the Great Depression were replaced by some of the lowest rates recorded in decades. Michigan's 18% unemployment rate, for example, fell below 8%; Illinois and Ohio managed to achieve 7.2% and 6.3% unemployment rates. And Massachusetts—once a troubled state with high unemployment—took the honors with one of the lowest unemployment rates in the country—2.9%—until this so-called "economic miracle" state slid back into high unemployment during the recession of 1990. But these unemployment figures were only low in comparison to historical highs. With more than 10 million Americans unemployed and unproductive each day, the actual numbers of unemployed remained high. The goal of full employment remained elusive.

While unemployment in Michigan, Illinois, Ohio, West Virginia, and Pennsylvania decreased during the later half of the 1980s, many communities in these states, as well as throughout much of the Northeast, remained vulnerable in the boom and bust economy of the 1990s. Economic recovery in these states would take time given continuing plant closures, depressed real estate and financial markets, and the high costs of doing new business. By the mid-1990s, major bright spots were emerging among manufacturing industries in the Midwest, especially near Chicago, that benefitted from increased U.S. exports and the transformation of their "rust belt" industries.

The second sector points us toward a more promising yet unpredictable future. Located mainly in younger suburban areas and in the rapidly grow- ing cities of the West and Southwest, as well as in a few cities in the East, Midwest, and Southeast, this sector is based on high-tech, communication, and service industries requiring a highly educated and skilled work force. In contrast to the first sector, this one is characterized by dynamic growth and relatively high employment. It is populated by a disproportionate number of well educated, skilled, and affluent people. Growth in these communities is mainly constrained by shortages of highly skilled workers and the overall boom and bust nature of the local economies. Communities heavily dependent on the energy and computer industries, such as Houston, Denver, and the Silicon Valley of California, witnessed both high employ- ment and high unemployment in the 1980s as their local economies went bust due to major downturns in the energy and computer industries. Simi- lar patterns have recently occurred in communities heavily dependent upon defense industries, especially in Texas and California, and may occur for so- called "hot" communities in the 1990s —Seattle and Las Vegas. Other more economically diversified communities, such as metropolitan Washington DC,

> **The emerging high-tech and service economy will require individuals with marketable skills who are willing to retrain and relocate when necessary.**

Atlanta, San Diego, and Los Angeles, led the way with strong economic performance throughout the 1980s. Except for temporary economic downturns in 1990-1995—due to a depressed housing market and major cutbacks in defense spending—suburban communities ringing these and many other metropolitan areas will most likely rebound in the near future. More and more individuals will relocate from the first sector into the second sector of America's dual society.

Similar to the 1980s, the most serious economic and employment problems in the 1990s and the beginning of the 21st century will be dispro- portionately felt by the unskilled poor who live in decaying central cities and rural areas. Lacking sufficient education, skills, and work experience as well as access to effective retraining programs and funding mechanisms for relocation and job search activities, the majority of these individuals will continue to live in and burden first sector communities. Their plight is further evidence of the inability and unwillingness of the political system to deal seriously with the pressing issues of productivity and income generation. Time-honored welfare and income support programs, scattered with a few train-the-poor initiatives, remain classic American subsidy approaches to the unemployed and poor. Such approaches have produced few cases of success. New welfare-to-work initiatives begun in 1996 are at best interesting political statements and photo opps about the state of America's troubled welfare system. Solutions to the hard-core unemployment problem remain elusive.

Lest we forget, America is an entrepreneurial skills-based society where individuals market their skills in exchange for money and position. Without the proper skills to function in such a society—or the means to acquire the necessary training, relocation, and job search assistance—many people will remain permanently displaced or take jobs which neither generate adequate income nor promote long-term skills development. The emerging high-tech and service economy in the decade ahead will require individuals with marketable skills who are willing to retrain and relocate when necessary.

Face Increased Structural Unemployment

Much of America's unemployment problem is structural in nature. The economy has entered into a major period of *structural unemployment*. While the normal pattern of unemployment is *cyclical*—people lose their jobs because of temporary business downtowns and then are rehired when business rebounds—structural unemployment has permanent features. Moreover, this type of unemployment has far reaching consequences for the economy, workers, and employment strategies in the 1990s and into the 21st century. It's the type of unemployment associated with popular "downsizing" and "restructuring processes" taking place in both business and government in the 1990s. These processes are closely associated with the application of new technology to the workplace and increased emphasis on worker productivity, decentralized decision-making, and efficient management and networking systems.

Structural unemployment is caused when industries and skills become obsolete due to technological advances. In the past, street sweepers, buggy-whip makers, tailors, and shoemakers became victims of such unemployment. More recently, aerospace scientists and engineers, auto workers, tire makers, steel workers, farm laborers, slide-rule makers, and middle managers have experienced structural unemployment. Like yesterday's buggy-whip maker and shoemaker counterparts, the recent victims must acquire new skills and change careers to become gainfully employed.

Unfortunately, few people are prepared or willing to deal with the changing structure of employment in America. Many unemployed auto and textile workers, for example, still believe their condition is due to cyclical unemployment, with "unfair" Japanese, Taiwanese, Korean, Hong Kong, Chinese, and Mexican competition being the major culprits. They expect to be rehired when the business cycle improves—hopefully brought about through protectionist trade policies. While union leaders have begun to recognize the significance of structural unemployment by negotiating for more job security, give-backs, and retraining programs for their members, management introduces the latest industrial robot technology as well as total quality management (TQM) systems in a continuing effort to improve the productivity and competitiveness of the American auto industry. During the 1980s the major American automakers spent billions of dollars to modernize their production lines with robot technology as well as introduce new and more productive management systems. The end result of such modernization would be to permanently displace workers—from the assembly line to the boardroom—throughout the 1990s. Such displaced workers must acquire new skills and find new jobs and careers if they are to survive and prosper in the job markets of tomorrow.

Following a pattern developing in the 1980s, the 1990s and the early 21st century will be a period of accelerated structural unemployment. The dual issues of productivity and competitiveness tied to an increasingly internationalized economy and a newly shaping world political order are forcing corporate America to apply the latest cost-saving technology to the work place. Protectionist labor unions are correct in their analysis of the problem: increases in productivity displace high-cost labor which, in turn, erode union membership. But at the same time, more than 1.5 million new jobs are created each year to absorb many of the structurally unemployed. And without industry's ability to remain competitive in a global marketplace, those jobs and the businesses will both be lost.

The major issue for the 1990s and the beginning of the 21st century began in the 1980s: how to retrain and relocate an increasing number of structurally unemployed individuals in a relatively unplanned and unpredictable economy subject to a highly volatile international arena that is likely to make and break millions of jobs. Assuming continuing public policy failures to deal with economic and employment problems, individuals in the decade ahead must develop their own strategies for navigating their careers in the boom and bust economy of the early 21st century.

Take Initiative in a Fundamentally Flawed System

Some experts estimate that somewhere between 50 and 75 percent of American factory workers will be displaced by robots by the end of this century! Millions of others will be displaced by more efficient and effective management, networking, and communication systems. Contrary to popular perception of an American manufacturing sector in decline, manufacturing has strengthened itself through the application of new technology which displaces factory workers. Beginning in the 1950s and further accelerating today, the real source of new jobs is found in the rapidly growing service sector, especially in health care, food service, and retail sales.

But few people, especially displaced workers facing structural unemployment, are taking the initiative to provide or acquire the necessary skills training and retraining—and for good reasons. The tax, unemployment insurance, health care, and pension systems were designed for a different era when structural unemployment was not a major issue. Such systems have yet to adjust to the employment realities of a profoundly different society of the 1990s which is based upon high technology and service industries and which experiences a high level of structural unemployment.

The tax, unemployment insurance, health care, and pension systems provide few incentives for retraining, relocation, and job search. Few employers, for example, are given tax incentives to retrain or outplace displaced workers. The unemployment insurance system is designed to give temporary income support for individuals facing cyclical unemployment. It does little to encourage the structurally unemployed to seek retraining, develop job search skills, or relocate. And the limited portability of most health care and pension systems discourages individuals from changing jobs and relocating.

As structural unemployment becomes more pervasive in the decade ahead, the problem of what to do with millions of unemployed workers with little education and obsolete skills may become a national crisis. Some analysts believe a major national training and retraining program, which goes far beyond the limited scope of the Jobs Training Partnership Act (JTPA), is desperately needed. Others see this as naive and nearly impossible to implement given the highly decentralized and fragmented nature of policy-making and implementation in America.

> **The tax, unemployment insurance, health care, and pension systems were designed for a different era when structural unemployment was not a major issue.**

What will displaced workers do—many of whom are highly skilled in older technologies? What actions can be taken now, and by whom, to make a positive transition to the job market of the high-tech and service society?

We believe the answers to these questions primarily lie with the *individual* rather than with government or corporations. Indeed, one of our major purposes in writing this book is to urge you to become *self-reliant and effective* in dealing with the job markets of today and tomorrow. While government and the private sector may provide incentives and opportunities as well as a few limited-scale programs, the individual ultimately must be responsible for his or her own employment fate. We assume that both government and the private sector will be slow in responding to the obvious retraining, relocation, and job search needs of individuals and society. In the meantime, a serious national employment and economic development crisis is brewing, and many people are being hurt by public and private sector inaction. Individuals, therefore, must take their own initiative to acquire the necessary skills for success in the job markets of today and tomorrow.

Predict and Prepare For an Uncertain Future

We see seven major developments in the decade ahead which will have important implications for the employment futures of most Americans:

PREDICTION 1: **The restructuring of the world political and economic order creates new opportunities and challenges for jobs relating to a more export-oriented economy.**

IMPLICATION: While new international job and career opportunities will arise throughout the 1990s, domestic jobs will become increasingly dependent on U.S. trade abroad. Great job opportunities will be available with U.S. companies doing business in Asia, Europe, and Mexico.

PREDICTION 2: **Boom and bust economic cycles will continue throughout the 1990s and into the 21st century as the economy experiences a combination of good times and bad times which, in turn, create a great deal of uncertainty for planning careers and lifestyles.**

IMPLICATION: You need to acquire the necessary work-content and job search skills for quickly changing jobs and careers. Also, be prepared to relocate to more prosperous communities as well as develop greater financial security to bridge the bust-boom cycles.

PREDICTION 3: **Millions of jobs will be created and eliminated throughout the 1990s. New jobs will be created at the rate of 1 to 2 million each year. At the same time, nearly 1 million jobs will be eliminated each year. In the midst of these changes nearly 20 million Americans will experience some form of unemployment each year; between 6 and 12 million Americans will be unemployed each day.**

IMPLICATION: While you have a high probability of experiencing some form of unemployment in the decade ahead, new opportunities for careering and re-careering will abound for those who know the "what," "where," and "how" of finding jobs and changing careers.

PREDICTION 4: **The rapidly expanding service sector will create the largest number of new jobs. These will be disproportionately found at the two extreme ends of the job market— high paying jobs requiring high-level skills and low paying jobs requiring few specialized skills.**

IMPLICATION: You should focus on acquiring specialized education and skills for the high-end of the job market. Many of your skills also should be sufficiently general and marketable so you can easily make job and career transitions without becoming a victim of structural unemployment and boom-bust cycles.

PREDICTION 5: **Structural unemployment will accelerate due to a combination of business failures in the boom/bust economy and continuing productivity improvements in both the manufacturing and service sectors as new technology and improved decision-making and management systems are introduced to the work place. Structural unemployment also will be exacerbated by the increased movement of both manufacturing and service jobs off-shore to low-wage countries in Asia, the Caribbean, Central America, and Latin America.**

IMPLICATION: You need to acquire the necessary skills to adjust to the coming changes in the work place and job market. Careering and re-careering should become your central focus in deciding which skills to acquire.

PREDICTION 6: **Thousands of stagnant communities and inner-city neighborhoods will generate too few jobs to provide sufficient careering and re-careering opportunities. "Rust belt" and "welfare-subsidy" communities, as well as**

those lacking a diversified service economy, will provide few job opportunities in
the decade ahead.

IMPLICATION: Individuals in stagnant communities must
find ways to create their own employment or
relocate to those communities offering long-
term careering opportunities. The most likely
candidates will be growing metropolitan areas
with diversified suburban economies.

PREDICTION 7:   **Public policy failures to resolve education,
training, and unemployment problems—as
well as initiate effective job generation,
relocation, and job search approaches for
promoting a more employable society—will
continue throughout the 1990s and the
early 21st century.**

IMPLICATION: Given the highly decentralized and fragmented governmental and policy systems in the
United States, politicians and public policy
relevant to promoting full employment will
remain relatively inert. Since most politicians
will continue to be preoccupied with form
and style rather than with substance and
results in dealing with pressing economic and
employment issues, individuals must take
their own initiative in acquiring skills, finding
jobs, changing careers, and relocating to communities offering better job opportunities.

These predictions form a set of assumptions upon which we propose
strategies for managing your career(s) throughout the 1990s and into the
21st century. Our careering and re-careering approaches are especially
relevant to a job market undergoing the types of turbulent changes we
foresee for the coming decade.

Whether our predictions turn out to be 30, 70, or 100 percent accurate
is beside the point. What is important is that you be aware, anticipate, and
prepare for change. In so doing, you will be ready to seize new opportunities regardless of whatever direction the economy and employment situation
takes in the decade ahead.

The changes taking place in the work place have important implications
for individuals in planning their future. As more and more jobs become
obsolete and new opportunities arise in the high-tech and service economy,
workers must be better prepared to function in today's evolving job market.

At the very least, they must learn how to career and re-career throughout the 1990s and into the 21st century.

Beware of Incomplete Approaches

The nature of work and the process of finding employment have changed dramatically during the past few decades. For those who lived through the Great Depression, a job—indeed, any job—was something you were lucky to have. A good job—one you enjoyed and earned a good living from—was something only a few people were lucky enough to have.

As white-collar employment expanded in the 1950s and 1960s, a new philosophy of work evolved. Work was to be enjoyed and based upon one's strongest skills. Individuals also were advised to change jobs and careers when they were no longer happy with their work.

Pioneered in the career planning methods of Bernard Haldane in the 1950s and 1960s and popularized in Richard Bolles' self-directed *What Color Is Your Parachute?* in the 1970s and 1980s, job search was placed on center stage as a skill that could be learned and applied with considerable success. Reflecting the do-your-own-thing philosophy of the 1960s and primarily emphasizing the importance of self-assessment and self-reliance, individuals were strongly advised to identify what they do well—their strengths—and enjoy doing. Based on this knowledge, they were further advised to take initiative in seeking employment outside the formal job market of classified ads and employment agencies by engaging in informational interviews, that is, asking people for information and advice about jobs and employment. The key principles for successful job search were the familiar sales approaches of *prospecting and networking*—methods for developing job contacts and acquiring job information, advice, and referrals. Changing careers primarily involved a strategy of identifying and communicating transferable skills to employers rather than acquiring new job-related skills.

The process identified by Haldane, Bolles, and other career counselors for finding employment is what Adele Scheele (*Skills For Success*) calls "successful careering." It requires the use of certain marketing skills and strategies for selling yourself. According to Scheele, these skills consist of (1) self-presentation, (2) positioning, and (3) connecting. Other writers refer to these same skills as (1) role playing, (2) risk taking, and (3) networking—key skills, principles, or strategies applicable to most sales and marketing situations.

The job search skills promoted during the past three decades are based on a business-sales analogy. According to many career advisors, finding a job is like selling—you sell yourself in exchange for status, position, and money. The emphases here are on the process of selling and the methods of self-presentation—not the substance of work-content skills. Seldom, if ever, does this group of career advisors address the equally critical issues of job generation and relocation nor advise individuals to acquire new work-content skills which are more responsive to the changing job market. Doing so requires more comprehensive approaches as well as a major investment of time and effort, especially in education and training, which may seem beyond the immediate employment needs of many individuals.

As more and more jobs require technical skills, and as the job market becomes restructured in response to the emerging high-tech and service economy, the career planning approaches of the past three decades need to be reoriented in light of new realities for the 1990s. Emphasizing process and form to the exclusion of such critical issues as job generation, relocation, and work-content skills, these approaches are at best incomplete in today's job market. Few individuals, for example, who use networking to market only such soft functional skills as reading, writing, and interpersonal communication will be successful in finding employment with a pro-mising future. As many displaced homemakers and liberal arts students learned in the 1980s, such strategies have limitations in a job market requiring concrete technical skills applicable to specific work settings. Lacking an appropriate set of work-content skills, these individuals may become the new displaced, underemployed, and discontented workers of tomorrow.

> **Emphasizing process and form to the exclusion of such critical issues as job generation, relocation, and work-content skills, these approaches are at best incomplete.**

The dual issues of job generation and relocation are critical in planning one's career future. We should never forget that people work in or from specific communities from which they rent or own property and develop particular lifestyles which may or may not be more important than their jobs or careers. If, for example, you live in an economically stagnant community that generates few job opportunities for someone with your interests and skills, using job search skills to find a great job in such a community would be frustrating, if not useless. Your options and approaches in such a situation come down to four:

1. Find a local job that may not fit well with your particular mix of interests and skills while hoping that more appropriate opportunities will eventually open for you in the future as this community generates more job and career options.

2. Commute to a job in another community within your region that offers opportunities appropriate for your interests and skills.

3. Start a business that is not dependent on local economic cycles —one that is broadly based with a diversified regional, national, or international clientele.

4. Relocate to a growing community that appears to be capable of generating many new jobs in the future. Such communities offer an ideal setting where job generation, relocation, and job search come together in providing individuals with numerous opportunities for careering and re-careering in the future.

Career and Re-Career For Today and Tomorrow

The processes we call "careering" and "re-careering" address present and future job realities and enable individuals to change their lives. Re-careering goes beyond the standard "careering" skills popularized during the past three decades, which were based upon an understanding of a job market in an industrial economy. As the job market becomes restructured in the direction of high technology and services, a new approach to job hunting, responsive to new economic realities, is required for the 1990s and beyond.

We anticipate a very different and intensely competitive job market in the future. The major dynamic for restructuring the job market is the emergence of a high-tech and service society, increasingly dependent upon international trade, requiring highly specialized and skilled workers who are prepared for job and career changes. These workers must not be overly specialized nor too narrow in their perception of the future demand for their present skills. Instead, tomorrow's workers must be flexible in learning new skills, for their specialized jobs may become obsolete with the continuing advancement and adaptation of technology to the work place and movement of both manufacturing and service jobs offshore. Furthermore, tomorrow's workers must be adaptive to new jobs and careers. Overall, success in tomorrow's job market will require a new breed of worker who anticipates, prepares, and eagerly adapts to change. Such individuals prepare for career transitions by acquiring new skills and actively seeking new work environments through the use of effective job search strategies and relocating to new communities and work settings.

> **Success in tomorrow's job market will require a new breed of worker who anticipates, prepares, and eagerly adapts to change.**

Careering is the process of preparing to enter the job market with marketable skills to land the job you want. **Re-careering** is the process of repeatedly acquiring marketable skills and changing careers in response to a turbulent job market. The standard careering process of the past three decades, therefore, must be modified with four new re-careering emphases:

1. Acquiring marketable skills through regular retraining.

2. Changing careers several times based on a combination of job search skills, new work-content skills, and relocation actions.

3. Using more efficient communication networks for finding jobs.

4. Relocating to communities experiencing long-term job growth.

Approach the Subject Differently

This book departs from much of the standard career literature of the past three decades as well as some of the newer approaches advanced for today's so-called new job market. Many such books are extremely useful yet redundant and static—largely focused on individual self-assessment within a never-changing job search process perhaps most relevant for the 1970s and 1980s. Newer approaches go to the other extreme—focus primarily on electronic techniques for navigating a job market found on the Internet or advance trendy theories about the "end of jobs" or the shape of a new "employment revolution." Preoccupied with one or two techniques, few such books relate one technique to another nor look beyond the individual in attempting to develop strategies for finding employment. Most lack a critical context and analysis. Many overstate reality in order to be different.

We offer what we believe is a realistic approach for the 1990s and beyond. We place career planning and job search within a more comprehensive employment framework—careering and re-careering—than previously examined. In so doing, we outline effective job search strategies within the context of new job market realities for the 1990s and the 21st century. The result is a new synthesis and approach for career planning that (1) links the individual and job search strategies to larger employment issues, and (2) focuses on managing an uncertain future. We feel such an approach will better prepare individuals for finding employment and changing careers in the years ahead than the much narrower focus on individual self-assessment within the job search process.

The following chapters address the problems of jobs and careers in the decade ahead as well as outline the necessary skills and strategies for finding jobs. Written for every working individual in the decade ahead, the book gives practical advice on how to prepare for new jobs and careers as well as how to make career changes. Individual chapters outline ways to identify and acquire marketable skills, state goals, write resumes and letters, prospect, network, interview, negotiate salaries, and advance and change careers. Special chapters address the challenges of career advancement, relocation, starting a business, and achieving results. Taken together, these chapters offer a recipe for changing your job and career as well as your life.

Achieve Results

Our goals in writing this book are concrete, specific, and oriented toward action and results. You should acquire certain careering and re-careering skills. Upon completing this book you should be able to:

- Understand the changing nature of jobs and careers in the decade ahead and how they relate to your future.

- Identify desirable jobs and careers you may wish to pursue.

- Assess your goals in relation to your values and the demands of the job market.

- Identify your present interests and skills as well as the skills you can best transfer to other jobs and careers.

- Specify your need for skills training as well as know how to acquire the necessary training.

- Communicate your goals, skills, and qualifications to employers.

- Conduct research on alternative jobs, careers, organizations, and communities.

- Write different types of resumes and job search letters.

- Prospect and network for job information, advice, referrals, and job leads.

- Conduct informational and job interviews.

- Negotiate salaries and the terms of employment.

- Advance your career.

- Relocate to other communities.

- Start your own business.

- Implement your plan of action.

- Identify and use additional useful resources, both conventional and electronic, for careering and re-careering in the future.

In the end, our goal is to get you to take actions that will have a positive impact on your future. While most of this book focuses on understanding concepts, following processes, and developing effective job search strategies, the real rewards of this book come when you put these concepts and processes into practice by implementing a realistic plan of action. We'll return to this key issue of implementation in Chapter 19. In the meantime, get ready to put together a realistic plan that will give you the power to change both your job and your life.

3

Prepare For New Career Challenges

W hether or not we realize it, we all have some image of the future that influences important decisions in our lives. Assuming you are like most people, you would not, for example, purchase a new home, relocate to another community, or change jobs unless you first projected what the future might hold for you over the next three, five, or ten years. You want to predict your future to some degree.

Images of the Future

Individuals orient themselves to the future in different ways. Some people always view the future pessimistically. They find numerous reasons for doing what they always do—not taking risks. Others fantasize about the future and "hope" a prosperous future will come to them without taking action or risking the unknown. And others set goals and work toward achieving an image of a positive future.

Finding employment and charting careers in the job markets of today and tomorrow require strategies based on an understanding of new realities as well as a different image of the future. But few people know how to plan for uncertainty. Denying new realities, many continue to operate on old assumptions. Not surprising, their adjustment to change is at best difficult.

Turn Turbulence Into New Opportunities

How do you anticipate the future and plan accordingly? During relatively stable times, planning proceeds along a relatively predictable path: assume the future will be very similar to the past and present. Therefore, a good plan is one that is based on an analysis of historical patterns—you follow the lessons of the past in charting your future.

But during turbulent times, planning based on historical patterns is a problem. Peter Drucker's observations on planning for turbulent times are especially relevant for the decade ahead. Traditional planning:

assumes a high degree of continuity. Planning starts out, as a rule, with the trends of yesterday and projects them into the future—using a different "mix" perhaps, but with very much the same elements and the same configuration. This is no longer going to work. The most probable assumption in a period of turbulence is the unique event, which changes the configuration—and unique events cannot, by definition, be "planned." But they can often be foreseen. This requires strategies for tomorrow, strategies that anticipate where the greatest changes are likely to occur and what they are likely to be, strategies that enable a business—or a hospital, a school, a university—to take advantage of new realities and to convert turbulence into opportunity. (from *Managing in Turbulent Times*)

Turbulent times can be dangerous times for people who fail to anticipate and adjust to new changes. Assuming continuity, or a return to previous times, they engage in wishful thinking. Many of these people are today's victims of structural unemployment. For others, who take action based upon an understanding of coming realities, turbulent times can offer new and exciting opportunities. These people anticipate where the greatest changes will take place and accordingly adapt to change as they advance with the new jobs and careers of tomorrow.

The economic transformation of American society has far reaching social and political implications which you should be aware of in planning your future. The projected changes are discussed at length by Toffler (*The Third Wave*), Naisbett (*Megatrends* and *Megatrends 2000*), Ferguson (*The Aquarian Conspiracy*), Cetron (*Jobs of the Future*), Feingold and Atwater (*New Emerging Careers*), Bridges (*Job Shift*), and Harkness (*The Career Chase*). Our major concern is not in predicting the future with precision. Rather, we are concerned with formulating an image of the future and outlining the implications of turbulent times for jobs, careers, and you.

The major question we need to address here is this:

What future should you prepare for in the world of work?

Based on an understanding of new trends in the work place and anticipating the impact of unique events on the economy, we believe you can develop strategies for converting turbulence into new opportunities.

Two powerful currents—one demographic and another technical—are converging at present in the work place and affecting the future of work in America. These changes, in turn, are precipitating the emergence of 33 new trends for careering and re-careering in the 1990s.

Face New Demographics

The paradox of major labor shortages in the midst of high unemployment is partly due to the impact of demographic changes on today's labor market.

For the American population is undergoing fundamental changes at the same time the economy shifts from an industrial to a high-tech and service base.

The major demographic changes characterizing today's labor force are found at the entry-level: fewer young people are filling entry-level jobs while more females, minorities, and immigrants are entering the job market.

The major implication of these demographic changes for the coming high-tech and service society will be continuing labor shortages for entry-level jobs. However, the paradox of high unemployment may continue if millions of displaced workers are not retrained for new jobs.

Forces

Two major demographic changes took place in the post-World War II period to help shape the present labor force. The first change was the baby-boom. As birth rates increased nearly 50 percent between 1947 and 1949, a new labor force was created for the latter part of the twentieth century. American industry in the 1960s and 1970s absorbed some of this new labor force, but the rapidly growing service sector absorbed most of it. The U.S. economy, especially the service and high-tech sectors, was able to provide employment for 10 million new workers between 1963 and 1980—a remarkable achievement for such a short time span. Between 1983 and 1988 the economy generated 16 million new jobs—the best performance in the history of the labor market. Between 1989 and 1996 the economy generated between 1 and 2 million new jobs each year.

The second major demographic change has been the rapid increase of women, minorities, and immigrants entering the labor force. This demographic current continues. For example, in 1980 over 50 percent of women worked outside the home. By 1990 more than 60 percent of women were in the labor force. Today nearly 75 percent of women are in the workforce.

By the year 2000 the baby-boom generation will reach middle age. The number of traditional 16 to 21 year olds entering the labor market will fall dramatically. About 80 percent of all new labor force entrees will be women, minorities, and immigrants. These groups will be less educated and skilled than the new job entrees of previous decades. For example, despite the $400 billion spent each year on education in the United States, basic literacy and skill levels remain alarming for industries that must dip deeper into the entry-level labor pool. In a 1994 assessment of literacy among 21-to 25-year-olds, the Education Department found these alarming statistics:

- Only 60 percent of whites, 40 percent of Hispanics, 25 percent of blacks can find specific information in a news article or almanac.

- Only 25 percent of whites, 7 percent of Hispanics, and 3 percent of blacks can understand a bus schedule.

Furthermore, 63 percent of white and 14 percent of black high school graduates have only attained a "basic" skill level required by the armed forces for training.

The implications of these trends will be costly for industries in the coming decade. Given rising skill requirements for entry-level jobs, coupled with the low skill levels of job applicants, many industries will experience severe labor shortages. They will most likely respond to this problem by cutting back on services and production and/or investing more resources on educating and training what is basically an entry-level labor force ill-prepared for the jobs of today and tomorrow.

Implications

Declining birth rates between the 1960s and 1980s, with America now approaching a zero-population growth rate, have important implications for the future labor market. Assuming the American economy will continue to expand, despite temporary setbacks, stimulated by the high-tech and service industries, major labor shortages are likely to occur during the coming decade. The continuing entry of women, minorities, and immigrants into the labor force, as well as the expansion of automation in the work place, will not significantly offset this labor deficiency.

Since birth rates declined in the 1960s and 1970s and immigration laws were changed in 1986, there are fewer young people and immigrants available for entry-level and low wage positions. In addition, women, who used to take part-time, low paying sales positions, are fast leaving this labor scene for better paying full-time positions. Teenagers, who make up a disproportionate share of the labor forces of fast-food restaurants, are scarcer because there are fewer teenagers in the population as a whole than during the previous 30 years.

Adjustments in the changing labor force have already begun. Fast-food restaurants employ older workers and introduce more self-service menus. Department stores recruit lower quality sales clerks—generally individuals who are less educated, skilled, stable, and responsible; training demands increase accordingly. Many small businesses, especially the "Mom and Pop" stores with fewer than five employees, experience difficulty recruiting and retaining the traditional young, low-salaried entry-level workers. Instead, many businesses cut back services and production as well as look toward the elderly, particularly retired individuals, for new recruits.

The changing population structure also has important implications for the quality of the labor force. While the private sector spends over $200 billion each year on training and retraining, much of this expenditure goes to training inexperienced entry-level personnel. Given the growing shortage of this traditional labor pool, high-tech industries will be forced to recruit and then retrain displaced workers. This will require a new emphasis on training—as well as a greater expenditure on retraining.

Other population dynamics have additional implications for the work force of tomorrow. Minorities, especially blacks and Hispanics, will enter the labor force at a faster rate because of their higher birth rates. As a result, minorities will disproportionately occupy entry-level positions. Furthermore, there will be greater pressure from minorities for advancement up the ranks, even though the upper ranks have become glutted with middle age managers and executives who were rapidly promoted when they were young people during the 1970s and 1980s.

With the entry of more women into the labor force and the concomitant emergence of the two-career family, individuals have greater freedom of choice to change jobs or careers, take part-time positions, retire, or drop out of the labor force altogether. Job-hopping may increase accordingly. In addition, employee benefit programs, many of which are still based on the model of the traditional male head of household supporting a family, will change in response to the two-career family with one, two, or no children.

> **Mid-life crises may well disappear as more individuals experience re-careering transitions.**

Careering and re-careering are directly related to these changing demographics. As the work force ages, life expectancy lengthens, the social security system becomes modified, and labor shortages abound, fewer people will enter traditional retirement in their 60s or retire at all. An individual's work life may well become one's total adult life. Re-careering will become a standard way of functioning within tomorrow's labor markets. Thus, it will not be unusual for individuals to change careers in their 40s, 50s, and 60s. Mid-life crises may well disappear as more individuals experience re-careering transitions.

Responses

Population changes also will create a more heterogeneous work force. Along with increased minority representation in entry-level positions, more and more immigrants will come to the United States—both legally and illegally—to meet the expanding labor needs. Despite the 1986 changes in immigration laws to document illegal immigrants and stem the tide of illegal immigration into the United States—political efforts totally at odds with America's growing labor needs—nearly 600,000 immigrants enter the U.S. legally each year and another 600,000 immigrants, mainly from Mexico and the Caribbean, probably enter the U.S. illegally. Most of these people initially take low-paying, manual, and service jobs which non-minorities avoid. Hispanic-Americans, who now number about 20 million, are expected to constitute one-fifth of the population, or 50 million out of 250 million, in the year 2000.

Assuming continuing low birth rates among middle class white Americans which, in turn, may contribute to labor shortages in the future, the government may be forced into a major policy reversal: relax enforcement of the 1986 immigration laws as well as open the doors to immigrants in order to alleviate the coming labor shortages. If and when this happens, training and retraining programs will become more urgently needed for the future of the high-tech and service society.

Peter Drucker, however, outlines another scenario which is by far one of the most interesting organizational forms for coping with the coming labor shortages in developed countries and the explosive expansion of working-age people in the less developed countries. Under a production sharing system, less developed countries with surplus labor would be responsible for labor-intensive aspects of production. Developed countries, such as the United States, would provide the needed capital, technology, and managerial skills for operating transnational companies. Such an arrangement would fully employ the surplus educated and skilled people in the developed countries without experiencing the social, economic, and political dislocation attendant with large scale migration.

Production sharing forms of organization are already in place for various industries in the United States, Japan, Singapore, Hong Kong, Malaysia, Taiwan, Korea, and Brazil—the so-called First and Second World countries. They are likely to develop in many other countries, especially those in the Third World. As Drucker sees this system,

> Production sharing is the best hope—perhaps the only hope—for most of the developing countries to survive without catastrophe the explosive expansion of working-age people in search of a job . . . for the standard of living of the developed world can also be maintained only if it succeeds in mobilizing the labor resources of the developing world. It has the technical resources, the entrepreneurial resources, the managerial resources—and the markets. But it lacks, and will increasingly lack, the labor resources to do the traditional stages of production.

Whether or not production sharing becomes a predominate organizational form, the changing population dynamics over the next two decades provide further evidence of the need for major skills training and retraining of the American labor force. Population dynamics undoubtedly will be a major force affecting the turbulent employment environment.

Experience the Impact of New Technologies

The second major current transforming the American work place is technical in nature. The electronics revolution began in 1948 in Western Electric Company's Allentown, Pennsylvania manufacturing plant. There, the transistor was produced, and it began an electronics revolution which has continued to evolve into even more revolutionary forms since the invention and application of the microprocessor in the 1970s. The end of this revolution is nowhere in sight. Many experts believe we are just at the initial stages of a profound transformation which will sweep across our society during the next two decades.

Evidence of a coming transformation began in the 1950s as white-collar workers began to outnumber blue-collar workers. The electronics revolution helped initiate an information and communication revolution. In 1950, for example, approximately 17 percent of the population worked in information-related jobs. Today this proportion has increased to over 50 percent. During the 1970s, when nearly 19 new jobs were created, only 16 percent were in the manufacturing and goods-producing sector.

As John Naisbett (*Megatrends*) and other futurists have noted, during the 1980s we began to move full-force into the second stage of technological development—the application of technology to old industrial tasks. Recognizing the urgent need to increase productivity in order to become more competitive in international markets, manufacturing industries have made major efforts to retool their plants with the latest labor-saving technologies and have thereby displaced workers skilled in the technologies of previous decades. Today, America's manufacturing plants are second to none in terms of technological adaptation.

Movement into third stage technological development—innovation, making new discoveries with second stage technologies—should proceed throughout the 1990s and into the 21st century. By the year 2000 many American manufacturing and service industries will be completely transformed by second and third stage technological developments. Entry into the labor market in the year 2000 will require a much higher level of education and skills than in the 1980s. Those who will be in the best position to advance into the best jobs for the year 2000 will be those who seriously focus on careering and re-careering issues by:

- acquiring new work-content skills through regular training and retraining

- developing effective job search skills

- relocating when necessary

The impact of the high-tech revolution is structural in nature. As computers, fiber optics, robotics, and genetic engineering generate new businesses and integrate into everyday life, the economy and work place will be fundamentally altered. For example, fiber optics, which makes copper wire obsolete, will further revolutionize communication. Genetic engineering will create major changes in agriculture and medicine. The main-frame computer, which was developed for practical use in 1945, in the form of today's microcomputer is now a common tool in many work places. With the continuing impact of fiber optics and new generation microprocessing chips—not to mention some still unknown technological breakthroughs—computers with vastly expanded capabilities will become common tools in the home over the next decade. Powerful laptop computers will increasingly displace standard desktop computers. And the continuing innovations and adaptation of the Internet may well transform the whole software industry within the next few years. Indeed, long-distance carriers such as AT&T and MCI, are in a race for survival as the Internet transforms long distance communications. Many in this industry predict that all long distance phone calls will be free in the not-too-distant future as telephone companies increasingly compete to become business service providers.

The microprocessor has dramatically altered the work place—from robots replacing assembly line workers to word processors displacing traditional typists. Office automation has transformed many secretaries into area managers, who are now in charge of coordinating work flows and managing equipment. Factory workers either become displaced or are retrained to deal with the new technology. Unfortunately, many displaced workers, who have not been retrained, have become permanently displaced or have moved into lower paying, high turnover, unskilled service jobs—the negative unemployment and underemployment consequences of structural changes.

Many futurists have predicted what seems to be an even more radical transformation of the work place—the emergence of the electronic cottage. According to these predictors, computers and word processors will create a decentralized work place where individuals can work from their homes on assignments received and processed via computer terminals. The electronic cottage, in turn, will alter family relationships, especially child rearing practices, and the structure of the traditional central business district. Many workers no longer will need to commute to the office, face traffic jams, and experience the accompanying office stress. Such changes, however, do not bode well for owners of downtown office buildings, parking lots, and businesses frequented by the noontime employee-shopper. The communication revolution may be the final death blow for some cities hoping to revitalize their downtown areas. In fact, the fastest growing business sector today is the home-based business which now employs over 25 million individuals. With the recent emergence of the Internet as a new business arena, these numbers will probably increase in the future. While only talked about as a future reality 10 or 15 years ago, today the electronic cottage has become a significant reality for millions of individuals in the space of only a decade.

These technological changes, coupled with the demographic currents, are transforming the nature of jobs. Yesterday's and today's workers are increasingly being displaced into an environment which is ill-equipped to help them gain advantages in tomorrow's high-tech society. Instead, a new class of individuals, skilled in the technology of previous decades, may become permanently displaced in the turbulent job market of tomorrow. Their major hope for career success is to become savvy in the technologies of today and tomorrow.

Prepare For 33 Coming Changes

Several additional trends are evident, and they will affect both the work force and the work place in years ahead. These trends are mainly stimulated by the larger demographic and technological changes taking place within society. We see 33 changes emerging in the areas of job creation, youth, elderly, minorities, women, immigrants, part-time employment, service jobs, education and training, unions and labor-management relations, urban-rural shifts, regionalism, small businesses and entrepreneurship, compensation, advancement opportunities, and relocation. Together these changes point to both dangers and new opportunities.

TREND 1: **Shortage of competent workers, with basic literacy and learning skills, creates serious problems in developing an economy with an adequate work force for the jobs of the 1990s and the 21st century.**

Given the double-whammy of over 20 million functionally illiterate adults—or 1/6 of the potential labor force unable to read, write, or perform simple computations—and the availability of fewer easily trainable young entry-level workers, a large portion of the work force is destined to remain at the lowest end of the job market despite the fact that over 15 million new jobs will be created in the 1990s. Most of these adults will remain permanently unemployed or underemployed while major labor shortages exist. As skill requirements rise rapidly for both entering and advancing within the work force, the nation's economic development will slow due to the lack of skilled workers. Both public and private sector worker literacy, basic education, and training programs will continue to expand, but their contribution to improving the overall skill levels of the work force will be minimal. The American economy and work force begin showing classic signs of Second and Third World economies—potential economic performance out-strips the availability of a skilled work force.

TREND 2: **A renewed and strong U.S. manufacturing sector will create few new jobs; service industries will be responsible for most job growth in the decade ahead.**

Despite popular notions of the "decline" of American manufacturing industries, these industries are following the model of America agriculture—increased productivity accompanied by the increased displacement of workers. American manufacturing industry is becoming one of the strongest economic sectors in terms of production output but the weakest sector in terms of its contribution to job growth and job creation. At the same time, American manufacturing is moving in the direction of Drucker's "production sharing system" by exporting the remaining high-cost, labor intensive aspects of the industries. As large manufacturing companies rebound in the 1990s by becoming productive with smaller and more highly skilled work forces, most new manufacturing jobs will develop among small manufacturing "job shops" employing fewer than 50 workers. The service industries, especially those in finance, retail, food, and healthcare, will continue to expand their work forces during the first half of the 1990s. The second half of the 1990s will witness major "productivity" and "management" improvement movements among service industries that developed among large manufacturing industries in the 1980s—a push for greater productivity because of (1) major labor shortages, and (2) the adaptation of new technology to increasingly inefficient, high-cost, labor intensive service industries, especially in the retail and healthcare industries.

TREND 3: **Unemployment remains cyclical, fluctuating between a low of 5 percent and a high of 9 percent.**

These fluctuations are attributed to a combination of boom and bust cycles in the economy as well as the persistence of structural unemployment exacerbated by millions of functionally illiterate adults on the periphery of the economy. In addition, millions of other Americans will be underemployed in low paying entry-level positions which offer little or no career advancement.

TREND 4: **Government efforts to stimulate employment growth continues to be concentrated at the periphery of the job market.**

Most government programs aimed at generating jobs and resolving unemployment problems will be aimed at the poor and unskilled. These groups also are the least likely to relocate, use job search skills, develop standard work habits, or be trained in skills for tomorrow's job market.

Given the mixed results from such programs and political pressures to experiment with some form of government-sponsored workfare programs, the government finally develops programs to directly employ the poor and unskilled on government programs as well as contract-out this class of unemployed to government contractors who will provide them with education and training along with work experience.

TREND 5: **After difficult economic times during the first half of the 1990s, the U.S. deficit significantly declines and trade becomes more balanced as the U.S. slowly regains a more competitive international trade and debt position due to improved productivity of U.S. manufacturing industries and the devaluation of the U.S. dollar.**

International and domestic issues become closely tied to employment issues. Emphasis shifts to issues of unemployment, productivity, population growth, consumption, and regional conflicts in Eastern Europe, the newly independent states of the former Soviet Union, the Middle East, and other Third and Fourth World countries that threaten the stability of international markets and thus long-term economic and employment growth in the U.S. New regional trading blocks play the most important role in redefining the post-Cold War era. Economic, trade, and employment issues take center stage in defining a highly unstable yet emerging structure of a newly emerging post-Cold War order. Major labor shortages in the U.S. become evident as a sluggish economy turns around in the second half of the 1990s. Another recession, reminiscent of the early 1990s, begins in 1997 as a result of declining markets for U.S. products in the over-heated economies of the Pacific Rim and the melt-down of a highly speculative and over-valued stock market. Higher levels of unemployment result in the U.S.

TREND 6: **A series of domestic and international crises—shocks and "unique events," some that already occurred in the 1980s—emerge in the 1990s and early 21st century to create new boom and bust cycles contributing to unemployment.**

The most likely sources for the international crises will be problems developing among former communist regimes and poor Third and Fourth World nations: the disintegration of the nation-states in the former Soviet Union and a few former communist regimes in Eastern Europe; energy and precious metals shortages due to a depletion of current stocks and regional military conflicts; the collapse of financial markets due to default on international debts; and dislocation of lucrative resource and consumption markets due to continued wars in the Middle East, Africa, and South Asia. The most likely domestic crises center on financial markets, real estate, energy, water, and the environment. Crises in the banking and real estate markets continue to create major debt, credit, and bankruptcy problems for the economy. An energy crisis once again revitalizes the economies of Texas, Colorado, and Alaska. A new crisis—water shortages—in the rapidly developing Southwest, further slows employment growth in the once booming economies of Southern California and Arizona. Environmental issues, such as acid rain and air and water pollution, emerge as important international and domestic crises.

TREND 7: **New jobs will be created at the rate of 1 to 2 million each year, with some boom years resulting in the creation of more than 3 million jobs each year.**

The good news is that employment will increase in most occupations throughout the 1990s and the early 21st century with export industries leading the way toward economic growth. Economic expansion in the service sector, coupled with the low productivity and low cost of labor in many parts of the service sector, contributes over 90 percent of all new jobs. Large scale manufacturing experiences labor declines while small scale manufacturing "job shops" contribute most of the minimal job growth in the manufacturing sector. The labor declines will be offset by increases in related service jobs, especially in manufacturing sales and marketing.

TREND 8: **A major shortage of skilled craftspeople will create numerous production, distribution, and service problems throughout the coming decade.**

During the 1980s the number of apprenticeship programs declined significantly; fewer individuals received training in blue-collar occupations; and interest among the young in blue-collar trades declined markedly. The impact of these changes will be felt throughout the 1990s and early 21st century as production and service industries requiring critically skilled craftspeople experience major labor shortages; distribution of products and services will be uneven. Despite government efforts to revitalize apprenticeship programs, expect to personally encounter the effects of such labor shortages—long waits for servicing your automobile and for repairing your home and major appliances as well as very expensive charges for such services.

TREND 9: **As the baby-boomers reach middle age and as the birth-rate continues at a near zero-population growth rate, fewer young people within the U.S. will be available for entry-level positions in the coming decade.**

Businesses will recruit and train more of the hard-core unemployed, unskilled, and the elderly; they will automate; and/or they will contract for cheap off-shore labor for everything from accounting and marketing to manufacturing jobs. As a result, more stopgap job opportunities will be available for individuals losing their jobs or wishing to change jobs or careers.

TREND 10: **Retirement practices undergo a major transformation. More job and career choices will be available for the elderly who are either dissatisfied with traditional retirement or who no longer can afford the high costs of retirement.**

As the work force increasingly ages, the trend toward early retirement will decrease. Many people will never retire, preferring instead part-time or self-employment in their later years. Others will retire from one job and then start new careers after age 50. A continuing financial crisis in the social security system results in declining social security benefits. Fewer social security benefits and higher costs of retirement will further transform retirement practices and systems throughout the 1990s. Expect to see more elderly working in the McDonald's and 7-Eleven stores of tomorrow.

TREND 11: **More minorities and immigrants—especially those with disproportionate high birth rates, low education** and skill levels, and poor economic status—will enter the job market.

A large proportion of minorities will occupy the less skilled entry-level, service positions where they will exhibit marked language, class, and cultural differences. Upwardly mobile minorities may find advancement opportunities blocked because of the glut of supervisors, managers, and executives already in most organizations.

TREND 12: Women will continue to enter the labor market, accounting for nearly 80 percent female participation in the labor force by the year 2000.

The entry of women into the work force during the 1990s will be due less to the changing role of women than to the economic necessity of women to generate family income in order to survive in an expensive consumer-oriented society. Women will account for two-thirds of the growth in all occupations. They will continue to expand into non-traditional jobs, especially production and management positions. Both men and women in a growing number of two-career families will have greater flexibility to change jobs and careers frequently.

TREND 13: More immigrants will enter the U.S.—both documented and undocumented—to meet labor shortages at all levels.

Despite major efforts of the INS to stem the flow of illegal immigrants, labor market demands will require more immigrants to occupy low-paying, entry-level service jobs in the decade ahead. The brain drain of highly skilled scientific and technical workers from developing countries to the U.S. will accelerate. Unskilled immigrants will move into service positions vacated by upwardly mobile Americans.

TREND 14: Part-time and temporary employment opportunities will increase.

With the increase in two-career families, the emergence of electronic cottages, and the smaller number of retirees, part-time and temporary employment will become a more normal pattern of employment for millions of Americans. More women, who wish to enter the job market but not as full-time employees, will seek new part-time employment opportunities. Temporary employment services will continue to experience a boom in business as more and more companies attempt to lower personnel costs as well as achieve greater personnel flexibility by hiring larger numbers of temporary employees.

TREND 15: Part-time and contingency workers will constitute a new and desired class of workers.

The number of contingency workers—part-time, temporary, or contract workers—will steadily increase in the decade ahead as more and more businesses cut back costly full-time employees, eliminate generous benefit packages, and seek greater flexibility in hiring and firing employees. Given economic uncertainties, the high costs of hiring, and the advantages of working with employment firms that field contingency workers, more and more employers will replace full-time employees with contingency workers. By the year 2000 many businesses employing 100 or fewer employees will routinely use contingency workers to staff at least 30 percent of their positions.

TREND 16: White-collar employment will continue to expand in the fast growing service sector.

Dramatic growth in clerical and service jobs will take place in response to new information technology. The classification of workers into blue and white-collar occupations, as well as into manufacturing and service jobs will become meaningless in a service economy dominated by white-collar workers.

TREND 17: The need for a smarter work force with specific technical skills will continue to impact on the traditional American education system as both businesses and parents demand greater job and career relevance in educational curriculum.

Four-year colleges and universities will face stable to declining enrollments as well as the flight of quality faculty to more challenging and lucrative jobs outside education. Declining enrollments will be due to the inability of these institutions to adjust to the educational and training skill requirements of the high-tech society as well as to the demographics of fewer numbers in the traditional 18-21 year-old student age population. The flight of quality faculty will be replaced by less qualified and inexpensive part-time faculty. Most community colleges, as well as specialized private vocational-technical institutions, will adapt to the changing demographics and labor market needs and flourish with programs most responsive to community employment needs. As declining enrollments, budgetary crises, and flight of quality faculty accelerates, many of the traditional four-year colleges and universities will attempt to shut down or limit the educational scope of community colleges in heated state political struggles for survival of traditional educational programs. More and more emphasis will be placed on providing efficient short-term, intensive skills training programs than on providing traditional degree programs—especially in the liberal arts. Career planning will become a major emphasis in education programs; a new emphasis will be placed on specialization and flexibility in career preparation.

TREND 18:   **Union membership will continue to decline as more blue-collar manufacturing jobs disappear and interest in unions wanes among both blue and white-collar employees.**

As unions attempt to survive and adjust to the new society, labor-management relations will go through a turbulent period of conflict, co-optation, and cooperation. Given declining union membership and the threat to lay-off employees unless unions agree to give-back arrangements, unions will continue to find themselves on the defensive, with little choice other than to agree to management demands for greater worker productivity. In the long-run, labor-management relations will shift from the traditional adversarial relationship to one of greater cooperation and participation of labor and management in the decision-making process. Profit sharing, employee ownership, and quality circles will become prominent features of labor-management relations. These changes will contribute to the continuing decline, and eventual disappearance, of traditional unions in many industries.

New organizational forms, such as private law firms specializing in the representation of employees' interests and the negotiation of employment contracts, will replace the traditional unions.

TREND 19:   **The population will continue to move into suburban and semi-rural communities as new high-tech industries and services move in this direction.**

The large, older central cities, especially in the Northeast and North Central regions, will continue to bear disproportionate welfare, tax, and criminal justice burdens due to their declining industrial bases, deteriorating infrastructures, relatively poor and unskilled populations, and high rates of crime. Cutbacks in their city government programs will require the retraining of public employees for private sector jobs. Urban populations will continue to move into suburban and semi-rural communities. Developing their own economic base, these communities will provide employment for the majority of local residents rather than serve as bedroom communities from which workers commute to the central city. With few exceptions, and despite noble attempts to "revitalize" downtown areas with new office, shopping, and entertainment complexes, most large central cities will continue to decline as their upwardly mobile residential populations move to the suburbs where they find good jobs, housing, and education; enjoy attractive lifestyles; and experience lower crime rates.

TREND 20:   **The population, as well as wealth and economic activity, will continue to shift into the Northwest, Southwest, and Florida at the expense of the Northeast and North Central regions.**

By the year 2000 the South and West will have about 60 percent of the U.S. population. These areas will also be the home for the nation's youngest population. Florida, Georgia, Texas, Colorado, Arizona, Nevada, Utah, and Washington will be the growth states for the decade ahead; construction and local government in these states will experience major employment increases. Many states in the Northeast and Midwest, and parts of the South, will be in for continuing difficult times due to their declining industrial base, excessive welfare burdens, older population, aging infrastructure, and shrinkage of non-cyclical economic sectors—services, retail trade, and public employment. However, some Midwest states (Ohio, Indiana, Iillinois, Wisconsin) will experience strong growth—based on the Massachusetts model of the 1980s—due to important linkages developing between their exceptionally well developed higher educational institutions and high-tech industries which depend on such institutions. Many manufacturing industries in the Midwest, especially auto, will continue to expand as they play an increasingly important role in the expanding U.S. export economy. Some states in the Midwest and Northwest will out-perform the rest of the economy during the second half of the 1990s.

The growth regions also will experience turbulence as they see-saw between shortages of skilled labor, surpluses of unskilled labor, and urban growth problems. A "unique event"—devastating earthquake in Southern California or major water shortages in California and Arizona—could result in a sudden reversal of rapid economic and employment growth in the Southwest region.

The problems of the declining regions are relatively predictable: they will become an economic drain on the nation's scarce resources; tax dollars from the growth areas will be increasingly transferred for nonproductive support payments. A new regionalism, characterized by numerous regional political conflicts, will likely arise centered around questions concerning the inequitable distribution of public costs and benefits.

TREND 21: **The number of small businesses will continue to increase as new opportunities for entrepreneurs arise in response to the high-tech and service revolutions and as more individuals find new opportunities to experiment with changing careers.**

As during the past decade, over 700,000 new businesses will be started each year during the coming decade. These businesses will generate 90 percent of all new jobs created each year. The number of business failures will increase accordingly, especially during the bust cycles of the boom/bust economy. Increases in self-employment and small businesses will not provide many new opportunities for career advancement. The small promotion hierarchies of these businesses will help accelerate increased job-hopping and career changes. This new entrepreneurship is likely to breed greater innovation, competition, and productivity.

TREND 22: **As large companies continue to downsize, major job growth will take place among small companies and millions of new start-up businesses.**

Between 1979 and 1993, Fortune 500 companies reduced their personnel by 4.8 million while firms with fewer than 500 employees generated 16 million new jobs. This trend will continue in the foreseeable future. The best job opportunities in terms of challenges, salaries, and future opportunities will be with growing companies

> **The best employment opportunities will be found among growing companies employing fewer than 50 employees.**

employing fewer than 50 employees. Large Fortune 500 companies, especially service industries, will continue to cut jobs as they attempt to survive intense competition by becoming more productive through the application of new technology to the work place and through the introduction of more efficient management systems. Cutbacks will further lower the morale of remaining employees who will seek new job and career opportunities—and many will start their own businesses.

TREND 23: **Opportunities for career advancement will be increasingly limited within most organizations.**

Organizations will have difficulty providing career advancement for employees due to (1) the growth of small businesses with short advancement hierarchies, (2) the postponement of retirement, (3) the continuing focus on nonhierarchical forms of organization, and (4) the already glutted managerial ranks. In the future, many of today's managers will have to find nonmanagerial positions. Job satisfaction will become less oriented toward advancement up the organizational ladder and more toward such organizational perks as club memberships, sabbaticals, vacations, retraining opportunities, flexible working hours, family services, and health care packages.

TREND 24: **Job satisfaction will become a major problem as many organizations will experience difficulty in retaining highly qualified personnel.**

Greater competition, fewer promotions, frustrated expectations, greater discontent, and job-hopping will arise in executive ranks due to limited advancement opportunities. As middle-management positions continue to be eliminated as part of overall downsizing efforts, managerial and executive turnover will increase accordingly. The problem will be especially pronounced for many women and minorities who have traditional aspirations to advance to the top but will be blocked by the glut of managers and executives from the baby-boom generation who are trying to survive at both the middle and top of their organizations. Many of these frustrated individuals will initiate affirmative action cases to open the closed upper ranks as well as become entrepreneurs by starting their own businesses in competition with their former employers.

TREND 25: **Many employers will resort to new and unorthodox hiring practices, improved working conditions, and flexible benefit packages in order to recruit and retain critical personnel.**

In an increasingly tight job market for skilled workers, employers will use new and more effective ways of finding and keeping personnel: job fair weekends; headhunters and executive search firms; temporary employment services; raids of competition's personnel; bonuses to present employees for finding needed personnel; entry-level hiring bonuses for new recruits; attractive profit-sharing packages for long-term commitments; vacation and travel packages; relocation and housing services; flex-time and job-sharing; home-based work; and day care services.

TREND 26: **Job-hopping will increase as more and more individuals learn how to change careers.**

As more job and career opportunities become available for the skilled and savvy worker, as pension systems become more portable, and as job search and relocation techniques become more widely known, more and more individuals will change jobs and careers in the decade ahead. The typical employee will work in one job and organization for four years and then move on to a similar job in another organization. Within 12 years this individual will have acquired new interests and skills and thus decide to change to a new career. Similar four and 12-year cycles of job and career changes will be repeated by the same individual. Job-hopping will become an accepted and necessary way of getting ahead in the job and career markets of tomorrow.

TREND 27: **Geographic relocation will accelerate as more and more individuals become drawn to growing communities offering attractive job opportunities.**

As the real estate market slowly rebounds across the nation, individuals will have a greater incentive to pull up stakes in one community to relocate to another. More and more people will move into the southeast and west in pursuit of better job and career opportunities.

TREND 28: **The hot jobs in the decade ahead—those offering excellent pay, advancement, and security—will be in healthcare and high-tech service industries.**

These jobs will require substantial amounts of education, training, and retraining. They also will command top salaries and benefits as well as offer attractive advancement opportunities and numerous career options for individuals interested in careering and re-careering.

TREND 29: **Salaries will only incrementally increase in the coming decade. In many organizations, executive level compensation will actually decline as well as be more closely tied to productivity indicators.**

The large salary gains of the 1980s are all but over for most occupations in the 1990s, excepting those requiring high level skills which will be difficult to recruit, such as computer science and engineering. Indeed, many chemical engineering graduates in 1997 will start at $43,000 a year! Salary increments will more and more be tied to annual performance evaluations which link pay raises to quantifiable performance indicators. More attractive and portable benefit packages will be offered by organizations seeking to recruit and retain highly skilled workers.

TREND 30: **Benefit packages will decline as more and more organizations cut back on personnel expenses.**

Health insurance and pensions will be the major targets of these cutbacks. More and more employers will require employees to make significant contributions to health insurance and retirement plans. While most employers will offer some form of health insurance, fewer employers will provide company-sponsored retirement plans. Workers can expect to contribute at least 20 percent to the cost of health insurance as well as develop their own retirement plans which will include little or no contribution from employers. More and more employers will opt to hire contingency workers whose benefits are handled by contractors.

TREND 31: **Apprenticeship programs will increase in number as the nation attempts to train and retrain a skilled labor pool for high-demand service industries.**

The coming shortage of skilled labor to service everything, from air-conditioners to automobiles, is directly related to the decline of apprenticeship programs and the lack of interest in pursuing careers in the trades. The government in cooperation with industry will make a major effort to revitalize such programs. Individuals not pursuing higher education degrees will find excellent career opportunities available through such programs.

TREND 32: **More and more skilled and high-tech service jobs will move off-shore as U.S. businesses take advantage of both cheap skilled labor and high-speed communications.**

The next decade with be the decade of the global job market for both skilled and unskilled labor. The stereotypical manufacturing sweat shops with cheap and relatively unskilled labor producing garments, footwear, and toys in China, Indonesia, and India will give way to more high-tech sweatshops in these and many other countries. However, the high-tech sweatshops will focus more and more on the service industries and use skilled labor in Third World countries. For example, given inexpensive high-speed communications, many businesses can now export their accounting, design, telemarketing, and data management functions to India, the Philippines, Mexico, and countries in the Caribbean via faxes, the Internet, and special two and three-day delivery services (DHL, UPS, Federal Express). Skilled cheap labor will pose a new challenge to the U.S. labor market. While it will help relieve some labor shortages, it also will compete directly with high wage skilled workers in the U.S.

TREND 33: Fewer people will be obsessed with chasing traditional careers. More and more people want satisfying jobs that enable them to pursue interesting lifestyle goals.

The concept of a "career" is deeply rooted in the post-World War II era of big manufacturing corporations. Until the 1990s, many individuals pursued careers, often within a single organizational setting. Given the changing structure of the job market, the decline of traditional career paths, and the increased interest in pursuing statisfying lifestyles, the 1990s has witnessed the gradual erosion of careers. More and more individuals today and in the decade ahead will be interested in finding specific jobs which may or may not be related to careers.

Be Realistic

While many individuals look toward the future with unquestioned optimism, there are good reasons to be cautious and less than enthusiastic. The decade ahead may be the worst of times for many people. Take several examples which indicate a need to be cautiously optimistic. Factory workers who remain unemployed after five years will have received an industrial death sentence of continuing unemployment, underemployment, or socio-economic decline. Many of the nation's poor, with high birth rates, are destined to remain at the bottom of society; their children may fare no better. Large cities in the Northeast and North Central regions, and even small communities in these and other regions, will have difficult adjustment problems. And we should not forget that America has not solved its energy and environmental problems, and a boom/bust economy is well and alive.

The best of times are when you are gainfully employed, enjoy your work, and look to your future with optimism. In the turbulent society, people experience both the best and worst of times at the same time. Those who are unprepared for the growing uncertainty and instability of the turbulent society may get hurt.

We lack a healthy sense of reality in facing change. Indeed, the future is seldom what we think it is. Only recently have we begun to take a second look at the high-tech and service revolutions and raised some sobering questions about their impact on work and the work place. We have not fully explored unanticipated consequences of new structural changes on individuals and society.

The 33 changes we forecast will create dislocations for individuals, groups, organizations, communities, and regions. These dislocations will require some form of public-private intervention. For example, the question of renewable energy resources has not been adequately dealt with in relation to the high-tech revolution. Many of the key metals for fueling the high-tech economy are located in politically unstable regions of Africa and the former Soviet Union. Such resources must be secured or substitutions found in order for the revolution to proceed according to optimistic predictions. Capital formation, investment, and world markets must also be secure and stable. New management systems must evolve in response to the changes. In other words, these key factors are variables or "if's"—not the constants underlying most predictions of the future. As such, they are unpredictable.

> In the turbulent society, people experience both the best and worst of times at the same time.

The clearer picture of unanticipated consequences of technological changes are already evident on the changing assembly lines, in the automated offices, and in the electronic cottages of today. While automation often creates more jobs as it displaces workers—usually at higher skill levels—the jobs may be psychologically and financially less rewarding. Supervising robots eight hours a day can be tedious and boring work with few on-the-job rewards. The same is true for the much touted "office of the future." Interacting with a computer terminal eight hours a day is tedious, tiring, and boring work for many people; and job burnout may accelerate.

The electronic cottage has similar unanticipated consequences. Many people may miss the daily interaction with fellow workers—the gossip, the politics, the strokes. Instead of being rewarding, work at home can become drudgery and low paying work, a 21st century version of the sweat shop.

The optimists often neglect the fact that the nature of work itself provides rewards. Many people intrinsically enjoy the particular job they perform. Furthermore, many rewards are tied to the human dimension of work—the interaction with others. Thus, the high-tech and service society will have to deal with serious management and motivational problems arising from the changing nature of work and the work place.

Many workers may need to re-career in order to overcome the boredom and burnout accompanying many of the new jobs or work situations of tomorrow. And even if the high-tech and service society does not emerge in the form outlined by us and other forecasters, the need to re-career will become necessary given the job and career uncertainty of a turbulent society largely shaped by a cyclical boom/bust economy.

Identify the Jobs of Tomorrow

Where are the jobs, and *how* do I get one? These are the first two questions most people ask when seeking employment. But one other equally important question should precede these traditional questions:

"What are the jobs of tomorrow?"

For the nature of jobs is changing rapidly in response to (1) technological innovations, (2) the development and application of new technology to the work place, and (3) the demand for a greater variety of consumer services. Today's job seeker needs answers to the "what," "where," and "how" of jobs for the 1990s and beyond.

Many jobs in the year 2000 will look very different from those in the 1980s. Indeed, if we project present trends into the future and believe what futurists tell us about emerging new careers, the 21st century will offer unprecedented and exciting careering and re-careering opportunities.

But such changes and opportunities have costs. The change in jobs and occupations will be so rapid that skills learned today may become obsolete in another five to ten years. Therefore, knowing what the jobs are becomes a prerequisite to knowing how to prepare for them, find them, and change them in the future.

Beware of Changing Occupational Profiles

A few words of caution are in order on how you should and should not use the information in this chapter. If you wish to identify a growing career field to plan your own career, do so only after you identify your interests, skills, and abilities—the subjects of Chapters 7, 8, and 9. You need to determine if you have the proper skills or the aptitude and interests to acquire the necessary skills. The next step is to acquire the training before conducting a job search. Only then should you seriously consider pursuing what appears to be a growing field.

At the same time, you should be aware that the statistics and projections on growing industrial and occupational fields may be inaccurate. First, they are based on traditional models and economic studies conducted by the U.S. Department of Labor, Bureau of Labor Statistics. Unlike fortune tellers and soothsayers who communicate in another world and many futurists who engage in "informed flights of fancy" and "brainstorming," the Bureau conducts "empirical studies" which assume a steady rate of economic growth throughout the 1990s—similar to the 1950s. Such occupational projections are nothing more than "best guesses" based upon a traditional model which assumes continual, linear growth. This planning model does not deal well with the reality of cyclical changes, as evidenced by its failures during the turbulent 1980s when boom and bust cycles, coupled with the emergence of unique events and crises, invalidated many of the Bureau's employment and occupational forecasts. For example, the Department of Labor projected a high unemployment rate of 7.6 percent for 1982; but in 1982 unemployment stood a 10.8 percent. In addition, the deepening recession and the government program cuts brought on by a series of international crises, domestic economic failures, and ideological changes were unanticipated developments which resulted in the actual decline in public employment for the first time since World War II. Thus, in 1982 there were 316,000 fewer public employees than in the year before! The decade ahead may well provide us with more unique economic scenarios which produce similar unpredictable outcomes.

> If you wish to identify a growing career field to plan your own career, do so only after you identify your interests, skills, and abilities.

Second, during a period of turbulent change, occupational profiles may become quickly outdated. Training requirements change, and thus individuals encounter greater uncertainty in career choices. For example, based on trend analyses, many people believe that promising careers lie ahead for computer programmers. This may be true if thousands of newly trained individuals do not glut the job market with computer programming skills. Moreover, it may be true if computer technology remains stagnant and the coming generation of self-programmed computers does not make computer programmers—like their keypunch counterparts in the 1960s and 1970s—obsolete. If either, let alone both, of these "if's" occur, many computer programming jobs may disappear, and many newly trained computer programmers may become displaced workers in need of re-careering.

A similar situation arises for students pursuing the much glamorized MBA and law degrees. Today, as more MBA's graduate and glut the job market with questionable skills, the glitter surrounding this degree has

diminished, and the MBA may fast become an obsolete degree as employers turn to degree fields that emphasize greater communication and
analytical skills.

A similar situation appears relevant to the law field. While the demand
for lawyers increased substantially in the 1980s and a large number of
students continue to enroll in law schools, competition for legal positions
has been keen during the past few years as more and more law graduates
flooded a shrinking job market. Opportunities for lawyers may not increase
much in the decade ahead. The demand for lawyers may actually decline
due to substantial restructuring of the legal profession as lawyers become
more competitive, promote more efficient legal services, hire more
paralegals, change fee and billing practices, introduce more technology to
traditional legal tasks, and develop more do-it-yourself legal approaches; as
the criminal justice system undergoes restructuring; and as Americans
become less litigious due to the high costs of pursuing legal action.

Expect Job Growth in Most
Occupations and For Most Groups

The growth in jobs has been steady during the past three to four decades.
From 1955 to 1980, for example, the number of jobs increased from 68.7
to 105.6 million. This represented an average annual increase of about 1.5
million new jobs. During the 1970s the number of jobs increased by over
2 million per year. And between the years 1983 and 1994 the number of
jobs increased by 24.6 million, a strong growth rate of 24 percent over an
11-year period or over 2 millions new jobs each year.

Job growth during the 1990s slowed but remained steady at about 1.5
million new jobs each year. The slow down reflected demographic changes
in society. By the year 2005 the labor force should consist of nearly 151
million workers—up 14 percent from 1994.

Highlighting these patterns of job growth are 16 forecasts, based on U.S.
Department of Labor data and projections and other recent analyses, which
represent the confluence of demographic, economic, and technological
changes in society during the 1990s:

❖ Employment Forecasts to the Year 2005 ❖

1. Growth of the labor force slows during the 1990s.

The growth in the labor force will slow to 151 million by the
year 2005—a 14 percent increase over the 1994 level. This
represents half the rate of increase during the previous 15-year
period, and it reflects the overall slow growth of the population,
with a less than zero population birth rate of 0.7 percent per
year.

2. **Labor force will be racially and ethnically more diverse.**

The racial and ethnic mix of the work force in the year 2005 will be even more diverse than in the year 1990 given the differential birth and immigration rates of various racial and ethnic groups. Blacks, Hispanics, Asians, and other minority groups will represent 27 percent of the work force—up from 22 percent in 1990. These groups also will account for 35 percent of labor force entrants between 1990 and 2005. Hispanics, Asians, and other minorities will increase at a faster rate than blacks and white non-Hispanics.

3. **Fewer young people will enter the job market.**

The number of 16 to 24 year-olds entering the job market declined between 1975 and 1990 by 1.4 million or 6 percent. Their numbers will increase by 2.8 million during 1990-2005, reflecting a change of 13 percent. These new entrants represent the children of the baby-boom generation who began entering the job market after 1992. The number of 22 to 24 year-olds entering the job market will continue to decline until 1998. The youth share of the labor force will fall to 16 percent by 2005. This represents a significant decline—down from 23 percent in 1972, 20 percent in 1987, and 17 percent in 1990. Businesses depending on this age group for students, recruits, customers, and part-time workers—especially colleges, the Armed Forces, eating and drinking establishments, and retail stores—must draw from a smaller pool of young people. Competition among young people for entry-level jobs will decline accordingly.

4. **The work force will continue to gray as it becomes older.**

As the baby-boom generation of the 1960s and 1970s becomes more middle-aged, the number of 25 to 54 year olds in the labor force will increase substantially by the year 2000—with 72 percent or nearly 3 of every 4 workers, being between the ages of 25 and 54. This represents a significant increase from 40 percent in 1988 and 36 percent in 1976. Between 1990 and 2005 the number of older workers, aged 55 years and above, will grow twice as fast as the labor force as a whole.

5. **Women will enter the labor force in growing numbers.**

Women will represent over half of all entrants into the labor force during the 1990s. While accounting for 39 percent of the labor force in 1972 and 41 percent of the labor force in 1976, women in the year 2005 are projected to constitute 48 percent of the labor force. By the year 2005, 4 out of 5 women between the ages of 25 and 54 will be in the labor force.

6. **Education requirements for most new jobs will continue to rise.**

Most new jobs will require strong basic education skills, such as reading, writing, oral communication, and computation. Many of these jobs will include important high-tech components which will require previous specialized education and training as well as the demonstrated ability to learn and acquire nontraditional education and training to continuously re-tool skills.

7. **The fastest growing occupations will be in executive, managerial, professional, and technical fields—all requiring the highest levels of education and skill.**

Three-quarters of the fastest growing occupational groups will be executive, administrative, and managerial; professional specialty; and technicians and related support occupations— occupations that require the highest levels of education and skill. Few opportunities will be available for high school dropouts or those who cannot read or follow directions. A combination of greater emphasis on productivity in the work place, increased automation, technological advances, innovations, changes in consumer demands, and import substitutions will decrease the need for workers with little formal education and few skills—helpers, laborers, assemblers, and machine operators.

8. **Employment will increase for most occupations in the 1990s.**

As the population continues to grow and become more middle-aged and affluent, demands for more services will increase accordingly. Except in the cases of agriculture, mining, and traditional manufacturing, the 1990s will be a period of steady to significant job growth in all occupations. Over 25 million jobs will be added to the U.S. economy between the years 1990 and 2005. However, new jobs will be unevenly distributed across major industrial and occupational groups due to the restructuring of the economy and the increased education and training requirements for most jobs.

9. **The greatest growth in jobs will take place in service industries and occupations.**

   Over 90 percent of all new jobs in the 1990s will be in the service-producing industries with services such as legal, business (advertising, accounting, word processing, and computer support), and healthcare leading the way. The number of jobs in services is expected to rise by 35 percent between 1990 and 2005, from 38 to 50.5 million. Health and business will be the fastest growing service industries during this period. Social, legal, and engineering and management services industries will also exhibit strong growth.

10. **Retail trade will be the second fastest growing industrial sector in the 1990s.**

    Employment in the retail trade is expected to increase by 26 percent, from 19.7 to 24.8 million during the 1990-2005 period.

11. **Federal government employment will decline but state and local government employment will increase at different rates for different levels of government as well as for governmental units in different regions of the country.**

    Federal government employment will continue to decline, reflecting the overall strategy to contract-out government services, downsize federal agencies, eliminate programs, and decentralize federal functions to state and local governments. The decline will average nearly 1.0 percent each year over the next five years. Except during recessionary periods, state and local government employment will increase by 1 to 2 percent each year with local governments in the rapidly developing and relatively affluent cities and counties of the West and Southwest experiencing the largest employment growth rates. State and local government employment is likely to decline in many areas of the Northeast. Excluding public education and public hospitals, for the period 1990 to 2005 government employment is expected to increase by 14 percent, from 9.5 million to 10.8 million jobs.

12. **Employment growth in education at all levels will be incremental.**

    Both public and private education is expected to add 2.3 million jobs to the 9.4 million employed in 1990. Employment in education will increase slightly at all levels due to projected population and enrollment increases. Between 1990 and 2005, elementary school age population should rise by 3.8 million, secondary by 3.2 million, and postsecondary by 1.4 million. Accordingly, job opportunities should increase for teachers, teacher aides, counselors, and administrative staff.

13. **Jobs in manufacturing will decline throughout the 1990s.**

    Manufacturing jobs are expected to decline by 3 percent, from the 1990 level of 19.1 million. Most of the decline will affect production jobs; professional, technical, and managerial positions in manufacturing will increase. These declines will be due to productivity gains achieved through automation and improved management as well as the closing of less efficient plants.

14. **Employment in agriculture, forestry, fishing, and mining jobs will continue to decline.**

    Employment in agriculture, forestry, and fishing is expected to decline by 6 percent, from 3.3 to 3.1 million, reflecting a decrease of nearly 410,000 self-employed workers. Wage and salary positions in agricultural, forestry, and fishing services will increase by 214,000. Strong growth will take place in agricultural services industries, especially landscape, horticultural, and farm management services. Much of the self-employment decline in agriculture will be due to the closing of lucrative export markets as the productivity of agriculture abroad improves and new hybrid crops are introduced from genetic engineering breakthroughs to solve many of the world's food problems. Employment in mining is expected to decline by 6 percent—from 712,000 to 669,000. These figures assume that domestic oil production will drop and oil imports will rise sharply.

15. **Glamorous new occupations, responding to new technological developments and consumer demands, will offer exciting new careering and re-careering opportunities for future job seekers who are well educated and skilled in the jobs of tomorrow.**

    New occupations, created through a combination of technological innovations and new service demands, will provide excellent career opportunities for those who possess the necessary skills and drive to succeed in the 1990s. New occupations with such names as bionic-electronic technician, holographic inspector, cryonics technician, and aquaculturist will enter our occupational vocabulary during the coming decade.

16. **The hottest career fields for the first five years of the 21st century will be in science, engineering, computer technology, and health services.**

Look for these jobs to be the highest demand and highest paying jobs in the coming decade: biological scientist, physician, mechanical engineer, chemical engineer, computer scientist, computer engineer, materials engineer, medical technologist. Demand also will be high for these less well paid jobs: special education teachers, personal and home care aides, home health aides, and physical therapists.

Examine Growing and Declining Occupations

The Department of Labor divides occupations into 16 broad groups based on the Standard Occupational Classification, the classification system used by all government agencies for collecting occupational employment information:

- Executive, administrative, and managerial occupations
- Engineers, scientists, and related occupations
- Social science, social service, and related occupations
- Teachers, librarians, and counselors
- Health-related occupations
- Writers, artists, and entertainers
- Technologists and technicians
- Marketing and sales occupations
- Administrative support occupations, including clerical
- Service occupations
- Agricultural and forestry occupations
- Mechanics and repairers
- Construction occupations
- Production occupations
- Transportation and material moving occupations
- Handlers, equipment cleaners, helpers, and laborers

Assuming a moderate rate of economic growth throughout the 1990s—not boom and bust cycles—the U.S. Department of Labor projects an average growth rate of 20 percent for all occupations. Technical and service occupations will grow the fastest during the 1990-2005 period:

Projected Employment Changes in Broad Occupational Groups, 1990-2005

Occupational group	Total increase/decrease in new jobs	Percentage change
All occupations	38,851,000	+20
■ Services	7,403,000	+29
■ Administrative support	6,413,000	+13
■ Operators	5,449,000	+4
■ Marketing and sales	5,379,000	+24
■ Precision production	4,764,000	+13
■ Professional specialty	4,281,000	+32
■ Managerial	3,085,000	+27
■ Technicians	1,200,000	+37
■ Agriculture-related	863,000	+5

More than one-half of all job growth in the 1990-2005 period will be contributed by 30 fast growing occupations:

Fastest Growing Occupations Contributing More Than 50% to Job Growth, 1990-2005

Occupation	New jobs created
■ Sales workers, retail	887,000
■ Registered nurses	767,000
■ Cashiers	685,000
■ General office clerks	670,000
■ Truck drivers, light and heavy	617,000
■ General managers and top executives	598,000
■ Janitors and cleaners	555,000
■ Nursing aides, orderlies, and attendants	552,000
■ Food counter, fountain, and related workers	550,000
■ Waiters and waitresses	449,000
■ Teachers, secondary school	437,000
■ Receptionists and information clerks	422,000
■ Systems analysts and computer scientists	366,000
■ Food preparation workers	365,000
■ Childcare workers	353,000
■ Gardeners and groundskeepers	348,000
■ Accountants and auditors	340,000
■ Teachers, elementary school	313,000
■ Guards	298,000
■ Teachers aids and educational assistants	278,000
■ Licensed practical nurses	269,000
■ Clerical supervisors and managers	263,000
■ Home health aids	263,000

- Maintenance repairers, general utility 251,000
- Secretaries except legal and medical 248,000
- Cooks, short order and fast food 246,000
- Stock clerks, sales floor 209,000
- Lawyers 206,000

The patterns of growth and decline in industries and occupations during the 1990s generally follow the larger changes in the economy we discussed earlier. The U.S. Department of Labor studies have identified the fastest growing and declining occupations for the years 1990-2005. Occupations, for example, contributing the largest job growth in terms of the actual number of new jobs generated will be in service industries requiring a wide range of skills. Nearly half of the 30 fastest growing occupations will be in the health services alone, and most of the jobs will require advanced education and training:

30 Fastest Growing Occupations, 1990-2005

Occupation	Percent growth
Home health aides	92
Paralegals	85
Systems analysts and computer scientists	79
Personal and home care aides	77
Physical therapists	76
Medical assistants	74
Operations research analysts	73
Human services workers	71
Radiological technologists and technicians	70
Medical secretaries	68
Physical and corrective therapy assistants and aides	64
Psychologists	64
Travel agents	62
Correction officers	61
Data processing equipment repairers	60
Flight attendants	59
Computer programmers	56
Occupational therapists	55
Surgical technologists	55
Medical records technicians	54
Management analysts	52
Respiratory therapists	52
Childcare workers	49
Marketing, advertising, and public relations managers	47
Legal secretaries	47
Receptionists and information clerks	47
Registered nurses	44

▪ Nursing aides, orderlies, and attendants	43
▪ Licensed practical nurses	42
▪ Cooks, restaurant	42

On the other hand, nearly half of the 30 fastest declining occupations will be in declining industries affected by technological change:

30 Fastest Declining Occupations, 1990-2005

Occupation	Numerical decline
▪ Farmers	224,000
▪ Bookkeeping, accounting, and auditing clerks	133,000
▪ Childcare workers, private household	124,000
▪ Sewing machine operators, garment	116,000
▪ Electrical and electronic assemblers	105,000
▪ Typists and word processors	103,000
▪ Cleaners and servants, private household	101,000
▪ Farm workers	92,000
▪ Electrical and electronic equipment assembler	81,000
▪ Textile draw-out and winding machine operators	61,000
▪ Switchboard operators	57,000
▪ Machine forming operators	43,000
▪ Machine tool cutting operators	42,000
▪ Telephone and cable TV line installers and repairers	40,000
▪ Central office and PBX installers and repairers	34,000
▪ Central office operators	31,000
▪ Statistical clerks	31,000
▪ Packaging and filling machine operators	27,000
▪ Station installers and repairers, telephone	26,000
▪ Bank tellers	25,000
▪ Lathe turning machine tool setters	20,000
▪ Grinders and polishers, hand	19,000
▪ Electromechanical equipment assemblers	18,000
▪ Grinding machine setters	18,000
▪ Service station attendants	17,000
▪ Directory assistance operators	16,000
▪ Butchers and meatcutters	14,000
▪ Chemical equipment controllers	14,000
▪ Drilling and boring machine tool setters	13,000
▪ Meter readers, utilities	12,000

Determine "The Best" Jobs For You

The fastest growing occupational fields are not necessarily the best ones to enter. The best job and career for you will depend on your particular mix of skills, interests, and work and lifestyle values. Money, for example, is only one of many determiners of whether or not a job and career is particularly desirable. A job may pay a great deal of money, but it also may be very stressful and insecure, or it is found in an undesirable location. "The best" job for you will be one you find very rewarding in terms of your own criteria and priorities.

Periodically some observers of the labor market attempt to identify what are the best, the worst, the hottest, the most lucrative, or the most promising jobs and careers of the decade. The latest and most objective attempt to assemble a list of "the best" jobs in America is presented in *The Jobs Rated Almanac*. Similar in methodology to *The Places Rated Almanac* for identifying the best places to live in America, the latest edition (1995) of *The Jobs Rated Almanac* evaluates and ranks 250 jobs in terms of six primary "job quality" criteria: income, stress, physical demands, environment, outlook, and security. According to their analyses, the 20 highest ranking jobs by accumulated score of these criteria are:

"The Best" Jobs in America

Job title	Overall rank	Overall score
▪ Actuary	1	118
▪ Software engineer	2	124
▪ Computer systems analyst	3	131
▪ Accountant	4	218
▪ Paralegal assistant	5	222
▪ Mathematician	6	223
▪ Medical secretary	7	230
▪ Computer Programmer	8	263
▪ Parole officer	9	279
▪ Medical Records Technician	10	294
▪ Dietician	11	310
▪ Medical Technologist	12	335
▪ Statistican	13	336
▪ Audiologist	14	342
▪ Hospital administrator	15	349
▪ Dental Hygienist	16	350
▪ Medical Laboratory Technician	17	365
▪ Urban/Regional Planner	18	367
▪ Biologist	19	370
▪ Sociologist	20	374

For the relative rankings of the remaining 230 jobs as well as the ratings of each job on individual criterion, consult the latest edition of *The Jobs Rated*

Almanac, which should be available in your local library or bookstore. It can also be ordered from Impact Publications by completing the order form at the end of this book.

Look For Exciting New Occupations in the 21st Century

In the early 1980s the auto and related industries—steel, rubber, glass, aluminum, railroads and auto dealers—accounted for one-fifth of all employment in the United States. Today that percentage continues to decline as service occupations further dominate America's occupational structure.

New occupations for the 1990s and beyond will center around information, energy, high-tech, healthcare, and financial industries. They promise to create a new occupational structure and vocabulary relating to computers, robotics, biotechnology, lasers, and fiber optics. And as these fields begin to apply new technologies to developing new innovations, they in turn will generate other new occupations in the 21st century. While most new occupations are not major growth fields, because they do not initially generate a large number of new jobs, they will present individuals with fascinating new opportunities to become leaders in pioneering new fields and industries.

Futurists identify several emerging occupations for the coming decades. Most tend to brainstorm lists of occupational titles they feel will emerge in the next decade based on present trends. Others identify additional occupations which may be created from new, unforeseen technological breakthroughs. Feingold and Miller (*Emerging Careers*), for example, see 30 new careers emerging:

Emerging Careers For the 21st Century

- artificial intelligence technician
- aquaculturist
- automotive fuel cell battery technician
- benefits analyst
- bionic electron technician
- computational linguist
- computer microprocessor
- cryonics technician
- dialysis technologist
- electronic mail technician
- fiber optic technician
- fusion engineer
- hazardous waste technician
- horticulture therapy
- image consultant
- information broker
- information center manager
- job developer
- leisure consultant
- materials utilization specialist
- medical diagnostic imaging technician
- myotherapist
- relocation counselor
- retirement counselor
- robot technician
- shyness consultant
- software club director
- space mechanic
- underwater archaeologist
- water quality specialist

Most futurists agree that such new occupations will have two dominant characteristics during the 1990s and into the 21st century:

- **They will generate fewer new jobs** in comparison to the overall growth of jobs in hundreds of more traditional service fields, such as sales workers, office clerks, truck drivers, and janitors.

- **They require a high level of education and skills** for entry into the fields as well as continuing training and retraining as each field transforms itself into additional growth fields.

If you plan to pursue any of these occupations, expect to first acquire highly specialized skills which may require years of higher education and training.

Consider the Implications of Future Trends For You

Most growth industries and occupations require skills training and experience. Moving into one of these fields will require knowledge of job qualifications, the nature of the work, and sources of employment. Fortunately, the U.S. Department of Labor publishes several useful sources of information available in most libraries to help you. These include the *Dictionary of Occupational Titles*, which identifies over 13,000 job titles. The *Occupational Outlook Handbook* provides an overview of current labor market conditions and projections as well as discusses nearly 250 occupations that account for 107 million jobs, or 87 percent of the nation's total jobs, according to several useful informational categories: nature of work; working conditions; employment; training, other qualifications, and achievement; job outlook; earnings; related occupations; and sources of additional information. Anyone seeking to enter the job market or change careers should initially consult these publications for information on trends and occupations.

However, remember that labor market statistics are for industries and occupations *as a whole*. They tell you little about the shift in employment emphasis *within the industry*, and nothing about the outlook of particular jobs for you, *the individual*. For example, employment in agriculture is expected to decline by 14 percent between 1985 and 2000, but the decline consists of an important shift in employment emphasis within the industry: there will be 500,000 fewer self-employed workers but 150,000 more wage and salary earners in the service end of agriculture. The employment statistics also assume a steady-state of economic growth with consumers having more and more disposable income to stimulate a wide variety of service and trade industries.

Therefore, be careful in how you interpret and use this information in making your own job and career decisions. If, for example, you want to become a college teacher, and the data tells you there will be a 10 percent decline in this occupation during the next 10 years, this does not mean you could not find employment, as well as advance, in this field. It merely means that, on the whole, competition may be keen for these jobs, and that future advancement and mobility in this occupation may not be very good—on the whole. At the same time, there may be numerous job opportunities available in a declining occupational field as many individuals abandon the field for more attractive occupations. In fact, you may do much better in this declining occupation than in a growing field depending on your interests, motivations, abilities, job search savvy, and level of competition. And if the decade ahead experiences more boom and bust cycles, expect most of these U.S. Department of Labor statistics and projections to be invalid for the economic realities of this decade.

As we emphasized earlier, use this industrial and occupational data to expand your awareness of various job and career options. By no means should you make critical education, training, and occupational choices based upon this information alone. Such choices require additional types of information—subjects of the next six chapters—on you, the individual.

5

Acquire Skills Appropriate For Today's Economy

The American economy and work force have faced numerous challenges and crises in the past. Most relate to occasional economic downturns that generate temporary high unemployment rates. During bad economic times, unemployment increases as jobs are eliminated; during good economic times, unemployment decreases as new jobs are created. This cyclical employment pattern appears to be a permanent feature of America's relatively unplanned and spontaneous economic system.

Skills Imbalance

The economic challenge in the decade ahead will be quite different from the previous cyclical patterns of growth and decline. The cyclical patterns will continue in a boom/bust economy. However, as already witnessed in the recession of 1990-1993, non-cyclical parts of the economy, which are normally resistant to recessions—services, retail trade, and public employment—will experience shrinkage; these sectors may not rebound in the foreseeable future. Led by over-expanded real estate and construction markets, and exacerbated by a severe credit crunch brought about by highly leveraged, speculative, and bankrupted banking and financial markets, these non-cyclical sectors of the economy will experience long-term unemployment in areas that were considered "hot" job markets in the overheated economy of the 1980s. Real estate, construction, banking, and related industries will experience employment decreases throughout the 1990s.

At the same time, structural unemployment will increase due to transformations in the economy brought about with the introduction of new technologies in the work place and the decline of traditional industries. The new crisis will be the imbalance between skills workers possess and those employers need. Widening in recent years, this imbalance is expected to continue, if not increase, into the 21st century.

The skills imbalance is due to several training failures—and failures to train—on the part of both government and industry. Traditional educational institutions fail to teach the skills needed for the new jobs of today and tomorrow. Government policies, emphasizing redistributive subsidy and welfare programs designed for the economies of the 1960s and 1970s, provide little incentive for individuals to seek retraining. And present training programs offered by the private sector tend to be oriented toward managers in the soft skill areas; training of production workers in the hard technical skill areas is relatively neglected.

In the meantime, a large segment of the work force is still oriented to the job market with skills and expectations best suited for the past three decades. Rather than take initiative to acquire new skills, many people do nothing; they remain unemployed, underemployed, or unhappy with their work. Others, unwilling to accept responsibility, seek scapegoats for their plight.

In this chapter we address the problem of training as well as outline how individuals can acquire the necessary education and training for the jobs and careers of tomorrow— essential knowledge for the decade ahead.

> **These non-cyclical sectors of the economy will experience long-term unemployment in areas that were considered "hot" job markets in the overheated economy of the 1980s.**

On Your Own in a Sea of Good Intentions

The structure of education and training in the United States is highly fragmented. Its scope, quality, and effectiveness vary greatly among regions, communities, and institutions. As a result, many people have difficulty understanding and using education and training opportunities.

Federal government-sponsored training programs consist of a maze of over 20 programs ranging from Trade Adjustment Assistance to programs for redwood forest lumberjacks. The major federal program which replaced the controversial Comprehensive Employment and Training Act (CETA) program in 1982, is the Jobs Training Partnership Act (JTPA). This program, like its predecessor, is limited in scope. It focuses primarily on providing training and employment assistance for the poor and hardcore unemployed.

Employment observers and policy analysts Pat Choate and Noel Epstein best characterize federal training programs as being subject to "confusion, fragmentation, bureaucracy and the political pork barrel." While much needed, such programs will not have a great effect on the overall training and retraining needs of the nation.

But politicians, journalists, employment specialists, and many other "experts" continue to propose more government-sponsored training and retraining programs to deal with the problems of unemployment and displaced workers. Such well-meaning proposals have limitations. They fail to take into account the capabilities of the government to develop and manage such programs. First, the costs of training and retraining are so massive that the government could not sustain them for long. Second, the intergovernmental system through which retraining must take place—state and local governments—is already too fragmented, decentralized, and political to allow for effective *implementation* of a government-sponsored program. Third, given these constraints, any realistic government-sponsored program would be small in scale; consequently, it would have little impact on the overall training and retraining needs of the country. These are real—not ideological or philosophical—constraints.

Overall educational reforms still remain at the policy debate stage with trendy institutional proposals such as eliminating the U.S. Department of Education, privatizing public schools, and initiating an educational voucher system allowing families to easily finance private education. However, it remains unclear how such structural changes would affect both the process and performance of education in reference to skills needed for the job markets of the coming decade. Indeed, more and more studies pinpoint the real culprit affecting education performance which has nothing to do with such institutional reforms—the continuing decline of the American family.

Despite its failures and limitations, government still has a major role to play in promoting training and retraining. For instance, it would be ideal if both government and the private sector provided new incentives to encourage more people to re-career by acquiring new skills and relocating to new jobs and communities. These incentives might include tax breaks for individuals engaged in retraining and for corporations sponsoring training programs. Another incentive, outlined by Choate and Epstein, would be to create Individual Training Accounts (ITA), structured similarly to a pension fund. Jointly financed by employers and employees, the innovative ITA would provide money for retraining displaced workers. The individual could use this money—perhaps in the form of a retraining voucher—to enroll in a specialized program of his or her own choosing. The problem of *how to finance retraining* will have to be addressed with these and other public policy options in the not-too-distant future.

The problem with most government policies and programs is that they are inevitably political. They are controversial, reflecting competing values in American society. They take time to develop and implement. And they often fail. In the meantime, individuals must be responsible for their own employment fate by taking appropriate actions to solve their own employment problems. Government is not likely to solve these problems.

The old cliche that *"there is no such thing as a free lunch"* should be reinforced with a new saying for the coming re-careering era: *"Times will be tough for those who don't get off their duff!"* At the very least, re-careering requires individuals to:

- take risks
- invest time and money in their future
- learn something new and usable
- apply new skills to changing employment situations

Train and Retrain For an Uncertain Future

Retraining needs in the decade ahead are difficult to estimate. Indeed, conducting a survey on the present state of training is difficult, if not impossible, given the fragmented nature of organizations in America. Nonetheless, certain trends are evident in the work place, and some statistics are available on the scope and depth of training in the United States. For example, during the past 30 years, blue-collar employment has steadily declined to the point where the traditional distinction between blue-collar and white-collar workers has become somewhat meaningless for describing critical characteristics of the labor force.

Changes have been evident during the past two decades, and they will likely accelerate in the decade ahead. For example, Bluestone and Harrison (*The Decentralization of America*) found that between 35 and 40 million Americans lost their jobs in the 1970s; many were forced to relocate as plants closed and industries moved South. The U.S. Department of Labor found that 11.5 million Americans lost their jobs between 1979 and 1984 due to plant shut downs or relocation, rising productivity, and shrinking output. Between 1979 and 1993, Fortune 500 companies reduced their staffs from 16.2 to 11.4 million employees, reducing their share of the civilian workforce from 17 to 10 percent. A study by Carnegie-Mellon University predicts that robots will supplant 3 million factory workers by the year 2000. Many factories may be completely automated—requiring only a handful of technicians to supervise the robots. In fact, the Japanese already have totally automated factories. While many low-wage manufacturing jobs have continued to move abroad, especially in the textile, footwear, toy, and electronic assembly industries, within the past three years many companies have moved a new level of skilled jobs off-shore to low-wage countries—accounting, data processing, and telemarketing.

Where will the displaced workers of today and tomorrow go? The fear—justifiably so—is that many workers will be permanently displaced by the new technology. For example, Harvard University economist James L. Medoff points to Commerce Department statistics: between 1969 and 1978 job-related training provided by employers for workers aged 25 to 49 increased to 6 percent from 5.2 percent. A further indication of a growing skills imbalance in the labor market since 1969 is found in Medoff's study of unemployment. Prior to 1969, when unemployment increased among 25 to 64 year-old men, the number of help-wanted ads declined as employers hired from the excess pool of skilled unemployed workers. However, since 1969 the number of help-wanted ads has not declined proportionately during a period of high unemployment. Medoff believes this indicates there is now a decreasing demand for the skills of present unemployed workers, a clear sign of worsening structural unemployment.

On the other hand, the emphasis on productivity and the introduction of new technology promise to create new jobs and career opportunities. Many people hope these changes will create a sufficient number of new jobs to absorb displaced workers and that employers will retrain them for the new technology.

Both the fear and the hope will probably come true, but for different groups in the society. The fears are indeed real. For example, at present over 20 million Americans are estimated to be functionally illiterate—they can't read nor write. Add to this number the fact that nearly 1 million students drop out of high school each year, and the U.S. Department of Education Secretary's warning to Congress:

> up to 75 percent of the unemployed lack the basic skills of communication, personal relations, motivation, self-confidence, reading and computing that would enable employers to train them for the jobs that will open up in the next few years.

Therefore, a large segment of the population will require remedial training prior to receiving job skills training.

For poor inner city and rural people, the consequences of productivity improvements and the introduction of new technology in the work place are frightening. Many of these people may become hopeless wards of the state, ill-equipped to function in a highly literate and efficient information society. Facing a vicious circle of circumstances which prevent them from taking initiative, they will constitute a major problem for society. In the end, government may be the only institution willing and able to provide basic training in functional skills for these individuals.

The worldwide problem of unemployment is even more frightening. Third World nations, with nearly 500 million unemployed at present, are expected to have nearly 1 billion unemployed in the year 2000. Twice this number are underemployed—performing jobs at low productivity and skill levels. Not surprising, jobs are increasingly becoming the top priority problem for all nations.

Question Public Education Performance

Public educational institutions have been slow in responding to the obvious training and retraining needs of employers. Despite billions of dollars expended on university education, the quality of reading, writing, and communication skills, as well as analytical and problem-solving abilities, seems to be declining compared to previous generations of graduates. The critical high-tech programs of engineering and computer science are not producing enough graduates to meet the demands of private industry. The result is a mismatch of college and university educational programs with the employment needs of companies.

Colleges and universities continue to graduate students in fields where there are few job opportunities. For example, while most college graduates in the 1960s found jobs in their chosen occupations, more graduates in the 1970s, 1980s, and 1990s were forced to seek employment outside their fields.

The transition for public education will be slow and difficult. Many public schools are too tradition-laden as well as insulated from the realities of the labor market to place a major emphasis on vocational-skills training within their academic programs. Lacking accountability, many public colleges and universities continue to teach a disproportionate number of subjects, courses, and disciplines which are favorites of the faculty, simply considered necessary for a "well-rounded" graduate, or at best "interesting" rather than emphasize skills for a turbulent job market. Education remains one of the few archaic bureaucratic institutions where producers, who have little or no market experience, dictate demand for consumers who compliantly acquire many questionable skills. Not surprising, the skills they acquire tend to be the very ones that keep faculty employed as well as insulated from the noneducational job market. More surprising, education and educators get away with such unaccountable, nonperformance behavior with little or no public outcry!

> **Education remains one of the few archaic bureaucratic institutions where producers, who have little or no market experience, dictate demands for consumers who compliantly acquire many questionable skills.**

On the other hand, community colleges, business colleges, vocational-technical schools, specialized training institutes, and university-sponsored conferences and workshops have been more responsive to training individuals in relation to job market needs. Many of these institutions provide practical, intensive skills training programs as well as placement services for their graduates. Over 25 million people participate in these programs each year.

Learn More About Private Efforts

If public educational institutions fail to respond to real needs, the private sector will have to provide the bulk of the training and retraining necessary for the decades ahead. More private educational and professional training organizations will be required to provide short two to five-day workshops, four-week refresher courses, or 15-week intensive training programs.

The private sector is equipped to provide training alternatives. Thousands of private organizations already provide off-the-shelf, custom-designed, and generic training seminars. Most of these programs last one to five days and stress intensive training in particular subject and skill areas.

A few companies are preparing for the future with their own in-house training programs. For example, Ford Motor Company and the United Auto Workers work with a nationwide network of community colleges in providing retraining for displaced automakers. Polaroid Corporation conducts reading labs and math tutorials for assembly line workers in order to prepare them for new technology in the work place. In the private sector AT&T maintains the largest number of in-house trainers for a trainer-to-employee ratio of 1:100. The U.S. Navy maintains the highest trainer-to-employee ratio: 26,000 full-time trainers for 565,000 enlisted personnel or a 1:21 ratio. Altogether, the private sector spends over $200 billion a year on training and retraining. This figure is likely to increase as the skills required in the work place change in response to the changing technology.

Most training taking place within organizations is either on-the-job or classroom training. Most firms with 500 or more employees have at least one full-time trainer in their organization; many of these organizations also have training departments. Organizations with more than 25,000 employees have an average of 50 full-time trainers. Organizations with 100 or fewer employees normally use part-time trainers or contract with private firms to conduct specific training programs for their employees.

While billions of dollars are spent each year on training and education, neither the public nor private sectors are adequately meeting the new retraining needs of society. From the perspective of training professionals, we are rapidly approaching a "human capital crisis."

Become a Generalist-Specialist

As we noted earlier, individuals must take the initiative to acquire the training and retraining necessary for a turbulent job market. No longer will knowledge of job hunting techniques alone be sufficient to function in such a job market. Specific work-content skills—mostly technical in nature—must accompany well-defined job search strategies. And promising trends have begun. For example, each year over 3 million Americans enroll in courses specifically designed to help them change careers.

So where do you go for skills training in a highly fragmented, decentralized, and chaotic educational and training market? While many organizations provide their own in-service training and retraining programs, they assume one possesses a certain level of skill proficiency prior to being hired. In other words, they expect the employee is easily trainable. For many jobs, this means one needs a well-rounded educational background which develops basic reading, writing, and communication skills as well as interpersonal, analytical, organizational, and problem-solving abilities—the major thrust of a good generalist liberal arts education. Given the changing nature of the job market, such an educational background can best prepare you for the flexibility you will need in the future.

At the same time, while providing a good foundation, a generalist background is insufficient for functioning in today's job market. Individuals need a strong background in scientific-technical skills. These skills are in math, science, computers, and technical fields. In addition, individuals are expected to have developed basic work attitudes which translate into positive behaviors such as: coming to work, being on time, managing time, meeting deadlines, getting along with superiors and co-workers, and being courteous to the public.

The changing job market requires more generalist-specialists who are trainable and thus can adapt to rapidly changing work places. For example, it is estimated that 40 million office workers will be using some type of electronic equipment in the 1990s—an increase of 30 million from the 1980s. Given the rapidly changing office technologies, employers may need to retrain the same workers five to ten times during a 20-year period. Therefore, regardless of what type of word processor an individual is trained on in a secretarial school today, the same individual can expect to operate one of a new generation of word processors five years from now. The important question for employers will be: "Is this individual, who is now a specialist in technology X, flexible enough to learn and adapt to technology Y tomorrow?" The answer requires a merging of the generalist and specialist traditions in individuals' educational and training programs.

Identify Your Major Training Options

The U.S. Department of Labor identifies nine structured training programs individuals should familiarize themselves with prior to making educational and training choices. Most of these sources emphasize practical hands-on training in specific occupational fields. Private trade schools, for example, are flourishing—an indication of the shift to practical skills training in education. Each alternative has various advantages and disadvantages, and costs differ considerably.

1. Public vocational education:

Public vocational education is provided through secondary, postsecondary, and adult vocational and technical programs. The emphasis in many secondary schools is to give high school students vocational training in addition to the regular academic program. Postsecondary vocational education is provided for individuals who have left high school but who are not seeking a baccalaureate degree. Adult vocational and technical programs emphasize retraining or upgrading the skills of individuals in the labor force. The traditional agricultural, trade, and industrial emphasis of vocational education has been vastly expanded to include training in distribution, health, home economics, office, and technical occupations. Most programs train individuals for specific occupations, which are outlined in the *Occupational Outlook Handbook*. Each year over 20 million people enroll in public vocational education programs.

2. Noncollegiate postsecondary vocational education:

Nearly 2 million people enroll in over 6,500 noncollegiate postsecondary schools with occupational programs each year. Most of these schools specialize in one of eight vocational areas: cosmetology/barber, business/commercial, trade, hospital, vocational/technical, allied health, arts/design, and technical. They offer programs in seven major areas: agribusiness, marketing and distribution, health, home economics, technical, business and office, and trade and industrial. Over 75 percent of these schools are privately owned institutions. And over 70 percent of the privately owned schools are either cosmetology/barber schools or business and commercial schools. Over 75 percent of the independent nonprofit schools are hospital schools. Over 1 million people complete occupational programs in noncollegiate postsecondary schools each year.

3. Employer training:

Employers spend over $200 billion a year on in-house training and education programs. These programs usually involve training new employees, improving employee performance, or preparing employees for new jobs. Skilled and semi-skilled workers are trained through apprenticeship programs, learning-by-doing, and structured on-the-job instruction. Structured classroom training is increasingly offered to skilled workers by in-house trainers, professional associations, private firms, or colleges and universities. Tuition-aid programs are used frequently among firms lacking in-house training capabilities.

4. Apprenticeship programs:

Apprenticeship programs normally range from one to six years, depending on the particular trade and organization. These programs are used most extensively in the trade occupations, especially in construction and metalworking. They involve planned on-the-job training in conjunction with classroom instruction and supervision. Over 500,000 individuals are involved in apprenticeship programs each year. These numbers are likely to increase in the coming decade as America faces an acute shortage of skilled trade workers. Expect apprenticeship programs to expand accordingly.

5. Federal employment and training programs:

Federal employment and training programs largely function through state and local governments. The major federal program is the Job Training Partnership Act (JTPA) program. Working through Private Industry Councils (PICs), the JTPA program is designed to train the economically disadvantaged as well as displaced workers who need assistance with skills training, job search, and job relocation. JTPA also operates two youth programs—The Job Corps and the Summer Youth Employment Program. Other major Federal programs include two administered through the Employment and Training Administration: The Trade Adjustment Act program to assist workers displaced by foreign competition, and the Work Incentive (WIN) program for employable recipients of Aid to Families with Dependent Children, migrant and seasonal farm workers, Native Americans, and workers 55 and over.

6. Armed Forces Training:

The Armed Forces provide training in numerous occupational skills that may or may not be directly transferred to civilian occupations. Thousands of military recruits complete training programs in several transferable areas each year, such as computer repair, medical care, food service, metalworking, communications, and administration. Occupations unique to the military, such as infantry and guncrew, are less transferable to civilian occupations.

7. Home study (correspondence) schools:

Home study or correspondence schools provide a variety of training options. Most programs concentrate on acquiring a single skill; others may even offer a BA, MA, or Ph.D. by mail! Some programs are of questionable quality while others may be revolutionizing the education and training landscape of America. For many people, this is a convenient, inexpensive, and effective way to acquire new skills. Over 5 million people enroll in home study courses each year. Colleges and universities are quickly moving into the home study business by offering numerous televised courses for academic credit. The Public Broadcast System (PBS) offers several home study courses through its Adult Learning Service: computer literacy and applications, basic skills and personal enrichment, sales and customer service, effective communication skills, and management skills.

8. Community and junior colleges:

Community and junior colleges in recent years have broadened their missions from primarily preparing individuals for university degree programs to preparing them with skills appropriate for the job market. Accordingly, more of their programs emphasize vocational and occupational curriculums, such as data processing or dental hygiene, which are typically two-year programs resulting in an associate degree. Community and junior colleges will probably continue to expand their program offerings as they further adjust to the employment needs of communities. Nearly 5 million students enroll in community and junior college programs each year.

9. Colleges and universities:

Colleges and universities continue to provide the traditional four-year and graduate degree programs in various subject fields. While many of the fields are occupational-specific and require some form of certification—such as engineering, law, medicine, and business—many other fields are not. The exact relationship of the degree program to the job market varies with different disciplines. As noted earlier, in recent years, graduates of many programs have had difficulty finding employment in their chosen fields. This is particularly true for students who only have a generalist background in the liberal arts. During the past decade many colleges and universities have adjusted to declining enrollments by offering several nontraditional occupational-related courses and programs. Continuing education, special skills training courses, short courses, evening course offerings, "telecourses," and workshops and seminars on job-related matters have become popular with nontraditional, older students who seek specific skills training rather than degrees. At the same time, traditional academic programs are placing greater emphasis on internships and cooperative education programs in order to give students work experience related to their academic programs.

Additional training programs may be sponsored by local governments, professional associations, women's centers, YWCA's, and religious and civic groups. As training and retraining become more acceptable to the general public, we can expect different forms and types of training programs to be sponsored by various groups.

We also can expect a revolution in the training field, closely related to high-tech developments. Televised education and training courses should continue to increase in number and scope. Computer-based training, similar in some respects to traditional home study programs, will become more prevalent as computer software and interactive video training packages are developed in response to the new technology and the rising demand for skills training.

Individuals in tomorrow's education training markets will become examples of Toffler's "prosumer society": in a decentralized information market, individuals will choose what training they most desire as well as control when and where they will receive it. With the development of interactive video and computer training programs, individuals will manage the training process in a more efficient and effective manner than with the more centralized, time consuming, and expensive use of traditional student-teacher classroom instruction. This type of training may eventually make many of the previously discussed categories of education and training obsolete.

Become an Informed Consumer

Several resources can help you decide which training path is more appropriate for you. If you use the popular *Discover II* computerized career planning system, for example, you will find it includes a section that matches education and training programs with career interests. A few other computer software programs also match career interests with education and training programs. Contact your local secondary school, community college, or library for information on these programs.

You should begin your search for useful education and training information by consulting several useful publications. The major sources will be found in the reference section of libraries as well as in guidance offices and career planning centers of schools, colleges, universities, and specialized employment assistance centers. Most of these organizations maintain catalogues, directories, and files listing educational and training opportunities.

Two useful sources for information on education and training programs are *Peterson's Guides* and *Barron's Educational Series* which publish several excellent directories. Most of the directories are updated annually and include basic information on choosing programs and institutions best suited to your interests. Among the many titles offered by Peterson's and Barron's are:

- *Guide to Four-Year Colleges*
- *Guide to Two-Year Colleges*

- *The College Money Handbook*
- *Guides to Graduate Study:*
  —*Graduate and Professional Programs*
  —*Humanities and Social Sciences*
  —*Biological Agricultural and Health Sciences*
  —*Physical Sciences and Mathematics*
  —*Engineering and Applied Sciences*
- *Regional Guides to Colleges*
  —*Middle Atlantic*
  —*Midwest*
  —*New England*
  —*New York*
  —*Southeast*
  —*Southwest*
  —*West*
- *Winning Money For College*
- *How to Write Your Way Into College*
- *Job Opportunities in Engineering and Technology*
- *Job Opportunities in Health Care*
- *Job Opportunities Business*
- *Guide to Medical and Dental Schools*
- *How to Prepare for the SAT*
- *Guide to Law Schools*
- *Profiles of American Colleges*
- *Guide to Graduate Business Schools*
- *Competitive Colleges*
- *Colleges With Programs For Learning-Disabled Students*
- *National College Databank*
- *Handbook For College Admissions*
- *Guide to College Admissions*
- *How the Military Will Help You Pay For College*
- *Corporate Tuition Aid Programs*
- *Graduate Education Directory*

Most major libraries have copies of these publications in their reference section. If you cannot find them in your local library, check with your local bookstore or contact the publishers directly. Ask for copies of their latest catalogs: Peterson's, P.O. Box 2123, Princeton, NJ 08543-2123, Tel. 800/338-3282; and Barron's Educational Series, 250 Wireless Blvd., Hauppauge, NY 11788, Tel. 516/434-3311.

If you decide you need to acquire a specific skill, consult various professional or trade associations; many can provide you with a list of reputable institutions providing skills training in particular fields. The names, addresses, and telephone numbers of all major associations are listed in the *Encyclopedia of Associations* (Gale Publishers) and *National Trade and Professional Associations* (Columbia Books), two extremely useful directories found in the reference section of most libraries.

The U.S. Department of Labor's *Occupational Outlook Handbook* also lists useful names and addresses relating to employment training in specific fields. Consult the *"Sources of Career Information"* section in the latest edition of this biannual directory. This book is also available in most libraries or can be purchased from Impact Publications by completing the order form at the end of this book or by consulting their World Wide Web site: http://www.impactpublications.com.

For information on **private trade and technical schools**, be sure to get a copy of the *Handbook of Accredited Private Trade and Technical Schools* which is distributed by the Career College Association: 750 1st St., NE., Washington, DC 20002, Tel. 202/336-6700.

For information on **apprenticeship programs**, get a copy of *The National Apprenticeship Program and Apprenticeship Information* through the Bureau of Apprenticeships and Training (BAT), U.S. Department of Labor, 200 Constitution Ave., NW, Room N-4649, Washington, DC 20210, Tel. 202/219-5921. BAT offices are also found in each state. To find if there is a BAT office near you, consult the White or Blue Pages of your telephone directory under *"United States Government—Department of Labor."* Your local library and public employment service office should also have information on apprenticeship programs.

If you are interested in **home study and correspondence courses**, contact the National Home Study Council (NHSC) for information on home study programs. NHSC distributes copies of a useful publication entitled *Directory of Accredited Home Study Programs*. For information on this and other NHSC publications, contact: National Home Study Council, 1601 18th St., NW, Washington, DC 20009, Tel. 202/234-5100.

You also need to determine the quality and suitability of these education and training programs. Many programs have reputations for fraud, abuse, and incompetence—primarily take your time and money in exchange for broken promises. After all, this is a business transaction—your money in exchange for their services. As an informed consumer, you must demand quality performance for your money. Therefore, when contacting a particular institution, ask to speak to former students and graduates. Write to the Council on Postsecondary Accreditation (One Dupont Circle, Suite 760, Washington, DC 20036) to inquire about the school's credentials. Focus your attention on the *results* or *outcomes* the institution achieves. Instead of asking workload questions—how many faculty have Master's or Ph.D. degrees, or how many students are enrolled—ask these performance or outcome questions:

- What are last year's graduates doing today?
- Where do they work and for whom?
- How much do they earn?
- How many were placed in jobs through this institution?

Institutions that can answer these questions focus on *performance.* Beware of those that can't answer these questions, for they may not be doing an adequate job to meet your needs.

Most colleges and universities will provide assistance to adult learners. Contact student services, continuing education, academic advising, adult services, or women's offices at your local community college, college, or university. Be sure to talk to present and former students about the *expectations and results* of the programs for them. Always remember that educators are first in the business of keeping themselves employed and, second, in the business of delivering educational services. And today, more than ever, educational institutions need students to keep their programs alive. Don't necessarily expect professional educators to be objective about your future vis-a-vis their interests, skills, and programs. At the very least, you must do a critical evaluation of their programs and services.

Other useful sources of information on education and training programs are your telephone book and employers. Look under "Schools" in the Yellow Pages of your telephone directory. Call the schools and ask them to send you literature and application forms and discuss the relevance of their programs to the job market. You should also talk to employers and individuals who have work experience in the field that interests you. Ask them how best to acquire the necessary skills for particular occupations. Most important, thoroughly research education and training alternatives before you invest any money, time, or effort.

> **Thoroughly research education and training alternatives before you invest any money, time, or effort.**

Know How to Finance Your Future

Most people can take advantage of training opportunities in order to better function in today's job market. Lack of information and money are often excuses based upon ignorance of available resources and costs. Education and training may not be cheap, but neither need they be excessively expensive. It is best to view education and training as good investments in your future.

You will find many alternatives to expensive training. For example, adult education programs sponsored by the public school system and community colleges are relatively inexpensive to attend. If you have the will, you usually can find the way in the U.S. education and training systems.

Financial aid for education and training is somewhat bewildering and confusing. It requires research and perseverance on your part. You should begin by contacting the financial aid officers at various institutions that offer the training you desire for advice on financial aid. The particular institutions as well as many other organizations provide scholarships, fellowships, grants, loans, and work-study programs. The American Legion, for example, publishes a useful booklet—*Need a Lift?*—on careers and scholarships for undergraduate and graduate students. To get a single free copy, call 317/630-1200 or write to: American Legion, ATTN: National Emblem Sales, 700 N. Pennsylvania St., P.O. Box 1055, Indianapolis, IN 46204. The College Board also publishes information on student aid. Among its many publications is its annual *Meeting College Costs*. For information on this and other College Board publications, contact: College Board Publications, Box 886, New York, NY 10101.

Information on federal government financial aid programs—grants, loans, work study, and benefits—can be obtained by writing to the U.S. Department of Education for a pamphlet entitled *The Student Guide to Federal Financial Aid Programs*. Revised yearly, this publication can be obtained by calling or writing to: Federal Student Aid Programs, P.O. Box 84, Washington, DC 20044, or call 800/433-3243.

For information on financial assistance for specific groups, such as Hispanics, blacks, Native Americans, and women, get a copy of the U.S. Department of Education's *Higher Education Opportunities for Minorities and Women* (Superintendent of Documents, U.S. Government Printing Office, Washington, DC 20402, Tel. 202/783-3238 for order information). You should also consider examining three useful resources published by Ferguson (previous editions published by Garrett Park Press) relevant to minorities:

- *The Big Book of Minority Opportunities*, Willis L. Johnson (ed.), (Chicago: Ferguson)

- *Financial Aid For Minority Students* (a series of booklets on Allied Health, Business, Education, Engineering, Law, Journalism/Communications, Medicine, Science), Ruth V. Swann (ed.), (Chicago: Ferguson)

- *The National Directory of Minority Organizations*, Katherine W. Cole (ed.) (Chicago: Ferguson)

Gale Research also publishes a series of directories on four minority groups: Asian Americans, Black Americans, Hispanic Americans, and Native Americans. These books can be ordered directly from Impact Publications by completing the order information at the end of this book or through their World Wide Web site: http://www.impactpublications.com.

Compare Costs and Performance Options

Don't forget to compare the different costs of various educational and training programs. Many are inexpensive whereas others are extremely costly. Keep in mind that there is no necessary correlation between educational costs and performance; you may well get your best performance at the lowest cost and the worst performance at the highest cost—and vice versa. Indeed, one of the major characteristics of the American education and training system is the variety of *options* it offers individuals. These include different choices in terms of programs, quality, costs, and expected outcomes. Therefore, you must do your research in order to identify your options and make informed choices.

> **There is no necessary correlation between educational costs and performance.**

Beware of Myths

Beware of education and training myths. Additional education and training is not always the answer for entry or advancement within the job market. Remember, education is a big $400 billion a year business. Exhibiting a great deal of inertia, few educational institutions are prepared to describe their performance in relation to today's job market. At best, educational institutions are most adept at keeping their businesses well and alive through the marketing of degree programs to relatively uninformed, accepting, and compliant consumers.

Contrary to what educators may tell you, additional education and training may not be necessary for entering or advancing within today's job market. But it is a good investment for the job markets of tomorrow. To determine if you need additional education and training, you should first learn what it is you do well and enjoy doing (through self-assessment) and then identify what it is you need to do to get what you want (through research). Education and training may be only one of several things you need to do. You may, for example, determine that you need to change your behavior by setting goals, becoming more focused on achieving results, and improving your dress and appearance. Or you may need to develop effective job search skills as well as relocate to a new community. After all, employers spend more than $200 billion each year on employee training and retraining—much of which is spent because of the failure of traditional educational institutions.

You may learn it is best to find an apprenticeship program or get into a particular organization that provides excellent training for its employees. Such training will be both up-to-date and relevant to the job market. Most of the best run corporations rely on their own in-house training rather than on institutions outside the corporation. When making hiring decisions, such organizations are more concerned with your overall level of intelligence as reflected in your ability to learn, acquire new skills, and grow within the organization than with the specific work-content skills you initially bring to the job—our basic careering and re-careering concerns for the 1990s.

6

Myths, Realities, and Planning Your Success

Making future occupational projections and knowing "what" jobs are available and "where" to find them in society as a whole tells you little about the critical "how" to find a job in your particular situation. Answers to general "what" and "where" questions may be interesting in describing and explaining reality, but they may or may not be useful in developing specific strategies for taking action.

If you are to be effective in the job markets of the decade ahead, you must link the "how" to the "what" and "where." At the very least, you must plan and organize specific activities in relation to your future goals.

Identify the Prerequisites to Success

Achieving job and career success in the decade ahead will depend on how well you understand and implement key processes for planning your future. Directly related to on-going job market realities, these processes constitute a set of how-to strategies for developing an effective job search, organizing specific job search activities, and achieving success. Examined separately, they are important prerequisites for developing effective careering and re-careering skills. Taken together, they constitute a well-organized framework for achieving successful careering and re-careering today and tomorrow.

This chapter relates our previous overview of careering and re-careering to the practical aspects of planning and implementing an effective job search. Here we examine the basic prerequisites for launching a successful job search. Each constitutes a skill that you can learn and apply:

- Understand job market realities
- Develop a well-organized job search
- Identify your careering and re-careering competencies

- Seek assistance when necessary
- Manage your time
- Organize a plan of action
- Follow principles for achieving success
- Take risks
- Handle rejections
- Form a support group

Above all, you must organize and implement to achieve success. You must translate your understanding of problems, approaches, and solutions into concrete action steps for achieving results.

Understand Key Myths and Realities

What do you know about the job market? Is it a place that has jobs for you? Where do you start? How will you approach it? What do you do when you get there? Whom do you talk to? What do you say?

The abstract notion of a "job market" generates several images of structures, processes, decision points, and outcomes. In one sense it appears to be well structured for dispensing job information and assistance. After all, you will find various elements that supposedly make up the structure of the job market: classified ads listing job vacancies; personnel offices with vacancy announcements; employment agencies and electronic databases linking candidates to job openings; and a variety of helpers known as career counselors, employment specialists, and executive recruiters who make a living by serving as gatekeepers to the "job market." At the same time, we know various processes are key to making this job market function: self-assessment, objective setting, research, applications, resume and letter writing, networking, interviewing, negotiating, and hiring. You need to become very familiar with each process as well as integrate each into a coherent job search.

Understanding the job market is like the blind person exploring an elephant: you may recognize a trunk, a leg, and a tail, but you're not sure what it is as a whole. As we will see shortly, the job market is anything but organized, centralized, and coherent. It is more an abstraction, or convenient short-hand way of talking about finding jobs, than a set of well defined and related structures.

Most people have an image of how the job market works as well as how they should relate to it. This image is based upon a combination of facts, stereotypes, and myths learned from experience and from the advice of well-meaning individuals. It's an unfortunate image when it guides people into unproductive job search channels by advising them to spend most of their time responding to vacancy announcements and waiting to hear from employers. In so doing, it reconfirms the often-heard lament of the unsuccessful job searcher—*"What more can I do—there are no jobs out there for me."*

Let's examine 30 myths about jobs, careers, and the job search before you proceed to organize yourself for today's and tomorrow's employment realities. These myths illustrate important points for organizing and implementing your job search:

MYTH 1: **Nearly 85 percent of Americans are unhappy with their jobs. They would change jobs if only they felt they could.**

REALITY: This is one of those phoney statistics thrown out by so-called career specialists who want to make themselves and their services highly visible. Unfortunately, such false assertions get quoted by others as employment "facts" and evidence of a job "crisis" in America. The truth, based upon numerous yearly studies of worker attitudes, is that over 80 percent of workers are relatively happy with their jobs. Less than 15 percent report they may be interested in making a job change. Half of that number indicate they are unhappy with their current jobs. The statistical distribution of these supposedly happy/unhappy workers has been very consistent over the past three decades.

MYTH 2: **We are now in a revolutionary period where we are witnessing the end of jobs.**

REALITY: Let's not get carried away with another trendy concept based on a skewed, anecdotal view of the job market. Jobs are here to stay and in a very big way. However, careers are clearly disappearing for many people. It's careers, not jobs, that may become obsolete. While traditional manufacturing jobs have been transformed in terms of skills required, jobs are still the basic activities by which work gets organized and accomplished. Employers still fill *positions* which consist of various assigned duties and responsibilities that define particular jobs. Certain jobs in certain industries, especially those using nontraditional organizational forms, have become less well defined and thus do not conform to the traditional concept of an assigned job. But such changes are no reason for thinking that jobs are ending. What is ending is the notion of a career. As we've already seen in the first half of the 1990s, jobs are "in" but careers are "out." Individuals entering the job market today expect to have many different jobs throughout their worklife. These jobs may or may not constitute a well-defined career.

MYTH 3: Anyone can find a job; all you need to know is how to find a job.

REALITY: This classic "form versus substance" myth is often associated with popular career planning exhortations of the 1970s and 1980s that stressed the importance of having positive attitudes and self-esteem, setting goals, dressing for success, and using interpersonal strategies for finding jobs. While such approaches may work well in an industrial society with low unemployment, they constitute myths in a post-industrial, high-tech society which requires employees to demonstrate both *intelligence and concrete work skills* as well as a *willingness to relocate* to new communities offering greater job opportunities. For example, many of today's unemployed are highly skilled in the old technology of the industrial society, but they live and own homes in economically depressed communities. These people

> The job market is highly decentralized, fragmented, and chaotic.

lack the necessary *skills and mobility* required for getting jobs in high-tech, growth communities. Knowing job search skills alone will not help these people. Indeed, such advice and knowledge will most likely frustrate such highly motivated and immobile individuals who possess skills of the old technology.

MYTH 4: The best way to find a job is to respond to classified ads, use employment agencies, and submit applications to personnel offices.

REALITY: Except for certain types of organizations, such as government, these formal application procedures are not the most effective ways of finding jobs. Such approaches assume the presence of an organized, coherent, and centralized job market—but no such thing exists. The job market is highly decentralized, fragmented, and chaotic. Classified ads, employment agencies, and personnel offices tend to list low paying yet highly competitive jobs or high paying highly skilled positions that are hard to fill. Most jobs are neither listed nor advertised; they are most likely found through word-of-mouth. Your most fruitful strategy will be to conduct research and informational interviews on what career counselors call the "hidden job market."

MYTH 5: Few jobs are available for me in today's competitive job market.

REALITY: This may be true if you lack marketable skills and insist on applying for jobs listed in newspapers, employment agencies, personnel offices, or online (the Internet). Competition in the advertised job market usually is high, especially for jobs requiring few skills. Numerous jobs with little competition are available on the hidden job market. Jobs requiring advanced technical skills often go begging. Little competition may occur during periods of high unemployment, because many people quit job hunting after a few disappointing weeks of concentrating job search efforts on working the advertised job market.

MYTH 6: I know how to find a job, but opportunities are not available for me.

REALITY: Most people don't know the best way to find a job, or they lack marketable job skills. They continue to use ineffective job search methods, such as only responding to classified ads with resumes and cover letters. Opportunities are readily available for individuals who understand the structure and operation of the job market, have appropriate work-content skills, and use job search methods designed for the hidden job market. They must learn to develop an effective networking and informational interviewing campaign for uncovering promising job leads. And they must persist in prospecting for new job leads as well as learn to handle rejections.

MYTH 7: I'm over-qualified in the eyes of many employers. They don't want to hire over-qualified individuals.

REALITY: Yes, if you're seeking a $25,000 a year job but you have experience and qualifications for a $60,000 a year job! Why would you even want to consider such a job? Who wants to hire someone who is over-qualified and thus likely to leave for greener pastures once they get their wake-up call that they are underemployed and undercompensated? This is the classic self-fulfilling prophecy of many career changers who don't know how to best communicate their qualifications to prospective employers. You're never over-qualified if you seek jobs for your level of skills and experience. Employers who view you as over-qualified are the wrong employers to whom to apply. They do you a favor by not giving you a job. Thank them for being so discriminating. They serve as your wake-up call. You need to get a better sense of where you fit into the job market. Stop under-selling yourself and thus contributing to this over-qualification myth. You need some job market smarts before you approach any more employers.

MYTH 8: **Employers are in the driver's seat; they have the upper-hand with applicants.**

REALITY: Most often no one is in the driver's seat. Not knowing what they want, many employers make poor hiring decisions. They frequently let applicants define their hiring needs. If you can define employers' needs as your skills, you might end up in the driver's seat!

MYTH 9: **Employers hire the best qualified candidates. Without a great deal of experience and numerous qualifications, I don't have a chance.**

REALITY: Employers hire people for all kinds of reasons. Most rank experience and qualifications third or fourth in their pecking order of hiring criteria. Employers seldom hire the best qualified candidate, because "qualifications" are difficult to define and measure. Employers normally seek people with the following characteristics: competent, intelligent, honest, enthusiastic, and likable. "Likability" tends to be an overall concern of employers—will you "fit in" and get along well with your superiors, co-workers, and clients? Employers want *value* for their money. Therefore, you must communicate to employers that you are such a person. You must overcome employers' objections to any lack of experience or qualifications. But never volunteer your weaknesses. The best qualified person is the one who knows how to get the job—convinces employers that he or she is the *most* desirable for the job.

MYTH 10: **It is best to go into a growing field where jobs are plentiful.**

REALITY: Be careful in following the masses to the "in" fields. First, many so-called growth fields can quickly become no-growth fields, such as aerospace engineering, nuclear energy, defense contracting, and nursing. Second, by the time you acquire the necessary skills, you may experience the "disappearing job" phenomenon: too many people did the same thing you did and consequently glut the job market. Third, since many people leave no-growth fields, new opportunities may arise for you. Fourth, if you go after a growth field, you will try to fit into a job rather than find a job fit for you. If you know what you do well and enjoy doing (Chapters 7 and 8), and what additional training you may need, you should look for a

> **If you go after a growth field, you will try to fit into a job rather than find a job fit for you.**

job or career conducive to your particular mix of skills, interests, and motivations. In the long-run you will be much happier and more productive finding a job fit for you. If you find a job you really love, you will be better compensated emotionally than if you only focused on finding a job that pays a high salary.

MYTH 11: **People over 40 have difficulty finding a good job; employers prefer hiring younger and less expensive workers.**

REALITY: Yes, if they apply for youth jobs. Age should be an insignificant barrier to employment if you conduct a well organized job search and are prepared to handle this potential negative with employers. Age should be a positive and must be communicated as such. After all, employers want experience, maturity, and stability. People over 40 generally possess these qualities. As the population ages and birth rates decline, older individuals should have a much easier time changing jobs and careers.

MYTH 12: **It's best to use an employment firm to find a job.**

REALITY: It depends on the firm and the nature of employment you are seeking. Employment firms that specialize in your skill area may be well worth contacting. For example, many law firms use employment firms to hire paralegals rather than directly recruit such personnel themselves. Many employers now use temporary employment firms to recruit both temporary and full-time employees at several different levels, from clerical to professional. Indeed, many temporary employment firms have temp-to-perm programs that link qualified candidates to employers who are looking for full-time employees. But make sure you are working with a legitimate employment firm. Legitimate firms get paid by employers or they collect placement fees from applicants only *after* the applicant has accepted a position. Beware of firms that want up-front fees for promised job placement assistance.

MYTH 13: I must be aggressive in order to find a job.

REALITY: Aggressive people tend to be offensive and obnoxious people. They also make pests of themselves. Try being purposeful, persistent, and pleasant in all job search activities. Such behavior is well received by potential employers!

MYTH 14: There are no jobs available in California's recessionary economy.

REALITY: While California's economy has been hard hit with the double-whammy of defense cutbacks and recessions in the Pacific Rim economies, California still has a large job market. California's current high unemployment rates will gradually recede during the next five years as the State's economy rebounds. However, don't expect California to return to the go-go employment years of the 60's, 70's, and 80's. It still has a tough job market. You'll simply have to spend more time looking for a job in California than in most other states.

MYTH 15: I should not change jobs and careers more than once or twice. Job-changers are discriminated against in hiring.

REALITY: While this may have been generally true 30 years ago, it is no longer true today. America is a skills-based society: individuals market their skills to organizations in exchange for money and position. Furthermore, since most organizations are small businesses with limited advancement opportunities, careers quickly plateau for most people. For them, the only way up is to get out and into another organization. Therefore, the best way to advance careers in a society of small businesses is to change jobs frequently. Job-changing is okay as long as such changes demonstrate career advancement and one isn't changing jobs every few months. Most individuals entering the job market today will undergo several career and job changes regardless of their initial desire for a one-job, one-career life plan.

MYTH 16: **People get ahead by working hard and putting in long hours.**

REALITY: Success patterns differ. Many people who are honest, work hard, and put in long hours also get fired, have ulcers, and die young. Some people get ahead even though they are dishonest and lazy. Others simply have good luck or a helpful patron. Moderation in both work and play will probably get you just as far as the extremes. There are other ways, as outlined near the end of this chapter, to become successful in addition to hard work and long hours.

MYTH 17: **I should not try to use "connections" to get a job. I should apply through the front door like everyone else. If I'm the best qualified, I'll get the job.**

REALITY: While you may wish to stand in line for tickets, bank deposits, and loans—because you have no clout—standing in line for a job is not the best approach. Every employer has a front door as well as a back door. Try using the back door if you can. It works in many cases. Chapter 12 details how you can develop your contacts, use connections, and enter *both* the front and back doors.

MYTH 18: **I need to get more education and training to qualify for today's jobs.**

REALITY: You may or may not need more education and training, depending on your present skill levels and the needs of employers. What many employers are looking for are individuals who are intelligent, communicate well, take initiative, and are trainable; they train their employees to respond to the needs of their organization. You first need to know what skills you already possess and if they appear appropriate for the types of jobs you are seeking.

MYTH 19: **Once I apply for a job, it's best to wait to hear from an employer.**

REALITY: Waiting is not a good job search strategy. If you want action on the part of the employer, you must first take action. The key to getting a job interview and offer is follow-up, follow-up, follow-up. You do this by making follow-up telephone calls as well as writing follow-up and thank you letters to employers.

MYTH 20: **I don't need a resume. I can get a job based solely on my network contacts.**

REALITY: While networking is one of the most effective methods for finding employment, it does not erase the need for a resume. The resume is your calling card; it provides a prospective employer with a snapshot of your background and skills. Employers often want to first see you on paper (resume) before meeting you in person (interview). Whether you like it or not, chances are you'll need a resume very early in your job search, especially when a contact asks you to "Send me a copy of your resume."

MYTH 21: **A good resume is the key to getting a job.**

REALITY: While resumes play an important role in the job search process, they are often overrated. The purpose of a resume is to communicate your qualifications to employers who, in turn, invite you to job interviews. The key to getting a job is the job interview. No job interview, no job offer.

MYTH 22: **I should include my salary expectations on my resume or in my cover letter.**

REALITY: You should never include your salary expectations on your resume or in a cover letter, unless specifically requested to do so. Salary should be the very last thing you discuss with a prospective employer. You do so only after you have had a chance to assess the worth of the position and communicate your value to the employer. This usually comes at the end of your final job interview, just before or after being offered the job. If you prematurely raise the salary issue, you may devalue your worth.

MYTH 23: **My resume should emphasize my work history.**

REALITY: Employers are interested in hiring your future rather than your past. Therefore, your resume should emphasize the skills and abilities you will bring to the job as well as your interests and goals. Let employers know what you are likely to do for them *in the future*. When you present your work history, do so in terms of your major skills and accomplishments.

MYTH 24: It's not necessary to write letters to employers—just send a resume or complete an application.

REALITY: You should be prepared to write several types of job search letters—cover, approach, resume, thank you, follow-up, and acceptance. In addition to communicating your level of literacy, these job search letters enable you to express important values sought after by employers—your tactfulness, thought-fulness, enthusiasm, likability, and fol-

> **Employers are interested in hiring your future rather than your past.**

low-up ability. Sending a resume without a cover letter devalues both your resume and your application.

MYTH 25: Electronic resumes are the wave of the future. You must have one in order to get a good job.

REALITY: Electronic resumes are increasingly important for job seekers and employers alike. More and more employers use the latest resume scanning technology to quickly screen hundreds of resumes. Therefore, it also may be in your interest to write a "computer friendly" resume based on the principles of electronic resumes. These are outlined in three relatively new books on this subject—Peter D. Weddle, *Electronic Resumes For the New Job Market: Resumes That Work for You 24 Hours a Day* (Impact Publications, 1995); and Joyce Lain Kennedy and Thomas J. Morrow, *Electronic Resume Revolution* (Wiley, 1996); and James Gonyea, *Electronic Resumes* (McGraw, 1996). These are very different resumes compared to conventional resumes. Structured around "keywords" or nouns which stress capabilities, electronic resumes may be excellent candidates for resume scanners but weak documents for human readers. Keep in mind that electronic resumes are primarily written for electronic scanners and high-tech distribution systems (job banks) rather than for human beings. Since human beings interview and hire, you should first create a high impact resume that follows the principles of human communication and intelligence. We also recommend developing a separate electronic resume designed for electronic scanners.

MYTH 26: **Individuals who join resume banks are more likely to get high paying jobs than those that don't.**

REALITY: Electronic resume banks, such as Career Net Graduate, Cors, SkillSearch, and University ProNet, offer alternative ways of distributing resumes to employers. Essentially a high-tech approach to broadcasting resumes, membership in one of these groups means your resume literally works 24 hours a day. Major employers increasingly use these resume banks for locating qualified candidates, especially for screening individuals with technical skills. And we know some individuals who join these resume banks do get jobs. However, there is no evidence that most people belonging to these groups ever get interviews or jobs through such membership. Nor is there any evidence that membership results in higher paying jobs than non-membership. The real advantage of such groups is this: they open new channels for contacting employers whom you might not otherwise come into contact with. Indeed, some employers only use these resume banks for locating certain types of candidates rather than use more traditional channels, such as newspapers and employment offices, for advertising positions and recruiting candidates.

MYTH 27: **Salaries are pre-determined by employers.**

REALITY: Most salaries are negotiable within certain ranges and limits. Before you ever apply or interview for a position, you should know what the salary range is for the type of position you seek. When you finally discuss the salary question—preferably at the end of the final job inter-view—do so with this range in mind. Assuming you have adequately demonstrated your value to the employer, try to negotiate the highest possible salary within the range.

MYTH 28: **Bigger employers will provide better benefits than smaller employers.**

REALITY: It depends on the employer and situation. Overall, both large and small employers are cutting back on benefits, especially in the high costs areas of healthcare and pensions. You should expect to contribute a larger percentage of your compensation to employer-sponsored benefit packages. When negotiating salary, it's best to concentrate on the total annual salary figure. At the same time, you may want to target your job search on small companies that offer some of today's most exciting job and career opportunities. Since many of these companies have little public visibility and thus may not be listed in the standard corporate or employer directories, you will need to do a lot of research to identify these companies.

MYTH 29: **It's best to relocate to a booming community.**

REALITY: Similar to the "disappearing job" phenomenon for college majors, today's economically booming communities may be tomorrow's busts. It's best to select a community that is conducive to your lifestyle preferences as well as has a sufficiently diversified economy to weather boom and bust economic cycles.

MYTH 30: **It's best to broadcast or "shotgun" my resume to as many employers as possible.**

REALITY: Broadcasting your resume to employers is a game of chance in which you usually waste your time and money. It's always best to target your resume on those employers who have vacancies or who might have openings in the near future. Your single best approach for uncovering job leads will be the process called networking.

You also should be aware of several other realities which will affect your job search or which you might find helpful in developing your plan of action for finding a job or changing a career:

Additional Realities

- **You will find less competition for high-level jobs than for middle and low-level jobs.** If you aim high yet are realistic, you may be pleasantly surprised with the results.

- **Personnel offices seldom hire.** They primarily screen candidates for employers who are found in operating units of organizations. Knowing this, you should focus your job search efforts on those who do the actual hiring.

- **Politics are both ubiquitous and dangerous in many organizations.** If you think you are above politics, you may quickly become one of its victims. Unfortunately, you only learn about "local politics" *after* you accept a position and begin relating to the different players in the organization.

- **It is best to narrow or "rifle" your job search on particular organizations and individuals rather than broaden or "shotgun"** it to many alternatives. If you remain focused, you will be better able to accomplish your goals.

- **Employment firms and personnel agencies may not help you.** Most work for employers and themselves rather than for applicants. Few have your best interests at heart. Use them only after you have investigated their effectiveness. Avoid firms that require up-front money for vague promises of performance.

- **Most people can make satisfying job and career changes.** They should minimize efforts in the advertised job market and concentrate instead on planning and implementing a well organized job search tailored to the realities of the hidden job market.

- **Jobs and careers tend to be fluid and changing.** Knowing this, you should concentrate on acquiring and marketing skills, talents, and abilities which can be transferred from one job to another.

- **Millions of job vacancies are available every day** because new jobs are created every day, and people resign, retire, get fired, or die.

- **Most people, regardless of their position or status, love to talk about their work and give advice** to both friends and strangers. You can learn the most about job opportunities and alternative careers by talking to such people.

As you conduct your job search, you will encounter many of these and other myths and realities about how you should relate to the job market. Several people will give you advice. While much of this advice will be useful, a great deal of it will be useless and misleading. You should be skeptical of well-meaning individuals who most likely will reiterate the same job and career myths. You should be particularly leery of those who try to *sell* you their advice. Always remember you are entering a relatively disorganized and chaotic job market where you can find numerous job opportunities. Your task is to organize the chaos around your skills and interests. You must convince prospective employers that they will like you more than other "qualified" candidates.

Find Jobs and Change Careers

If you are looking for your first job, re-entering the job market after a lengthy absence, or planning a job or career change, you will join an army of millions of individuals who do so each year. Indeed, between 15 and 20 million people find themselves unemployed each year. Millions of others try to increase their satisfaction within the work place as well as advance their careers by looking for alternative jobs and careers. If you are like most other Americans, you will make more than 10 job changes and between 3 and 5 career changes during your lifetime.

Most people make job or career transitions by accident. They do little other than take advantage of opportunities that may arise unexpectedly. While chance and luck do play important roles in finding employment, we recommend that you *plan* for future job and career changes so that you will experience even greater degrees of chance and luck!

> If you seek comprehensive, accurate, and timely job information, the job market will frustrate you.

Finding a job or changing a career in a systematic and well-planned manner is hard yet rewarding work. The task should first be based upon a clear understanding of the key ingredients that define jobs and careers. Starting with this understanding, you should next convert key concepts into action steps for implementing your job search.

A career is a series of related jobs which have common skill, interest, and motivational bases. You may change jobs several times without changing careers. But once you change skills, interests, and motivations, you change careers.

It's not easy to find a job given the present structure of the job market. You will find the job market to be relatively disorganized, although it projects an outward appearance of coherence. If you seek comprehensive, accurate, and timely job information, the job market will frustrate you with its poor communication. While you will find many employment services ready to assist you, such services tend to be fragmented and their performance is often disappointing. Job search methods are controversial and many are ineffective.

No system is organized to give people jobs. At best you will encounter a *decentralized and fragmented system* consisting of job listings in newspapers, trade journals, employment offices, or computerized job data banks—all designed to link potential candidates with available job openings. Many people will try to sell you job information as well as questionable job search services. While efforts are underway to create a nationwide computerized job bank which would list available job vacancies on a daily basis, don't expect such data to become available soon nor to be very useful. Many of the listed jobs may be nonexistent, or at a low skill and salary level, or represent only a few employers. In the end, most systems organized to help you find a job do not provide you with the information you need in order to land a job that is most related to your skills and interests.

Understand the Career Development Process

Finding a job is both an art and a science; it encompasses a variety of basic facts, principles, and skills which can be learned but which also must be adapted to individual situations. Thus, *learning how to find a job* can be as important to career success as *knowing*

> **Job finding skills are often as important to career success as job performance or work-content skills.**

how to perform a job. Indeed, job finding skills are often as important to career success as job performance or work-content skills.

Our understanding of how to find jobs and change careers is illustrated on pages 101 and 102. As outlined on page 101, you should involve yourself in a four-step career development process as you prepare to move from one job to another.

Career Development Process

1. **Conduct a self-assessment:**

   This first step involves assessing your skills, abilities, motivations, interests, values, temperaments, experience, and accomplishments—the major concern of this book. Your basic strategy is to develop a firm foundation of information on *yourself* before proceeding to other stages in the career development process. This self-assessment develops the necessary self-awareness upon which you can effectively communicate your qualifications to employers as well as focus and build your career.

2. **Gather career and job information:**

   Closely related to the first step, this second step is an exploratory, research phase of your career development. Here you need to formulate goals, gather information about alternative jobs and careers through reading and talking to informed people, and then narrow your alternatives to specific jobs.

THE CAREER DEVELOPMENT PROCESS

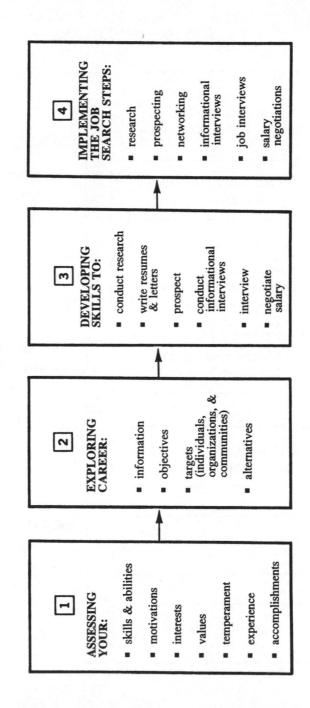

1 ASSESSING YOUR:
- skills & abilities
- motivations
- interests
- values
- temperament
- experience
- accomplishments

2 EXPLORING CAREER:
- information
- objectives
- targets (individuals, organizations, & communities)
- alternatives

3 DEVELOPING SKILLS TO:
- conduct research
- write resumes & letters
- prospect
- conduct informational interviews
- interview
- negotiate salary

4 IMPLEMENTING THE JOB SEARCH STEPS:
- research
- prospecting
- networking
- informational interviews
- job interviews
- salary negotiations

JOB SEARCH STEPS

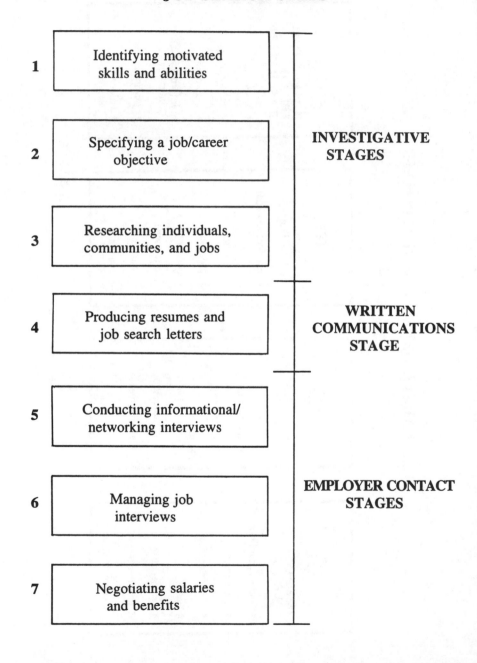

3. **Develop job search skills:**

   The third step focuses your career around specific job search skills for landing the job you want. As further outlined on page 101, these job search skills are closely related to one another as a series of *job search steps*. They involve conducting research, writing resumes and letters, prospecting and networking, conducting informational interviews, interviewing for a job, and negotiating salary and terms of employment. Each of these job search skills involves well-defined strategies and tactics you must learn in order to be effective in the job market.

4. **Implement each job search step:**

   The final career development step emphasizes the importance of transforming understanding into *action*. You do this by implementing each job search step which already incorporates the knowledge, skills, and abilities you acquired in Steps 1, 2, and 3.

Organize and Sequence Your Job Search

The figure on page 102 further expands our career development process by examining the key elements in a successful job search. It consists of a seven-step process which relates your past, present, and future. We cover all of these steps in subsequent chapters which deal with skills assessment, research, resume writing, networking, interviewing, and salary negotiations.

Based on this concept, *your past* is well integrated into the process of finding a job or changing your career. Therefore, you should feel comfortable conducting your job search: it represents the best of what you are in terms of your past and present accomplishments as these relate to your present and future goals. If you base your job search on this process concept, you will communicate your *best self* to employers as well as focus on *your strengths* both during the job search and on the job.

Since the individual job search steps are interrelated, they should be followed in sequence. If you fail to properly complete the initial self-assessment steps, your job search may become haphazard, aimless, and costly. For example, you should never write a resume (Step 3) before first conducting an assessment of your skills (Step 1) and identifying your objective (Step 2). Relating Step 1 to Step 2 is especially critical to the successful implementation of all other job search steps. You *must* complete Steps 1 and 2 *before* continuing on to the other steps. Steps 3 to 6 may be conducted simultaneously because they complement and reinforce one another.

Try to sequence your job search as close to these steps as possible. The true value of this sequencing will become very apparent as you implement your plan.

The processes and steps identified on pages 101 and 102 represent the careering and re-careering processes used successfully by thousands of job-seekers during the past 30 years. They are equally applicable as careering and re-careering processes for the decade ahead as long as you recognize the importance of acquiring work-content skills along with job search skills.

You must do much more than just know how to find a job. In the job markets of today and tomorrow, you need to constantly review your work-content skills to make sure they are appropriate for the changing job market. Assuming you have the necessary work-content skills, you should be ready to target your skills on particular jobs and careers that you do well and enjoy doing. You will be able to avoid the trap of trying to fit into jobs that are not conducive to your particular mix of interests, abilities, skills, and motivations.

Test Your Careering Competencies

Knowing *where* the jobs are is important to your job search. But knowing *how to find a job* is even more important. Before you acquire names, addresses, and phone numbers of potential employers, you should possess the necessary job search knowledge and skills for gathering and using job information effectively.

Answers to many of your job related questions are found by examining your present level of job search knowledge and skills. Successful job seekers, for example, use a great deal of information as well as specific skills and strategies for getting the jobs they want.

Let's begin by testing for the level of job search information, skills, and strategies you currently possess as well as those you need to develop and improve. You can easily identify your level of job search competence by completing the exercise on pages 105-106.

After you finish this exercise, calculate your overall careering competencies by adding the numbers you circled for a composite score. If your total is more than 75 points, you need to work on developing your careering skills. How you scored each item will indicate to what degree you need to work on improving specific job search skills. If your score is under 50 points, you are well on your way toward job search success. In either case, this book should help you better focus your job search as well as identify job search skills you need to acquire or strengthen.

Your Careering Competencies

INSTRUCTIONS: Respond to each statement by circling which number at the right best represents your situation.

SCALE: 1 = strongly agree   4 = disagree
             2 = agree   5 = strongly disagree
             3 = maybe, not certain

1. I know what motivates me to excel at work.   1 2 3 4 5

2. I can identify my strongest abilities and skills.   1 2 3 4 5

3. I have seven major achievements that clarify
   a pattern of interests and abilities that
   are relevant to my job and career.   1 2 3 4 5

4. I know what I both like and dislike in work.   1 2 3 4 5

5. I know what I want to do during the next
   10 years.   1 2 3 4 5

6. I have a well defined career objective that
   focuses my job search on particular
   organizations and employers.   1 2 3 4 5

7. I know what skills I can offer employers in
   different occupations.   1 2 3 4 5

8. I know what skills employers most seek in
   candidates.   1 2 3 4 5

9. I can clearly explain to employers what I do
   well and enjoy doing.   1 2 3 4 5

10. I can specify why employers should hire me.   1 2 3 4 5

11. I can gain the support of family and friends
    for making a job or career change.   1 2 3 4 5

12. I can find 10 to 20 hours a week to
    conduct a part-time job search.   1 2 3 4 5

13. I have the financial ability to sustain a
    three-month job search.   1 2 3 4 5

14. I can conduct library and interview research on different occupations, employers, organizations, and communities.   1 2 3 4 5

15. I can write different types of effective resumes and job search/thank you letters.   1 2 3 4 5

16. I can produce and distribute resumes and letters to the right people.   1 2 3 4 5

17. I can list my major accomplishments in action terms.   1 2 3 4 5

18. I can identify and target employers I want to interview.   1 2 3 4 5

19. I can develop a job referral network.   1 2 3 4 5

20. I can persuade others to join in forming a job search support group.   1 2 3 4 5

21. I can prospect for job leads.   1 2 3 4 5

22. I can use the telephone to develop prospects and get referrals and interviews.   1 2 3 4 5

23. I can plan and implement an effective direct-mail job search campaign.   1 2 3 4 5

24. I can generate one job interview for every 10 job search contacts I make.   1 2 3 4 5

25. I can follow-up on job interviews.   1 2 3 4 5

26. I can negotiate a salary 10-20% above what an employer initially offers.   1 2 3 4 5

27. I can persuade an employer to renegotiate my salary after six months on the job.   1 2 3 4 5

28. I can create a position for myself in an organization.   1 2 3 4 5

TOTAL _____

Seek Professional Assistance When Necessary

While some people can successfully conduct a job search based on the advice of books such as this, many others also need the assistance of various professional groups that offer specific career planning and job search services. These groups offer everything from testing and assessment services to offering contacts with potential employers, including job vacancy information and temporary employment services. Some do one-on-one career counseling while others sponsor one to three-day workshops or six to twelve-week courses on the various steps in the career planning process. You should know something about these services before you invest your time and money beyond this and other career planning and job search books.

Options

You have two options in organizing your job search. First, you can follow the principles and advice outlined in this and many other self-directed books. Just read the chapters and then put them into practice by following the step-by-step instructions. Second, you may wish to seek professional help to either supplement or replace this book. Indeed, many people will read parts of this book—perhaps all of it—and do nothing. Unwilling to take

> **While many services are excellent, other services are useless.**

initiative, lacking sufficient time or motivation, or failing to follow-through, many people will eventually seek professional help to organize and implement their job search. They will pay good money to get someone else to tell them to follow the advice found in this book. Some people need this type of expensive motivation and organization.

At the same time, we recognize the value of professional assistance. Especially with the critical assessment and objective setting steps (Chapters 7, 8, and 9), some individuals may need more assistance than our advice and exercises provide. You may, for example, want to take a battery of tests to better understand your interests and values in relation to alternative jobs and careers. And still others, due to a combination of job loss, failed relationships, or depression, may need therapy best provided by a trained psychologist or psychiatrist rather than career testing and information services provided by career counselors. If any of these situations pertain to you, by all means seek professional help.

You also should beware of pitfalls in seeking professional advice. While many services are excellent, other services are useless and fraudulent. Remember, career planning and job assistance are big businesses involving millions of dollars each year. Many people enter these businesses without expertise. Professional certification in these areas is extremely weak to nonexistent in some states. Indeed, many so-called "professionals" get into the business because they are unemployed. In other words, they major in their own problem! Others are frauds and hucksters who prey on vulnerable and naive people who feel they need a "specialist" or "expert" to get them a job. They will take your money in exchange for promises. You will find several types of services promising to assist you in finding all types of jobs. You should know something about these professional services before you venture beyond this book.

If you are interested in exploring the services of job specialists, begin by looking in the Yellow Pages of your telephone directory under these headings: Management Consultants, Employment, Resumes, Career Planning, and Social Services. Several career planning and employment services are available, ranging from highly generalized to very specific services. Most services claim they can help you. If you read this book, you will be in a better position to seek out specific services as well as ask the right questions for screening the services. You may even discover you know more about finding a job than many of the so-called professionals!

Alternative Services

At least 11 different career planning and employment services are available to assist you with your job search. Each has certain advantages and disadvantages. Approach them with caution. Never sign a contract before you read the fine print, get a second opinion, and talk to former clients about the *results* they achieved through the service. With these words of caution in mind, let's take a look at the variety of services available.

1. Public employment services:

Public employment services usually consist of a state agency which provides employment assistance as well as dispenses unemployment compensation benefits. Employment assistance largely consists of job listings and counseling services. However, counseling services often screen individuals for employers who list with the public employment agency. If you are looking for an entry-level job in the $15,000 to $35,000 range, contact this service. Most employers still do not list with this service, especially for positions paying more than $35,000 a year. Although the main purpose of these offices is to dispense unemployment benefits, don't overlook these offices because of past stereotypes. Many of these offices are literally "reinventing" themselves for today's new job market. Many of them offer useful employment services, including self-assessment and job search workshops as well as electronic job banks that match skills and experience with available job vacancies. Many of these offices are linked to America's Job Bank, an electronic database which includes job listings throughout the U.S. and abroad. If you are a veteran, you will find many of the jobs listed with state employment offices are designated for veterans. Go see for yourself if your state employment office offers useful services for you.

2. Private employment agencies:

Private employment agencies work for money, either from applicants or employers. Approximately 8,000 such agencies operate nationwide. Many are highly specialized in technical, scientific, and financial fields. The majority of these firms serve the interests of employers since employers—not applicants—represent repeat business. While employers normally pay the placement fee, many agencies charge applicants 10 to 15 percent of their first year salary. These firms have one major advantage: job leads which you may have difficulty uncovering elsewhere. Especially for highly specialized fields, a good firm can be extremely helpful. The major disadvantages are that they can be costly and the quality of the firms varies. Be careful in how you deal with them. Make sure you understand the fee structure and what they will do for you before you sign anything.

3. Temporary employment firms:

During the past decade temporary employment firms have come of age as more and more turn to them for recruitment assistance. They offer a variety of employment services to both applicants and employers who are either looking for temporary work and workers or who want to better screen applicants and employers. Many of these firms recruit individuals for a wide range of positions and skill levels as well as full-time employment. If you are interested in "testing the job waters," you may want to contact these firms for information on their services. Employers—not job seekers—pay for these services.

4. College/university placement offices:

College and university placement offices provide in-house career planning services for graduating students. While some give assistance to alumni, don't expect too much help if you have already graduated. Many of these offices are under-

staffed or provide only rudimentary services, such as maintaining a career planning library, coordinating on-campus
interviews for graduating seniors, and conducting workshops
on how to write resumes and interview. Others provide a full
range of well supported services including testing and one-
on-one counseling. Indeed, many community colleges offer
such services to members of the community on a walk-in
basis. You can use their libraries and computerized career
assessment programs, take personality and interest inventories, or attend special workshops or full-semester career
planning courses which will take you through each step of
the career planning and job search processes. You are well
advised to enroll in such a course since it is likely to provide
just enough structure and content to assess your motivated
abilities and skills and to assist you in implementing a successful job search plan. Check with your local campus to see
what services you might use.

5. Private career and job search firms:

Private career and job search firms help individuals acquire
job search skills. They do not find you a job. In other words,
they teach you much—maybe more but possibly less—of
what is outlined in this book. Expect to pay anywhere from
$1,500 to $10,000 for this service. If you need a structured
environment for conducting your job search, contract with
one of these firms. One of the oldest and most popular firms
is Haldane Associates. Many of their pioneering career
planning and job search methods are incorporated in this
book. You will find branches of this nationwide firm in many
major cities.

6. Executive search firms and headhunters:

Executive search firms work for employers in finding
employees to fill critical positions in the $60,000 plus salary
range. They also are called "headhunters," "management
consultants," and "executive recruiters." These firms play an
important role in linking high level technical and managerial
talent to organizations. Don't expect to contract for these
services. Executive recruiters work for employers—not
applicants. If a friend or relative is in this business or you
have relevant skills of interest to these firms, let them know
you are available—and ask for their advice. On the other
hand, you may want to contact firms that specialize in

recruiting individuals with your skill specialty. Several books identify how you can best approach "headhunters" on your own: *How to Select and Use an Executive Search Firm* (A. R. Taylor); *How to Answer a Headhunter's Call* (Robert H. Perry); *The Headhunter Strategy* (Kenneth J. Cole); *The Directory of Executive Recruiters* (Kennedy Publications); and *How to Get a Headhunter to Call* (Howard S. Freedman).

7. Marketing services:

Marketing services represent an interesting combination of job search and executive search activities. They can cost $2,500 or more, and they work with individuals anticipating a starting salary of at least $75,000 but preferably over $100,000. These firms try to minimize the time and risk of applying for jobs. A typical operation begins with a client paying a $150 fee for developing psychological, skills, and interests profiles. Next, a marketing plan is outlined and a contract signed for specific services. Using word processing equipment, the firm normally develops a slick "professional" resume and mails it along with a cover letter, to hundreds—maybe thousands—of firms. Clients are then briefed and sent to interview with interested employers. While you can save money and achieve the same results on your own, these firms do have one major advantage. They save you *time* by doing most of the work for you. Again, approach these services with caution and with the knowledge that you can probably do just as well—if not better—on your own by following the step-by-step advice of this and other job search books.

8. Women's Centers and special career services:

Women's Centers and special career services have been established to respond to the employment needs of special groups. Women's Centers are particularly active in sponsoring career planning workshops and job information networks. These centers tend to be geared toward elementary job search activities, because their clientele largely consists of homemakers who are entering or re-entering the work force with little knowledge of the job market. Special career services arise at times for different categories of employees. For example, unemployed aerospace engineers, teachers, veterans, air traffic controllers, and government employees have formed special groups for developing job search skills and sharing job leads.

9. Testing and assessment centers:

Testing and assessment centers provide assistance for identifying vocational skills, interests, and objectives. Usually staffed by trained professionals, these centers administer several types of tests and charge from $300 to $800 per person. You may wish to use some of these services if you feel our activities in Chapters 7, 8, and 9 generate insufficient information on your skills and interests to formulate your job objective. If you use such services, make sure you are given one or both of the two most popular and reliable tests: *Myers-Briggs Type Indicator* and the *Strong Interest Inventory*. You should find both tests helpful in better understanding your interests and decision-making styles. However, try our exercises before you hire a psychologist or visit a testing center. If you first complete these exercises, you will be in a better position to know exactly what you need from such centers. In many cases the career office at your local community college or women's center can administer these tests at minimum cost.

10. Job fairs or career conferences:

Job fairs or career conferences are organized by employment agencies to link applicants to employers. Usually consisting of one to two-day meetings in a hotel, employers meet with applicants as a group and on a one-to-one basis. Employers give presentations on their companies, applicants circulate resumes, and employers interview candidates. Many such conferences are organized to attract hard-to-recruit groups, such as engineers, computer programmers, and clerical and service workers. While private companies typically organize job fairs, the federal government increasingly uses job fairs for quickly recruiting many specialized personnel. These are excellent sources for job leads and information—if you get invited to the meeting or they are open to the public. Employers pay for this service—not applicants.

11. Professional associations:

Professional associations often provide placement assistance. This usually consists of listing job vacancies and organizing a job information exchange at annual conferences. These meetings are good sources for making job contacts in different geographic locations within a particular professional field. But don't expect too much. Talking to people (network-ing) at professional conferences may yield better results than reading job listings and interviewing at conference placement centers.

Choose the Best

Other types of career planning and employment services are growing and specializing in particular occupational fields. You may wish to use these services as a supplement to this book.

Whatever you do, proceed with caution, know exactly what you are getting into, and choose the best. Remember, there is no such thing as a free lunch, and you often get less than what you pay for. At the same time, the most expensive services are not necessarily the best. Indeed, the free and inexpensive career planning services offered by many community colleges—libraries, computerized career assessment programs, testing, and workshops—are often superior to alternative services which can be expensive.

After reading this book, you should be able to make intelligent decisions about what, when, where, and with what results you can use professional assistance. Shop around, compare services and costs, ask questions, talk to former clients, and read the fine print with your lawyer before giving an employment expert a job using your hard earned money!

When in Doubt, Take Purposeful Action

The old adage "When in doubt, do something" is especially relevant when expanded to include a thoughtful plan of action related to the job search process: "When in doubt, engage in a concrete activity related to the sequence of job search steps." This might include conducting research on communities, companies, positions, and salaries; surveying job vacancy announcements; writing a resume and job search letters; or contacting three employers each day.

But developing a plan and taking action is much easier said than done. If conducted properly, a job search can become an extremely time consum-ing activity. It inevitably competes with other personal and professional priorities. That's why you need to make some initial decisions as to how and when you will conduct a job search. How much time, for example, are you willing to set aside each day or week to engage in each of the seven job search activities outlined at the beginning of this chapter? After you've spent numerous hours identifying your abilities and skills and formulating an objective, are you willing to commit yourself to 20 hours a week to network for information and advice? If you are unwilling to commit both your time and yourself to each activity within the process, you may remain stuck, and inevitably frustrated, at the initial stages of self-awareness and understanding. Success only comes to those who take action at other stages in the job search process.

Use Time Wisely

If you decide to conduct your own job search with minimum assistance from professionals, your major cost will be your time. Therefore, you must find sufficient time to devote to your job search. Ask yourself this question:

> "How valuable is my time in relation to finding a job
> or changing my career?"

Assign a dollar value to your time. For example, is your time worth $3, $5, $10, $25, $50, or $100 an hour? Compare your figure with what you might pay a professional for doing much of the job search work for you. Normal professional fees range from $2,000 to $12,000.

The time you devote to your job search will depend on whether you want to work at it on a full-time or part-time basis. If you are unemployed, by all means make this a full-time endeavor—40 to 80 hours per week. If you are presently employed, we do not recommend quitting your job in order to look for employment. You will probably need the steady income and attendant health benefits during your transition period. Furthermore, it is easier to find new employment by appearing employed. Unemployed people project a negative image in the eyes of many employers—they appear to need a job. *Your goal is to find a job based on your strengths rather than your needs.*

However, if you go back to school for skills retraining, your present employment status may be less relevant to employers. Your major strength is the fact that you have acquired a skill the employer needs. If you quit your job and spend money retraining, you will communicate a certain degree of risk-taking, drive, responsibility, and dedication which employers readily seek, but seldom find, in candidates today.

Assuming you will be conducting a job search on a part-time basis—15 to 25 hours per week—you will need to find the necessary time for these job activities. Unfortunately, most people are busy, having programmed every hour to "important" personal and professional activities. Thus, conducting a job search for 15 or more hours a week means that some things will have to go or receive low priority in relation to your job search.

This is easier said than done. The job search often gets low priority. It competes with other important daily routines, such as attending meetings, taking children to games, going shopping, and watching favorite TV programs. Rather than fight with your routines—and create family disharmony and stress—make your job search part of your daily routines by improving your overall management of time.

Certain time management techniques will help you make your job search a high priority activity in your daily schedule. These practices may actually lower your present stress level and thus enhance your overall effectiveness.

Time management experts estimate that most people waste their time on unimportant matters. Lacking priorities, people spend 80 percent of their time on trivia and 20 percent of their time on the important matters which should get the most attention. If you reverse this emphasis, you could have a great deal of excess time—and probably experience less stress attendant with the common practice of crisis managing the critical 20 percent.

Before reorganizing your time, you must know how you normally use your time. Therefore, complete the exercise on pages 116-117 to assess your time management behavior. While many of these statements are relevant to individuals in managerial positions, respond to those statements that are most relevant to your employment situation. If you answered "no" to many of these statements, you should consider incorporating a few basic time management principles and practices into your daily schedule.

Don't go to extremes by drastically restructuring your life around the "religion" of time management. If you followed all the advice of time management experts, you would probably alienate your family, friends, and colleagues with your narrow efficiency mentality! A realistic approach is to start monitoring your time use and then gradually re-organize your time according to goals and priorities. This is all you need to do. Forget the elaborate flow charts that are the stuff of expensive time management workshops and consultants. Start by developing a time management log that helps you monitor your present use of time. Keep daily records of how you use your time over a two week period. Identify who controls your time and the results of your time utilization. Within two weeks, clear patterns will emerge. You may learn that you have an "open door" policy that enables others to control your time, leaving little time to do your own work. Based on this information, you may need to close your door and be more selective about access. You may find from your analysis that you use most time for activities that have few if any important outcomes. If this is the case, then you may need to set goals and prioritize daily activities.

A simple yet effective technique for improving your time management practices is to complete a "to do" list for each day. You can purchase tablets of these forms in many stationery and office supply stores, or you can develop your own "Things To Do Today" list. This list also should prioritize which activities are most important to accomplish each day. Include at the top of your list a particular job search activity or several activities that should be completed on each day. If you follow this simple time management practice, you will find the necessary time to include your job search in your daily routines. You can give your job search top priority. Better still, you will accomplish more in less time, and with better results.

Your Time Management Inventory

Respond to each statement by circling "yes" or "no," depending on which response best represents your normal pattern of behavior.

1. I have a written set of long, intermediate, and short-range goals for myself (and my family).   Yes   No

2. I have a clear idea of what I will do today at work and at home.   Yes   No

3. I have a clear idea of what I want to accomplish at work this coming week and month.   Yes   No

4. I set priorities and follow-through on the most important tasks first.   Yes   No

5. I judge my success by the results I produce in relation to my goals.   Yes   No

6. I use a daily, weekly, and monthly calendar for scheduling appointments and setting work targets.   Yes   No

7. I delegate as much work as possible.   Yes   No

8. I get my subordinates to organize their time in relation to mine.   Yes   No

9. I file only those things which are essential to my work. When in doubt, I throw it out.   Yes   No

10. I throw away junk mail.   Yes   No

11. My briefcase is uncluttered, including only essential materials; it serves as my office away from the office.   Yes   No

12. I minimize the number of meetings and concentrate on making decisions rather than discussing aimlessly.   Yes   No

13. I make frequent use of the telephone and face-to-face encounters rather than written communications.   Yes   No

14. I make minor decisions quickly.   Yes   No

15. I concentrate on accomplishing one thing at a time.   Yes   No

16. I handle each piece of paper once and only once.   Yes   No

17. I answer most letters on the letter I receive with either a handwritten or typed message.   Yes   No

18. I set deadlines for myself and others and follow-through in meeting them.   Yes   No

19. I reserve time each week to plan.   Yes   No

20. My desk and work area are well organized and clear.   Yes   No

21. I know how to say "no" and do so.   Yes   No

22. I first skim books, articles, and other forms of written communication for ideas before reading further.   Yes   No

23. I monitor my time use during the day by asking myself "How can I best use my time at present?"   Yes   No

24. I deal with the present by getting things done that need to be done.   Yes   No

25. I maintain a time log to monitor the best use of my time.   Yes   No

26. I place a dollar value on my time and behave accordingly.   Yes   No

27. I—not others—control my time.   Yes   No

28. My briefcase includes items I can work on during spare time in waiting rooms, lines, and airports.   Yes   No

29. I keep my door shut when I'm working.   Yes   No

30. I regularly evaluate to what degree I am achieving my stated goals.   Yes   No

Plan to Take Action

While we recommend that you plan your job search, we also caution you to avoid the excesses of too much planning. Like time management, planning should not be all-consuming. Planning makes sense because it focuses attention and directs action toward specific goals and targets. It requires you to set goals and develop strategies for achieving the goals. However, too much planning can blind you to unexpected occurrences and opportunities—that wonderful experience called serendipity. Given the highly decentralized and chaotic nature of the job market, you want to do just enough planning so you will be in a position to take advantage of what will inevitably be unexpected occurrences and opportunities arising from your planned job search activities. Therefore, as you plan your job search, be sure you are flexible enough to take advantage of new opportunities.

Based on our previous discussion of the sequence of job search steps, we outline on page 119 a hypothetical plan for conducting an effective job search. This plan incorporates the individual job search activities over a six month period. If you phase in the first five job search steps during the initial three to four weeks and continue the final four steps in subsequent weeks and months, you should begin receiving job offers within two to three months after initiating your job search. Interviews and job offers can come anytime—often unexpectedly—as you conduct your job search. An average time is three months, but it can occur within a week or take as long as five months. If you plan, prepare, and persist at the job search, the pay-off will be job interviews and offers.

While three months may seem a long time, especially if you have just lost your job and you need work immediately, you can shorten your job search time by increasing the frequency of your individual job search activities. If you are job hunting on a full-time basis, you may be able to cut your job search time in half. But don't expect to get a job—especially a job that's right for you—within a week or two. Job hunting requires time and hard work—perhaps the hardest work you will ever do—but if done properly, it pays off with a job that is right for you.

Strategies For Success

Success is determined by more than just a good plan getting implemented. We know success is not determined primarily by intelligence, time management, or luck. Based upon experience, theory, research, common sense, and acceptance of some self-transformation principles, we believe you will achieve job search success by following most of these 20 principles (page 120):

ORGANIZATION OF JOB SEARCH ACTIVITIES

Activity	Weeks 1 2 3 4 5 6 7 8 9 10 11 12 13 14 15 16 17 18 19 20 21 22 23 24
■ Think, questioning, listening, evaluating, adjusting	
■ Identifying abilities & skills	
■ Setting objectives	
■ Writing resume	
■ Conducting research	
■ Prospecting, referrals, networking	
■ Interviewing	
■ Receiving and negotiating job offers	

1. **You should work hard at finding a job:** Make this a daily endeavor and involve your family. Focus on specifics.

2. **You should not be discouraged with set-backs:** You are playing the odds, so expect disappointments and handle them in stride. You will get many "no's" before finding the one "yes" which is right for you.

3. **You should be patient and persevere:** Expect three to six months of hard work before you connect with the job that's right for you.

4. **You should be honest with yourself and others:** Honesty is always the best policy. But don't be naive and stupid by confessing your negatives and shortcomings to others.

5. **You should develop a positive attitude toward yourself:** Nobody wants to employ guilt-ridden people with inferiority complexes. Focus on your positive characteristics.

6. **You should associate with positive and successful people:** Finding a job largely depends on how well you relate to others. Avoid associating with negative and depressing people who complain and have a "you-can't-do-it" attitude. Run with winners who have a positive "can-do" outlook on life.

7. **You should set goals:** You should have a clear idea of what you want and where you are going. Without these, you will present a confusing and indecisive image to others. Clear goals help direct your job search into productive channels. Moreover, setting high goals will help make you work hard in getting what you want.

8. **You should plan:** Convert your goals into action steps that are organized as short, intermediate, and long-range plans.

9. **You should get organized:** Translate your plans into activities, targets, names, addresses, telephone numbers, and materials. Develop an efficient and effective filing system and use a large calendar to set time targets, record appointments, and compile useful information.

10. **You should be a good communicator:** Take stock of your oral, written, and nonverbal communication skills. How well do you communicate? Since most aspects of your job search

involve communicating with others, and communication skills are one of the most sought-after skills, always present yourself well both verbally and nonverbally.

11. **You should be energetic and enthusiastic:** Employers are attracted to positive people. They don't like negative and depressing people who toil at their work. Generate enthusiasm both verbally and nonverbally. Check on your telephone voice—it may be more unenthusiastic than your voice in face-to-face situations.

12. **You should ask questions:** Your best information comes from asking questions. Learn to develop intelligent questions that are non-aggressive, polite, and interesting to others. But don't ask too many questions and thereby become a bore.

13. **You should be a good listener:** Being a good listener is often more important than being a good questioner or talker. Learn to improve your face-to-face listening behavior (nonverbal cues) as well as remember and use information gained from others. Make others feel they enjoyed talking with you, i.e., you are one of the few people who actually *listens* to what they say.

14. **You should be polite, courteous, and thoughtful:** Treat gatekeepers, especially receptionists and secretaries, like human beings. Avoid being aggressive or too assertive. Try to be polite, courteous, and gracious. Your social graces are being observed. Remember to send thank you letters—a very thoughtful thing to do in a job search. Even if rejected, thank employers for the "opportunity" given to you. After all, they may later have additional opportunities, and they will remember you.

15. **You should be tactful:** Watch what you say to others about other people and your background. Don't be a gossip, backstabber, or confessor.

16. **You should maintain a professional stance:** Be neat in what you do and wear, and speak with the confidence, authority, and maturity of a professional.

17. **You should demonstrate your intelligence and competence:** Present yourself as someone who gets things done and achieves results—a *producer*. Employers generally seek

people who are bright, hard working, responsible, communicate well, have positive personalities, maintain good interpersonal relations, are likable, observe dress and social codes, take initiative, are talented, possess expertise in particular areas, use good judgment, are cooperative, trustworthy, and loyal, generate confidence and credibility, and are conventional. In other words, they like people who score in the "excellent" to "outstanding" categories of the annual performance evaluation.

18. **You should not overdo your job search:** Don't engage in overkill and bore everyone with your "job search" stories. Achieve balance in everything you do. Occasionally take a few days off to do nothing related to your job search. Develop a system of incentives and rewards—such as two non-job search days a week, if you accomplish targets A, B, C, and D.

19. **You should be open-minded and keep an eye open for "luck":** Too much planning can blind you to unexpected and fruitful opportunities. You should welcome serendipity. Learn to re-evaluate your goals and strategies. Seize new opportunities if they appear appropriate.

20. **You should evaluate your progress and adjust:** Take two hours once every two weeks and evaluate what you are doing and accomplishing. If necessary, tinker with your plans and reorganize your activities and priorities. Don't become too routinized and thereby kill creativity and innovation.

These principles should provide you with an initial orientation for starting your job search. As you become more experienced, you will develop your own set of operating principles that should work for you in particular employment situations.

Take Risks and Handle Rejections

You can approach a job or career change in various ways. Some actions have higher pay-offs than others. Many people waste time by doing nothing, reconstructing the past, worrying about the future, and thinking about what they should have done. This negative approach impedes rather than advances careers.

A second approach is to do what most people do when looking for a job. They examine classified ads, respond to vacancy announcements, and complete applications in personnel offices. While this approach is better than doing nothing, it is relatively inefficient as well as ineffective. You compete with many others who are using the same approach. Furthermore, the vacancy announcements do not represent the true number of job vacancies nor do they offer the best opportunities. As we will see in Chapter 11, you should use this approach to some degree, but it should not preoccupy your time. Responding to vacancy announcements is a game of chance, and the odds are usually against you. It makes you too dependent upon others to give you a job.

The third approach to making a job change requires *taking creative action* on your part. You must become a self-reliant risk-taker. You identify what it is you want to do, what you have acquired skills to do, and organize yourself accordingly by following the methods outlined in subsequent chapters. You don't need to spend much time with classified ads, employment agencies, and personnel offices. And you don't need to worry about your future. You take charge of your future by initiating a job search which pays off with job offers. Your major investment is *time*. Your major risk is being turned down or rejected.

Job hunting is an ego-involving activity. You place your past, abilities, and self-image before strangers who don't know who you are or what you can do. Being rejected or having someone say "no" to you will probably be your greatest job hunting difficulty. We know most people can handle two or three "no's" before they get discouraged. If you approach your job search from a less ego-involved perspective, you can take "no's" in stride; they are a normal aspect of your job search experience. Be prepared to encounter 10, 20, or 50 "no's." Remember, the odds are in your favor. For every 20 "no's" you get, you also should uncover one or two "yeses." The more rejections you get, the more acceptances you also will get. Therefore, you must encounter rejection *before* you get acceptances.

This third approach is the approach of this book. Experience with thousands of clients shows that the most successful job seekers are those who develop a high degree of self-reliance, maintain a positive self-image, and are willing to risk being rejected time after time without becoming discouraged. This approach will work for you if you follow our advice on how to become a self-reliant risk-taker in today's job market. Better yet, use the networking strategies outlined in Chapter 13 as well as more fully developed in our *Interview For Success* and *Dynamite Networking For Dynamite Jobs* books, and you can significantly decrease the number of "no's" you receive on your way to a job that's right for you.

Form a Support Group

We believe most people can conduct a successful job search on their own by following the step-by-step procedures of this book. We know they work because these methods have been used by thousands of successful job hunters. But we know it is difficult to become a risk-taker, especially in an area where few people have a base of experience and knowledge from which to begin. Therefore, we recommend sharing the risks with others.

Our self-directed methods work well when you join others in forming a job search group or club. The group provides a certain degree of security which is often necessary when launching a new and unknown adventure. In addition, the group can provide important information on job leads. Members will critique your approach and progress. They will provide you with psychological supports as you experience the frustration of rejections and the joys of success. You also will be helping others who will be helping you. Some career counselors estimate that membership in such groups can cut one's job search time by as much as 50 percent!

You can form your own group by working with your spouse or by finding friends who are interested in looking for a new job. Your friends may know other friends or colleagues who are interested in doing the same. Some of your friends may surprise you by indicating they would like to join your group out of curiosity. If you are over 40 years of age, check to see if there is a chapter of the 40-Plus Club in your community. This group is organized as a job search club.

Your group should meet regularly—once a week. At the meetings discuss your experiences, critique each other's approaches and progress, and share information on what you are learning or what you feel you need to know more about and do more effectively. Include your spouse as part of this group. We will return to this subject in Chapter 13 when we discuss how to develop your networks for uncovering job leads.

One other aspect of this self-directed book should be clarified. While we do not immediately recommend that you seek professional assistance, such as a career counselor, this assistance can be useful at certain stages and depending on individual circumstances. For example, the next chapter focuses on skills identification. While we present the necessary information and exercises for you to identify your skills, some individuals may wish to enhance this step of the job search by seeking the assistance of a professional career counselor who may have more sophisticated testing instruments for meeting these needs.

On the other hand, if you bring to your job search certain health and psychological problems which affect your job performance, you should seek professional help rather than try to solve your problems with this book. This is especially true for those with alcohol or drug problems who really need some form of professional therapy before putting in practice the job search steps identified in this book. If you are in serious financial trouble or a separation or divorce is greatly troubling you, seek professional help. Only after you get yourself together physically and mentally will this book produce its intended results for you. Remember, no employer wants to hire alcohol, drug, financial, or marital problems. They want productive, job-centered individuals who are capable of handling their personal problems rather than bringing them to work.

You must be honest with yourself before you can be honest with others. The whole philosophy underlying this book is one of personal honesty and integrity in everything you do related to your job search.

Part II

DEVELOP POWERFUL CAREERING AND RE-CAREERING SKILLS

Identify Your Skills and Abilities

We live in a skills-based society where individuals market their skills to employers in exchange for money, position, and power. The ease by which individuals change jobs and careers is directly related to their ability to communicate their skills to employers and then transfer their skills to new work settings.

To best position yourself in the job markets of today and tomorrow, you should pay particular attention to refining your present skills as well as acquiring new and more marketable skills.

Identify Your Skills

But before you can refine your skills or acquire additional skills, you need to know what skills you presently possess. Unfortunately, few people can identify and talk about their skills even though they possess hundreds of skills which they use on a regular basis. This becomes a real problem when they must write a resume or go to a job interview. Since employers want to know about your specific abilities and skills, you must learn to both identify and communicate your skills to employers. You should be able to explain what it is you do well and give examples relevant to employers' needs.

What skills do you already have to offer employers? If you have just completed an educational program, the skills you have to offer are most likely related to the subject matter you studied. If you are changing jobs or careers, the skills you wish to communicate to employers will be those things you already have demonstrated you can do in specific jobs.

We earlier addressed the question of how to acquire skills training for careering and re-careering in the years ahead by noting that the skills required for *finding a job* are no substitute for the skills necessary for *doing the job*. Learning new skills requires a major investment of time, money, and effort. Nonetheless, the long-term pay-off should more than justify the initial costs. Indeed, research continues to show that well selected education and training provide the best returns on individual and societal investment.

Types of Skills

Most people possess two types of skills that define their accomplishments and strengths as well as enable them to enter and advance within the job market: work-content skills and functional skills. You need to acquaint yourself with these skills before communicating them to employers. These skills become the key language for communicating your qualifications to employers through your resumes and letters as well as in interviews. They can be expressed in the form of both verbs and nouns—an important distinction that differentiates conventional resumes in Chapter 11 from new electronic resumes in Chapter 21.

We assume you have already acquired certain *work-content skills* necessary to function effectively in today's job market. These "hard skills" are easy to recognize since they are often identified as "qualifications" for specific jobs; they are the subject of most educational and training pro- grams. Work-content skills tend to be technical and job-specific in nature. Examples of such skills include proficiency in word processing, program- ming computers, teaching history, or operating an X-ray machine. They may require formal training, are associated with specific trades or professions, and are used only in certain job and career settings. One uses a separate skills vocabulary, jargon, and subject matter for specifying technical qualifications of individuals entering and advancing in an occupation. While these skills do not transfer well from one occupation to another, they are critical for entering and advancing within certain occupations.

At the same time, you possess numerous *functional/transferable skills* employers readily seek along with your work-content skills. These "soft skills" are associated with numerous job settings, are mainly acquired through experience rather than formal training, and can be communicated through a general vocabulary. Functional/transferable skills are less easy to recognize since they tend to be linked to certain *personal characteristics* (energetic, intelligent, likable) and the ability to *deal with processes* (communicating, problem-solving, motivating) rather than *do things* (programming a computer, building a house, repairing air-conditioners). While most people have only a few work-content skills, they may have numerous—as many as 300—functional/transferable skills. These skills enable job seekers to more easily change jobs. But you must first be aware of your functional skills before you can relate them to the job market.

Most people view the world of work in traditional occupational job skill terms. This is a *structural view* of occupational realities. Occupational fields are seen as consisting of separate and distinct jobs which, in turn, require specific work-content skills. From this perspective, occupations and jobs are relatively self-contained entities. Social work, for example, is seen as being different from paralegal work; social workers, therefore, are not "qualified" to seek paralegal work.

On the other hand, a *functional view* of occupations and jobs emphasizes the similarity of job characteristics as well as common linkages between different occupations. Although the structure of occupations and jobs may differ, they have similar functions. They involve working with people, data, processes, and objects. If you work with people, data, processes, and objects in one occupation, you can transfer that experience to other occupations which have similar functions. Once you understand how your skills relate to the functions as well as investigate the structure of different occupations, you should be prepared to make job changes from one occupational field to another. Whether you possess the necessary work-content skills to qualify for entry into the other occupational field is another question altogether.

The skills we identify and help you organize in this chapter are the functional skills career counselors normally emphasize when advising clients to assess their *strengths*. In contrast to work-content skills, functional skills can be transferred from one job or career to another. They enable individuals to make some job and career changes without acquiring

> **Functional skills can be transferred from one job or career to another.**

additional education and training. They constitute an important bridge for moving from one occupation to another.

Before you decide if you need more education or training, you should first assess both your functional and work-content skills to see how they can be transferred to other jobs and occupations. Once you do this, you should be better prepared to communicate your qualifications to employers with a rich skills-based vocabulary.

Your Strengths

Regardless of what combination of work-content and functional skills you possess, a job search must begin with identifying your strengths. Without knowing these, your job search will lack content and focus. After all, your goal should be to find a job that is fit for you rather than one you think you might be able to fit into. Of course, you also want to find a job for which there is a demand. This particular focus requires a well-defined approach to identifying and communicating your skills to others. You can best do this by asking the right questions about your strengths and then conducting a systematic self-assessment of what you do best.

Ask the Right Questions

Knowing the right questions to ask will save you time and steer you into productive job search channels from the very beginning. Asking the wrong questions can cripple your job search efforts and leave you frustrated. The questions must be understood from the perspectives of both employers and applicants.

Two of the most humbling questions you will encounter in your job search are "Why should I hire you?" and "What are your weaknesses?"

While employers may not directly ask these questions, they are asking them nonetheless. If you can't answer these questions in a positive manner—directly, indirectly, verbally, or nonverbally—your job search will likely founder and you will join the ranks of the unsuccessful and disillusioned job searchers who feel something is wrong with them. Individuals who have lost their jobs are particularly vulnerable to these questions since many have lowered self-esteem and self-image as a result of the job loss. Many such people focus on what is wrong rather than what is right about themselves. Such thinking creates self-fulfilling prophecies and is self-destructive in the job market. By all means avoid such negative thinking.

Employers want to hire your *value or strengths*—not your weaknesses. Since it is easier to identify and interpret weaknesses, employers look for indicators of your strengths by trying to identify your weaknesses. The more successful you are in communicating your strengths to employers, the better off you will be in relation to both employers and fellow applicants.

Unfortunately, many people work against their own best interests. Not knowing their strengths, they market their weaknesses by first identifying job vacancies and then trying to fit their "qualifications" into job descriptions. This approach often frustrates applicants; it presents a picture of a job market which is not interested in the applicant's strengths. This leads some people toward acquiring new skills which they hope will be marketable, even though they do not enjoy using them. Millions of individuals find themselves in such misplaced situations. Your task is to avoid joining the ranks of the misplaced and unhappy work force by first understanding your skills and then relating them to your interests and goals. In so doing, you will be in a better position to target your job search toward jobs that should become especially rewarding and fulfilling.

> **Your goal should be to find a job that is fit for you rather than one you think you might be able to fit into.**

Functional/Transferable Skills

We know most people stumble into jobs by accident. Some are at the right place at the right time to take advantage of opportunities. Others work hard at trying to fit into jobs listed in classified ads, employment agencies, and personnel offices; identified through friends and acquaintances; or found by knocking on doors. After 15 to 20 years in the work world, many people wish they had better planned their careers from the very start. All of a sudden they are unhappily locked into jobs because of retirement benefits and family responsibilities of raising children and meeting monthly mortgage payments.

After 10 or 20 years of work experience, most people have a good idea of what they don't like to do. While their values are more set than when they first began working, many people are still unclear as to what they do well and how their skills fit into the job market. What other jobs, for example, might they be qualified to perform? If they have the opportunity to change jobs or careers—either voluntarily or forced through termination—and find the time to plan the change, they can move into jobs and careers which fit their skills.

The key to understanding your non-technical strengths is to identify your transferable or functional skills. Once you have done this, you will be better prepared to identify what it is you want to do. Moreover, your self-image and self-esteem will improve. Better still, you will be prepared to communicate your strengths to others through a rich skills-based vocabulary. These outcomes are critically important for writing your resume and letters as well as for conducting informational and job interviews.

Let's illustrate the concept of functional/transferable skills for educators. Many educators view their skills in strict work-content terms—knowledge of a particular subject matter such as math, history, English, physics, or music. When looking for jobs outside education, many seek employment which will use their subject matter skills. But they soon discover non-educational institutions are not a ready market for such "skills."

> **Employers want to hire your value or strengths—not your weaknesses.**

On the other hand, educators possess many other skills that are directly transferable to business and industry. Unaware of these skills, many educators fail to communicate their strengths to others. For example, research shows that graduate students in the humanities most frequently possess these transferable skills, in order of importance:

- critical thinking
- research techniques
- perseverance
- self-discipline
- insight
- writing

- general knowledge
- cultural perspective
- teaching ability
- self-confidence
- imagination
- leadership ability

Most functional/transferable skills can be classified into two general skills and trait categories—organizational/interpersonal skills and personality/ work-style traits:

Types of Transferable Skills

Organizational and Interpersonal Skills

___ communicating
___ problem solving
___ analyzing/assessing
___ planning
___ decision-making

___ trouble shooting
___ implementing
___ self-understanding
___ understanding
___ setting goals

___ innovating
___ thinking logically
___ evaluating
___ identifying problems
___ synthesizing
___ forecasting
___ tolerating ambiguity
___ motivating
___ leading
___ selling
___ performing
___ reviewing
___ attaining
___ team building
___ updating
___ coaching
___ supervising
___ estimating
___ negotiating
___ administering

___ conceptualizing
___ generalizing
___ managing time
___ creating
___ judging
___ controlling
___ organizing
___ persuading
___ encouraging
___ improving
___ designing
___ consulting
___ teaching
___ cultivating
___ advising
___ training
___ interpreting
___ achieving
___ reporting
___ managing

Personality and Work-Style Traits

___ diligent
___ patient
___ innovative
___ persistent
___ tactful
___ loyal
___ successful
___ versatile
___ enthusiastic
___ out-going
___ expressive
___ adaptable
___ democratic
___ resourceful
___ determining
___ creative
___ open
___ objective
___ warm
___ orderly
___ tolerant
___ frank
___ cooperative

___ honest
___ reliable
___ perceptive
___ assertive
___ sensitive
___ astute
___ risk taker
___ easy going
___ calm
___ flexible
___ competent
___ punctual
___ receptive
___ diplomatic
___ self-confident
___ tenacious
___ discrete
___ talented
___ empathic
___ tidy
___ candid
___ adventuresome
___ firm

__ dynamic	__ sincere
__ self-starter	__ initiator
__ precise	__ competent
__ sophisticated	__ diplomatic
__ effective	__ efficient

These are the types of skills you need to identify and then communicate to employers in your resumes and letters as well as during interviews.

Identify Your Skills

If you are just graduating from high school or college and do not know what you want to do, you probably should take a battery of vocational tests and psychological inventories to identify your interests and skills. These tests are listed in Chapter 9. If you don't fall into these categories of job seekers, chances are you don't need complex testing. You have experience, you have well defined values, and you know what you don't like in a job. Therefore, we outline several alternative skills identification exercises—from simple to complex—for assisting you at this stage. We recommend using the most complete and extensive activity—the Motivated Skills Exercise—to gain a thorough understanding of your strengths.

Use the following exercises to identify both your work-content and transferable skills. These self-assessment techniques stress your positives or strengths rather than identify your negatives or weaknesses. They should generate a rich vocabulary for communicating your "qualifications" to employers. Each exercise requires different investments of your time and effort as well as varying degrees of assistance from other people.

These exercises, however, should be used with caution. There is nothing magical nor particularly profound about them. Most are based upon a very simple and somewhat naive *deterministic theory of behavior*—your past patterns of behavior are good predictors of your future behavior. Not a bad theory for most individuals, but it is rather simplistic and disheartening for individuals who wish to, and can, break out of past patterns as they embark on a new future. Furthermore, most exercises are *historical devices.* They provide you with a clear picture of your past, which may or may not be particularly useful for charting your future. Nonetheless, these exercises do help individuals (1) organize data on themselves, (2) target their job search around clear objectives and skills, and (3) generate a rich vocabulary of skills and accomplishments for communicating strengths to potential employers.

If you feel these exercises are inadequate for your needs, by all means seek professional assistance from a testing or assessment center staffed by a licensed psychologist. These centers do in-depth testing which goes further than these self-directed skill exercises.

When using the following exercises, keep in mind that some individuals can and do change—often very dramatically—their behavior regardless of such deterministic and historical assessment devices. Much of the "motivation and success," "power of positive thinking," "thinking big," and "empowerment" literature, for example, challenges the validity of these standardized assessment tests that are used to predict or pattern future individual behavior. So be careful how you use such information for charting your career future. You *can* change your future. But at least get to know yourself before making the changes. Critiques of, as well as alternatives to, these exercises are outlined in our book, *Discover the Best Jobs For You!*

Checklist Method

This is the simplest method for identifying your strengths. Review the different types of transferable skills outlined on pages 133-135. Place a "1" in front of the skills that *strongly* characterize you; assign a "2" to those skills that describe you to a *large extent*; put a "3" before those that describe you to *some extent.* After completing this exercise, review the lists and rank order the 10 characteristics that best describe you on each list.

Skills Map

Richard N. Bolles has produced two well-known exercises for identifying transferable skills based upon John Holland's typology of work environments. Both are historical devices structured around a deterministic theory of behavior. In his book, *The Three Boxes of Life* (Ten Speed Press), he develops a checklist of 100 transferable skills. They are organized into 12 categories or types of skills: using hands, body, words, senses, numbers, intuition, analytical thinking, creativity, helpfulness, artistic abilities, leadership, and follow-through.

Bolles' second exercise, *"The Quick Job Hunting Map,"* expands upon this first one. The *"Map"* is a checklist of 222 skills. This exercise requires you to identify seven of your most satisfying accomplishments, achievements, jobs, or roles. After writing a page about each experience, you relate each to the checklist of 222 skills. The *"Map"* should give you a comprehensive picture of what skills you (1) use most frequently, and (2) enjoy using in satisfying and successful settings. While this exercise may take six hours to complete, it yields an enormous amount of data on past strengths. Furthermore, the *"Map"* generates a rich skills vocabulary for communicating your strengths to others. The *"Map"* is found in the appendix of Bolles' *What Color Is Your Parachute?* (Ten Speed Press) or it can be purchased separately in beginning, advanced, or new versions from Ten Speed Press. His books, as well as the latest version (1990) of his popular *New Quick Job Hunting Map*, can be ordered directly from Impact Publications by completing the order form at the end of this book.

Autobiography of Accomplishments

Write a lengthy essay about your life accomplishments. This could range from 20 to 100 pages. After completing the essay, go through it page by page to identify what you most enjoyed doing (working with different kinds of information, people, and things) and what skills you used most frequently as well as enjoyed using. Finally, identify those skills you wish to continue using. After analyzing and synthesizing this data, you should have a relatively clear picture of your strongest skills.

Computerized Assessment Systems

While the previous self-directed exercises required you to either respond to checklists of skills or reconstruct and analyze your past job experiences, several computerized self-assessment programs are designed to help individuals identify their skills. Many of the programs are available in schools, colleges, and libraries. Some of the most widely used programs include:

- *Cambridge Career Counseling System*
- *Career Information System* (CIS)
- *Career Navigator*
- *Choices*
- *Discover II*
- *Guidance Information System* (GIS)
- *SIGI-Plus* (System of Interactive Guidance and Information)

Most of these comprehensive career planning programs do much more than just assess skills. As we will see in Chapter 9, they also integrate other key components in the career planning process—interests, goals, related jobs, college majors, education and training programs, and job search plans. These programs are widely available in schools, colleges, and libraries across the country. You might check with the career or counseling center at your local community college to see what computerized career assessment systems are available for your use. Relatively easy to use, they generate a great deal of useful career planning information. Many will print out a useful analysis of how your interests and skills are related to specific jobs and careers.

8

Specify Your Interests and Values

Knowing what you do well is essential for understanding your strengths and for linking your capabilities to specific jobs. However, just knowing your abilities and skills will not give your job search the direction it needs for finding the right job. You also need to know your work values and interests. These are the basic building blocks for setting goals and targeting your abilities toward certain jobs and careers.

Take, for example, the individual who types 120 words a minute. While this person possesses a highly marketable skill, if the person doesn't enjoy using this skill and is more interested in working outdoors, this will not become a *motivated skill*; the individual will most likely not pursue a typing job. Your interests and values will determine whether or not certain skills should play a central role in your job search.

Vocational Interests

We all have interests. Most change over time. Many of your interests may center on your present job whereas others relate to activities that define your hobbies and leisure activities. A good place to start identifying your interests is by examining the information and exercises found in both *The Guide to Occupational Exploration* and *The Enhanced Guide to Occupational Exploration*. Widely used by students and others first entering the job market, it is also relevant to individuals who already have work experience. The guide classifies all jobs in the United States into 12 interest areas. Examine the following list of interest areas. In the first column check those work areas that appeal to you. In the second column rank order those areas you checked in the first column. Start with "1" to indicate the most interesting:

Your Work Interests

Yes/No (x)	Ranking (1-12)	Interest Area
___	___	**Artistic:** An interest in creative expression of feelings or ideas.
___	___	**Scientific:** An interest in discovering, collecting, and analyzing information about the natural world, and in applying scientific research findings to problems in medicine, the life sciences, and the nature sciences.
___	___	**Plants and animals:** An interest in working with plants and animals, usually outdoors.
___	___	**Protective:** An interest in using authority to protect people and property.
___	___	**Mechanical:** An interest in applying mechanical principles to practical situations by using machines or hand tools.
___	___	**Industrial:** An interest in repetitive, concrete, organized activities done in a factory setting.
___	___	**Business detail:** An interest in organized, clearly defined activities requiring accuracy and attention to details (office settings).
___	___	**Selling:** An interest in bringing others to a particular point of view by personal persuasion, using sales and promotion techniques.
___	___	**Accommodating:** An interest in catering to the wishes and needs of others, usually on a one-to-one basis.
___	___	**Humanitarian:** An interest in helping others with their mental, spiritual, social, physical, or vocational needs.

___   ___   **Leading and influencing:** An interest in leading
and influencing others by using high-level verbal
or numerical abilities.

___   ___   **Physical performing:** An interest in physical
activities performed before an audience.

The Guide to Occupational Exploration also includes other checklists
relating to home-based and leisure activities that may or may not relate to
your work interests. If you are unclear about your work interests, you might
want to consult these other interest exercises. You may discover that some
of your home-based and leisure activity interests should become your work
interests. Examples of such interests include:

Leisure and Home-Based Interests

___ Acting in a play or amateur variety show.

___ Advising family members on their personal problems.

___ Announcing or emceeing a program.

___ Applying first aid in emergencies as a volunteer.

___ Building model airplanes, automobiles, or boats.

___ Building or repairing radio or television sets.

___ Buying large quantities of food or other
     products for an organization.

___ Campaigning for political candidates or issues.

___ Canning and preserving food.

___ Carving small wooden objects.

___ Coaching children or youth in sports activities.

___ Collecting experiments involving plants.

___ Conducting house-to-house or telephone
     surveys for a PTA or other organization.

___ Creating or styling hairdos for friends.

___ Designing your own greeting cards and writing
     original verses.

___ Developing film.

___ Doing impersonations.

___ Doing public speaking or debating.

___ Entertaining at parties or other events.

___ Helping conduct physical exercises for disabled people.

___ Making ceramic objects.

___ Modeling clothes for a fashion show.

___ Mounting and framing pictures.

___ Nursing sick pets.

___ Painting the interior or exterior of a home.

___ Playing a musical instrument.

___ Refinishing or re-upholstering furniture.

___ Repairing electrical household appliances.

___ Repairing the family car.

___ Repairing or assembling bicycles.

___ Repairing plumbing in the house.

___ Speaking on radio or television.

___ Taking photographs.

___ Teaching in Sunday School.

___ Tutoring pupils in school subjects.

___ Weaving rugs or making quilts.

___ Writing articles, stories, or plays.

___ Writing songs for club socials or amateur plays.

Indeed, many people turn hobbies or home activities into full-time jobs after deciding that such "work" is what they really enjoy doing.

Other popular exercises designed to identify your work interests include John Holland's *"The Self-Directed Search"* which is found in his book, *Making Vocational Choices: A Theory of Careers*. It is also published as a separate testing instrument, *The Self-Directed Search—A Guide to Educational and Vocational Planning*. Developed from Holland's Vocational Preference Inventory, this popular self-administered, self-scored, and self-interpreted inventory helps individuals quickly identify what type of work environment they are motivated to seek—realistic, investigative, artistic, social, enterprising, or conventional—and aligns these work environments with lists of common occupational titles. An easy exercise to use, it gives you a quick overview of your orientation toward different types of work settings that interest you.

Holland's self-directed search is also the basic framework used in developing Bolles' *"The Quick Job Hunting Map"* as found in his *What Color Is Your Parachute?* and *The New Quick Job Hunting Map* books (see discussion on page 136).

For more sophisticated treatments of work interests, which are also validated through testing procedures, contact a career counselor, women's center, or testing and assessment center for information on these tests:

- *Strong Interest Inventory*
- *Myers-Briggs Type Indicator*
- *Edwards Personal Preference Schedule*
- *Kuder Occupational Interest Survey*
- *APTICOM*
- *Jackson Vocational Interest Survey*
- *Ramak Inventory*
- *Vocational Interest Inventory*
- *Career Assessment Inventory*
- *Temperament and Values Inventory*

Numerous other job and career interest inventories are also available. For further information, contact a career counselor or consult Educational Testing Service which compiles such tests. *The ETS Test Collection Catalog* (New York: Oryx Press), which is available in many library reference sections, lists most of these tests. The *Mental Measurements Yearbook* (Lincoln, NE: University of Nebraska Press) also surveys many of the major testing and assessment instruments.

Keep in mind that not all testing and assessment instruments used by career counselors are equally valid for career planning purposes. While the Strong Interest Inventory appears to be the most relevant for career decision-making, the Myers-Briggs Type Indicator has become extremely popular during the past ten years. Based on Carl Gustav Jung's personality preference theory, the Myers-Briggs Type Indicator is used extensively by psychologists and career counselors for identifying personality types. However, it is more useful for measuring individual personality and decision-making styles than for predicting career choices. It is most widely used in pastoral counseling, student personnel, and business and religious organizations for measuring personality and decision-making styles. For more information on this test, contact: Consulting Psychologists Press, Inc. At 3803 East Bayshore Road, Palo Alto, CA 94303, Tel. 800/624-1765. A version of the test is also available online through CompuServe. In the meantime, many career counselors find Holland's *The Self-Directed Search* an excellent self-directed alternative to these professionally administered and interpreted tests.

Work Values

Work values are those things you like to do. They give you pleasure and enjoyment. Most jobs involve a combination of likes and dislikes. By identifying what you both like and dislike about jobs, you should be able to better identify jobs that involve tasks that you will most enjoy.

Several exercises can help you identify your work values. First, identify what most satisfies you about work by completing the following exercise:

My Work Values

I prefer employment which enables me to:

____ contribute to society	____ be creative
____ have contact with people	____ supervise others
____ work alone	____ work with details
____ work with a team	____ gain recognition
____ compete with others	____ acquire security
____ make decisions	____ make money
____ work under pressure	____ help others
____ use power and authority	____ solve problems
____ acquire new knowledge	____ take risks
____ be a recognized expert	____ work at own pace

Select four work values from the above list which are the most important to you and list them in the space below. List any other work values (desired satisfactions) which were not listed above but are nonetheless important to you:

1. _____

2. _____

3. _____

4. _____

   _____

   _____

Another approach to identifying work values is outlined in *The Guide to Occupational Exploration*. If you feel you need to go beyond the above exercises, try this one. In the first column check those values that are most important to you. In the second column rank order the five most important values:

Ranking Work Values

Yes/No (x)	Ranking (1-5)	Work Values
——	——	**Adventure:** Working in a job that requires taking risks.
——	——	**Authority:** Working in a job in which you use your position to control others.
——	——	**Competition:** Working in a job in which you compete with others.
——	——	**Creativity and self-expression:** Working in a job in which you use your imagination to find new ways to do or say something.
——	——	**Flexible work schedule:** Working in a job in which you choose your hours to work.
——	——	**Helping others:** Working in a job in which you provide direct services to persons with problems.
——	——	**High salary:** Working in a job where many workers earn a large amount of money.
——	——	**Independence:** Working in a job in which you decide for yourself what work to do and how to do it.
——	——	**Influencing others:** Working in a job in which you influence the opinions of others or decisions of others.
——	——	**Intellectual stimulation:** Working in a job which requires a great amount of thought and reasoning.

___ ___ **Leadership:** Working in a job in which you direct, manage, or supervise the activities of others.

___ ___ **Outside work:** Working out-of-doors.

___ ___ **Persuading:** Working in a job in which you personally convince others to take certain actions.

___ ___ **Physical work:** Working in a job which requires substantial physical activity.

___ ___ **Prestige:** Working in a job which gives you status and respect in the community.

___ ___ **Public attention:** Working in a job in which you attract immediate notice because of appearance or activity.

___ ___ **Public contact:** Working in a job in which you daily deal with the public.

___ ___ **Recognition:** Working in a job in which you gain public notice.

___ ___ **Research work:** Working in a job in which you search for and discover new facts and develop ways to apply them.

___ ___ **Routine work:** Working in a job in which you follow established procedures requiring little change.

___ ___ **Seasonal work:** Working in a job in which you are employed only at certain times of the year.

___ ___ **Travel:** Working in a job in which you take frequent trips.

___ ___ **Variety:** Working in a job in which your duties change frequently.

___ ___ **Work with children:** Working in a job in which you teach or care for children.

___   ___   **Work with hands:** Working in a job in which you use your hands or hand tools.

___   ___   **Work with machines or equipment:** Working in a job in which you use machines or equipment.

___   ___   **Work with numbers:** Working in a job in which you use mathematics or statistics.

Second, develop a comprehensive list of your past and present *job frustrations and dissatisfactions*. This should help you identify negative factors you should avoid in future jobs.

My Job Frustrations and Dissatisfactions

List as well as rank order as many past and present things that frustrate or make you dissatisfied and unhappy in job situations:

Rank

1. _____ ____
2. _____ ____
3. _____ ____
4. _____ ____
5. _____ ____
6. _____ ____
7. _____ ____
8. _____ ____
9. _____ ____
10. _____ ____
11. _____ ____
12. _____ ____
13. _____ ____
14. _____ ____
15. _____ ____

Third, brainstorm a list of "Ten or More Things I Love to Do". Identify which ones could be incorporated into what kinds of work environments:

Ten or More Things I Love To Do

Item	Related Work Environment
1. _____	_____
2. _____	_____
3. _____	_____
4. _____	_____
5. _____	_____
6. _____	_____
7. _____	_____
8. _____	_____
9. _____	_____
10. _____	_____

Fourth, list at least ten things you most enjoy about work and rank each item accordingly:

Ten Things I Enjoy the Most About Work

Rank

1. _____ ____
2. _____ ____
3. _____ ____
4. _____ ____
5. _____ ____
6. _____ ____
7. _____ ____
8. _____ ____
9. _____ ____
10. _____ ____

Fifth, you should also identify the types of interpersonal environments you prefer working in. Do this by specifying the types of people you like and dislike associating with:

Interpersonal Environments

Characteristics of people I like working with:	Characteristics of people I dislike working with:
_____	_____
_____	_____
_____	_____
_____	_____
_____	_____
_____	_____
_____	_____
_____	_____
_____	_____

Computerized Systems

Several computerized self-assessment programs identified in Chapter 7 (page 137) largely focus on career interests and values. Again, you may be able to get access to these and other relevant computerized assessment programs through your local community college, career center, or library.

Your Future As Objectives

All of these exercises are designed to explore your past and present work-related values. At the same time, you need to project your values into the *future*. What, for example, do you want to do over the next 10 to 20 years? We'll return to this type of value question when we address in Chapter 10 the critical objective setting stage of the job search process.

9

Know Your Motivated Abilities and Skills (MAS)

Once you know what you do well and enjoy doing, you next need to analyze those interests, values, abilities, and skills that form a **recurring motivated pattern**. This "pattern" is the single most important piece of information you need to know about yourself in the whole self-assessment process. Knowing your skills and abilities alone without knowing how they relate to your interests and values will not give you the necessary direction for finding the job you want. You simply *must* know your pattern.

What's Your MAS?

The concept of motivated abilities and skills (MAS) enables us to relate your interests and values to your skills and abilities. But how do we identify your MAS beyond the questions and exercises outlined thus far?

Your pattern of motivated abilities and skills becomes evident once you analyze your *achievements or accomplishments.* For it is your achievements that tell us what you both did well and enjoyed doing. If we analyze and synthesize many of your achievements, we are likely to identify a *recurring pattern* that most likely goes back to your childhood and which will continue to characterize your achievements in the future.

An equally useful exercise would be to identify your weaknesses by analyzing your failures. These, too, would fall into recurring patterns. Understanding what your weaknesses are might help you avoid jobs and work situations that bring out the worst in you. Indeed, you may learn more about yourself by analyzing your failures than by focusing solely on your accomplishments.

For now, let's focus on your positives rather than identify your negatives. After you complete the strength exercises in this chapter, you may want to reverse the procedures to identify your weaknesses.

Numerous self-directed exercises can assist you in identifying your pattern of motivated abilities and skills. The basic requirements for making these exercises work for you are time and analytical ability. You must spend a great deal of time detailing your achievements by looking at your history of accomplishments. Once you complete the historical reconstruction task, you must comb through your "stories" to identify recurring themes and patterns. This requires a high level of analytical ability which you may or may not possess. If analysis and synthesis are not two of your strong skills, you may want to seek assistance from a friend or professional who is good at analyzing and synthesizing information presented in narrative form. Career counseling firms such as Haldane Associates (nationwide) and People Management, Inc. (Snohomish, WA) are known for their use of this type of motivated pattern approach; they should be able to assist you.

Several paper and pencil exercises are designed to help identify your pattern of motivated abilities and skills. We outline some of the most popular and thorough such exercises that have proved useful to thousands of people.

The Skills Map

Richard Bolles' *"Quick Job Hunting Map"* has become a standard self-assessment tool for thousands of job seekers and career changers who are willing to spend the time and effort necessary for discovering their pattern of motivated abilities and skills. Offering a checklist of over 200 skills organized around John Holland's concept of *"The Self-Directed Search"* for defining work environments (realistic, investigative, artistic, social, enterprising, and conventional), the *"Map"* requires you to identify seven of your most satisfying accomplishments, achievements, jobs, or roles. After detailing each achievement, you analyze the details of each in relation to the checklist of skills. Once you do this for all seven achievements, you should have a comprehensive picture of what skills you (1) use most frequently, and (2) enjoy using in satisfying and successful settings. This exercise not only yields an enormous amount of information on your interests, values, skills, and abilities, it also assists you in the process of analyzing the data. If done properly, the *"Map"* should also generate a rich "skills" vocabulary which you should use in your resumes and letters as well as in interviews.

The *"Map"* is available in different forms and for different levels of experience. The most popular versions are found in the Appendix of Bolles' *What Color Is Your Parachute?* and *The Three Boxes of Life* as well as in a separate publication entitled *The New Quick Job Hunting Map*. These three publications can be ordered directly from Impact Publications by completing the order information at the end of this book. The map is also available in three other versions: *The Beginning Quick Job-Hunting Map, How to Create a Picture of Your Ideal Job or Next Career*, and *The Classic Quick Job-Hunting Map*. These versions of the *"Map"* are most conveniently available directly from the publisher, Ten Speed Press (P.O. Box 7123, Berkeley, CA 94707).

We highly recommend using the Map because of the ease in which it can be used. If you will spend the six to 20 hours necessary to complete it properly, the *"Map"* will give you some important information about yourself. Unfortunately, many people become overwhelmed by the exercise and either decide not to complete it, or they try to save time by not doing it according to the directions. You simply must follow the directions and spend the time and effort necessary if you want to get the maximum benefit from this exercise.

> **Once you uncover your pattern, get prepared to acknowledge it and live with it in the future.**

Keep in mind that like most self-assessment devices, there is nothing magical about the *"Map"*. Its basic organizing principles are simple. Like other exercises designed to uncover your pattern of motivated abilities and skills, this one is based on a theory of historical determinism and probability. In other words, once you uncover your pattern, get prepared to acknowledge it and live with it in the future.

Autobiography of Accomplishments

Less structured than the *"Map"* device, this exercise requires you to write a lengthy essay about your life accomplishments. Your essay may run anywhere from 20 to 200 pages. After completing it, go through it page by page to identify what you most enjoyed doing (working with different kinds of data, people, processes, and objects) and what skills you used most frequently as well as enjoyed using. Finally, identify those skills you wish to continue using. After analyzing and synthesizing this data, you should have a relatively clear picture of your strongest skills.

This exercise requires a great deal of self-discipline and analytic skill. To do it properly, you must write as much as possible, and in as much detail as possible, about your accomplishments. The richer the detail, the better will be your analysis.

Motivated Skills Exercise

Our final exercise is one of the most complex and time consuming self-assessment exercises. However, it yields some of the best data on motivated abilities and skills, and it is especially useful for those who feel they need a more thorough analysis of their past achievements. This device is widely used by career counselors. Initially developed by Haldane Associates, this particular exercise is variously referred to as *"Success Factor Analysis,"* *"System to Identify Motivated Skills,"* or *"Intensive Skills Identification."*

This technique helps you identify which skills you *enjoy* using. While you can use this technique on your own, it is best to work with someone else. Since you will need six to eight hours to properly complete this exercise, divide your time into two or three work sessions.

The exercise consists of six steps. The steps follow the basic pattern of generating raw data, identifying patterns, analyzing the data through reduction techniques, and synthesizing the patterns into a transferable skills vocabulary. You need strong analytical skills to complete this exercise on your own. The six steps include:

1. **Identify 15-20 achievements:** These consist of things you enjoyed doing, believe you did well, and felt a sense of satisfaction, pride, or accomplishment in doing. You can see yourself performing at your best and enjoying your experiences when you analyze your achievements. This information reveals your motivations since it deals entirely with your voluntary behavior. In addition, it identifies what is right with you by focusing on your positives and strengths. Identify achievements throughout your life, beginning with your childhood. Your achievements should relate to specific experiences—not general ones—and may be drawn from work, leisure, education, military, or home life. Put each achievement at the top of a separate sheet of paper. For example, your achievements might appear as follows:

Sample Achievement Statements

"When I was 10 years old, I started a small paper route and built it up to the largest in my district."

———————————

"I started playing chess in ninth grade and earned the right to play first board on my high school chess team in my junior year."

———————————

"Learned to play the piano and often played for church services while in high school."

———————————

"Designed and constructed a dress for a 4-H demonstration project."

———————————

"Although I was small compared to other guys, I made the first string on my high school football team."

———————————

"I graduated from high school with honors even though I was very active in school clubs and had to work part-time."

———————————

"I was the first in my family to go to college and one of the few from my high school. Worked part-time and summers. A real struggle, but I made it."

———————————

"Earned an 'A' grade on my senior psychology project from a real tough professor."

———————————

"Finished my master's degree while working full-time and attending to my family responsibilities."

———————————

"Proposed a chef's course for junior high boys. Got it approved. Developed it into a very popular elective."

———————————

"Designed the plans for our house and had it constructed within budget."

2. Prioritize your seven most significant achievements.

Your Most Significant Achievements

1. _____

2. _____

3. _____

4. _____

5. _____

6. _____

7. _____

3. **Write a full page on each of your prioritized achievements.**
   You should describe:

   ▪ How you initially became involved.
   ▪ The details of *what you did* and *how you did it.*
   ▪ What was especially enjoyable or satisfying to you.

   Use copies of the "Detailing Your Achievements" form on page 155 to outline your achievements.

4. **Elaborate on your achievements:** Have one or two other people interview you. For each achievement have them note on a separate sheet of paper any terms used to reveal your skills, abilities, and personal qualities. To elaborate details, the interviewer(s) may ask:

   ▪ What was involved in the achievement?
   ▪ What was your part?
   ▪ What did you actually do?
   ▪ How did you go about that?

   Clarify any vague areas by providing an example or illustration of what you actually did. Probe with the following questions:

   ▪ Would you elaborate on one example of what you mean?
   ▪ Could you give me an illustration?
   ▪ What were you good at doing?

   This interview should clarify the details of your activities by asking only "what" and "how" questions. It should take 45 to 90 minutes to complete. Make copies of the "Strength Identification Interview" form on page 157 to guide you through this interview.

5. **Identify patterns by examining the interviewer's notes:** Together identify the recurring skills, abilities, and personal qualities *demonstrated* in your achievements. Search for patterns. Your skills pattern should be clear at this point; you should feel comfortable with it. If you have questions, review the data. If you disagree with a conclusion, disregard it. The results must accurately and honestly reflect how you operate.

6. **Synthesize the information by clustering similar skills into categories:** For example, your skills might be grouped in the following manner (page 156):

Detailing Your Achievement

ACHIEVEMENT # ___: _____

_____

_____

1. How did I initially become involved? _____

_____

_____

_____

2. What did I do? _____

_____

_____

_____

_____

3. How did I do it? _____

_____

_____

_____

_____

4. What was especially enjoyable about doing it?

_____

_____

_____

_____

Synthesized Skill Clusters

Investigate/Survey/Read Inquire/Probe/Question	Teach/Train/Drill Perform/Show/Demonstrate
Learn/Memorize/Practice Evaluate/Appraise/Assess Compare	Construct/Assemble/Put together
	Organize/Structure/Provide definition/Plan/Chart course Strategize/Coordinate
Influence/Involve/Get participation/Publicize Promote	
	Create/Design/Adapt/Modify

This exercise yields a relatively comprehensive inventory of your skills. The information will better enable you to use a *skills vocabulary* when identifying your objective, writing your resume and letters, and interviewing. Your self-confidence and self-esteem should increase accordingly.

Other Alternatives

Several other techniques also can help you identify your motivated abilities and skills:

1. List all of your hobbies and analyze what you do in each, which ones you like the most, what skills you use, and your accomplishments.

2. Conduct a job analysis by writing about your past jobs and identifying which skills you used in each job. Cluster the skills into related categories and prioritize them according to your preferences.

3. Purchase a copy of Arthur F. Miller and Ralph T. Mattson's *The Truth About You* and work through the exercises found in the Appendix. While its overt religious message, extreme deterministic approach, and laborious exercises may turn off some users, you may find this book useful nonetheless. This is an abbreviated version of the authors' SIMA (System for Identifying Motivated Abilities) technique used by their career counseling firm, People Management, Inc. (924 First Street, Suite A, Snohomish, WA 98290, Tel. 206/563-0105). If you need professional assistance, contact this firm directly. They can provide you with several alternative services consistent with the career planning philosophy and approach outlined in this chapter.

Strength Identification Interview

Interviewee _____ Interviewer _____

INSTRUCTIONS: For each achievement experience, identify the **skills** and abilities the achiever actually demonstrated. Obtain details of the experience by asking *what* was involved with the achievement and *how* the individual made the achievement happen. Avoid "why" questions which tend to mislead. Ask for examples or illustrations of what and how.

Achievement #1:

Achievement #2:

Achievement #3:

Recurring abilities and skills:

4. Complete John Holland's *"The Self-Directed Search."* You'll find it in his book, *Making Vocational Choices: A Theory of Careers* or in a separate publication entitled *The Self-Directed Search—A Guide to Educational and Vocational Planning.*

Benefit From Redundancy

The self-directed MAS exercises generate similar information. They identify interests, values, abilities, and skills you already possess. While aptitude and achievement tests may yield similar information, the self-directed exercises have three major advantages over the standardized tests: less expensive, self-monitored and evaluated, and measure motivation *and* ability.

Completing each exercise demands a different investment of your time. Writing your life history and completing the Motivated Skills Exercise as well as Bolles' *"Map"* are the most time consuming. On the other hand, Holland's *"Self-Directed Search"* can be completed in a few minutes. But the more time you invest with each technique, the more useful information you will generate.

We recommend creating redundancy by using at least two or three different techniques. This will help reinforce and confirm the validity of your observations and interpretations. If you have a great deal of work experience, we recommend using the more thorough exercises. The more you put into these techniques and exercises, the greater the benefit to other stages of your job search. You will be well prepared to target your job search toward specific jobs that fit your MAS as well as communicate your qualifications loud and clear to employers. A carefully planned career or career change should not do less than this.

Bridging Your Past and Future

Many people want to know about their future. If you expect the self-assessment techniques in Chapters 7, 8, and 9 to spell out your future, you will be disappointed. Fortune tellers, horoscopes, and various forms of mysticism may be what you need.

These are historical devices which integrate past achievements, abilities, and motivations into a coherent framework for projecting future performance. They clarify past strengths and recurring motivations for targeting future jobs. Abilities and motivations are the *qualifications* employers expect for particular jobs. Qualifications consist of your past experience *and* your motivated abilities and skills.

The assessment techniques provide a bridge between your past and future. As such, they treat your future preferences and performance as functions of your past experiences and demonstrated abilities. This common sense notion is shared among employers: past performance is the best predictor of future performance.

Yet, employers hire a person's *future* rather than their past. And herein lies an important problem you can help employers overcome. Getting the job that is right for you entails communicating to prospective employers that you have the necessary qualifications. Indeed, employers will look for signs of your future productivity *for them*. You are an unknown and risky quantity. Therefore, you must communicate evidence of your past productivity. This evidence is revealed clearly in your past achievements as outlined in our assessment techniques.

> **Past performance is the best predictor of future performance.**

The overall value of using these assessment techniques is that they should enhance your occupational mobility over the long-run. The major thrust of all these techniques is to identify abilities and skills which are *transferable* to different work environments. This is particularly important if you are making a career change. You must overcome employers' negative expectations and objections toward career changers by clearly communicating your transferable abilities and skills in the most positive terms possible. These assessment techniques are designed to do precisely that.

10

Develop a Realistic Objective

Once you identify your interests, skills, and abilities, you should be well prepared to develop a clear and purposeful objective for targeting your job search toward specific organizations and employers. With a renewed sense of direction and versed in an appropriate language, you should be able to communicate to employers that you are a talented and purposeful individual who *achieves results*. Your objective must tell employers what you will *do for them* rather than what you want from them. It targets your accomplishments around employers' needs. In other words, your objective should become employer-centered rather than self-centered.

Goals and Objectives

Goals and objectives are statements of what you want to do in the future. When combined with an assessment of your interests, values, abilities and skills and related to specific jobs, they give your job search needed direction and meaning for the purpose of targeting specific employers. Without them, your job search may founder as you present an image of uncertainty and confusion to potential employers.

When you identify your strengths, you also create the necessary data base and vocabulary for developing your job objective. Using this vocabulary, you should be able to communicate to employers that you are a talented and purposeful individual who achieves results.

If you fail to do the preliminary self-assessment work necessary for developing a clear objective, you will probably wander aimlessly in a highly decentralized, fragmented, and chaotic job market looking for interesting jobs you might fit into. Your goal, instead, should be to find a job or career that is compatible with your interests, motivations, skills, and talents as well as related to a vision of your future. In other words, try to find a job fit for you and your future rather than try to fit into a job that happens to be advertised and for which you think you can qualify.

Examine Your Past, Present, and Future

Depending on how you approach your job search, your goals can be largely a restatement of your past MAS patterns or a vision of your future. If you base your job search on an analysis of your motivated abilities and skills, you may prefer restating your past patterns as your present and future goals. On the other hand, you may want to establish a vision of your future and set goals that motivate you to achieve that vision through a process of self-transformation.

The type of goals you choose to establish will involve different processes. However, the strongest goals will be those that combine your motivated abilities and skills with a realistic vision of your future.

Orient Yourself to Employers' Needs

Your objective should be a concise statement of what you want to do and what you have to offer to an employer. The position you seek is "what you want to do"; your qualifications are "what you have to offer." Your objective should state your strongest qualifications for meeting employers' needs. It should communicate what you have to offer an employer without emphasizing what you expect the employer to do for you. In other words, your objective should be *work-centered*, not self-centered; it should not contain trite terms which emphasize what you want, such as give me a(n) "opportunity for advancement," "position working with people," "progressive company," or "creative position." Such terms are viewed as "canned" job search language which say little of value about you. Above all, your objective should reflect your honesty and integrity; it should not be *"hyped."*

> **Your objective should be employer- or work-centered rather than self-centered. Above all, it should reflect your honesty and integrity; it should not be "hyped."**

Identifying what it is you want to do can be one of the most difficult job search tasks. Indeed, most job hunters lack clear objectives. Many engage in a random, and somewhat mindless, search for jobs by identifying available job opportunities and then adjusting their skills and objectives to fit specific job openings. While you can get a job using this approach, you may be misplaced and unhappy with what you find. You will fit into a job rather than find a job that is fit for you.

Knowing what you want to do can have numerous benefits. First, you define the job market rather than let it define you. The inherent fragmentation and chaos of the job market should be advantageous for you, because it enables you to systematically organize job opportunities around your specific objectives and skills. Second, you will communicate professionalism to prospective employers. They will receive a precise indication of your interests, qualifications, and purposes, which places you ahead of most other applicants. Third, being purposeful means being able to communicate to employers what you want to do. Employers are not interested in hiring indecisive and confused individuals. They want to know what it is you can do for them. With a clear objective, based upon a thorough understanding of your motivated skills and interests, you can take control of the situation as you demonstrate your value to employers.

> **The strongest goals will be those that combine your motivated abilities and skills with a realistic vision of your future.**

Finally, few employers really know what they want in a candidate. Like most job seekers, employers lack clear employment objectives and knowledge about how the job market operates. If you know what you want and can help the employer define his or her "needs" as your objective, you will have achieved a tremendously advantageous position in the job market.

Be Purposeful and Realistic

Your objective should communicate that you are a *purposeful individual who achieves results*. It can be stated over different time periods as well as at various levels of abstraction and specificity. You can identify short, intermediate, and long-range objectives and very general to very specific objectives. Whatever the case, it is best to know your prospective audience before deciding on the type of objective. Your objective should reflect your career interests as well as employers' needs.

Objectives also should be *realistic*. You may want to become President of the United States or solve all the world's problems. However, these objectives are probably unrealistic. While they may represent your ideals and fantasies, you need to be more realistic in terms of what you can personally accomplish in the immediate future. What, for example, are you prepared to deliver to prospective employers over the next few months? While it is good to set challenging objectives, you can overdo it. Refine your objective by thinking about the next major step or two you would like to make in your career advancement—not some grandiose leap outside reality!

Project Yourself Into the Future

Even after identifying your abilities and skills, specifying an objective can be the most difficult and tedious step in the job search process; it can stall the resume writing process indefinitely. This simple one-sentence, 25-word statement can take days or weeks to formulate and clearly define. Yet, it must be specified prior to writing the resume and engaging in other job search steps. An objective gives meaning and direction to all other activities.

Your objective should be viewed as a function of several influences. Since you want to build upon your strengths and you want to be realistic, your abilities and skills will play a central role in formulating your work objective. At the same time, you do not want your objective to become a function solely of your past accomplishments and skills. You may be very skilled in certain areas, but you may not want to use these skills in the future. As a result, your values and interests filter which skills you will or will not incorporate into your work objective.

Overcoming the problem of historical determinism—your future merely reflecting your past—requires incorporating additional components into defining your objective. One of the most important is your ideals, fantasies, or dreams. Everyone engages in these, and sometimes they come true. Your ideals, fantasies, or dreams may include making $1,000,000 by age 45; owning a Mercedes-Benz and a Porsche; taking trips to Rio, Hong Kong, and Rome; owning your own business; developing financial independence; writing a best-selling novel; solving major social problems; or winning the Nobel Peace Prize. If your fantasies require more money than you are now making, you will need to incorporate monetary considerations into your work objective. For example, if you have these fantasies, but your sense of realism tells you that your objective is to move from a $40,000 a year position to a $42,000 a year position you will be going nowhere, unless you can fast-track in your new position. Therefore, you will need to set a higher objective to satisfy your fantasies.

You can develop realistic objectives many different ways. We don't claim to have a new or magical formula, only one which has worked for many individuals. We assume you are capable of making intelligent career decisions if given sufficient data. Using redundancy once again, our approach is designed to provide you with sufficient corroborating data from several sources and perspectives so that you can make preliminary decisions. If you follow our steps in setting a realistic objective, you should be able to give your job search clear direction.

Four major steps are involved in developing a work objective. Each step can be implemented in a variety of ways:

STEP 1: Develop or obtain basic data on your functional/transferable skills, which we discussed in Chapter 7.

STEP 2: Acquire corroborating data about yourself from others, tests, and yourself. Several resources are available for this purpose:

A. **From others:** Ask three to five individuals whom you know well to evaluate you according to the questions in the "Strength Evaluation" form on page 165. Explain to these people that you believe their candid appraisal will help you gain a better understanding of your strengths and weaknesses from the perspectives of others. Make copies of this form and ask your evaluators to complete and return it to a designated third party who will share the information—but not the respondent's name—with you.

B. **From vocational tests:** Although we prefer self-generated data, vocationally-oriented tests can help clarify, confirm, and translate your understanding of yourself into occupational directions. If you decide to use vocational tests, contact a professional career counselor who can administer and interpret the tests. We suggest several of the following tests:

   ■ *Strong Interest Inventory*
   ■ *Myers-Briggs Type Indicator*
   ■ *Edwards Personal Preference Schedule*
   ■ *Kuder Occupational Interest Survey*
   ■ *APTICOM*
   ■ *Jackson Vocational Interest Survey*
   ■ *Ramak Inventory*
   ■ *Vocational Interest Inventory*
   ■ *Career Assessment Inventory*
   ■ *Temperament and Values Inventory*

C. **From yourself:** Numerous alternatives are available for you to practice redundancy. Refer to the exercises in Chapter 8 that assist you in identifying your work values, job frustrations and dissatisfactions, things you love to do, things you enjoy most about work, and your preferred interpersonal environments.

STEP 3: Project your values and preferences into the future by completing simulation and creative thinking exercises:

A. **Ten Million Dollar Exercise:** First, assume that you are given a $10,000,000 gift; now you don't have to work. Since the gift is restricted to your use only, you cannot give any part of it away. What will you do with your time! At first? Later on?

Strength Evaluation

TO: _____

FROM: _____

I am going through a career assessment process and thought you would be an appropriate person to ask for assistance. Would you please candidly respond to the questions below? Your comments will be given to me by the individual designed below; s/he will not reveal your name. Your comments will be used for advising purposes only. Thank you.

What are my strengths?

What weak areas might I need to improve?

In your opinion, what do I need in a job or career to make me satisfied?

Please return to: _____

Second, assume that you are given another $10,000,000, but this time you are required to give it all away. What kinds of causes, organizations, charities, etc. would you support? Complete the following form in which you answer these questions:

What Will I Do With Two $10,000,000 Gifts?

First gift is restricted to my use only:

_____

_____

_____

Second gift must be given away:

_____

_____

_____

SOURCE: John C. Crystal, *"Life/Work Planning Workshop"*

B.   Obituary Exercise: Make a list of the most important things you would like to do or accomplish before you die. Two alternatives are available for doing this. First, make a list in response to this lead-in statement: "Before I die, I want to..."

Before I Die, I Want to . . .

1.   _____

_____

2.   _____

_____

3.   _____

_____

4.   _____

_____

5. _____

6. _____

7. _____

8. _____

9. _____

10. _____

Second, write a newspaper article which is actually your obituary for 10 years from now. Stress your accomplishments over the coming ten year period.

My Obituary

Obituary for Mr./Ms. _____ to appear in the _____ Newspaper in 2007.

_____

_____

_____

_____

_____

_____

_____

_____

_____

_____

_____

_____

_____

C. **My Ideal Work Week:** Starting with Monday, place each day of the week as the headings of seven sheets of paper. Develop a daily calendar with 30-minute intervals, beginning at 7am and ending at midnight. Your calendar should consist of a 118-hour week. Next, beginning at 7am on Monday (sheet one), identify the *ideal activities* you would enjoy doing, or need to do for each 30-minute segment during the day. Assume you are capable of doing anything; you have no constraints except those you impose on yourself. Furthermore, assume that your work schedule consists of 40 hours per week. How will you fill your time? Be specific.

My Ideal Work Week

Monday

am		pm	
7:00	_____	4:00	_____
7:30	_____	4:30	_____
8:00	_____	5:00	_____
8:30	_____	5:30	_____
9:00	_____	6:00	_____
9:30	_____	6:30	_____
10:00	_____	7:00	_____
10:30	_____	7:30	_____
11:00	_____	8:00	_____
11:30	_____	8:30	_____
12:00	_____	9:00	_____
p.m.	_____	9:30	_____

12:30 _____	10:00 _____
1:00 _____	10:30 _____
1:30 _____	11:00 _____
2:00 _____	11:30 _____
2:30 _____	12:00 _____
3:00 _____	Continue for Tuesday, Wednesday, Thursday, and Friday
3:30 _____	

D.   My Ideal Job Description: Develop your ideal future job. Be sure you include:

- Specific interests you want to build into your job.
- Work responsibilities.
- Working conditions.
- Earnings and benefits.
- Interpersonal environment.
- Working circumstances, opportunities, and goals.

Use "My Ideal Job Specifications" on page 170 to outline your ideal job. After completing this exercise, synthesize the job and write a detailed paragraph which describes the kind of job you would most enjoy:

Description of My Ideal Job

_____

_____

_____

_____

_____

_____

_____

_____

_____

MY IDEAL JOB SPECIFICATIONS

Job Interests	Work Responsibilities	Working Conditions	Earnings/ Benefits	Interpersonal Environment	Circumstances/ Opportunities/ Goals

_____

_____

_____

_____

_____

_____

_____

_____

_____

_____

STEP 4: Test your objective against reality. Evaluate and refine it by conducting market research, a force field analysis, library research, and informational interviews.

A. **Market Research:** Four steps are involved in conducting this research:

1. **Products or services:** Based upon all other assessment activities, make a list of what you *do* or *make*:

Products/Services I Do or Make

1. _____

2. _____

3. _____

4. _____

5. _____

6. _____

7. _____

8. _____

9. _____

10. _____

2. **Market:** Identify who needs, wants, or buys what you do or make. Be specific. Include individuals, groups, and organizations. Then, identify *what* specific *needs* your products or services fill. Next, assess the *results* you achieve with your products or services.

The Market For My Products/Services

Individuals, groups, organizations needing me:

1. _____
2. _____
3. _____
4. _____
5. _____

Needs I fulfill:

1. _____
2. _____
3. _____
4. _____
5. _____

Results/Outcomes/Impacts of my products/services:

1. _____
2. _____
3. _____
4. _____
5. _____

3. **New Markets:** Brainstorm a list of *who else* needs your products or services. Think about ways of expanding your market. Next, list any new needs your current or new market has which you might be able to fill:

Developing New Needs

Who else needs my products/services?

1. _____
2. _____
3. _____
4. _____
5. _____

New ways to expand my market:

1. _____
2. _____
3. _____
4. _____
5. _____

New needs I should fulfill:

1. _____
2. _____
3. _____
4. _____
5. _____

4. **New products and/or services:** List any new products or services you can offer and any new needs you can satisfy:

New Products/Services I Can Offer

1. _____
2. _____
3. _____
4. _____
5. _____

New Needs I Can Meet

1. _____
2. _____
3. _____
4. _____
5. _____

B. **Force Field Analysis:** Once you have developed a tentative or firm objective, force field analysis can help you understand the various internal and external forces affecting the achievement of your objective. Force field analysis follows a specific sequence of activities:

- Clearly state your objective or course of action.

- List the positive and negative forces affecting your objective. Specify the internal and external forces working *for* and *against* you in terms of who, what, where, when, and how much. Estimate the impact of each force upon your objective.

- Analyze the forces. Assess the importance of each force upon your objective and its probable affect upon you. Some forces may be irrelevant to your goal. You may need additional information to make a thorough analysis.

- Maximize positive forces and minimize negative ones. Identify actions you can take to strengthen positive forces and to neutralize, overcome, or reverse negative forces. Focus on real, important, and probable key forces.

- Assess the feasibility of attaining your objective and, if necessary, modifying it in light of new information.

C. **Conduct Library and On-Line Research:** This research should strengthen and clarify your objective. Consult various reference materials on alternative jobs and careers. Most of these resources are available in print form at your local or college library. Some are available in electronic versions on-line. If you explore the numerous company profiles and career sites available on the Internet, you should be able to tap into a wealth of information on alternative jobs and careers. One of the best resources for initiating on-line research is Margaret Riley, Frances Roehm, and Steve Oserman's *The Guide to Internet Job Search* (Lincolnwood, IL: National Textbook, 1996). We identify other resources in Chapters 20 and 21.

Career and Job Alternatives

- *Dictionary of Occupational Titles*
- *Encyclopedia of Careers and Vocational Guidance*
- *Enhanced Guide For Occupational Exploration*
- *Guide to Occupational Exploration*
- *Occupational Outlook Handbook*
- *Occupational Outlook Quarterly*

Industrial Directories

- *Bernard Klein's Guide to American Directories*
- *Dun and Bradstreet's Middle Market Directory*
- *Dun and Bradstreet's Million Dollar Directory*
- *Encyclopedia of Business Information Sources*
- *Geography Index*
- *Poor's Register of Corporations, Directors, and Executives*
- *Standard Directory of Advertisers*
- *The Standard Periodical Directory*
- *Standard and Poor's Industrial Index*
- *Standard Rate & Data Business Publications Directory*
- *Thomas' Register of American Manufacturers*

Associations

- *Directory of Professional and Trade Associations*
- *Encyclopedia of Associations*

Government Sources

- *The Book of the States*
- *Congressional Directory*
- *Congressional Staff Directory*
- *Congressional Yellow Book*
- *Federal Directory*
- *Federal Yellow Book*
- *Municipal Yearbook*
- *Taylor's Encyclopedia of Government Officials*
- *United Nations Yearbook*
- *United States Government Manual*
- *Washington Information Directory*

Newspapers

- *The Wall Street Journal*
- Major city newspapers
- Trade newspapers
- Any city newspaper—especially the Sunday edition.

Business Publications

- *Barron's, Business Week, Business World, Forbes, Fortune, Harvard Business Review, Time, Newsweek*
- Annual issues of publications surveying the best jobs for the year: *Money, Working Women, U.S. News and World Report*

Other Library Resources

- Trade journals (refer to the *Directory of Special Libraries and Information Centers* and *Subject Collections: A Guide to Specialized Libraries of Businesses, Governments, and Associations*).
- Publications of Chambers of Commerce; State Manufacturing Associations; and federal, state, and local government agencies
- Telephone books—The Yellow Pages
- Trade books on "How to get a job"

4. **Conduct Informational Interviews:** This may be the most useful way to clarify and refine your objective. We'll discuss this procedure in Chapters 13 and 14.

After completing these steps, you will have identified what it is you *can* do (abilities and skills), enlarged your thinking to include what it is you would *like* to do (aspirations), and probed the realities of implementing your objective. Thus, setting a realistic work objective is a function of the diverse considerations represented on page 178.

Your work objective is a function of both subjective and objective information as well as idealism and realism. We believe the strongest emphasis should be placed on your competencies and should include a broad data-base. Your work objective is realistic in that it is tempered by your past experiences, accomplishments, skills, and current research. An objective formulated in this manner permits you to think beyond your past experiences.

State a Functional Objectives

Your job objective should be oriented toward skills and results or outcomes. You can begin by stating a functional job objective at two different levels: a general objective and a specific one for communicating your qualifications to employers both on resumes and in interviews. Thus, this objective setting process sets the stage for other key job search activities. For the general objective, begin with the statement:

Stating Your General Objective

I would like a job where I can use my ability to _____which will result in _____.

SOURCE: Richard Germann and Peter Arnold, *Bernard Haldane Associates Job & Career Building* (New York: Harper and Row, 1980), 54-55.

The objective in this statement is both a *skill* and an *outcome*. For example, you might state:

Skills-Based and Results-Oriented Objective

I would like a job where my experience in program development, supported by innovative decision-making and systems engineering abilities, will result in an expanded clientele and a more profitable organization.

At a second level you may wish to re-write this objective in order to target it at various consulting firms. For example, on your resume it becomes (page 179):

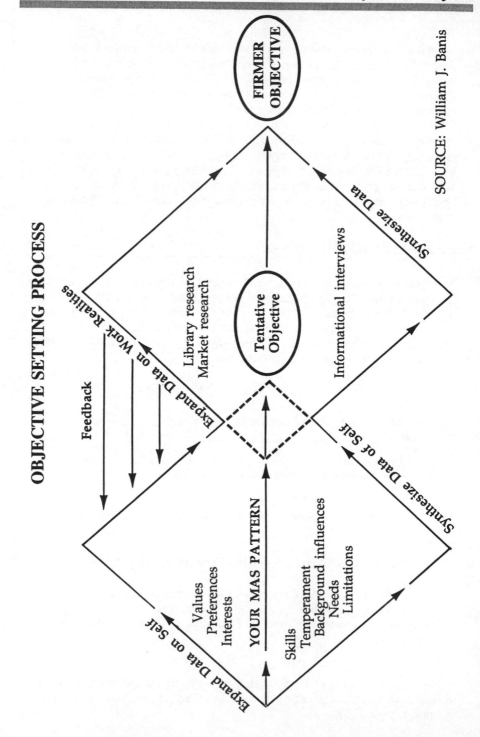

OBJECTIVE SETTING PROCESS

FIRMER OBJECTIVE

Tentative Objective

Library research
Market research

Informational interviews

Expand Data on Work Realities

Synthesize Data

Feedback

Synthesize Data of Self

YOUR MAS PATTERN

Values
Preferences
Interests

Skills
Temperament
Background influences
Needs
Limitations

Expand Data on Self

SOURCE: William J. Banis

Job-Targeted Objective

An increasingly responsible research position in consulting, where proven decision-making and system engineering abilities will be used for improving organizational productivity.

The following are examples of weak and strong objective statements. Various styles are also presented:

Weak Objectives

Management position which will use business administration degree and will provide opportunities for rapid advancement.

A position in social services which will allow me to work with people in a helping capacity.

A position in Personnel Administration with a progressive firm.

Sales Representative with opportunity for advancement.

Stronger Objectives

*To use computer science training in **software development** for designing and implementing operating systems.*

A public relations position which will maximize opportunities to develop and implement programs, to organize people and events, and to communicate positive ideas and images. Effective in public speaking and in managing a publicity/promotional campaign.

A position as a General Sales Representative with a pharmaceutical house which will use chemistry background and ability to work on a self-directed basis in managing a marketing territory.

A position in data analysis where skills in mathematics, computer programming, and deductive reasoning will contribute to new systems development.

Retail Management position which will use sales/customer service experience and creative abilities for product display and merchandising. Long term goal: Progression to merchandise manager with corporate-wide responsibilities for product line.

———————

Responsible position in investment research and analysis. Interests and skills include securities analysis, financial planning, and portfolio management. Long range goal: to become a Chartered Financial Analyst.

———————

It is important to relate your objective to your audience. While you definitely want a good job, your audience wants to know what you can do for them. Remember, your objective should be work-centered, not self-centered.

We will return to this discussion when we examine how to develop the objective section on your resume. Your objective will become the key element for organizing all other elements on your resume. It gives meaning and direction to your job search. Your objective says something very important about how you want to change your life.

11

Produce Effective Resumes and Letters

Now that you know (1) what you do well, (2) what you enjoy doing, and (3) what you want to do in the future—based on your work in the four previous chapters—you have the basic information necessary for communicating your qualifications to employers. But what will you do with this information? What messages do you want to send to employers about yourself? How will you convey these messages—by telephone, letter, or in face-to-face meetings?

Communicating Positive Images

At every stage in the job search you must communicate a positive image to potential employers. The initial impression you make on an employer through applications, resumes, letters, telephone calls, or informational interviews will determine whether the employer is interested in interviewing you and offering you a position.

Developing and managing effective job search communication should play a central role in everything you do related to finding employment. While this communication will take several verbal and nonverbal forms, your first communication with employers will most likely be by letter, telephone, or in a face-to-face meeting. Job search letters often include your calling card—the resume. Essentially nonverbal forms of communication, these documents should be written and distributed with impact.

Writing Resumes

Resumes are important tools for communicating your purpose and capabilities to employers. While many jobs only require a completed application form, you definitely should prepare a resume for influencing the hiring process. Application forms do not substitute for resumes.

Many myths surround resumes and letters. Some people still believe a resume should summarize one's history. Others believe it will get them a job. And still others believe a resume should be mailed or e-mailed in response to classified ads, job listings, or resume databases. The reality is this: A resume advertises your qualifications to prospective employers. It is your calling card for getting interviews which hopefully lead to job offers.

> **A resume advertises your qualifications to prospective employers. It is your calling card for getting interviews.**

Ineffective Resumes

Most people write ineffective resumes. Misunderstanding the purpose of resumes, they make numerous mistakes commonly associated with weak resumes and poor advertising copy. Their resumes often lack an objective, include unrelated categories of information, are too long, and appear unattractive. Other common pitfalls identified by employers include:

- Poor layout
- Misspellings and punctuation errors
- Poor grammar
- Unclear purpose
- Too much jargon
- Irrelevant data
- Too long or too short
- Poorly typed and reproduced
- Unexplained time gaps
- Too boastful
- Deceptive or dishonest
- Difficult to understand or interpret

Your resume, instead, should incorporate the characteristics of strong and effective resumes:

- Clearly communicate your purpose and competencies in relation to employers' needs.
- Are concise and easy to read.
- Motivate the reader to read it in-depth.
- Tell employers that you are a responsible and purposeful individual—a doer who can solve their problems.

Keep in mind that most employers are busy people who normally glance at a resume for only 20 to 30 seconds. Your resume, therefore, must sufficiently catch their attention to pass the 20 to 30 second evaluation test. When writing your resume, ask yourself the same question asked by employers: "Why should I read this or contact this person for an interview?" Your answer should result in an attractive, interesting, unique, and skills-based resume.

Types of Resumes

You have four types of resumes to choose from: chronological, functional, combination, or resume letter. Each form has various advantages and disadvantages, depending on your background and purpose. For example, someone first entering the job market or making a major career change should use a functional resume. On the other hand, a person who wants to target a particular job may choose to use a resume letter. Examples of these different types of resumes are included at the end of this chapter. Further

> **Employers are busy people who normally only glance at a resume for 20 or 30 seconds.**

assistance in developing each section of your resume is found in our two comprehensive resume development books, *High Impact Resumes and Letters* and *Dynamite Resumes*.

The **chronological resume** is the standard resume used by most applicants. It comes in two forms: traditional and improved. The **traditional chronological resume** is also known as the "obituary resume," because it both "kills" your chances of getting a job and is a good source for writing your obituary. Summarizing your work history, this resume lists dates and names first and duties and responsibilities second; it includes extraneous information such as height, weight, age, marital status, sex, and hobbies. While relatively easy to write, this is the most ineffective resume you can produce. Its purpose at best is to inform people of what you have done in the past as well as where, when, and with whom. It tells employers little or nothing about what you want to do, can do, and will do for them.

The **improved chronological resume** communicates directly to employers your purpose, past achievements, and probable future performance. You should use this type of resume when you have extensive experience directly related to a position you seek. This resume should include a work objective which reflects both your work experience and professional goals. The work experience section should include the names and addresses of former employers followed by a brief description of your accomplishments, skills, and responsibilities; inclusive employment dates should appear at the end. Do not begin with dates; they are the least significant element in the descriptions. Be sure to stress your *accomplishments* and *skills* rather than your formal duties and responsibilities. You want to inform your audience that you are a productive and responsible person who gets things done—a doer.

Functional resumes should be used by individuals making a significant career change, first entering the work force, or re-entering the job market after a lengthy absence. This resume should stress your accomplishments and transferable skills regardless of previous work settings and job titles. This could include accomplishments as a housewife, volunteer worker, or Sunday school teacher. Names of employers and dates of employment should not appear on this resume.

Functional resumes have certain weaknesses. While they are important bridges for the inexperienced and for those making a career change, some employers dislike these resumes. Since many employers still look for names, dates, and direct job experience, this resume does not meet their expectations. You should use a functional resume only if you have limited work experience or your past work experience does not strengthen your objective when making a major career change.

> Functional resumes should be used by individuals making a significant career change.

Combination resumes are a compromise between chronological and functional resumes. Having more advantages than disadvantages, this resume may be exactly what you need if you are making a career change with related experience from one career to another.

Combination resumes have the potential to both *meet* and *raise* the expectations of employers. You should stress your accomplishments and skills as well as include your work history. Your work history should appear as a separate section immediately following your presentation of accomplishments and skills in the "Areas of Effectiveness" or "Experience" section. It is not necessary to include dates unless they enhance your resume. This is the perfect resume for someone with work experience who wishes to change to a job in a related career field.

Resume letters are substitutes for resumes. Appearing as a job inquiry or application letter, resume letters highlight various sections of your resume, such as work history, experience, areas of effectiveness, objective, or education, in relation to employers' needs. These letters are used when you prefer not sending your more general resume. Resume letters have one major weakness: they give employers insufficient information and thus may prematurely eliminate you from consideration.

Structuring Resume Content

After choosing an appropriate resume format, you should generate the necessary information for structuring each category of your resume. You developed much of this information when you identified your motivated abilities and skills and specified your objective in Chapters 7 through 10. Include the following information on separate sheets of paper:

CONTACT INFO: name, address, and telephone number.

WORK OBJECTIVE: refer to your data in Chapter 10 on writing an objective.

EDUCATION: degrees, schools, dates, highlights, special training.

WORK EXPERIENCE: paid, unpaid, civilian, military, and part-time employment. Include job titles, employers, locations, dates, skills, accomplishments, duties, and responsibilities. Use the functional language in Chapters 7 and 8.

OTHER EXPERIENCE: volunteer, civic, and professional memberships. Include your contributions, demonstrated skills, offices held, names, and dates.

SPECIAL SKILLS OR LICENSES/ CERTIFICATES: foreign languages, teaching, paramedical, etc. relevant to your objective

OTHER INFORMATION: references, expected salary, willingness to relocate/travel, availability dates, and other information supporting your objective.

Producing Drafts

Once you generate the basic data for constructing your resume, your next task is to reduce this data into draft resumes. If, for example, you write a combination resume, the internal organization of the resume should be as follows:

- Contact information
- Work objective
- Qualifications or functional experience
- Work history or employment
- Education

Be careful in including any other type of information on your resume. Other information most often is extraneous or negative information. You should only include information designed to strengthen your objective.

While your first draft may run more than two pages, try to get everything into one or two pages for the final draft. Most employers lose interest after reading the first page. If you produce a two-page resume, one of the best formats is to attach a single supplemental page to a self-contained one-page resume.

Your final draft should conform to the following rules for creating an excellent resume:

Rules For Effective Resumes

Resume "Don'ts"

- **Don't** use abbreviations except for your middle name.
- **Don't** make the resume cramped and crowded; it should be pleasing to the eyes.
- **Don't** make statements you can't document.
- **Don't** use the passive voice.
- **Don't** change tense of verbs.
- **Don't** use lengthy sentences and descriptions.
- **Don't** refer to yourself as "I."
- **Don't** include negative information.
- **Don't** include extraneous information.

Resume "Dos"

- **Do** use action verbs and the active voice.
- **Do** include strong keywords (nouns) so your resume is scannable.
- **Do** be direct, succinct, and expressive with your language.
- **Do** appear neat, well organized, and professional.
- **Do** use ample spacing and highlights (all caps, underlining, bulleting) for different emphases.
- **Do** maintain an eye pleasing balance. Try centering your contact information at the top, keeping information categories on the left in all caps, and describing the categories in the center and on the right.
- **Do** check carefully your spelling, grammar, and punctuation.
- **Do** clearly communicate your purpose and value to employers.
- **Do** communicate your strongest points first.

Evaluating the Final Product

You should subject your resume drafts to two types of evaluations. An *internal evaluation* consists of reviewing our lists of "dos" and "don'ts" to make sure your resume conforms to these rules. An *external evaluation* should be conducted by circulating your resume to three or more individuals whom you believe will give you frank, objective, and useful feedback. Avoid people who tend to flatter you. The best evaluator would be someone in a hiring position similar to one you will encounter in the actual interview. Ask these people to critique your draft resume and suggest improvements in both form and content. This will be your most important evaluation. After all, the only evaluation that counts is the one that helps get you an interview. Asking someone to critique your resume is one way to spread the word that you are job hunting. As we will see in Chapter 13, this is one method for getting invited to an interview!

Final Production

Your final resume can be typed, word processed, or typeset. If you produce it the old fashion way—type it on a typewriter—make the final product look as professional as possible. Being old technology, it's difficult to achieve a top professional look with a typewriter. Furthermore, producing a resume in this manner communicates that you are probably a generation behind with your communication skills—still using a typewriter rather than a computer. Nonetheless, if this is your only choice, be sure to use an electric typewriter with a carbon ribbon. Varying the typing elements and styles can produce an attractive copy. Do not use a portable typewriter with a nylon ribbon since it does not produce professional copy.

The best alternative is to have your resume word processed and printed on a laser printer (600 dpi preferred). Dot matrix and near letter quality printers make your resume look both unprofessional and mass produced. Word processed resumes give you the greatest flexibility to custom design your resume for individual employers.

Alternatively, you can have a printer typeset your resume. This may cost anywhere from $20 to $50. The final product should look first-class. However, it may look *too* professional or *too* slick; some employers may think you had someone else write the resume for you.

Whichever method you use, be sure to proofread the final copy. Many people spend good money on production only to later find typing errors.

When reproducing the resume, you must consider the quality and color of paper as well as the number of copies you need. By all means use good quality paper. You should use 20-pound or heavier bond paper. Costing 3¢ to 7¢ per sheet, this paper can be purchased through stationery stores and printers. It is important not to cut corners at this point by purchasing cheap paper or using copy machine paper. You may save $5 on 100 copies, but you also will communicate an unprofessional image to employers.

Use one of the following paper colors: white, cream, light tan, light gray, or light blue. Avoid blue, yellow, green, pink, orange, red, or any other bright or pastel colors. Conservative, light, neutral colors are the best. Any of these colors can be complemented with black ink. In the case of light gray—our first choice—a navy blue ink looks best. Dark brown ink is especially attractive on light tan paper.

Your choices of paper quality and color say something about your personality and professional style. They communicate nonverbally your potential strengths and weaknesses. Employers will use these as indicators for screening you in or out of an interview. At the same time, these choices may make your resume stand out from the crowd of standard black-on-white resumes.

You have three choices in reproducing your resume: laser printer, a copy machine, or an offset process. Assuming you are having your resume word processed, it's probably cheaper and more convenient to have multiple copies produced on a laser printer. In addition, the copies will have a crisper look because each one will be a first-generation copy. Many of the newer copy machines give good reproductions on the quality paper you need—nearly the same quality as the offset process. You should be able to make such copies for 10-20¢ per page. The offset process produces the best quality because it uses a printing plate. It also is relatively inexpensive—5 to 10¢ per copy with a minimum run of 100 copies. The cost per copy decreases with large runs of 300, 500, or 1000. In the end, you should be able to have your resume typed and 100 copies reproduced on high quality colored bond paper for less than $25. If you have it typeset, the same number of copies may cost you $50.

> **Remember, your resume is your calling card—it should represent your best professional image.**

Whatever your choices, do not try to cut costs when it comes to producing your resume. It simply is not worth it. Remember, your resume is your calling card—it should represent your best professional image. Put your best foot forward at this stage. Go in style; spend a few dollars on producing a first-class resume.

Job Search Letters

Resumes sent through the mail are normally accompanied by a cover letter. After interviewing for information or a position, you should send a thank-you letter. Other occasions will arise when it is both proper and necessary for you to write different types of job search letters. Examples of these letters are presented in our *High Impact Resumes and Letters, Dynamite Cover Letters*, and *201 Dynamite Job Search Letters*.

Your letter writing should follow the principles of good resume and business writing. Job hunting letters are like resumes—they advertise you for interviews. Like good advertisements, these letters should follow four basic principles for effectiveness:

1. Catch the reader's attention.
2. Persuade the reader of your benefits or value.
3. Convince the reader with evidence.
4. Move the reader to acquire the product.

Basic Preparation Rules

Before you begin writing a job search letter, ask yourself several questions to clarify the content of your letter:

- What is the *purpose* of the letter?
- What are the *needs* of my audience?
- What *benefits* will my audience gain from me?
- What is a good opening sentence or paragraph for grabbing the *attention* of my audience?
- How can I maintain the *interests* of my audience?
- How can I best end the letter so that the audience will be *persuaded* to contact me?
- If a resume is enclosed, how can my letter best *advertise the resume*?
- Have I spent enough *time* revising and proofreading the letter?
- Does the letter represent my *best professional effort*?

Since your letters are a form of business communication, they should conform to the rules of good business correspondence:

Principles of Good Business Communication

- Plan and organize what you will say by outlining the content of your letter.
- Know your purpose and structure your letter accordingly.
- Communicate your message in a logical and sequential manner.
- State your purpose immediately in the first sentence and paragraph; main ideas always go first.
- End by stating what your reader can expect next from you.
- Use short paragraphs and sentences; avoid complex sentences.
- Punctuate properly and use correct grammar and spelling.
- Use simple and straight forward language; avoid jargon.
- Communicate your message as directly and briefly as possible.

The rules stress how to both *organize and communicate* your message with impact. At the same time, you should always have a specific purpose in mind as well as know the needs of your audience.

Types of Letters

Cover letters provide cover for your resume. You should avoid overwhelming a one-page resume with a two-page letter or repeating the contents of the resume in the letter. A short and succinct one-page letter which highlights one or two points in your resume is sufficient. Three paragraphs will suffice. The first paragraph should state your interests and purposes for writing. The second paragraph should highlight your possible value to the employer. The third paragraph should state that you will call the individual at a particular time to schedule an interview.

However, do not expect great results from cover letters. Many professional job search firms use word processing equipment and mailing lists to flood the job market with resumes and cover letters. Other job seekers use "canned" job search letters produced by computer software programs designed to generate model letters. As a result, employers are increasingly suspicious of the authenticity of such letters.

> **Approach letters should get employers to engage in the 5R's of informational interviewing.**

Approach letters are written for the purpose of developing job contacts, leads, or information as well as for organizing networks and getting interviews—the subjects of Chapter 13. Your primary purposes should be to get employers to engage in the 5R's of informational interviewing:

- *Reveal* useful information and advice.
- *Refer* you to others.
- *Read* and *revise* your resume.
- *Remember* you for future reference.

These letters help you gain access to the hidden job market by making important networking contacts that lead to those all-important informational interviews.

Approach letters can be sent out en masse to uncover job leads, or they can target particular individuals or organizations. It is best to target these letters since they have maximum impact when personalized in reference to particular positions.

The structure of approach letters is similar to other letters. The first paragraph states your purpose. In so doing, you may want to use a personal statement for openers, such as *"Mary Tillis recommended that I write to you..."* or *"I am familiar with your..."* State your purpose, but do not suggest that you are asking for a job—only career advice or information. In your final paragraph, request a meeting and indicate you will call to schedule such a meeting at a mutually convenient time.

Thank you letters may well become your most effective job search letters. They especially communicate your thoughtfulness. These letters come in different forms and are written for various occasions. The most common thank you letter is written after receiving assistance, such as job search information and advice or a critique of your resume. Other occasions include:

- **Immediately following an interview:** Thank the interviewer for the opportunity to interview for the position. Repeat your interest in the position.

- **Receive a job offer:** Thank the employer for his or her faith in you and express your appreciation.

- **Rejected for a job:** Thank the employer for giving you the "opportunity" to interview for the job. Ask to be remembered for future reference.

> **Being remembered by employers is the closest thing to being invited to an interview and offered a job.**

- **Terminate employment:** Thank the employer for the experience and ask to be remembered for future reference.

- **Begin a new job:** Thank the employer for giving you this new opportunity and express your confidence in producing the value he or she is expecting from you.

Examples of these letters are included at the end of this chapter.

Several of these thank you letters are unusual, but they all have the same goal in mind—to be remembered by potential employers in a positive light. In a job search, being remembered by employers is the closest thing to being invited to an interview and offered a job.

Distribution and Management

The only good resumes are the ones that get read, remembered, referred, and result in a job interview. Therefore, after completing a first-rate resume, you must decide what to do with it. Are you planning to only respond to classified ads with a standard mailing piece consisting of your a conventional or electronic resume and a formal cover letter? Do you prefer posting your resume online with resume databases or e-mailing it to potential employers? But wait a minute; classified ads and resume databases only represent once portion of the job market. What other creative distribution methods might you use, such as sending it to friends, relatives, and former employers? What is the best way to proceed?

Responding to Classified Ads

Most of your writing activities should focus on the hidden job market. At the same time, you should respond to job listings in newspapers, magazines, and personnel offices. While this is largely a numbers game, you can increase your odds by the way you respond to the listings.

You should be selective in your responses. Since you know what you want to do, you will be looking for only certain types of positions. Once you identify them, your response entails little expenditure of time and effort—an envelope, letter, stamp, resume, and maybe 20 minutes of your time. You have little to lose. While you have the potential to gain by sending a letter and resume in response to an ad, remember the odds are usually against you.

It is difficult to interpret job listings. Some employers place blind ads with P.O. Box numbers in order to collect resumes for future reference. Others wish to avoid aggressive applicants who telephone or "drop-in" for interviews. Many employers work through professional recruiters who place these ads or they post job listings on electronic bulletin boards. While you may try to second guess the rationale behind such ads, respond to them as you would to ads with an employer's name, address, or telephone number. Assume there is a real job behind each ad.

> Keep your letter brief and concise and highlight your qualifications as stated in the employer's ad.

Most ads request a copy of your resume. You should respond with a cover letter and resume as soon as you see the ad. Depending on how much information about the position is revealed in the ad, your letter should be tailored to emphasize your qualifications vis-a-vis the ad. Examine the ad carefully. Underline any words or phrases which relate to your qualifications. In your cover letter, you should use similar terminology in emphasizing your qualifications. Keep the letter brief and to the point.

If the ad asks you to state your salary history or salary requirements, state "negotiable" or "open." Alternatively, you can include a figure by stating a salary range 20 percent above your present salary base. For example, if you are making $40,000 a year, you can state this as *"in the $40,000 to $45,000 range."* Use your own judgment in addressing the salary question. There is no hard and fast rule on stating a figure or range. A figure helps the employer screen-out individuals with too high a salary expectation. However, most people prefer to keep salary considerations to the end of the interview—after you have demonstrated your value and have more information about the position.

You may be able to increase your odds by sending a second copy of your letter and resume two or three weeks after your initial response. Most applicants normally reply to an ad during the seven day period immediately after it appears in print. Since employers often are swamped with responses, your letter and resume may get lost in the crowd. If you send a second copy of your application two or three weeks later, the employer will have more time to give you special attention. By then, he or she also will have a better basis on which to compare you to the others.

Keep in mind that your cover letter and resume may be screened among 400 other resumes and letters. Thus, you want your cover letter to be eye catching and easy to read. Keep it brief and concise and highlight your qualifications as stated in the employer's ad. Don't spend a great deal of time responding to an ad or waiting anxiously at your mailbox or telephone for a reply. Keep moving on to other job search activities.

Self-Initiated Methods

Your letters and resumes can be distributed and managed in various ways. Many people shotgun hundreds of cover letters and resumes to prospective employers. This is a form of gambling where the odds are against you. For every 100 people you contact in this manner, expect one or two who might be interested in you. After all, successful direct-mail experts at best expect only a 2 percent return on their mass mailings!

If you choose to use the shotgun methods, you can increase your odds by using the *telephone*. Call the prospective employer within a week after he or she receives your letter. This technique will probably increase your effectiveness rate from 1 to 5 percent.

However, many people are shotgunning their resumes today. As more resumes and letters descend on employers with the increased use of word processing equipment, the effectiveness rates may be even lower. This also can be an expensive marketing method.

Your best distribution strategy will be your own modification of the following procedure:

1. Selectively identify with whom you are interested in working.
2. Send an approach letter.
3. Follow up with a telephone call requesting an interview.

In more than 50 percent of the cases, you will get an interview. It is best not to include a copy of your resume with the approach letter. If you include a resume, you communicate the wrong message—you want a job rather than information and advice. Keep your resume for the very end of the interview. Chapter 13 outlines procedures for conducting this informational interview.

Electronic Resume Databases

One of the newest approaches to resume distribution involves participation in an electronic resume database. Individuals either participate in them free of charge or they pay a monthly, quarterly, or annual membership fee for getting their resume into an electronic database; employers pay either an annual fee and/or a per-search fee to use the database for accessing resumes in response to their hiring needs. Using sophisticated search and retrieval software to "match" individuals' resumes to employers' vacancy requirements, these electronic database firms have become part of today's much touted "information highway" for job seekers. They offer an important avenue for marketing your resume on a nationwide and/or international basis to hundreds of potential employers.

Numerous organizations offer these electronic database services. Some of the largest and best known private firms charging annual membership fees include SkillSearch, University ProNet, and Cors. For more information on these electronic resume database services as well as the role of the Internet in the job search, see our extended and critical discussion in Chapter 21—"Join the Electronic Revolution."

For more information on the use of electronic resume databases, we recommend three books:

Peter D. Weddle, *Electronic Resumes For the New Job Market: Resumes That Work For You 24 Hours a Day* (Manassas Park, VA: Impact Publications, 1995)

Joyce Lain Kennedy and Thomas J. Morrow, *Electronic Resume Revolution* (New York: Wiley, 1996)

James C. Gonyea, *Electronic Resumes: Putting Your Resume On-Line* (New York: McGraw-Hill, 1996)

These books go into great detail on how to write a resume appropriate for electronic databases. They also identify various firms that offer electronic resume distribution services.

Recordkeeping

Once you begin distributing letters and resumes, you also will need to keep good records for managing your job search writing campaign. Purchase file folders for your correspondence and notes. Be sure to make copies of all letters you write since you may need to refer to them over the telephone or before interviews. Record your activities with each employer—letters, resumes, telephone calls, interviews—on a 4x6 card and file it according to the name of the organization or individual. These files will help you quickly access information and evaluate your job search progress.

If you use the computer, you may want to electronically organize your recordkeeping activities. Check your current software for a calendar or tracking/follow-up program. Several software programs are now available for networking and tracking activities. Some, such as *Sharkware, You're Hired!, Achieving Your Career,* and *Finding and Following Up Job Leads,* are designed specifically for tracking job leads and following up specific job search activities.

Always remember the purpose of resumes and letters—*advertise you for interviews.* They do not get jobs. Since most employers know nothing about you, *you must effectively communicate your value in writing prior to the critical interview.* While you should not overestimate the importance of this written communication, neither should you underestimate it.

TRADITIONAL CHRONOLOGICAL RESUME
(Obituary Type)

RESUME

James C. Astor	Weight: 190 lbs.
4921 Tyler Drive	Height: 6'0"
Washington, D.C. 20011	Born: June 2, 1964
	Health: Good
	Marital Status: Divorced

EDUCATION
1993-1994: M.A., Vocational Counseling, Virginia Commonwealth University, Richmond, Virginia.

1982-1986: B.A., Psychology, Roanoke College, Salem, Virginia.

1978-1982: High School Diploma, Richmond Community High School, Richmond, Virginia.

WORK EXPERIENCE
6/13/94 to 2/22/97: Supervisory Trainer, GS-12, U.S. Department of Labor, Washington, D.C. Responsible for all aspects of training. Terminated because of budget cuts.

9/10/92 to 11/21/93: Bartender, Johnnie's Disco, Richmond, Virginia. Part-time while attending college.

4/3/90 to 6/2/92: Counselor, Virginia Employment Commission, Richmond, Virginia. Responsible for interviewing unemployed for jobs. Resigned to work full-time on Master's degree.

8/15/87 to 6/15/89: Guidance counselor and teacher, Petersburg Junior High School, Petersburg, Virginia.

2/11/85 to 10/6/85: Cook and waiter, Big Mama's Pizza Parlor, Roanoke, Virginia. Part-time while attending college.

PROFESSIONAL AFFILIATIONS
American Personnel and Guidance Association
American Society for Training and Development
Personnel Management Association
Phi Delta Pi

HOBBIES
I like to play tennis, bicycle, and hike.

REFERENCES
David Ryan, Chief, Training Division, U.S. Department of Labor, Washington, D.C. 20012, (212) 735-0121.

Dr. Sara Thomas, Professor, Department of Psychology, George Washington University, Washington, D.C. 20030 (201) 621-4545.

Thomas V. Grant, Area Manager, Virginia Employment Commission, Richmond, Virginia 26412, (804) 261-4089.

IMPROVED CHRONOLOGICAL RESUME

_____ JAMES C. ASTOR _____
4921 Tyler Drive
Washington, D.C. 20011   212/422-8764

OBJECTIVE: A training and counseling position with a computer firm, where strong administrative, communication, and planning abilities will be used for improving the work performance and job satisfaction of employees.

EXPERIENCE: U.S. Department of Labor, Washington, D.C.
Planned and organized counseling programs for 5,000 employees. Developed training manuals and conducted workshops on interpersonal skills, stress management, and career planning; resulted in a 50 percent decrease in absenteeism. Supervised team of five instructors and counselors. Conducted individual counseling and referrals to community organizations. Advised government agencies and private firms on establishing in-house employee counseling and career development programs. Consistently evaluated as outstanding by supervisors and workshop participants. 1994 to present.

Virginia Employment Commission, Richmond, Virginia.
Conducted all aspects of employment counseling. Interviewed, screened, and counseled 2,500 jobseekers. Referred clients to employers and other agencies. Coordinated job vacancy and training information for businesses, industries, and schools. Reorganized interviewing and screening processes which improved the efficiency of operations by 50 percent. Cited in annual evaluation for "outstanding contributions to improving relations with employers and clients." 1990-1992.

Petersburg Junior High School, Petersburg, Virginia.
Guidance Counselor for 800 students. Developed program of individualized and group counseling. Taught special social science classes for socially maladjusted and slow learners. 1987-1989.

EDUCATION: M.A., Vocational Counseling, Virginia Commonwealth University, Richmond, Virginia, 1994.

B.A., Psychology, Roanoke College, Salem, Virginia, 1986.

REFERENCES: Available upon request.

FUNCTIONAL RESUME

JAMES C. ASTOR

4921 Tyler Drive	Washington, D.C. 20011	212/422-8764

OBJECTIVE A training and counseling position with a computer firm, where strong administrative, communication, and planning abilities will be used for improving the work performance and job satisfaction of employees.

EDUCATION Ph.D. in process, Industrial Psychology, George Washington University, Washington, D.C.

M.A., Vocational Counseling, Virginia Commonwealth University, Richmond, Virginia, 1994.

B.A., Psychology, Roanoke College, Salem, Virginia 1986.

AREAS OF EFFECTIVENESS

Administration
Supervised instructors and counselors. Coordinated job vacancy and training information for businesses, industries, and schools.

Communication
Conducted over 100 workshops on interpersonal skills, stress management, and career planning. Frequent guest speaker to various agencies and private firms. Experienced writer of training manuals and public relations materials.

Planning
Planned and developed counseling programs for 5,000 employees. Reorganized interviewing and screening processes for public employment agency. Developed program of individualized and group counseling for community school.

PERSONAL Enjoy challenges and working with people. . .interested in productivity. . .willing to relocate and travel.

REFERENCES: Available upon request.

COMBINATION RESUME

JAMES C. ASTOR
4921 Tyler Drive
Washington, D.C. 20011   212/422-8764

OBJECTIVE: A training and counseling position with a computer
firm, where strong administrative, communication,
and planning abilities will be used for improving the
work performance and job satisfaction of employees.

AREAS OF EFFECTIVENESS

ADMINISTRATION: Supervised instructors and counselors. Coordinated
job vacancy and training information for businesses,
industries, and schools.

COMMUNICATION: Conducted over 100 workshops on interpersonal
skills, stress management, and career planning. Frequent guest speaker to various agencies and private
firms. Experienced writer of training manuals and
public relations materials.

PLANNING: Planned and developed counseling programs for
5,000 employees. Reorganized interviewing and
screening processes for public employment agency.
Developed program of individualized and group
counseling for community school.

WORK HISTORY: Supervisory Trainer, U.S. Department of Labor,
Washington, D.C., 1994 to present.

Counselor, Virginia Employment Commission,
Richmond, Virginia, 1990-1992.

Guidance counselor and teacher, Petersburg Junior
High School, Petersburg, Virginia 1987-1989.

EDUCATION: M.A., Vocational Counseling, Virginia Commonwealth University, Richmond, Virginia, 1994.

B.A., Psychology, Roanoke College, Salem, Virginia, 1979.

PERSONAL: Enjoy challenges and working with people. . .inter-
ested in productivity. . .willing to relocate and travel.

COMBINATION RESUME—continued

SUPPLEMENTAL INFORMATION   JAMES C. ASTOR

Continuing Education and Training

- Completed 12 semester hours of computer science courses.
- Attended several workshops during past three years on employee counseling and administrative methods:

> "Career Development For Technical Personnel," Professional Management Association, 3 days, 1996.

> "Effective Supervisory Methods For Training Directors," National Training Associates, 3 days, 1995.

> "Training the Trainer," American Society For Training and Development, 3 days, 1993.

> "Time Management," U.S. Department of Labor, 3 days, 1992.

> "Career Development For Technical Personnel," Professional Management Associates, 3 days, 1991.

> "Counseling the Absentee Employee," American Management Association, 3 days, 1991.

Training Manuals Developed

- "Managing Employee Stress," U.S. Department of Labor, 1995.
- "Effective Interpersonal Communication in the Workplace," U.S. Department of Labor, 1991.
- "Planning Careers Within the Organization," U.S. Department of Labor, 1990.

Research Projects Completed

- "Employee Counseling Programs for Technical Personnel," U.S. Department of Labor, 1996. Incorporated into agency report on "New Directions in Employee Counseling."
- "Developing Training Programs for Problem Employees," M.A. thesis, Virginia Commonwealth University, 1994.

Professional Affiliations

- American Personnel and Guidance Association
- American Society for Training and Development
- Personnel Management Association

Educational Highlights

- Completing Ph.D. in Industrial Psychology, George Washington University, Washington,D.C., 1997.
- Earned 4.0/4.0 grade point average as a graduate student.

RESUME LETTER

4921 Tyler Drive
Washington,D.C. 20011
March 15, 19___

Doris Stevens
STR Corporation
179 South Trail
Rockville, Maryland 21101

Dear Ms. Stevens:

STR Corporation is one of the most dynamic computer companies in the nation. In addition to being a leader in the field of small business computer, STR has a progressive employee training and development program which could very well become a model for other organizations. This is the type of organization I am interested in joining.

I am seeking a training position with a computer firm which would utilize my administrative, communication, and planning abilities to develop effective training and counseling programs. My experience includes:

Administration: Supervised instructors and counselors. Coordinated job vacancy and training information for businesses, industries, and schools.

Communication: Conducted over 100 workshops on interpersonal skills, stress management, and career planning. Frequent guest speaker to various agencies and private firms. Experienced writer of training manuals and public relations materials.

Planning: Planned and developed counseling programs for 5,000 employees. Reorganized interviewing and screening processes for public employment agency. Developed program of individualized and group counseling for community school.

In addition, I am completing my Ph.D. in industrial psychology with emphasis on developing training and counseling programs for technical personnel.

Could we meet to discuss your program as well as how my experience might relate to your needs? I will call your office on Tuesday morning, March 23, to arrange a convenient time to meet with you.

I especially want to show you a model employee counseling and career development program I recently developed. Perhaps you may find it useful for your work with STR.

Sincerely yours,

James C. Astor

James C. Astor

COVER LETTER

2842 South Plaza
Chicago, Illinois 60228
March 12, 19 ___

David C. Johnson
Director of Personnel
Bank of Chicago
490 Michigan Avenue
Chicago, Illinois 60222

Dear Mr. Johnson:

The accompanying resume is in response to your listing in the Chicago Tribune for a loan officer.

I am especially interested in this position because my experience with the Small Business Administration has prepared me for understanding the financial needs and problems of the business community from the perspectives of both lenders and borrowers. I wish to use this experience with a growing and community-conscious bank such as yours.

I would appreciate an opportunity to meet with you to discuss how my experience will best meet your needs. My ideas on how to improve small business financing may be of particular interest to you. Therefore, I will call your office on the morning of March 17 to inquire if a meeting can be scheduled at a convenient time.

I look forward to meeting you.

Sincerely yours,

Joyce Pitman

Joyce Pitman

APPROACH LETTER
Referral

821 Stevens Points
Boston, MA 01990
April 14, 19 ___

Terri Fulton
Director of Personnel
TRS Corporation
6311 W. Dover
Boston, MA 01991

Dear Ms. Fulton:

Alice O'Brien suggested that I contact you about my interest in personnel management. She said you are one of the best people to talk to in regard to careers in personnel.

I am leaving government after seven years of increasingly responsible experience in personnel. I am especially interested in working with a large private firm. However, before I venture further into the job market. I want to benefit from the experience and knowledge of others in the field who might advise me on opportunities for someone with my qualifications.

Perhaps we could meet briefly sometime during the next two weeks to discuss my career plans. I have several questions which I believe you could help clarify. I will call your office on Tuesday, April 22, to schedule a meeting time.

I look forward to discussing my plans with you.

Sincerely yours,

Katherine Kelly

Katherine Kelly

APPROACH LETTER
Cold Turkey

2189 West Church Street
New York, NY 10011
May 3, 19 ____

Patricia Dotson, Director
Northeast Association for
  the Elderly
9930 Jefferson Street
New York, NY 10013

Dear Ms. Dotson:

I have been impressed with your work with the elderly. Your organization takes a community perspective in trying to integrate the concerns of the elderly with those of other community groups. Perhaps other organizations will soon follow your lead.

I am anxious to meet you and learn more about your work. My background with the city Volunteer Services Program involved frequent contacts with elderly volunteers. From this experience I decided I preferred working primarily with the elderly.

However, before I pursue my interest further, I need to talk to people with experience in gerontology. In particular, I would like to know more about careers with the elderly as well as how my background might best be used in the field of gerontology.

I am hoping you can assist me in this matter. I would like to meet with you briefly to discuss several of my concerns. I will call next week to see if your schedule permits such a meeting.

I look forward to meeting you.

Sincerely,

Carol Timms

Carol Timms

THANK YOU LETTER
Post-Informational Interview

9910 Thompson Drive
Cleveland, Ohio 43382
June 21, 19____

Jane Evans, Director
Evans Finance Corporation
2122 Forman Street
Cleveland, Ohio 43380

Dear Ms. Evans:

Your advice was most helpful in clarifying my questions on careers in finance. I am now reworking my resume and have included many of your thoughtful suggestions. I will send you a copy next week.

Thanks so much for taking time from your busy schedule to see me. I will keep in contact and follow through on your suggestion to see Sarah Cook about opportunities with the Cleveland-Akron Finance Company.

Sincerely,

Daryl Haines

Daryl Haines

THANK YOU LETTER
Post-Job Interview

2962 Forrest Drive
Denver, Colorado 82171
May 28, 19 ___

Thomas F. Harris
Director, Personnel Department
Coastal Products Incorporated
7229 Lakewood Drive
Denver, Colorado 82170

Dear Mr. Harris:

Thank you again for the opportunity to interview for the marketing position. I appreciated your hospitality and enjoyed meeting you and members of your staff.

The interview convinced me of how compatible my background, interest, and skills are with the goals of Coastal Products Incorporated. My prior marketing experience with the Department of Commerce has prepared me to take a major role in developing both domestic and international marketing strategies. I am confident my work for you will result in increased profits within the first two years.

For more information on the new product promotion program I mentioned, call David Garrett at the Department of Commerce; his number is 202/726-0132. I talked to Dave this morning and mentioned your interest in this program.

I look forward to meeting you again.

Sincerely,

Tim Potter

Tim Potter

THANK YOU LETTER
Job Rejection

564 Court Street
St. Louis, MO 53167
April 29, 19 ___

Ralph Ullman, President
S.T. Ayer Corporation
6921 Southern Blvd.
St. Louis, MO 53163

Dear Mr. Ullman:

I appreciated your consideration for the Research Associate position. While I am disappointed in not being selected, I learned a great deal about your corporation, and I enjoyed meeting with you and your staff. I felt particularly good about the professional manner in which you conducted the interview.

Please keep me in mind for future consideration. I have a strong interest in your company. I believe we would work well together. I will be closely following the progress of your company over the coming months. Perhaps we will be in touch with each other at some later date.

Best wishes.

Sincerely,

Martin Tollins

Martin Tollins

THANK YOU LETTER
Job Offer Acceptance

7694 James Court
San Francisco, CA 94826
June 7, 19___

Judith Greene
Vice President
West Coast Airlines
2400 Van Ness
San Francisco, CA 94829

Dear Ms. Greene:

I am pleased to accept your offer, and I am looking forward to joining you and your staff next month.

The customer relations position is ideally suited to my background and interests. I assure you I will give you my best effort in making this an effective position within your company.

I understand I will begin work on July. If, in the meantime, I need to complete any paper work or take care of any other matters, please contact me.

I enjoyed meeting with you and your staff and appreciated the professional manner in which the hiring was conducted.

Sincerely,

Joan Kitner

Joan Kitner

12

Research Alternative Jobs and Communities

T he old adage that "knowledge is power" is especially true when conducting a job search. Your job search is only as good as the knowledge you acquire and use for finding the job you want.

Gathering, processing, and using information is the lifeblood of any job search. Research integrates the individual job search activities and provides feedback for adapting strategies to the realities of the job market. Given the numerous individuals and organizations involved in your job search, you must develop an information gathering strategy that will help you gain knowledge about, as well as access to, those individuals and organizations that will play the most important role in your job search.

Research Purposes

Research is the key to gathering, processing, and using information in your job search. It is a skill that will point you in fruitful directions for minimizing job search frustrations and maximizing successes. Be sure to make research one of your top priorities.

However, most people are reluctant to initiate a research campaign which involves using libraries and computers, telephoning, and meeting new people. Such reluctance is due in part to the lack of knowledge on how to conduct research and where to find resources, and in part to a certain cultural shyness which inhibits individuals from initiating contacts with strangers. However, research is not a difficult process. After all, most people conduct research daily as they read and converse with others about problems. This daily research process needs to be specified and focused on your job search campaign.

Research serves several purposes when adapted to your job search. First, knowing the who, what, when, and where of organizations and individuals is essential for targeting your resume and conducting informational and job interviews. Second, the research component should broaden your perspective on the job market in relationship to your motivated abilities and skills and job objective. Since there are over 13,000 different job titles as well as several million job markets, even a full-time research campaign will uncover only a small segment of the job market relevant to your interests and skills.

A third purpose of research is to better understand how to relate your motivated abilities and skills to specific jobs and work environments. Once you research and understand the critical requirements of a given job in a specific work environment, you can assess the appropriateness of that job for you vis-a-vis your pattern of motivated abilities and skills (MAS).

Fourth, researching organizations and individuals should result in systematically uncovering a set of contacts for developing your job search network. One of your major research goals should be to compile names, addresses, and telephone numbers of individuals who may become important resources in your new network of job contacts.

A fifth purpose of research is to learn the *languages* of alternative jobs and careers. You can learn to better converse in these languages by reading trade journals, annual reports, pamphlets, and other organizational literature as well as talking with people in various occupational fields. Knowing these languages—especially asking and answering intelligent questions in the language of the employer—is important for conducting successful referral and job interviews.

Finally, research should result in bringing some degree of structure, coherence, and understanding to the inherently decentralized, fragmented, and chaotic job market. Without research, you place yourself at the mercy of chance and luck; thus, you become a subject of your environment. Research best enables you to take control of your situation. It is power.

Your research activities should focus on four major targets: occupational alternatives, organizations, individuals, and communities. If you give equal time to all four, you will be well on your way to getting job interviews and offers.

Investigate Alternative Jobs and Careers

Your initial research should help familiarize you with *job and career alternatives*. For example, the U.S. Department of Labor identifies approximately 13,000 job titles. Most individuals are occupationally illiterate and unaware of the vast array of available jobs and careers. Therefore, it is essential to investigate occupational alternatives in order to broaden your perspective on the job market.

You should start your research by examining several key directories that provide information on alternative jobs and careers:

- *The Occupational Outlook Handbook*
- *Dictionary of Occupational Titles*
- *Encyclopedia of Careers and Vocational Guidance*
- *Enhanced Guide to Occupational Exploration*
- *Guide to Occupational Exploration*

You will also find several books that focus on alternative jobs and careers. NTC Publishing, for example, produces one of the most comprehensive series of books on alternative jobs and careers. Their books now address 180 different job and career fields. Representative titles in their *"Opportunities in..."* series include:

- *Opportunities in Advertising*
- *Opportunities in Airline Careers*
- *Opportunities in Banking*
- *Opportunities in Business Management*
- *Opportunities in Child Care*
- *Opportunities in Craft Careers*
- *Opportunities in Electrical Trades*
- *Opportunities in Eye Care*
- *Opportunities in Gerontology*
- *Opportunities in Interior Design*
- *Opportunities in Laser Technology*
- *Opportunities in Microelectronics*
- *Opportunities in Optometry*
- *Opportunities in Pharmacy*
- *Opportunities in Public Relations*
- *Opportunities in Robotics*
- *Opportunities in Sports and Athletics*
- *Opportunities in Telecommunications*

NTC Publishing also publishes two other useful sets of books in a *"Careers in..."* and a *"Careers For You"* series. The titles in the *"Careers in..."* series consist of

- *Careers in Accounting*
- *Careers in Advertising*
- *Careers in Business*
- *Careers in Child Care*
- *Careers in Communications*
- *Careers in Computers*
- *Careers in Education*
- *Careers in Engineering*
- *Careers in Environment*
- *Careers in Government*

- *Careers in Health Care*
- *Careers in High Tech*
- *Careers in Horticulture*
- *Careers in International Business*
- *Careers in Journalism*
- *Careers in Law*
- *Careers in Marketing*
- *Careers in Medicine*
- *Careers in Science*
- *Careers in Social and Rehabilitation Services*

Books in the *"Careers For You"* series include:

- *Careers For Animal Lovers*
- *Careers For Bookworms*
- *Careers For Caring People*
- *Careers For Computer Buffs*
- *Careers For Crafty People*
- *Careers For Culture Lovers*
- *Careers For Environmental Types*
- *Careers For Fashion Plates*
- *Careers For Film Buffs*
- *Careers For Foreign Language Aficionados*
- *Careers For Good Samaritans*
- *Careers For Gourmets*
- *Careers For Health Nuts*
- *Careers For History Nuts*
- *Careers For Kids at Heart*
- *Careers For Music Lovers*
- *Careers For Mystery Lovers*
- *Careers For Nature Lovers*
- *Careers For Night Owls*
- *Careers For Numbers Crunchers*
- *Careers For Plant Lovers*
- *Careers For Shutterbugs*
- *Careers For Sports Nuts*
- *Careers For Travel Buffs*
- *Careers For Writers*

Peterson's publishes a *"Careers Without College"* series of books for students. They currently have fourteen books in this growing series:

- *Building*
- *Computers*
- *Cars*
- *Kids*

- *Emergencies*
- *Entertainment*
- *Fashion*
- *Fitness*
- *Health Care*

- *Money*
- *Music*
- *Office*
- *Sports*
- *Travel*

Facts on File publishes six books on alternative jobs and careers in various industries:

- *Career Opportunities in Advertising and Public Relations*
- *Career Opportunities in Art*
- *Career Opportunities in the Food and Beverage Industry*
- *Career Opportunities in the Music Industry*
- *Career Opportunities in Theater and Performing Arts*
- *Career Opportunities in Travel and Tourism*
- *Career Opportunities in Writing*

Impact Publications publishes twelve volumes on international, public service, and sports careers:

- *Almanac of International Jobs and Careers*
- *Directory of Federal Jobs and Employers*
- *Complete Guide to International Jobs and Careers*
- *Complete Guide to Public Employment*
- *Federal Applications That Get Results*
- *Federal Jobs in Law Enforcement*
- *Find a Federal Job Fast!*
- *Guide to Careers in World Affairs*
- *Jobs For People Who Love Travel*
- *Jobs in Russia and the Newly Independent States*
- *Jobs Worldwide*
- *You Can't Play the Game If You Don't Know the Rules*

Many other books examine a wide range of jobs and careers. Some are annual or biannual reviews of today's most popular jobs. You should find several of these books particularly helpful:

- *100 Best Careers For the 21st Century,* Shelly Fields (Arco)
- *American Almanac of Jobs and Salaries,* John W. Wright (Avon)
- *Best Jobs For the 1990s and Into the 21st Century,* Ron and Caryl Krannich (Impact)
- *The Best Jobs For the 1990s and Beyond,* Carol Kleiman (Dearborn)
- *Bob Adams Job Almanac 1997* (Adams Media)
- *Careers Encyclopedia,* Craig T. Norback ed. (NTC Publishing)

- *Jobs 1997,* Ross and Kathryne Petras (Simon and Schuster)
- *The Jobs Rated Almanac,* Les Krantz (Wiley & Sons)
- *Occupational Outlook Handbook,* U.S. Department of Labor (U.S. Government Printing Office)
- *World Almanac Job Finder's Guide 1997,* Les Krantz (St. Martin)

If you are unable to find these books in your local library or bookstore, they can be ordered directly from Impact Publications. Order information is found at the end of this book. You may also want to examine their online (World Wide Web) bookstore: http://www.impactpublications.com

Target Organizations

After completing research on occupational alternatives, you should identify specific organizations which you are interested in learning more about. Next compile lists of names, addresses, and telephone numbers of important individuals in each organization. Also, explore the home pages of various organizations on the World Wide Web and write or telephone them for information, such as an annual report and recruiting literature. The most important information you should be gathering concerns the organizations' goals, structures, functions, problems, and projected future opportunities and development. Since you invest part of your life in such organizations, treat them as you would a stock market investment. Compare and evaluate different organizations.

Several directories will assist you in researching organizations. Most are available in the reference sections of libraries; some, such as the Hoover's books, also are available online:

- *Directory of American Firms Operating in Foreign Countries*
- *The Directory of Corporate Affiliations: Who Owns Whom*
- *Dun & Bradstreet's Middle Market Directory*
- *Dun & Bradstreet's Million Dollar Directory*
- *Dun & Bradstreet's Reference Book of Corporate Managements*
- *Encyclopedia of Business Information Sources*
- *Fitch's Corporation Reports*
- *Hoover's 500*
- *Hoover's Emerging Companies*
- *Hoover's Handbook of World Business*
- *MacRae's Blue Book*
- *Moody's Manuals*
- *The Multinational Marketing and Employment Directory*
- *Standard & Poor's Industrial Index*
- *Standard Rate and Data Business Publications Directory*
- *Thomas' Register of American Manufacturers*

Peterson's Guides publishes three annual directories in their *"Job Opps"* series that are the definitive guides to organizations that hire business, engineering, and health care graduates:

- *Job Opps in Business*
- *Job Opps in Engineering and Technology*
- *Job Opps in Health Care*

The following trade books identify organizations that are considered to be some of the best to work for today:

- *100 Best Companies to Work For in America*
- *150 Best Companies For Liberal Arts Graduates*
- *America's Fastest Growing Employers*
- *Hidden Job Market 1997*
- *Hoover's Top 2,500 Employers*
- *Job Seekers Guide to 1000 Top Employers*

If you are interested in jobs with a particular organization, you should contact the personnel office for information on the types of jobs offered within the organization. You may be able to examine vacancy announcements which describe the duties and responsibilities of specific jobs. If you are interested in working for federal, state, or local governments, each agency will have a personnel office which can supply you with descriptions of their jobs. While gathering such information, be sure to ask people about their jobs.

Contact Individuals

While examining directories and reading books on alternative jobs and careers will provide you with useful job search information, much of this material may be too general for specifying the right job for you. In the end, the best information will come directly from people in specific jobs in specific organizations. To get this information you must interview people. You especially want to learn more about the people who make the hiring decisions.

You might begin your investigations by contacting various professional and trade associations for detailed information on jobs and careers relevant to their members. For names, addresses, and telephone numbers of such associations, consult the following key directories which are available in most libraries:

- *The Encyclopedia of Associations* (Gale Research)
- *National Trade and Professional Associations* (Columbia Books)

Your most productive research activity will be talking to people. Informal, word-of-mouth communication is still the most effective channel of job search information. In contrast to reading books, people have more current, detailed, and accurate information. Ask them about:

- Occupational fields
- Job requirements and training
- Interpersonal environments
- Performance expectations
- Their problems
- Salaries
- Advancement opportunities
- Future growth potential of the organization
- How best to acquire more information and contacts in a particular field

You may be surprised how willingly friends, acquaintances, and strangers will give you useful information. But before you talk to people, do your library research so that you are better able to ask thoughtful questions.

Ask the Right Questions

The quality of your research will only be as good as the questions you ask. Therefore, you should focus on a few key questions that will yield useful information for guiding your job search. Answers to these questions will help make important job search decisions relevant to informational and job interviews.

Who Has the Power to Hire?

Finding out who has the power to hire may take some research effort on your part. Keep in mind that personnel offices normally do not have the power to hire. They handle much of the paper work involved in announcing vacancies, taking applications, testing candidates, screening credentials, and placing new employees on the payroll. In other words, personnel offices tend to perform auxiliary support functions for those who do the actual hiring—usually individuals in operating units.

If you want to learn who really has the power to hire, you need to conduct research on the particular organization that interests you. You should ask specific questions concerning who normally is responsible for various parts of the hiring process:

- Who describes the positions?
- Who announces vacancies?
- Who receives applications?

- Who administers tests?
- Who selects eligible candidates?
- Who chooses whom to interview?
- Who offers the jobs?

If you ask these questions about a specific position you will quickly identify who has what powers to hire. Chances are the power to hire is *shared* between the personnel office and the operating unit. You should not neglect the personnel office, and in some cases it will play a powerful role in all aspects of the hiring. Your research will reveal to what degree the hiring function has been centralized, decentralized, or fragmented within a particular organization.

How Does Organization X Operate?

It's best to know something about the internal operation of an organization before joining it. Your research may uncover information that would convince you that a particular organization is not one in which you wish to invest your time and effort. You may learn, for example, that Company X has a history of terminating employees before they become vested in the company retirement system. Or Company X may be experiencing serious financial problems. Or advancement within Company X may be very political and company politics are vicious and debilitating.

You can get financial information about most companies by examining their annual reports as well as by talking to individuals who know the organization well. Information on the internal operations, especially company politics and power, must come from individuals who work within the organization. Ask them: "Is this a good organization to work for?" and let them expand on specific areas you wish to probe—advancement opportunities, working conditions, relationships among co-workers and supervisors, growth patterns, internal politics, management style, work values, opportunities for taking initiative.

What Do I Need to Do To
Get A Job With Organization X?

The best way to find how to get a job in a particular organization is to follow the advice in the next chapter on prospecting, networking, and informational interviewing. This question can only be answered by talking to people who know both the formal and informal hiring practices.

You can get information on the formal hiring system by contacting the personnel office. A telephone call should be sufficient for this information.

But you must go beyond the formal system and personnel office in order to learn how best to conduct your job search. This means contacting people who know how one really gets hired in the organization, which may or may

218   ❖ *Develop Powerful Careering and Re-Careering Skills*

not follow the formal procedures. The best sources of information will be individuals who play a major role in the hiring process.

Identify the Right Community

Your final research target is central to all other research targets and it may occur at any stage in your research. Identifying the geographical area where you would like to work will be one of your most important decisions. Once you make this decision, other job search decisions and activities become easier. For example, if you live in a small town, you may need to move in order to change careers. If you are a member of a two-career family, opportunities for both you and your spouse will be greater in a growing metropolitan area. If you decide to move to another community, you will need to develop a long-distance job search campaign which has different characteristics from a local campaign. It involves writing letters, making long-distance phone calls, and visiting a community for strategic one to two-week periods during your vacations.

Deciding where you want to live involves researching various communities and comparing advantages and disadvantages of each. In addition to identifying specific job alternatives, organizations, and individuals in the community, you need to do research on other aspects of the community. After all, you will live in the community, buy or rent a residence, perhaps send children to school, and participate in community organizations and events. Often these environmental factors are just as important to your happiness and well-being as the particular job you accept. For example, you may be leaving a $45,000 a year job for a position in your favorite community—San Francisco. But you may quickly find you are worse off with your new $57,000 a year job, because you must pay $350,000 for a home in San Francisco that is nearly identical to the $135,000 home in your small town community. Consequently, it would be foolish for you to take a new job without first researching several facets of the community other than job opportunities.

Research on different communities can be initiated from your local library or on your personal computer, if you are connected to the World Wide Web. While most of this research will be historical in nature, several resources will provide you with a current profile of various communities. Statistical overviews and comparisons of states and cities are found in the *U.S. Census Data, The Book for the States,* and the *Municipal Yearbook.* Many libraries have a reference section of telephone books on various cities. If this section is weak or absent in your local library, contact your local telephone company. They have a relatively comprehensive library of telephone books. In addition to giving you names, addresses, and telephone numbers, the Yellow Pages are invaluable sources of information on the specialized structures of the public and private sectors of individual communities. The library may also have state and community directories as well as subscriptions to some state and community magazines and city newspapers. Research magazine, journal, and newspaper articles on different communities by consulting references in the *Reader's Guide to Periodical Literature,* the *Social Science and Humanities Index,* the *New York Times Index,* and the *Wall Street Journal Index.*

Many communities now maintain home pages on the Internet's World Wide Web. If you have a computer with access to the Internet, you'll find a wealth of community-based information on such home pages, from housing information to local employers. If you don't have a computer or such access, check with your local library. Many libraries have computers connected to the Internet for use by their patrons.

If you are trying to determine the best place to live, you should start with the latest edition of David Savageau's and Richard Boyer's *Places Rated Almanac* (Simon & Schuster). This book ranks cities by various indicators. The *Moving and Relocation Sourcebook* (Omnigraphics) profiles the 100 largest metropolitan areas with information on population, education, recreation, arts, media, health care, taxes, transportation, and per capita income.

You should also consult several city job banks that will give you contact information on specific employers in major metropolitan communities. Adams Media annually publishes *The National JobBank* and *The JobBank Guide to Employment Services* as well as 27 annual job bank guides:

- *The Atlanta JobBank*
- *The Austin/San Antonio JobBank*
- *The Boston JobBank*
- *The Carolina JobBank*
- *The Chicago JobBank*
- *The Dallas/Fort Worth JobBank*
- *The Denver JobBank*
- *The Detroit JobBank*
- *The Florida JobBank*
- *The Houston JobBank*
- *The Indianapolis JobBank*
- *The Las Vegas JobBank*
- *The Los Angeles JobBank*
- *The Minneapolis/St. Paul JobBank*
- *The Missouri JobBank*
- *The New Mexico JobBank*
- *The New York JobBank*
- *The North New England JobBank*
- *The Ohio JobBank*
- *The Philadelphia JobBank*
- *The Phoenix JobBank*
- *The San Francisco JobBank*

- *The Seattle JobBank*
- *The Tennessee JobBank*
- *The Upstate New York JobBank*
- *The Virginia JobBank*
- *The Metro Washington D.C. JobBank*

Adams Media also has this information available on a CD-ROM program (*Adams Job Bank CD-ROM*) as well as on its online career service (Adams JobBank Online) which can be accessed through most commercial online services or directly on the Internet: http://www.adamsonline.com.

Surrey Books also publishes a similar job bank series for six major metropolitan areas:

- *How to Get a Job in Atlanta*
- *How to Get a Job in Chicago*
- *How to Get a Job in New York*
- *How to Get a Job in San Francisco*
- *How to Get a Job in Seattle/Portland*
- *How to Get a Job in Southern California*

Another series, published by NET Research, provides information on employment agencies and executive search firms in major regions, states, and cities throughout the country:

- *Boston and New England Job Seekers Sourcebook*
- *Chicago and Illinois Job Seekers Sourcebook*
- *Los Angeles and Southern California Job Seekers Sourcebook*
- *Mid-Atlantic Job Seekers Sourcebook*
- *Mountain and Plain States Job Seekers Sourcebook*
- *New York and New Jersey Job Seekers Sourcebook*
- *Pacific Northwest Job Seekers Sourcebook*
- *Southern States Job Seekers Sourcebook*
- *Southwest Job Seekers Sourcebook*

After narrowing the number of communities that interest you, further research them in depth. Start by exploring community home pages on the World Wide Web (search by community name). Ask your relatives, friends, and acquaintances for contacts in the particular community; they may know people whom you can write or telephone for information and referrals. Once you have decided to focus on one community, visit it in order to establish personal contacts with key reference points, such as the local Chamber of Commerce, real estate firms, schools, libraries, churches, Forty-Plus Club (if appropriate), government agencies, and business firms and associations. Begin developing personal networks based upon the research and referral strategies in the next chapter. Subscribe to the local newspaper and to any community magazines which help profile the community. Follow the help-wanted, society, financial, and real estate sections of the newspaper—especially the Sunday edition. Keep a list of names of individuals who appear to hold influential community positions; you may want to contact these people for referrals. Write letters to set up informational interviews with key people; give yourself two months of lead time to complete your letter writing campaign. Your overall community research should focus on developing personal contacts which may assist you in both your job search and your move to the community.

Know What's Important

Reviewing published resources can be extremely time consuming if taken to the extreme. While you should examine several of them, do not spend an inordinate amount of time reading and taking notes. Your time will be best spent in gathering information through meetings and conversations with key people. Your primary goals in conducting research should be identifying people to contact, setting appointments, and asking the right questions which lead to more information and contacts. If you engage in these activities you will know what is important when conducting research.

As you get further into your job search, networking for information, advice, and referrals will become an important element in your overall job search strategy. At that time you will come into closer contact with potential employers who can provide you with detailed information on their organizations and specific jobs. If you have a well defined MAS, specific job objectives, and a clearly focused resume, you should be in a good position to make networking pay off with useful information, advice, and referrals. You will quickly discover that the process of linking your MAS and objectives to specific jobs is an ongoing one involving several steps in your job search.

13

Network For Information, Advice, and Referrals

N
ow that you have identified your skills, specified your objective, written your resume, and conducted research, what should you do next? At this point let's examine where you are going so you don't get preoccupied with the trees and thus lose sight of the larger forest. Let's identify the most effective methods for linking your previous job search activities to job interviews and offers.

Focus on Getting Interviews

Everything you do up to this point in your job search should be aimed at *getting a job interview*. The skills you identified, the goals you set, the resume you wrote, and the information you gathered are carefully related to one another so you can clearly communicate your best qualifications to employers who, in turn, will decide to invite you to a job interview.

But there are secrets to getting a job interview you should know before continuing further with your job search. The most important secret is the *informational interview*—a type of interview which yields useful job search information and *may* lead to job interviews and offers. Based on prospecting and networking techniques, these interviews minimize rejections and competition as well as quickly open the doors to organizations and employers. If you want a job interview, you first need to understand the informational interview and how to initiate and use it for maximum impact.

Prospecting and Networking

What do you do after you complete your resume? Most people send cover letters and resumes in response to job listings; they then wait to be called for a job interview. Viewing the job search as basically a direct-mail operation, many are disappointed in discovering the realities of direct mail—a 5 percent response rate is considered outstanding!

Successful job seekers break out of this relatively passive job search role by orienting themselves toward face-to-face action. Being proactive, they develop interpersonal strategies in which the resume plays a *supportive* rather than a central role in the job search. They first present themselves to employers; the resume appears only at the end of a face-to-face conversation.

Throughout the job search you will acquire useful names and addresses as well as meet people who will assist you in contacting potential employers. Such information and contacts become key building blocks for generating job interviews and offers.

Since the best and most numerous jobs are found on the hidden job market, you must use methods appropriate for this job market. Indeed, research and experience clearly show the most effective means of communication are face-to-face and word-of-mouth. The informal, interpersonal system of communication is the central nervous system of the hidden job market. Your goal should be to penetrate this job market with proven methods for success. Appropriate methods for making important job contacts are

> **The most effective means of communication are face-to-face and word-of-mouth.**

prospecting and networking. Appropriate methods for getting these contacts to provide you with useful job information are *informational and referral interviews*.

Communicate Your Qualifications

Taken together, these interpersonal methods help you *communicate your qualifications to employers*. Although many job seekers may be reluctant to use this informal communication system, they greatly limit their potential for success if they do not.

Put yourself in the position of the employer for a moment. You have a job vacancy to fill. If you advertise the position, you may be bombarded with hundreds of resumes, applications, phone calls, faxes, and walk-ins. While you do want to hire the best qualified individual for the job, you simply don't have time nor patience to review scores of applications. Even if you use a P.O. Box number, the paperwork may quickly overwhelm you. Furthermore, with limited information from application forms, cover letters, and resumes, you find it hard to identify the best qualified individuals to invite for an interview; many look the same on paper.

So what do you do? You might hire a professional job search firm or use the services of a temporary employment agency to take on all of this additional work. On the other hand, you may want to better control the hiring process, especially since it appears to be filled with uncertainty and headaches. You want to minimize your risks and time so you can get back to what you do best—accomplishing the external goals of the organization. Like many other employers, you begin by calling your friends, acquaintances, and other business associates and ask if they or someone else might know of any good candidates for the position. If they can't help, you ask them to give you a call should they learn of anyone qualified for your vacancy. You, in effect, create your own hidden job market—an informal information network for locating desirable candidates. Your trusted contacts initially screen the candidates in the process of referring them to you. This both saves you time and minimizes your risks in hiring a stranger.

Based on this understanding of the employer's perspective, what should you do to best improve your chances of getting an interview and job offer? Networking for information, advice, and referrals should play a central role in your overall job search. Remember, employers need to solve personnel problems. By conducting *informational interviews and networking* you help employers identify their needs, limit their alternatives, and thus make decisions and save money. Most important, such interviews and networking activities help relieve their anxiety of hiring a career changer.

At the same time, you gain several advantages by conducting these interviews:

1. You are less likely to encounter rejections since you are not asking for a job—only information, advice, referrals, and to be remembered.

2. You go after high level positions.

3. You encounter little competition.

4. You go directly to the people who have the power to hire.

5. You are likely to be invited to job interviews based upon the referrals you receive.

Most employers want more information on candidates to supplement the "paper qualifications" represented in application forms, resumes, and letters. Studies show that employers in general seek candidates who have these skills: communication, problem solving, analytical, assessment, and planning. Surprising to many job seekers, technical expertise ranks third or fourth in employers' lists of most desired skills. These findings support a frequent observation made by employers: the major problems with employees relate to communication, problem solving, and analysis; individuals get fired because of political and interpersonal conflicts rather than technical incompetence.

Employers seek individuals they *like* both personally and professionally. Therefore, communicating your qualifications to employers entails more than just informing them of your technical competence. You must communicate that you have the requisite personal *and* professional skills for performing the job. Informal prospecting, networking, and informational interviewing activities are the best methods for communicating your "qualifications" to employers.

Develop Networks

Networking is the process of purposefully developing relations with others. Networking in the job search involves connecting and interacting with other individuals who can be helpful to you. Your network consists of you interacting with these other individuals. The more you develop, maintain, and expand your networks, the more successful should be your job search.

Your network is your interpersonal environment. While you know and interact with hundreds of people, on a day-to-day basis you may encounter no more than 20 people. You frequently contact these people in face-to-face situations. Some people are more *important* to you than others. You *like* some more than others. And some will be more *helpful* to you in your job search than others. Your basic network may encompass the following individuals and groups: friends, acquaintances, immediate family, distant relatives, professional colleagues, spouse, supervisor, fellow workers, close friends and colleagues, and local businessmen and professionals, such as your banker, lawyer, doctor, minister, and insurance agent. You should contact many of these individuals for advice relating to your job search.

You need to *identify everyone in your network* who might help you with your job search. You first need to expand your basic network to include individuals you know and have interacted with over the past 10 or more years. Make a list of at least 200 people you know. Include friends and relatives from your Christmas card list, past and present neighbors, former classmates, politicians, business persons, previous employers, professional associates, ministers, insurance agents, lawyers, bankers, doctors, dentists, accountants, and social acquaintances.

After identifying your extended network, you should try to *link your network to others' networks.* The figure on page 226 illustrates this linkage principle. Individuals in these other networks also have job information and contacts. Ask people in your basic network for referrals to individuals in their networks. This approach should greatly enlarge your basic job search network.

What do you do if individuals in your immediate and extended network cannot provide you with certain job information and contacts? While it is much easier and more effective to meet new people through personal contacts, on occasion you may need to *approach strangers without prior*

LINKING YOUR NETWORKS TO OTHERS

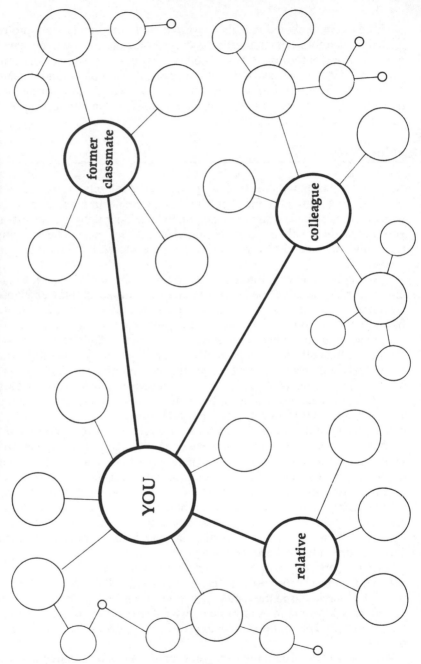

contacts. In this situation, try the "cold turkey" approach. Write a letter to someone you feel may be useful to your job search. Research this individual so you are acquainted with their background and accomplishments. In the letter, refer to their accomplishments, mention your need for job information, and specify a date and time you will call to schedule a meeting. Another approach is to introduce yourself to someone by tele-phone and request a meeting and/or job information. While you may exper-ience rejections in using these approaches, you also will experience successes. And those successes should lead to further expansion of your job search network.

Prospect For Leads

The key to successful networking is an active and routine *prospecting campaign*. Salespersons in insurance, real estate, Amway, Shaklee, and other direct-sales businesses understand the importance and principles of prospecting; indeed, many have turned the art of prospecting into a science! The basic operating principle is *probability*: the number of sales you make is a direct function of the amount of effort you put into developing new contacts and following-through. Expect no more than a 10 percent acceptance rate: for every 10 people you meet, 9 will reject you and 1 will accept you. Therefore, the more people you contact, the more acceptances you will receive. If you want to be successful, you must collect many more "nos" than "yeses." In a 10 percent probability situation, you need to contact 100 people for 10 successes.

These prospecting principles are extremely useful for making a career change. Like sales situations, the job search is a highly ego-involved activity often characterized by numerous rejections accompanied by a few acceptances. While no one wants to be rejected, few people are willing and able to handle more than a few rejections. They take a "no" as a sign of personal failure—and quit prematurely. If they persisted longer, they would achieve success after a few more "nos." Furthermore, if their prospecting activities were focused on gathering information rather than making sales, they would considerably minimize the number of rejections. Therefore, you should do the following:

- Prospect for job leads.
- Accept rejections as part of the game.
- Link prospecting to informational interviewing.
- Keep prospecting for more information and "yeses" which will eventually translate into job interviews and offers.

A good prospecting pace as you start your search is to make two new contacts each day. Start by contacting people in your immediate net-work. Let them know you are conducting a job search, but emphasize that you are only doing research. Ask for a few moments of their time to discuss your information needs. You are only seeking *information and advice* at this time—not a job.

It should take you about 20 minutes to make a contact by letter or telephone. If you make two contacts each day, by the end of the first week you will have 10 new contacts for a total investment of less than seven hours. By the second week you may want to increase your prospecting pace to four new contacts each day or 20 each week. The more contacts you make, the more useful information, advice, and job leads you will receive. If your job search bogs down, you probably need to increase your prospecting activities.

> **The job search is a highly ego-involved activity often characterized by numerous rejections accompanied by a few acceptances.**

Expect each contact to refer you to two or three others who will also refer you to others. Consequently, your contacts should multiply considerably within only a few weeks.

Handle and Minimize Rejections

These prospecting and networking methods are effective. While they are responsible for building, maintaining, and expanding multi-million dollar businesses, they work extremely well for job hunters. But they only work if you are patient and persist. *The key to networking success is to focus on gathering information while also learning to handle rejections.* Learn from rejections, forget them, and go on to more productive networking activities. The major reason direct-sales people fail is because they don't persist. The reason they don't persist is because they either can't take, or get tired of taking, rejections.

Rejections are no fun, especially in such an ego-involved activity as a job search. But you will encounter rejections as you travel on the road toward job search success. This road is strewn with individuals who quit prematurely because they were rejected four or five times. Don't be one of them!

Our prospecting and networking techniques differ from sales approaches in one major respect: we have special techniques for minimizing the number of rejections. If handled properly, at least 50 percent—maybe as many as 90 percent—of your prospects will turn into "yeses" rather than "nos." The reason for this unusually high acceptance rate is how you introduce and handle yourself before your prospects. Many insurance agents and direct distributors expect a 90 percent rejection rate, because they are trying to sell specific products potential clients may or may not need. Most people don't like to be put on the spot—especially when it is in their own home or office—to make a decision to buy a product.

Be Honest and Sincere

The principles of selling yourself in the job market are similar. People don't want to be put on the spot. They feel uncomfortable if they think you expect them to give you a job. Thus, you should never introduce yourself to a prospect by asking them for a job or a job lead. You should do just the opposite: relieve their anxiety by mentioning that you are not looking for a job from them—only job information and advice. You must be honest and sincere in communicating these intentions to your contact. The biggest turn-off for individuals targeted for informational interviews is insincere job seekers who try to use this as a mechanism to get a job.

Your approach to prospects must be subtle, honest, and professional. You are seeking *information, advice, and referrals* relating to several subjects: job opportunities, your job search approach, your resume, and contacts who may have similar information, advice, and referrals. Most people gladly volunteer such information. They generally like to talk about themselves, their careers, and others. They like to give advice. This approach flatters individuals by placing them in the role of the expert-advisor. Who doesn't want to be recognized as an expert-advisor, especially on such a critical topic as one's employment?

This approach should yield a great deal of information, advice, and referrals from your prospects. One other important outcome should result from using this approach: people will *remember* you as the person who made them feel at ease and who received their valuable advice. If they hear of job opportunities for someone with your qualifications, chances are they will contact you with the information. After contacting 100 prospects, you will have created 100 sets of eyes and ears to help you in your job search!

Practice the 5R's of Informational Interviewing

The guiding principle behind prospecting, networking, and informational interviews is this: the best way to get a job is to ask for job information, advice, and referrals; never ask for a job. Remember, you want your prospects to engage in the 5R's of informational interviewing:

- *Reveal* useful information and advice.
- *Refer* you to others.
- *Read* and *revise* your resume.
- *Remember* you for future reference.

If you follow this principle, you should join the ranks of thousands of successful job seekers who paid a great deal of money learning it from highly-paid professionals.

Approach Key People

Whom should you contact within an organization for an informational interview? Contact people who are busy, who have the power to hire, and who are knowledgeable about the organization. The least likely candidate will be someone in the personnel department. Most often the heads of operating units are the most busy, powerful, and knowledgeable individuals in the organization. However, getting access to such individuals may be difficult. Some people at the top may appear to be informed and powerful, but they may lack information on the day-to-day personnel changes or their influence is limited in the hiring process. It is difficult to give one best answer to this question.

Therefore, we recommend contacting several types of people. Aim for the busy, powerful, and informed, but be prepared to settle for less. Secretaries, receptionists, and the person you want to meet may refer you to others. From a practical standpoint, you may have to take whomever you can schedule an appointment with. Sometimes people who are less powerful can be helpful. Talk to a secretary or receptionist sometime about their boss or working in the organization.

> The best way to get a job is to ask for job information, advice, and referrals; never ask for a job.

You may be surprised with what you learn! Nonetheless, you will conduct informational interviews with different types of people. Some will be friends, relatives, or acquaintances. Others will be referrals or new contacts. You will gain the easiest access to people you already know. This can usually be done informally by telephone. You might meet at their home or office or at a restaurant.

You should use a more formal approach to gain access to referrals and new contacts. The best way to initiate a contact with a prospective employer is to *send an approach letter* and follow it up with a phone call. Examples of approach letters are found at the end of Chapter 11. This letter should include the following elements:

OPENERS   If you have a referral, tell the individual you are considering a career in _____. His or her name was given to you by _____ who suggested he or she might be a good person to give you useful information about careers in _____ _____. Should you lack a referral to the individual and thus must use a "cold turkey" approach to making this contact, you might begin your letter by stating that you are aware he or she has been at the forefront of _____ business—or whatever is both truthful and appropriate for the situation. A subtle form of flattery will be helpful at this stage.

REQUEST   Demonstrate your thoughtfulness and courtesy rather than aggressiveness by mentioning that you know he or she is busy. You hope to schedule a mutually convenient time for a brief meeting to discuss your questions and career plans. Most people will be flattered by such a request and happy to talk with you about their work—if they have time and are interested in you.

CLOSINGS   In closing the letter, mention that you will call the person to see if an appointment can be arranged. Be specific by stating the time and day you will call—for example, Thursday at 2pm. You must take initiative to follow-up the letter with a definite contact time. If you don't, you cannot expect to hear from the person. It is *your* responsibility to make the telephone call to schedule a meeting.

ENCLOSURE Do *not* enclose your resume with this approach letter. You should take your resume to the interview and present it as a topic of discussion near the end of your meeting. If you send it with the approach letter, you communicate a mixed and contradictory message. Remember your purpose for this interview: to gather information and advice. You are not—and never should be—asking for a job. A resume accompanying a letter appears to be an application or a job request.

Many people will meet with you, assuming you are sincere in your approach. On the other hand, many people also are very busy and simply don't have the time to meet with you. If the person puts you off when you telephone for an appointment, clearly state your purpose and emphasize that you are not looking for a job with this person—only information and advice. If the person insists on putting you off, make the best of the situation: try to conduct the informational interview over the telephone. Alternatively, write a nice thank you letter in which you again state your intended purpose; mention your disappointment in not being able to learn from the person's experience; and ask to be remembered for future reference. Enclose your resume with this letter.

While you are ostensibly seeking information and advice, treat this meeting as an important preliminary interview. You need to communicate your qualifications—that you are competent, intelligent, honest, and likeable. These are the same qualities you should communicate in a formal job interview. Hence, follow the same advice given for conducting a formal interview and dressing appropriately for a face-to-face meeting (Chapter 14).

Conduct the Interview Well

An informational interview will be relatively unstructured compared to a formal job interview. Since you want the interviewer to advise you, you reverse roles by asking questions which should give you useful information. You, in effect, become the interviewer. You should structure this interview with a particular sequence of questions. Most questions should be open-ended, requiring the individual to give specific answers based upon his or her experience.

The structure and dialogue for the informational interview might go something like this. You plan to take no more than 45 minutes for this interview. The first three to five minutes will be devoted to small talk—the weather, traffic, the office, mutual acquaintances, or an interesting or humorous observation. Since these are the most critical moments in the interview, be especially careful how you communicate nonverbally. Begin your interview by stating your appreciation for the individual's time:

> *"I want to thank you again for scheduling this meeting with me. I know you're busy. I appreciate the special arrangements you made to see me on a subject which is very important to my future."*

Your next comment should be a statement reiterating your purpose as stated in your letter:

> *"As you know, I am exploring job and career alternatives. I know what I do well and what I want to do. But before I commit myself to a new job, I need to know more about various career options. I thought you would be able to provide me with some insights into career opportunities, job requirements, and possible problems or promising directions in the field of _____."*

This statement normally will get a positive reaction from the individual who may want to know more about what it is you want to do. Be sure to clearly communicate your job objective. If you can't, you may communicate that you are lost, indecisive, or uncertain about yourself. The person may feel you are wasting his or her time.

Your next line of questioning should focus on "how" and "what" questions centering on (1) specific jobs and (2) the job search process. Begin by asking about various aspects of specific jobs:

- Duties and responsibilities
- Knowledge, skills, and abilities required
- Work environment relating to fellow employees, work flows, deadlines, stress, initiative
- Advantages and disadvantages
- Advancement opportunities and outlook
- Salary ranges

Your informer will probably take a great deal of time talking about his or her experience in each area. Be a good listener, but make sure you move along with the questions.

Your next line of questioning should focus on your job search activities. You need as much information as possible on how to:

- Acquire the necessary skills
- Best find a job in this field
- Overcome any objections employers may have to you
- Uncover job vacancies which may be advertised
- Develop job leads
- Approach prospective employers

Your final line of questioning should focus on your resume. Do not show your resume until you focus on this last set of questions. The purpose of these questions is to: (1) get the individual to read your resume in-depth, (2) acquire useful advice on how to strengthen it, (3) refer you to prospective employers, and (4) be remembered. With the resume in front of you and your interviewee, ask the following questions:

- Is this an appropriate type of resume for the jobs I have outlined?
- If an employer received this resume in the mail, how do you think he or she would react to it?
- What do you see as possible weaknesses or areas that need to be improved?
- What should I do with this resume? Shotgun it to hundreds of employers with a cover letter? Use resume letters instead?
- What about the length, paper quality and color, layout, and typing? Are they appropriate?
- How might I best improve the form and content of the resume?

You should receive useful advice on how to strengthen both the content and use of your resume. Most important, these questions force the individual to *read* your resume which, in turn, may be *remembered* for future reference.

Your last question is especially important in this interview. You want to be both *remembered* and *referred*. Some variation of the following question should help:

"I really appreciate all this advice. It is very helpful and it should improve my job search considerably. Could I ask you one more favor? Do you know two or three other people who could help me with my job search? I want to conduct as much research as possible, and their advice might be helpful also."

Before you leave, mention one more important item:

"During the next few months, should you hear of any job opportunities for someone with my interests and qualifications, I would appreciate being kept in mind. And please feel free to pass my name on to others."

Send a nice thank you letter within 48 hours of completing this informational interview. Express your genuine gratitude for the individual's time and advice. Reiterate your interests, and ask to be remembered and referred to others.

Follow-up on any useful advice you receive, particularly referrals. Approach referrals in the same manner you approached the person who gave you the referral. Write a letter requesting a meeting. Begin the letter by mentioning:

"Mr./Ms. _____ suggested that I contact you concerning my research on careers in _____."

If you continue prospecting, networking, and conducting informational interviews, soon you will be busy conducting interviews and receiving job offers. While 100 informational interviews over a two-month period should lead to several formal job interviews and offers, the pay-offs are uncertain because job vacancies are unpredictable. We know cases where the first referral turned into a formal interview and job offer. More typical cases require constant prospecting, networking, and informational interviewing activities. The telephone call or letter inviting you to a job interview can come at any time. While the timing may be unpredictable, your persistent job search activities will be largely responsible for the final outcome.

Telephone For Job Leads

Telephone communication should play an important role in prospecting, networking, and informational interviews. However, controversy centers around how and when to use the telephone for generating job leads and scheduling interviews. Some people recommend writing a letter and waiting for a written or telephone reply. Others suggest writing a letter and following it with a telephone call. Still others argue you should use the telephone exclusively rather than write letters.

How you use the telephone will indicate what type of job search you are conducting. Exclusive reliance on the telephone is a technique used by highly formalized job clubs which operate phone banks for generating job leads. Using the Yellow Pages as the guide to employers, a job club member may call as many as 50 employers a day to schedule job interviews. A rather aggressive yet typical telephone dialogue goes something like this:

"Hello, my name is Jim Morgan. I would like to speak to the head of the training department. By the way, what is the name of the training director?"

"You want to talk to Ms. Stevens. Her number is 723-8191 or I can connect you directly."

"Hello, Ms. Stevens. My name is Jim Morgan. I have several years of training experience as both a trainer and developer of training materials. I'd like to meet with you to discuss possible openings in your department for someone with my qualifications. Would it be possible to see you on Friday at 2pm?"

Not surprising, this telephone approach generates many "nos." If you have a hard time handling rejections, this telephone approach will help you confront your anxieties. The principle behind this approach is *probability*: for every 25 telephone "nos" you receive, you will probably get one or two "yeses." Success is just 25 telephone calls away! If you start calling prospective employers at 9am and finish your 25 calls by 12 noon, you should generate at least one or two interviews. That's not bad for three hours of job search work. It beats a direct-mail approach.

While the telephone is more efficient than writing letters, its effectiveness is questionable. When you use the telephone in this manner, you are basically asking for a job. You are asking the employer: "Do you have a job for me?" There is nothing subtle or particularly professional about this approach. It is effective in uncovering particular types of job leads for particular types of individuals. If you need a job—any job—in a hurry, this is one of the most efficient ways of finding employment. It sure beats standing in line at the state employment office! However, if you are more concerned with finding a job that is right for you—a job you do well and enjoy doing, one that is fit for you—this telephone approach is inappropriate.

You must use your own judgment in determining when and how to use the telephone in your job search. There are appropriate times and methods for using the telephone, and these should relate to your job search goals and needs. We prefer the more conventional approach of writing a letter requesting an informational interview and following it up with a telephone call. While you take the initiative in scheduling an appointment, you do not put the individual on the spot by asking for a job. You are only seeking information and advice. This low-keyed approach results in numerous acceptances and has a higher probability of paying off with interviews than the aggressive telephone request. You should be trying to uncover jobs that are right for you rather than any job that happens to pop up from a telephoning blitz.

Use Job Clubs and Support Groups

The techniques outlined thus far are designed for individuals conducting a self-directed job search. Job clubs and support groups are two important alternatives to these techniques.

Job clubs are designed to provide a group structure and support system to individuals seeking employment. These groups consist of about 12 individuals who are led by a trained counselor and supported with telephones, copying machines, and a resource center.

Highly formalized job clubs, such as the 40-Plus Club, organize job search activities for both the advertised and hidden job markets. As outlined by Azrin and Besalel in their book *Job Club Counselor's Manual*, job club activities include:

- Signing commitment agreements to achieve specific job search goals and targets.
- Contacting friends, relatives, and acquaintances for job leads.
- Completing activity forms.
- Using telephones, typewriters, photocopy machines, postage, and other equipment and supplies.
- Meeting with fellow participants to discuss job search progress.
- Telephoning to uncover job leads.
- Researching newspapers, telephone books, and directories.
- Developing research, telephone, interview, and social skills.
- Writing letters and resumes.
- Responding to want ads.
- Completing employment applications.

In other words, the job club formalizes many of the prospecting, networking, and informational interviewing activities within a group context and interjects the role of the telephone as the key communication device for developing and expanding networks.

Job clubs place excessive reliance on using the telephone for uncovering job leads. Members call prospective employers and ask about job openings. The Yellow Pages become the job hunting bible. During a two-week period, a job club member might spend most of his or her mornings telephoning for job leads and scheduling interviews. Afternoons are normally devoted to job interviewing.

We do not recommend joining such job clubs for obvious reasons. Most job club methods are designed for the hardcore unemployed or for individuals who need a job—any job—quickly. Individuals try to fit into available vacancies; their objectives and skills are of secondary concern. We recommend conducting your own job search or forming a support group which adapts some job club methods to our central concept of finding a job fit for you—one appropriate to your objective and in line with your particular mix of skills, abilities, and interests.

Support groups are a useful alternative to job clubs. They have one major advantage: they may cut your job search time in half. Forming or joining one of these groups can help direct as well as enhance your individual job search activities.

Your support group should consist of three or more individuals who are job hunting. Try to schedule regular meetings with specific purposes in mind. While the group may be highly social, especially if it involves close friends, it also should be *task-oriented*. Meet at least once a week and include your spouse. At each meeting set *performance goals* for the week. For example, your goal can be to make 20 new contacts and conduct five informational interviews. The contacts can be made by telephone, letter, or in person. Share your experiences and job information with each other. *Critique* each other's progress, make suggestions for improving the job search, and develop new strategies together. By doing this, you will be gaining valuable information and feedback which is normally difficult to gain on one's own. This group should provide important psychological supports to help you through your job search. After all, job hunting can be a lonely, frustrating, and exasperating experience. By sharing your experiences with others, you will find you are not alone. You will quickly learn that rejections are part of the game. The group will encourage you, and you will feel good about helping others achieve their goals. Try building small incentives into the group, such as the individual who receives the most job interviews for the month will be treated to dinner by other members of the group.

Explore Electronic Networking

Networking is increasingly taking on new communication forms in today's high-tech electronic revolution. As outlined in Chapters 11 and 21, job seekers can now take advantage of several electronic databases for conducting a job search, from gathering information on the job market to disseminating resumes to employers. The electronic revolution also allows job seekers to network for information, advice, and job leads. If you belong to one of the online computer information systems, such as America Online, Microsoft Network, CompuServe, or Prodigy or have direct access to the Internet's World Wide Web, you can use electronic bulletin boards, e-mail systems, and the Internet to gather job information and make contacts with potential employers. Using e-mail, you can make personal contacts which give you job leads for further networking via computer or through the more traditional networking methods outlined in this chapter.

We expect these electronic communication systems will play an increasingly important role in conducting job searches. They offer new networking options for individuals who are literate in today's computer technology and telecommunication systems. If you have access to any of the online telecommunications systems, we recommend exploring their electronic bulletin board, e-mail, and job vacancy ("career corner") options. Within just a few minutes of electronic networking you may pick up important job information, advice, and leads that could turn into a real job. For more information on these electronic networks, see Chapter 21.

14

Interview For Job Offers

Make no mistake—the job interview is *the* most important step in the job search process. All previous job search activities lead to this one. Put simply, no interview, no job offer; no job offer, no negotiations, no salary, and no job.

Your previous job search activities have assisted you in getting this far, but the interview itself will determine whether you will be invited to additional interviews and offered a position. How you approach the interview will make a difference in the outcome of the interview. Therefore, you need to know what best to do and not to do in order to make a good impression on your prospective employer.

Interviewing For the Job

Nearly 95 percent of all organizations require job interviews prior to hiring employees. In fact, employers consider an effective interview to be the most important hiring criteria—outranking grade point average, related work experience, and recommendations.

While the job interview is the most important job search activity, it also is the most stressful job search experience. Your application, resume, and letters may get you to the interview, but you must perform well in person in order to get a job offer. Knowing the stakes are high, most people face interviews with dry throats and sweaty palms; it is a time of great stress. You will be on stage, and you are expected to put on a good performance.

How do you prepare for the interview? First, you need to understand the nature and purpose of the interview. Second, you must prepare to respond to the interview situation and the interviewer. Make sure whoever assists you in preparing for the interview evaluates your performance. Practice the whole interviewing scenario, from the time you enter the door until you leave. You should sharpen your nonverbal communication skills and be prepared to give positive answers to questions as well as ask intelligent questions. The more you practice, the better prepared you will be for the real job interview.

Communication

An interview is a two-way communication exchange between an interviewer and interviewee. It involves both verbal and nonverbal communication. While we tend to concentrate on the content of what we say, research shows that approximately 65 percent of all communication is nonverbal. Furthermore, we tend to give more credibility to nonverbal than to verbal messages. Regardless of what you say, how you dress, sit, stand, use your hands, move your head and eyes, and listen communicates both positive and negative messages.

Job interviews can occur in many different settings and under various circumstances. You may write job interview letters, schedule interviews by telephone, be interviewed over the phone, and encounter one-on-one as well as panel, group, and series interviews. Each situation requires a different set of communication behaviors. For example, while telephone communication is efficient, it may be ineffective for interview purposes. Only certain types of information can be effectively communicated over the telephone because this medium is only verbal. Honesty, intelligence, and likability—three of the most important values you want to communicate to employers—are primarily communicated nonverbally. Therefore, you should be very careful of telephone interviews—whether giving or receiving them.

Job interviews have different purposes and can be negative in many ways. From your perspective, the purpose of an initial job interview is to get a second interview, and the purpose of the second interview is to get a job offer. However, for many employers, the purpose of the interview is to eliminate you from a second interview or job offer. The interviewer wants to know why he or she should *not* hire you. The interviewer tries to do this by identifying your weaknesses. These differing purposes can create an adversarial relationship and contribute to the overall interviewing stress experienced by both the applicant and the interviewer.

Since the interviewer wants to identify your weaknesses, you must counter by *communicating your strengths* to lessen the interviewer's fears of hiring you. Recognizing that you are an unknown quantity to the employer, you must raise the interviewer's expectations of you.

Answering Questions

Hopefully your prospecting, networking, informational interviewing, and resume and letter writing activities result in several invitations to interview for jobs appropriate to your objective. Once you receive an invitation to interview, you should do a great deal of work in preparation for your meeting. You should prepare for the interview as if it were a $1,000,000 prize. After all, that may be what you earn during your employment.

The invitation to interview will most likely come by telephone. In some cases, a preliminary interview will be conducted by telephone. The employer may want to shorten the list of eligible candidates from ten to three. By calling each individual, the employer can quickly eliminate marginal candidates as well as update the job status of each individual. When you get such a telephone call, you have no time to prepare. You may be dripping wet as you step from the shower or you may have a splitting headache as you pick up the phone. Telephone interviews always seem to occur at bad times. Whatever your situation, put your best foot forward

> **You should prepare for the interview as if it were a $1,000,000 prize.**

based upon your thorough preparation for an interview. You may want to keep a list of questions near the telephone just in case you receive such a telephone call.

Telephone interviews often result in a face-to-face interview at the employer's office. Once you confirm an interview time and place, you should do as much research on the organization and employer as possible as well as learn to lessen your anxiety and stress levels by practicing the interview situation. *Preparation and practice* are the keys to doing your best.

During the interview, you want to impress upon the interviewer your knowledge of the organization by asking insightful questions and giving intelligent answers. Your library and networking research should yield useful information on the organization and employer. Be sure you know something about the organization. Interviewers are normally impressed by interviewees who demonstrate knowledge and interest in their organization.

You should practice the actual interview by mentally addressing several questions most interviewers ask. Most of these questions will relate to your educational background, work experience, career goals, personality, and related concerns. The most frequently asked questions include:

Education

- Describe your educational background.
- Why did you attend _____ University (College or School)?
- Why did you major in _____?
- What was your grade point average?
- What subjects did you enjoy the most? The least? Why?
- What leadership positions did you hold?
- How did you finance your education?
- If you could start over, what would you change about your education?

- Why were your grades so low? So high?
- Did you do the best you could in school? If not, why not?

Work Experience

- What were your major achievements in each of your past jobs?
- Why did you change jobs before?
- What is your typical work day like?
- What functions do you enjoy doing the most?
- What did you like about your boss? Dislike?
- Which job did you enjoy the most? Why? Which job did you enjoy the least? Why?
- Have you ever been fired? Why?

Career Goals

- Why do you want to join our organization?
- Why do you think you are qualified for this position?
- Why are you looking for another job?
- Why do you want to make a career change?
- What ideally would you like to do?
- Why should we hire you?
- How would you improve our operations?
- What do you want to be doing five years from now?
- How much do you want to be making five years from now?
- What are your short-range and long-range career goals?
- If you could choose your job and organization, where would you go?
- What other types of jobs are you considering? What other companies?
- When will you be ready to begin work?
- How do you feel about relocating, traveling, working overtime, and spending weekends in the office?
- What attracted you to our organization?

Personality and Other Concerns

- Tell me about yourself.
- What are your major weaknesses? Your major strengths?
- What causes you to lose your temper?
- What do you do in your spare time? Any hobbies?
- What types of books do you read?
- What role does your family play in your career?
- How well do you work under pressure? In meeting deadlines?
- Tell me about your management philosophy.

- How much initiative do you take?
- What types of people do you prefer working with?
- How _____ (creative, analytical, tactful, etc.) are you?
- If you could change your life, what would you do differently?

Handle Objections and Negatives With Ease

Interviewers must have a healthy skepticism of job candidates. They expect people to exaggerate their competencies and overstate what they will do for the employer. They sometimes encounter dishonest applicants, and some people they hire fail to meet their expectations. Being realists who have made poor hiring decisions before, they want to know why they should *not* hire you. Although they do not always ask you these questions, they think about them nonetheless:

- Why should I hire you?
- What do you really want?
- What can you really do for me?
- What are your weaknesses?
- What problems will I have with you?

Underlying these questions are specific employers' objections to hiring you:

- You're not as good as you say you are; you probably hyped your resume or lied about yourself.
- All you want is a job and security.
- You have weaknesses like the rest of us. Is it alcohol, sex, drugs, finances, shiftlessness, petty politics?
- You'll probably want my job in another 5 months.
- You won't stay long with us. Ambitious people like you join the competition or *become* the competition.

Employers raise such suspicions and objections because it is difficult to trust strangers in the employment game and they may have been "burned" before. Indeed, there is an alarming rise in the number of individuals lying on their resumes or falsifying their credentials.

How can you best handle employers' objections? You must first recognize their biases and stereotypes and then *raise* their expectations. You do this by stressing your strengths and avoiding your weaknesses. You must be impeccably honest in doing so.

Your answers to employers' questions should be positive and emphasize your *strengths*. Remember, the interviewer wants to know what's wrong with you—your *weaknesses*. When answering questions, both the *substance* and *form* of your answers should be positive. For example, such words as "couldn't," "can't," "won't," and "don't" may create a negative tone and distract from the positive and enthusiastic image you are trying to create. While you cannot eliminate all negative words, at least recognize that the type of words you use makes a difference and therefore word choice should be better managed. Compare your reactions to the following interview answers:

QUESTION: **Why do you want to leave your present job?**

ANSWER 1:   *After working there three years, I don't feel I'm going anywhere. Morale isn't good, and management doesn't reward us according to our productivity. I really don't like working there anymore.*

ANSWER 2:   *After working there three years, I have learned a great deal about managing people and developing new markets. But it is time for me to move on to a larger and more progressive organization where I can use may marketing experience in several different areas. I am ready to take on more responsibilities. This change will be a positive step in my professional growth.*

Which one has the greatest impact in terms of projecting positives and strengths? The first answer communicates too many negatives. The second answer is positive and upbeat in its orientation toward skills, accomplishments, and the future.

In addition to choosing positive words, select *content information* which is positive and *adds* to the interviewer's knowledge about you. Avoid simplistic "yes/no" answers; they say nothing about you. Instead, provide information which explains your reasons and motivations behind specific events or activities. For example, how do you react to these two factual answers?

QUESTION: **I see from your resume that you've been working with Company X for 5 years. Are you one of the employees being affected by the recent budget cuts?**

ANSWER 1:   *Yes, that's correct.*

ANSWER 2:   *Yes. Like many others, I've been affected by the recent cutbacks. However, instead of looking at my situation as a crisis, I'm approaching it as an opportunity to explore several other strong interests of mine. I know my talents can be useful in any number of settings, and I'm particularly interested in the work your department does.*

Let's try another question reflecting possible objections to hiring you:

QUESTION: **Your background bothers me somewhat. You've been with this organization for 10 years. You know, it's different working in our organization. Why should I hire you?**

ANSWER 1:   *I can understand that.*

ANSWER 2:   *I understand your hesitation in hiring someone with my background. I would too, if I were you. Yes, many people don't do well in different occupational settings. But I don't believe I have that problem. I'm used to working with people. I work until the job gets done, which often means long hours and on weekends. I'm very concerned with achieving results. But most important, I've done a great deal of thinking about my goals. I've researched your organization as well as many others. From what I have learned, this is exactly what I want to do, and your organization is the one I'm most interested in joining. I know I will do a good job, as I have always done in the past.*

The first answer is incomplete. It misses an important opportunity to give evidence that you have resolved this issue in a positive manner which is clearly reflected in the second response.

The most difficult challenge to your positive strategy comes when the interviewer asks you to describe your negatives or weaknesses:

QUESTION: **We all have our negatives and weaknesses. What are some of yours?**

You can handle this question in any of five different ways, yet still give positive information on yourself:

1. Discuss a negative which is not related to the job being considered:

I don't enjoy accounting. I know it's important, but I find it boring. Even at home my wife takes care of our books. Marketing is what I like to do. Other people are much better at book-

keeping than I am. I'm glad this job doesn't involve any account-ing!

2. Discuss a negative which the interviewer already knows:

I spent a great deal of time working on advanced degrees, as indicated in my resume, and thus I lack extensive work experience. However, I believe my education has prepared me well for this job. My leadership experience in college taught me how to work with people, organize, and solve problems. I write well and quickly. My research experience helped me analyze, synthesize, and develop strategies.

3. Discuss a negative which you have improved upon:

I used to get over-committed and miss important deadlines. But then I read a book on time management and learned what I was doing wrong. Within three weeks I reorganized my use of time and found I could meet my deadlines with little difficulty. The quality of my work also improved. Now I have time to work out at the gym each day. I'm doing more and feeling better at the same time.

4. Discuss a "negative" which can also be a positive:

I'm somewhat of a workaholic. I love my work, but I sometime neglect my family because of it. I've been going into the office seven days a week, and I often put in 12 hour days. I'm now learning to better manage my time.

5. Discuss a negative outside yourself:

I don't feel that there is anything seriously wrong with me. Like most people, I have my ups and downs. But overall I have a positive outlook, feel good about myself and what I've accomplished so far in my life. However, I am somewhat concerned how you might view my wanting to change occupations. I want to assure you that I'm not making this change on a whim. I've taken my time in thinking through the issues and taking a hard look at what I do well and enjoy doing. Like a lot of young people, I guess I didn't have much life experience when I started my career ten years ago, and I got into sales because I enjoyed that kind of environment. However, as I got more experience and had opportunities to become involved in different areas, my interest in management training developed. I found that I not only enjoyed those activities, but that I had some natural talent for them. While I've enjoyed my years in sales, I am committed to finding work more in line with my interests and abilities.

All of these examples stress the basic point about effective interviewing. Your single best strategy for managing the interview is to *emphasize your strengths and positives.* Questions come in several forms. Anticipate these questions, especially the negative ones, and practice positive responses in order to project your best self in an interview situation.

Encountering Behavior-Based Interviews and Questions

More and more employers are conducting a different type of interview than they did five or ten years ago. Known as "behavior-based interviews," these interviews are filled with behavior-based questions designed to illicit *patterns of accomplishments* relevant to the employer's situation. They are specific and challenge interviewees to provide concrete examples of their achievements in different types of situations. Such interviews are based on the simply belief that how a job candidate has responded to certain types of situations in the past is a good predictor of how that person will behave in a similar future situation. Behavior-based questions are likely to begin with some variation of:

- Give me an example of a time when you . . .
- Give me an example of how you . . .
- Tell me about how you . . .

This is an opportunity for you to sell your positives with an example or two. Briefly describe the situation, enthusiastically explain what you did (adding information as to why if you think this would not be evident), and indicate the outcome.

For example, if the interviewer asks,

"Tell me about a time when you saved an account for your company."

The applicant might respond,

"Just last month I was observing a one-day training session conducted by one of our instructors I supervise. His class evaluations were lower than what we expect of our trainers and my boss told me the client was not happy with the way the training sessions were going. He was afraid we might lose the account.

As I observed the session it was apparent the instructor knew the material but was having trouble moving the participants through the material in the time allotted. They often broke into small groups to complete an activity, but it was taking a long time as some groups had to wait for others to finish. At the end of the day Joe and I met with the client who indicated his dissatisfaction and gave us an ultimatum: if the training of future groups couldn't be completed in a day and to his satisfaction, he would get another contractor.

I solved the problem by having Joe develop copies of the end product the participants should have formulated at the end of each activity. At the next training session he was able to pass these out at the end of the allotted time for each phase of the activity.

The seminar participants understood the information and gave the instructor excellent course evaluations and the client was pleased. We not only saved this contract, but got an additional contract from the client as well. My boss and I were both pleased with the outcome."

Obviously you want to select examples that promote your skills and have a positive outcome. Even if the interviewer asks about a time when something negative happened, try to select an example where you were able to turn the situation around and something positive came out of it. For example, if asked, *"Tell me about a time you made a bad decision."* Try to identify an example where:

- even though it wasn't the best decision, you were able to pull something positive out of the situation

- though it was a poor decision, you learned from it and in the next similar situation you made a good decision or know how you will handle it differently the next time a similar situation arises

- it was bad decision but the negative outcome had only minor impact

In other words, try to pull something positive—either that you did or that you learned—out of even a negative experience you are asked to relate. As you prepare for your interview, consider situations where you:

- demonstrated leadership
- solved a problem
- increased company profits
- made a good decision/made a poor decision
- handled change (not money, but changing events)
- handled criticism
- met a deadline/missed a deadline
- worked as part of a team

Add to this list other behavioral questions you think of that apply to the job for which you are applying. For example, if the job includes making presentations, expect questions about a speech where you achieved your goal or conversely about a time when your speech failed miserably.

Ask others who have interviewed with the company, if possible, to find out the types of questions to expect. You may encounter hypothetical questions in which you are asked not what you did, but what you would do *if* something occurred. With hypothetical questions the interviewer is usually not interested so much in your actual answer—often there is no correct or incorrect response—as in your thought process. The information is in how you would solve a problem or respond to a particular type of situation.

Individuals who do well in behavior-based interviews are those who have a rich background of accomplishments as well as are good story-tellers. Indeed, *story-telling* is one of the key communication skill involved in conducting effective such interviews. If you want to do well in this type of interview, be sure to anticipate questions you might be asked so you can prepare a well thought-out response—a set of revealing stories about your performance—prior to the interview. It is far easier to formulate positive responses to questions in the relaxed setting of your living room than in the stressful and time constrained setting of the job interview.

Illegal Questions

Many questions are illegal, but some employers ask them nonetheless. Consider how you would respond to these questions:

- Are you married, divorced, separated, or single?
- How old are you?
- Do you go to church regularly?
- Do you have many debts?
- Do you own or rent your home?
- What social and political organizations do you belong to?
- What does your spouse think about your career?
- Are you living with anyone?
- Are you practicing birth control?
- Were you ever arrested?
- How much insurance do you have?
- How much do you weigh?
- How tall are you?

Don't get upset and say *"That's an illegal question...I refuse to answer it!"* While you may be perfectly right in saying so, this response lacks tact, which may be what the employer is looking for. For example, if you are divorced and the interviewer asks about your divorce, you might respond with *"Does a divorce have a direct bearing on the responsibilities of this position?"* Some employers may ask such questions just to see how you answer or react under stress. Others may do so out of ignorance of the law. Whatever the case, be prepared to handle these questions with tact.

Asking Questions

Interviewers expect candidates to ask intelligent questions concerning the organization and the nature of the work. Moreover, you need information and should indicate your interest in the employer by asking questions. Consider asking some of these questions if they haven't been answered early in the interview:

- Tell me about the duties and responsibilities of this job.
- How does this position relate to other positions within this organization?
- How long has this position been in the organization?
- What would be the ideal type of person for this position? Skills? Personality? Working style? Background?
- Can you tell me about the people who have been in this position before? Backgrounds? Promotions? Terminations?
- Whom would I be working with in this position?
- Tell me something about these people? Their strengths? Their weaknesses? Their performance expectations?
- What am I expected to accomplish during the first year?
- How will I be evaluated?
- Are promotions and raises tied to performance criteria?
- Tell me how this operates?
- What is the normal salary range for such a position?
- Based on your experience, what type of problems would someone new in this position likely encounter?
- I'm interested in your career with this organization. When Did you start? What are your plans for the future?
- I would like to know how people get promoted and advance in this organization?
- What is particularly unique about working in this organization?
- What does the future look like for this organization?

You may want to write your questions on a 3 x 5 card and take them with you to the interview. While it is best to memorize these questions, you may need to refer to your list when the interviewer asks you if you have any questions. You might do this by saying: *"Yes, I jotted down a few questions which I want to make sure I ask you before leaving."* Then pull out your card and refer to the questions.

Dress Appropriately

Appearance is the first thing you communicate to others. Before you have a chance to speak, others notice how you dress and accordingly draw certain conclusions about your personality and competence. Indeed, research shows that appearance makes the greatest difference when an evaluator has little information about the other person. This is precisely the situation you find yourself in at the start of the interview.

Many people object to having their capabilities evaluated on the basis of their appearance and manner of dress. *"But that is not fair,"* they argue. *"People should be hired on the basis of their ability to do the job—not on how they look."* But debating the lack of merit or complaining about the unfairness of such behavior does not alter reality. Like it or not, people do make initial judgments about others based on their appearance. Since you cannot alter this fact and bemoaning it will get you nowhere, it is best to learn to use it to your advantage. If you learn to effectively manage your image, you can convey marvelous messages regarding your authority, credibility, and competence.

Some estimates indicate that as much as 65 percent of the hiring decision may be based on the nonverbal aspects of the interview! Employers sometimes refer to this phenomenon with such terms as "chemistry," "body warmth," or that "gut feeling" the individual is right for the job. This correlates with findings of communication studies that approximately 65 percent of a message is communicated nonverbally. The remaining 35 percent is communicated verbally.

Rules of the Game

Knowing how to dress appropriately for the interview requires knowing important rules of the game. Like it or not, employers play by these rules. Once you know the rules, you at least can make a conscious choice whether or not you want to play. If you decide to play, you will stand a better chance of winning by using the often unwritten rules to your advantage.

Much has been written on how to dress professionally, especially since John Molloy first wrote his books on dress for success in the 1970s. While this approach has been criticized for promoting a "cookie cutter" or "carbon copy" image, it is still valid for most interview situations. The degree to which employers adhere to these rules, however, will depend on particular individuals and situations. Your job is to know when, where, and to what extent the rules apply to you. When in doubt, follow our general advice on looking professional.

Knowing and playing by the rules does not imply incompetent people get jobs simply by dressing the part. Rather, it means qualified and competent job applicants can gain an extra edge over a field of other qualified, competent individuals by dressing to convey positive professional images.

Winning the Game

Much advice has been written about how to dress for success—some of it excellent. However, there is a major flaw in most of the advice you encounter. Researchers on the subject have looked at how people in positions of power view certain colors for professional attire. Few have gone beyond this to note that colors do different things on different people. Various shades or clarities of a color or combinations of contrast between light and dark colors when worn together may be unenhancing to some individuals and actually diminish that person's "power look."

If you combine the results of research done by John Molloy on how colors relate to one's power look and that done by JoAnne Nicholson and Judy Lewis-Crum as explained in their book *Color Wonderful* (New York: Bantam) on how colors relate to people as unique individuals, you can achieve a win-win situation. You can retain your individuality and look your most enhanced while, at the same time, achieving a look of success, power, and competence.

Your Winning Appearance

The key to effective dressing is to know how to relate the clothing you put on your body to your own natural coloring. Into which category does your coloring fit? Let's find out where you belong in terms of color type:

- **Contrast coloring:** If you are a contrast color type, you have a definite dark-light appearance. You have very dark brown or black hair and light to medium ivory or olive toned skin. Black men and women in this category will have clear light to dark skin tones and dark hair.

- **Light-bright coloring:** If you are of this color type, you have golden tones in your skin and golden tones in your blond or light to medium brown hair. Most of you had blond or light brown hair as children. Black men and women in this category will have clear golden skin in their face and dark hair.

- **Muted coloring:** If you are a muted color type, you have a definite brown-on-brown or red-on-brown appearance. Your skin tone is an ivory-beige, brown-beige, or golden-beige tone—that is, you have a beige skin with a golden-brown cast. Your hair could be red or light to dark brown with camel, bronze, or red highlights. Black men and women in this category will have golden or brown skin tones and dark hair.

- **Gentle coloring:** If you are of this color type, you have a soft, gentle looking appearance. Your skin tone is a light ivory or pink-beige tone and your hair is ash blond or ash brown. You probably had blond or ash brown hair as a child. Black men and women in this category will have pink tones in their skin and dark hair.

There are also some individuals who may be a combination of two color types. If your skin tone falls in one category and your hair color in another, you are a combination color type.

However, if you are not certain which hair or skin tone is yours and are hence undecided as to which color type category you belong to, you may wish to contact Color 1 Associates by calling their toll-free number: 1-800-523-8496. They can refer you to the Color 1 consultant nearest you.

A Color 1 associate can provide you with an individualized color chart that allows you to wear every color in the spectrum, but in your best *shade* and *clarity* as well as written material telling you how you can combine your colors for the best amounts of contrast for your natural coloring (color type).

The color chart is an excellent one-time investment considering the costs of buying the wrong colored suit, shirt, or blouse. It will more than pay for itself if it contributes to an effective interview as you wear your suit in your best shade and put your clothing together to work with, rather than against, your natural coloring. It can help you convey positive images during those crucial initial minutes of the interview—as well as over a lifetime.

Images of Success

John Molloy has conducted extensive research on how individuals can dress effectively. Aimed at individuals already working in professional positions who want to communicate a success image, his advice is just as relevant for someone interviewing for a job.

Basic attire for men or women interviewing for a position is a suit. Let's look at appropriate suits in terms of color, fabric, and style. The suit color can make a difference in creating an image of authority and competence. The suit colors that make the strongest positive statements for you are *your shade* of gray in a medium to charcoal depth or *your shade* of blue in a medium to navy depth of color. However, you may choose a less authoritative look for some interview settings. Camel or beige are also considered proper colors for men's suits and women have an even greater color range. Generally even women should select fairly conservative colors for a job interview unless you are interviewing for a job in a field where non-conformity is considered a plus.

When selecting your suit, choose a shade that appears enhancing to you. Should you wear a blue-gray, a taupe-gray, or a shade in-between? Do you look better in a somewhat bright navy or a more toned-down navy; a blue navy or a black navy; a navy with a purple or a yellow base to it?

In general, most people will look better in somewhat blue grays than in grays that are closer to the taupe side of the spectrum. Most people will be enhanced by a navy that is not too bright or contain so much black that it is difficult to distinguish whether the color is navy or black. When selecting a beige or a camel, select a tone that complements your skin color. If your skin has pink tones, avoid beiges and camels that contain gold hues and select pink based beiges/camels that enhance your skin color. Similarly, those of you who have gold/olive tones to your skin should avoid the pink based camel and beiges.

Your suit(s) should be made of a natural fiber. A good blend of a natural fiber with some synthetic is acceptable as long as it has the "look" of the natural fiber. The very best suit fabrics are wool, wool blends, or fabrics that look like them. Even for the warmer summer months, men can find summer weight wool suits that are comfortable and look marvelous. They are your best buy. For really hot climates, a linen/silk fabric can work well. Normally a linen will have to be blended with another fiber, often a synthetic, in order to retain a pressed, neat look. The major disadvantage of pure linen is that it wrinkles. Women's suits also should be made of a natural fiber or have the "look" of a natural fiber. The very best winter-weight suit fabrics are wool or wool blends. For the warmer climates or the summer months, women will find few, if any, summer weight wool suits made for them. Hence linen, blended with a synthetic so it will not look as if it needs constant pressing or a good silk or silk blend are good choices. Avoid 100 percent polyester materials, or anything that looks like it—especially double-knits—like the plague! It is a definite negative for your look of competence, power, and success.

The style of your suit should be classic. It should be well-tailored and well-styled. Avoid suits that appear "trendy" unless you are applying for a job in a field such as arts or perhaps advertising. A conservative suit that has a timeless classic styling and also looks up-to-date will serve you best not only for the interview, but it will give you several years wear once you land the job.

Men should select a shirt color that is lighter than the color of their suit. Ken Karpinski's book, *Red Socks Don't Work! Messages From the Real World About Men's Clothing*, and John Molloy's book on appearance and dress for men, *John Molloy's New Dress For Success*, go into great detail on shirts, ties, and practically everything you might wear or carry with you. We recommend both books over others because they are based on research rather than personal opinion and promotional fads.

When deciding on your professional wardrobe, always buy clothes to last and buy quality. For women quality means buying silk blouses if you can afford them. Keep in mind not only the price of the blouse itself, but the cleaning bill. There are many polyester blouse fabrics that have the look and feel of silk—this is an exception to the "no polyester" rule. Silk or a polyester that has the look and feel of silk are the fabrics for blouses to go with your suits. Choose your blouses in your most flattering shades and clarity of color. John Molloy's book on appearance and dress for women, *The New Woman's Dress or Success Book*, goes into great detail on the blouse styles that test best as well as expands on suit colors. It includes information on almost anything you might wear or carry with you to the interview or on the job. You might also want to consult Janet Wallach's *Looks That Work* for similar information.

Give your outfit a more "finished and polished" look by accessorizing it effectively. Collect silk scarves and necklaces of semiprecious stones in your suit colors. Wear scarves and necklaces with your suits and blouses in such a way that they repeat the color of the suit. For example, a woman wearing a navy suit and a red silk blouse could accent the look by wearing a necklace of navy sodalite beads or a silk scarf that has navy as a predominate color. The *Color Wonderful* book includes a great deal of information to help you accessorize your look geared to your color type.

> When deciding on your professional wardrobe, always buy clothes to last and buy quality.

Appear Likable

Remember, most people invited to a job interview have already been "screened in." They supposedly possess the basic qualifications for the job, such as education and work experience. At this point employers will look for several qualities in the candidates, such as honesty, credibility, intelligence, competence, enthusiasm, spontaneity, friendliness, and likability. Much of the message communicating these qualities will be conveyed through your dress as well as through other nonverbal behaviors.

In the end, employers hire people they *like* and who will interact well on an interpersonal basis with the rest of the staff. Therefore, you should communicate that you are a likable candidate who can get along well with others. You can communicate these messages by engaging in several nonverbal behaviors. Four of the most important ones include:

1. **Sit with a very slight forward lean toward the interviewer.** It should be so slight as to be almost imperceptible. If not overdone, it communicates your interest in what the interviewer is saying.

2. **Make eye contact frequently, but don't overdo it.** Good eye contact establishes rapport with the interviewer. You will be perceived as more trustworthy if you will look at the interviewer as you ask and answer questions. To say someone has "shifty

eyes" or cannot "look us in the eye" is to imply they may not be completely honest. To have a direct, though moderate eye gaze, conveys interest, as well as trustworthiness.

3. **A moderate amount of smiling will also help reinforce your positive image.** You should smile enough to convey your positive attitude, but not so much that you will not be taken seriously. Some people naturally smile often and others hardly ever smile. Monitor your behavior or ask a friend to give you frank feedback.

4. **Try to convey interest and enthusiasm through your vocal inflections.** Your tone of voice can say a lot about you and how interested you are in the interviewer and organization.

Close the Interview

Be prepared to end the interview. Many people don't know when or how to close interviews. They go on and on until someone breaks an uneasy moment of silence with an indication that it is time to go.

Interviewers normally will initiate the close by standing, shaking hands, and thanking you for coming to the interview. Don't end by saying *"Good-bye and thank you."* As this stage, you should summarize the interview in terms of your interests, strengths, and goals. Briefly restate your qualifications and continuing interest in working with the employer. At this point it is proper to ask the interviewer about selection plans:

"When do you anticipate making your final decision?"

Follow this question with your final one:

"May I call you next week (or whatever is appropriate in response to your question about timing of the final decision) to inquire about my status?"

By taking the initiative in this manner, the employer will be prompted to clarify your status soon, and you will have an opportunity to talk to her further.

Many interviewers will ask you for a list of references. Be sure to prepare such a list *prior to* the interview. Include the names, addresses, and phone numbers of four individuals who will give you positive professional and personal recommendations. If asked for references, you will appear well prepared by presenting a list in this manner. If you fail to prepare this information ahead of time, you may appear at best disorganized and at worst lacking good references. Always anticipate being asked for specific names, addresses, and phone numbers of your references.

Remember to Follow-Up

Once you have been interviewed, be sure to follow through to get nearer to the job offer. One of the best follow-up methods is the thank you letter; you will find examples of these letters at the end of Chapter 11. After talking to the employer over the telephone or in a face-to-face interview, send a thank you letter. This letter should be typed on good quality bond paper. In this letter express your gratitude for the opportunity to interview. Re-state your interest in the position and highlight any particularly noteworthy points made in your conversation or anything you wish to further clarify. Close the letter by mentioning that you will call in a few days to inquire about the employer's decision. When you do this, the employer should remember you as a thoughtful person.

If you call and the employer has not yet made a decision, follow through with another phone call in a few days. Send any additional information to the employer which may enhance your application. You might also want to ask one of your references to call the employer to further recommend you for the position. However, don't engage in overkill by making a pest of yourself. You want to tactfully communicate two things to the employer at this point: (1) you are interested in the job, and (2) you will do a good job.

For more information on developing interviewing skills, including follow-up and thank you letters, look for the Krannichs' *Interview For Success, 101 Dynamite Answers to Interview Questions, Dynamite Tele-Search,* and *201 Dynamite Job Search Letters* and Richard Fein's *111 Dynamite Ways to Ace Your Job Interview* and *111 Dynamite Questions to Ask At Your Job Interview* (all published by Impact Publications and included in the order form at the end of this book).

15

Negotiate Salary, Benefits, and Your Future

Throughout your job search you need to seriously consider several questions about your financial value and future income. What, for example, are you worth? How much should you be paid for your work? How can you best demonstrate your value to an employer? What dollar value will the employer assign to you? What salary are you willing to accept?

You think you are worth a lot. After impressing upon the employer that you are the right person for the job, the bottom line becomes money—your talent and labor in exchange for the employer's cash and benefits. How, then, are you going to deal with these questions in order to get more than the employer may initially be willing to offer?

Approach Salaries as Negotiable

Salary is one of the most important yet least understood considerations in the job search. Many individuals do very well in handling all interview questions except the salary question. They are either too shy to talk about money or they believe you must take what you are offered—because salary is predetermined by employers. As a result, many applicants may be paid much less than they are worth. Over the years, they will lose thousands of dollars by having failed to properly negotiate their salaries. Indeed, most employees are probably underpaid by $2,000 to $5,000 because they failed to properly negotiate their salaries.

Salary is seldom predetermined. Most employers have some flexibility to negotiate salary. While most employers do not try to exploit applicants, neither do they want to pay applicants more than what they are willing to accept.

Salaries are usually assigned to positions or jobs rather than to individuals. But not everyone is of equal value in performing the job; some are more productive than others. Since individual performance differs, you should attempt to establish your value in the eyes of the employer rather than accept a salary figure for the job. The art of salary negotiation will help you do this.

Look to Your Financial Future

We all have financial needs which our salary helps to meet. But salary has other significance too. It is an indicator of our worth to others. It also influences our future income. Therefore, it should be treated as one of the most serious considerations in the job interview.

The salary you receive today will influence your future earnings. Yearly salary increments will most likely be figured as a percentage of your base salary rather than reflect your actual job performance. When changing jobs, expect employers to offer you a salary similar to the one you earned in your last job. Once they learn what you made in your previous job, they will probably offer you no more than a 10% to 15% increase, regardless of your productivity. If you hope to improve your income in the long run, then you must be willing to negotiate your salary from a position of strength.

Prepare For the Salary Question

You should be well prepared to deal with the question of salary anytime during your job search but especially during the job interview. Based on your library research (Chapter 12) as well as salary information gained from your networking activities (Chapter 13), you should know the approximate salary range for the position you are seeking. If you fail to gather this salary information prior to the screening or job interview, you may do yourself a disservice by accepting too low a figure or pricing yourself out of consideration. It is always best to be informed so you will be in better control to negotiate salary and benefits.

Keep Salary Issues to the Very End

The question of salary may be raised anytime during the job search. Employers may want you to state a salary expectation figure on an application form, in a cover letter, or over the telephone. Most frequently, however, employers will talk about salary during the employment interview. If at all possible, keep the salary question open until the very last. Even with application forms, cover letters, and telephone screening interviews, try to delay the discussion of salary by stating "open" or "negotiable." After all, the ultimate purpose of your job search activities is to demonstrate your *value* to employers. You should not attempt to translate your value into dollar figures until you have had a chance to convince the employer of your worth. This is best done near the end of the job interview.

Although employers will have a salary figure or range in mind when they interview you, they still want to know your salary expectations. How much will you cost them? Will it be more or less than the job is worth? Employers preferably want to hire individuals for the least amount possible. You, on the other hand, want to be hired for as much as possible. Obviously, there is room for disagreement and unhappiness as well as negotiation and compromise.

One easy way employers screen you in or out of consideration is to raise the salary question early in the interview. A standard question is: "What are your salary requirements?" When asked, don't answer with a specific dollar figure. You should aim at establishing your value in the eyes of the employer prior to talking about a figure. If you give the employer a salary figure at this stage, you are likely to lock yourself into it, regardless of how much you impress the employer or what you find out about the duties and responsibilities of the job. Therefore, salary should be the last major item you discuss with the employer.

> Salary should be the last major item you discuss with the employer.

You should never ask about salary prior to being offered the job, even though it is one of your major concerns. Try to let the employer initiate the salary question. And when he or she does, take your time. Don't appear too anxious. While you may know—based on your previous research—approximately what the employer will offer, try to get the employer to state a figure first. If you do this, you will be in a stronger negotiating position.

Handle the Salary Question With Tact

When the salary question arises, assuming you do not want to put it off, your first step should be to clearly summarize the job responsibilities/duties as you understand them. At this point you are attempting to do three things:

1. Seek clarification from the interviewer as to the actual job and all it involves.

2. Emphasize the level of skills required in the most positive way. In other words, you emphasize the value and worth of this position to the organization and subtly this may help support the actual salary figure that the interviewer or you later provide.

3. Focus attention on your value in relation to the requirements of the position—the critical linkage for negotiating salary from a position of strength.

You might do this, for example, by saying,

> *"As I understand it, I would report directly to the vice-president in charge of marketing and I would have full authority for marketing decisions that involved expenditures of up to $50,000. I would have a staff of five people—a secretary, two copywriters, and two marketing assistants."*

Such a summary statement establishes for both you and the interviewer that (1) this position reports to the highest levels of authority; (2) this position is responsible for decision-making involving fairly large sums of money; and (3) this position involves supervision of staff.

Although you may not explicitly draw the connection, you are emphasizing the value of this position to the organization. This position should be worth a lot more than one in which the hiree will report to the marketing manager, be required to get approval for all expenditures over $100, and has no staff—just access to the secretarial pool! By doing this you will focus the salary question (that you have not yet responded to) around the exact work you must perform on the job in exchange for salary and benefits. You have also seized the opportunity to focus on the value of the person who will be selected to fill this vacancy.

Your conversation might go something like this. The employer poses the question:

> *"What are your salary requirements?"*

Your first response should be to summarize the responsibilities of the position. You might begin with a summary statement followed by a question:

> *"Let me see if I understand all that is involved with this position and job. I would be expected to _____. Have I covered everything or are there some other responsibilities I should know about?"*

This response focuses the salary question around the *value* of the position in relation to you. After the interviewer responds to your final question, answer the initial salary expectation question in this manner:

> *"What is the normal salary range in your company for a position such as this?"*

This question establishes the value, as well as the range, for the position or job—two important pieces of information you need before proceeding further into the salary negotiation stage. The employer normally will give you the requested salary range. Once he or she does, depending on how you feel about the figure, you can follow up with one more question.

"What would be the normal salary range for someone with my qualifications?"

This question further establishes the value for the individual versus the position. This line of questioning will yield the salary expectations of the employer without revealing your desired salary figure or range. It also will indicate whether the employer distinguishes between individuals and positions when establishing salary figures.

Reach Common Ground and Agreement

After finding out what the employer is prepared to offer, you have several choices. First, you can indicate that his or her figure is acceptable to you and thus conclude your final interview. Second, you can haggle for more money in the hope of reaching an acceptable compromise. Third, you can delay final action by asking for more time to consider the figure. Finally, you can tell the employer the figure is unacceptable and leave.

The first and the last options indicate you are either too eager or playing hard-to-get. We recommend the second and third options. If you decide to reach agreement on salary in this interview, haggle in a professional manner. You can do this best by establishing a salary range from which to bargain in relation to the employer's salary range. For example, if the employer indicates that he or she is prepared to offer $50,000 to $55,000, you should establish common ground for negotiation by placing your salary range into the employer's range. Your response to the employer's $50,000 to $55,000 range might be:

"Yes, that does come near what I was expecting. I was thinking more in terms of $54,000 to $59,000."

You, in effect, place the top of the employer's range into the bottom of your range. At this point you should be able to negotiate a salary of $55,000 to $57,000, depending on how much flexibility the employer has with salaries. Most employers have more flexibility than they are willing to admit.

Once you have placed your expectations at the top of the employer's salary range, you need to emphasize your value with *supports,* such as examples, illustrations, descriptions, definitions, statistics, comparisons, or testimonials. It is not enough to simply state you were "thinking" in a certain range; you must state why you believe you are worth what you want. Using statistics and comparisons as your supports, you might say, for example:

"The salary surveys I have read indicate that for the position of __ _____ in this industry and region the salary is between $54,000 and $59,000. Since, as we have discussed, I have extensive ex-

perience in all the areas you outlined, I would not need training in the job duties themselves—just a brief orientation to the operating procedures you use here at _____. I'm sure I could be up and running in this job within a week or two. Taking everything in consideration—especially my skills and experience and what I see as my future contributions here—I really feel a salary of $58,000 is fair compensation. Is this possible here at _____?"

Another option is to ask the employer for time to think about the salary offer. You want to sleep on it for a day or two. A common professional courtesy is to give you at least 48 hours to consider an offer. During this time, you may want to carefully examine the job. Is it worth what you are being offered? Can you do better? What are other employers offering for comparable positions? If one or two other employers are considering you for a job, let this employer know his or her job is not the only one under consideration. Let the employer know you may be in demand elsewhere. This should give you a better bargaining position. Contact the other employers and let them know you have a job offer and that you would like to have your application status with them clarified before you make any decisions with

> How you negotiate your salary will affect your future relations with the employer.

the other employer. Depending on how much flexibility an employer may have to accelerate a hiring decision, you may be able to go back to the first employer with another job offer. With a second job offer in hand, you should greatly enhance your bargaining position.

In both recommended options, you need to keep in mind that you should always negotiate from a position of knowledge and strength—not because of need or greed. Learn about salaries for your occupation, establish your value, discover what the employer is willing to pay, and negotiate in a professional manner. For how you negotiate your salary will affect your future relations with the employer. In general, applicants who negotiate well will be treated well on the job.

Treat Benefits as Standard

Many employer will try to impress candidates with the benefits offered by the company. These might include retirement, bonuses, stock options, medical and life insurance, and cost of living adjustments. If the employer includes these benefits in the salary negotiations, do not be overly impressed. Most benefits are standard—they come with the job. When negotiating salary, it is best to talk about specific dollar figures.

On the other hand, if the salary offered by the employer does not meet your expectations, but you still want the job, you might try to negotiate for some benefits which are not considered standard. These might include longer paid vacations, some flextime, and profit sharing.

Offer a Renegotiation Option

You should make sure your future salary reflects your value. One approach to doing this is to reach an agreement to renegotiate your salary at a later date, perhaps in another six to eight months. Use this technique especially when you feel the final salary offer is less than what you are worth, but you want to accept the job. Employers often will agree to this provision since they have nothing to lose and much to gain if you are as productive as you tell them.

However, be prepared to renegotiate in both directions—up and down. If the employer does not want to give you the salary figure you want, you can create good will by proposing to negotiate the higher salary figure down after six months, if your performance does not meet the employer's expectations. On the other hand, you may accept this lower figure with the provision that the two of you will negotiate your salary up after six months, if you exceed the employer's expectations. It is preferable to start out high and negotiate down rather than start low and negotiate up.

Renegotiation provisions stress one very important point: you want to be paid on the basis of your performance. You demonstrate your professionalism, self-confidence, and competence by negotiating in this manner. More important, you ensure that the question of your monetary value will not be closed in the future. As you negotiate the present, you also negotiate your future with this as well as other employers.

Take Time Before Accepting

You should accept an offer only after reaching a salary agreement. If you jump at an offer, you may appear needy. Take time to consider your options. Remember, you are committing your time and effort in exchange for money and status. Is this the job you really want? Take some time to think about the offer before giving the employer a definite answer. But don't play hard-to-get and thereby create ill-will with your new employer.

While considering the offer, ask yourself several of the same questions you asked at the beginning of your job search:

- What do I want to be doing five years from now?

- How will this job affect my personal life?

- Do I want to travel?

- Do I know enough about the employer and the future of this organization?

- How have previous occupants of this position fared? Why did they have problems?

- Are there other jobs I'm considering which would better meet my goals?

Accepting a job is serious business. If you make a mistake, you could be locked into a very unhappy situation for a long time.

If you receive one job offer while considering another, you will be able to compare relative advantages and disadvantages. You also will have some external leverage for negotiating salary and benefits. While you should not play games, let the employer know you have alternative job offers. This communicates that you are in demand, others also know your value, and the employer's price is not the only one in town. Use this leverage to negotiate your salary, benefits, and job responsibilities.

If you get a job offer but you are considering other employers, let the others know you have a job offer. Telephone them to inquire about your status as well as inform them of the job offer. Sometimes this will prompt employers to make a hiring decision sooner than anticipated. In addition you will be informing them that you are in demand; they should seriously consider you before you get away!

Some job seekers play a bluffing game by telling employers they have alternative job offers even though they don't. Some candidates do this and get away with it. We don't recommend this approach. Not only is it dishonest, it will work to your disadvantage if the employer learns that you were lying. But more important, you should be selling yourself on the basis of your strengths rather than your deceit and greed. If you can't sell yourself honestly, don't expect to get along well on the job. When you compromise your integrity, you demean your value to others and yourself.

Your job search is not over with the job offer and acceptance. You need to set the stage. Be thoughtful by sending your new employer a nice thank-you letter. As outlined at the end of Chapter 11, this is one of the most effective letters to write for getting your new job off on the right foot. The employer will remember you as a thoughtful individual whom he looks forward to working with.

The whole point of our job search methods is to clearly communicate to employers that you are competent and worthy of being paid top dollar. If you follow our advice, you should do very well with employers in interviews and negotiating your salary as well as working on the job.

Translate Your Value Into Productivity For Others

One final word of advice. Many job seekers have unrealistic salary expectations and exaggerated notions of their worth to potential employers. Furthermore, some occupational groups appear overpaid for the type of skills they use and the quality of the work they produce. In recent years several unions began renegotiating contracts in a new direction—downwards. Unions gave back salary increases and benefits won in previous years in order to maintain job security in the face of deepening recessions. Workers in many industries were not in a position to further increase their salaries. Many employers believed salaries had become extremely inflated in relation to profits. Such salaries, in turn, created even more inflated salary expectations among job hunters.

Given the declining power of unions, turbulent economic conditions, the increased prevalence of "give-back" schemes, and greater emphasis on productivity and performance in the work place, many employers are reluctant to negotiate salaries upwards prior to seeing you perform in their organization. Especially in a tight job market, many employers feel they can maintain their ground on salary offers. After all, as more well qualified candidates glut the job market, many job seekers are willing to take lower salaries.

Given this situation, you may find it increasingly difficult to negotiate better salaries with employers. You will need to stress your value more than ever. For example, if you think you are worth $50,000 a year in salary, will you be productive enough to generate $300,000 of business for the company to justify that amount? If you can't translate your salary expectations into dollars and cents profits for the employer, perhaps you should not be negotiating at all!

Part III

CREATE YOUR OWN OPPORTUNITIES

16

Advance Your Career

The career decisions you make today will affect your career development tomorrow. Indeed, throughout this book we have tried to prepare you for making critical career choices for today and tomorrow. While we cannot predict the future, we do know you will gain greater control over your future when you use our careering and re-careering methods.

After negotiating the job offer, shaking hands, and feeling great for having succeeded in getting a job that is right for you, what's next? How do you get started on the right foot and continue to advance your career? In this chapter we suggest how to best handle your job and career future after congratulating yourself on a job search well done.

Take More Positive Actions

If you managed your interviews and salary negotiations in a professional manner, your new employer should view you in a positive light. Once you've completed the interview, negotiated the salary, and accepted the offer, you should do two things:

1. Send your new employer a thank you letter.

Never underestimate the power of a simple thank you letter. It may be the single most important action you take. Mention your appreciation for the professional manner in which you were hired and how pleased you are to be joining the organization. Reaffirm your goals and your commitment to producing results. This letter should be well received. After all, employers seldom receive such thoughtful letters, and your reaffirmation helps ease the employer's fears of hiring an untested quantity.

269

2. **Send thank you letters to those individuals who assisted you with your job search, especially those with whom you conducted informational and referral interviews.**

Tell them of your new position, thank them for their assistance, and offer your assistance in the future. Not only is this a nice and thoughtful thing to do, it also is a wise thing to do for your future.

Always remember your networks. You work with people who can help you in many ways. Take good care of your networks by sending a thank you letter and keeping in contact. In another few years you may be looking for another position. In addition, people in your network may later want to hire you away from your present employer. Since they know what you can do and they like you, they may want to keep you informed of new opportunities. While you will be developing new contacts and expanding your network in your new job, your former contacts should be remembered for future reference. An occasional letter, New Years card, or telephone call are thoughtful things to do.

Be Alert to Changing Job Requirements

In today's highly competitive and fast-paced work environments, the skills required for the job you have today may change tomorrow. Always make sure your on-the-job skills are up-to-date and that you are doing more than what you consider to be "your job." This may mean acquiring new skills and redefining your job in reference to changing organizational requirements. Individuals who unexpectedly become victims of downsizing are often ones who did a particularly job well but suddenly discover they have the wrong set of skills for an organization undergoing transformation as it attempts to become more competitive. Never assume the skills and experience you have today will be sufficient for the job tomorrow. Always define what you are doing today in terms of the larger organization. Ask yourself, for example, am I a continuing asset to what may be a rapidly changing organization? Will I be needed as much tomorrow as I am today?

Beware of Office Politics

After three months on the job, you should know who's who, who has clout, whom to avoid, and how to get things done in spite of people and their positions. In other words, you will become inducted into the informal structure of the organization. You should become aware of this structure and use it to your advantage.

While it goes without saying that you should perform in your job, you need more than just performance. You should understand the informal organization, develop new networks, and use them to advance your career. This means conducting an internal career advancement campaign as well as an annual career check-up.

Don't expect to advance by sitting around and doing your job, however good you may be. Power is distributed in organizations, and politics is often ubiquitous. Learn the power structure as well as how to play positive politics. For sound advice on this subject, see Andres J. DuBrin's *Winning in Office Politics* (Van Nostrand Reinhold) and Marilyn Moats Kennedy's *Office Politics* (Follett).

After a while many organizations appear to be similar in terms of the quality and quantity of politics. Intensely interpersonal jobs are the most political. Indeed, people are normally fired because of politics—not incompetence. What do you do, for example, if you find yourself working for a tyrannical or incompetent boss or a jealous co-worker is out to get you? Some organizational environments can be unhealthy for your professional development.

Conduct an Annual Career Check-Up

We recommend an annual career check-up. Take out your resume and review it. Ask yourself several questions:

- Am I achieving my objective?
- Has my objective changed?
- Is this job meeting my expectations?
- Am I doing what I'm good at and enjoy doing?
- Are my skills up-to-date for this job and organization?
- Is this job worth keeping?
- How can I best achieve career satisfaction either on this job or in another job or career?
- What other opportunities elsewhere might be better than this job?

Individuals should increasingly ask these questions in the turbulent job market of today and tomorrow.

Perhaps changing jobs is not the best alternative for you. If you encounter difficulties with your job, you should first assess the nature of the problem. Perhaps the problem can be resolved by working with your present employer. Many employers prefer this approach. They are learning that increased job satisfaction translates into less job stress and absenteeism as well as more profits for the company. Progressive employers want happy workers because they are productive employees. They view job-keeping and job-revitalization as excellent investments in their futures.

Alternatively, you may want to participate in an electronic job bank where you can literally keep yourself in the job market 24 hours a day, 365 days a year. Whether you are actively looking for a job or just keeping in touch with potential opportunities, participation in such a group may be a good way to conduct a career check-up on a regular basis. Indeed, we expect more and more individuals will include their resume in such databases as they begin looking at their futures in terms of careering and re-careering. Such organizations offer a new approach to the job search: no longer will you need to activate a job search campaign only when you lose your job or decide to change jobs. Electronic job banks allow you to remain active on the job market throughout your worklife. New and unexpected job opportunities may come your way even though you are perfectly happy with your current job. In other words, membership in such a group may result in employers coming to you rather than you seeking out employers by using the job search strategies and techniques outlined in this book. The concept of an annual career check-up may be replaced with the concept of a lifetime membership in a career health or fitness club. You keep your career healthy and fit by always keeping yourself, via your electronic resume, on the job market.

Use Job-Keeping and Advancement Strategies

Assuming you enjoy your work, how can you best ensure keeping your job as well as advancing your career in the future? What job-keeping skills should you possess for the career environments of today and tomorrow? How can you best avoid becoming a victim of cutbacks, politics, and terminations?

As we noted in Chapter 14, most employers want their employees to perform according to certain expectations. Hecklinger and Curtin in *Training for Life* (Kendall/Hunt) further expand these expectations into 13 basic job-keeping skills:

Critical Job-Keeping Skills

1. **Ability to do the job well:** develop your know-how and competence.

2. **Initiative:** work on your own without constant direction.

3. **Dependability:** being there when you are needed.

4. **Reliability:** getting the job done.

5. **Efficiency:** being accurate and capable.

6. **Loyalty:** being faithful.

7. **Maturity:** handling problems well.

8. **Cheerfulness:** being pleasant to be with.

9. **Helpfulness:** willing to pitch in and help out.

10. **Unselfishness:** helping in a bind even though it is not your responsibility.

11. **Perseverance:** carrying on with a tedious project.

12. **Responsibility:** taking care of your duties.

13. **Creativity:** looking for new ways to solve your employer's problems.

While using these skills will not ensure job security, they will most likely enhance your security and potential for advancement.

A fourteenth job-keeping skill—managing your political environment—is one employers don't like to talk about. It may well be more important than all the other job-keeping skills. Many people who get fired are victims of political assassinations rather than failures at meeting the bosses' job performance expectations or scoring well on the annual performance appraisal.

You must become politically sophisticated at the game of office politics in order to survive in many jobs. For example, what might happen if the boss you have a good working relationship with today is replaced tomorrow by someone you don't know or by someone you know but don't like? By no fault of your own—except having been associated with a particular mentor or patron—you may become a victim of the new bosses' house cleaning. Accordingly, you get a two-hour notice to clean out your desk and get out. Such political assassinations are common occurrences in the publishing, advertising, media, and other businesses.

Hecklinger and Curtin identify eight survival tactics that can be used to minimize the uncertainty and instability surrounding many jobs today:

Eight Job Survival Tactics

1. **Learn to read danger signals.** Beware of cutbacks, layoffs, and firings before they occur. Adjust to the danger signals by securing your job or by looking for another job.

2. **Document your achievements.** Keep a record of what you accomplish—problems you solve, contributions you make to improving productivity and profits.

3. **Expand your horizons.** Become more aware of other areas in the company and acquire skills for performing other jobs. The more skills you have, the more valuable you should be to the company.

4. **Prepare for your next job.** Seek more training through:

   - apprenticeships
   - community colleges
   - weekend colleges
   - private, trade, or technical schools
   - home study through correspondence courses
   - industrial training programs
   - government training programs—U.S. Department of Agriculture, for example
   - military training
   - cooperative education
   - four-year college or university

5. **Promote yourself.** Talk about you accomplishments with co-workers and supervisors—but don't boast. Keep them informed of what you are doing; let them know you are available for promotion.

6. **Attach yourself to a mentor or sponsor.** Find someone in a position of influence and power whom you admire and who can help you acquire more responsibilities, skills, and advancement. Avoid currying favor.

7. **Continue informational interviewing.** Educate yourself as well as expand your interpersonal network of job contacts by regularly talking to people about their jobs and careers.

8. **Use your motivated abilities and skills.** Success tends to attract more success. Regularly use the abilities and skills you enjoy in different everyday settings.

The most important thing you can do now is to assess your present situation as well as identify what you want to do in the future with your career and life. You may conclude that your job is not worth keeping!

Assess and Change When Necessary

We are not proposing disloyalty to employers or regular job-hopping. Instead, we believe in the great American principle of "self-interest rightly understood"; your first obligation is to yourself. No one owes you a job, and neither should you feel you owe someone your career. Jobs and careers should not be life sentences. Periodically assess your career health and feel free to make changes when necessary. You owe it to yourself and others around you to be your very best self.

Since many jobs change for the worse, it may not be worth staying around for headaches and ulcers. If the organization does not meet your career expectations, use the same job search methods that got you into the organization. Be prepared to bail out for greener pastures by doing your job research and conducting informational and referral interviews. While the grass may not always be greener on the other side, many times it is; you will know by conducting another job search.

> **Jobs and careers should not be life sentences. Periodically assess your career health and feel free to make changes when necessary.**

Revitalize Your Job

Assuming you know how to survive on your job, what do you do if you experience burnout and high levels of job stress, or are just plain bored with your job? A job change, rather than resolving these problems, may lead to a repetition of the same patterns elsewhere. Techniques for changing the nature of your present job may prove to be your best option.

Most people will sometime experience what Marilyn Moats Kennedy (*Career Knockouts*, Follett) calls the "Killer Bs": blockage, boredom, and burnout. What can individuals do to make their jobs less stressful, more interesting, and more rewarding? One answer is found in techniques collectively referred to as "job revitalization."

Job-revitalization involves changing work patterns. It requires you to take risks. Again, you need to evaluate your present situation, outline your career and life goals, and develop and implement a plan of action. A job-revitalization campaign may include meeting with your superior to develop an on-the-job career development plan. Set goals with your boss and discuss with him or her how you can best meet these goals on the job. If your boss is not familiar with career development and job-revitalization alternatives, suggest some of these options:

- Rotating jobs
- Redesigning your job
- Creating a new position
- Promotions
- Enlarging your job duties and responsibilities
- Sabbatical or leave of absence
- Part-time work

- Flextime scheduling
- Job sharing
- Retraining or educational programs
- Internship

Perhaps your supervisor can think of other options which would be acceptable to company policy as well as productive for both you and the organization.

More and more companies are recognizing the value of introducing career development programs and encouraging job-revitalization among their employees. They are learning it is more cost-effective to retain good employees by offering them new job options for career growth within the organization than to see them go. Such programs and policies are congruent with the productivity and profit goals of organizations. They are good management practices. As organizations in the coming decade stress greater productivity, they will place more emphasis on career development and job-revitalization.

Prepare For Change

You should prepare yourself for the job realities associated with a society that is undergoing major structural changes. This means avoiding organizations, careers, and jobs that are declining as well as knowing what you do well and enjoy doing. It also means regularly acquiring the necessary training and retraining to function in a turbulent job market. And it means using your career planning skills to effectively career and re-career in the decades ahead. If you do this, you should be well prepared to turn turbulence into new opportunities and to acquire new jobs which will become exciting and satisfying challenges. Above all, you will be fit for the jobs and careers of the future.

17

Find Your Ideal Place to Live and Work

Relocation is an important job concern for millions of Americans. Indeed, most people change residences as frequently as they change jobs. One in every five families moves to a different residence each year; the average person changes addresses eleven times during their life. Each year approximately 7 million Americans move to another state. Relocation often means changing jobs and lifestyles.

People relocate for many reasons. Some are forced to relocate because of a company policy that routinely moves personnel from one branch office to another or from headquarters to field offices, and vice versa. Others choose to relocate when their company closes in one community, consolidates its operations in another community, or opens a new office elsewhere. And still others choose to seek employment in communities that offer better job opportunities or more attractive lifestyles. For them, relocation becomes another strategy in their arsenal of job search techniques.

Whether you are forced to relocate due to company policies or you seek new opportunities in other communities, chances are you will consider relocating sometime in the decade ahead. When you are faced with a relocation decision, you need to be prepared to deal with many new job, community, and lifestyle issues.

Relocate to Career and Re-Career

Where will you be working and living next year, five years, or ten years from today? If you had the freedom to pick up and move today, where would you love to live? Choosing where you want to live can be just as important as choosing what you want to do. Such a choice involves making career and lifestyle changes.

When you conduct a job search, you do so by targeting specific employers in particular communities. In most cases, individuals will conduct their job search in the same community in which they live. For other people, moving to another community is desirable for career and lifestyle purposes. And for others, unemployment may be preferred to leaving their present community.

Whatever your choices, you should weigh the relative costs and benefits of relocating to a new community where job opportunities for someone with your skills may be plentiful. If you live in a declining community or one experiencing little economic growth, job and career opportunities for you may be very limited. You should consider whether it would be better for you to examine job opportunities in other communities which may offer greater long-term career advancement as well as more opportunities for careering and re-careering in the future.

In recent years economic development has shifted toward the West, Southwest, and Southeast as well as to selected metropolitan areas in the East, South, Midwest, and Plains states. Millions of job seekers will continue to migrate to these areas in the decade ahead in response to growing job opportunities. Perhaps you, too, will look toward these areas as you change jobs and careers in the future.

In this chapter we examine how to conduct both a long-distance and a community-based job search campaign. We use the example of Washington, DC to illustrate the importance of conducting community research as well as for identifying alternative job networks. Nowhere do we recommend that you pull up stakes and take to the road in search of new opportunities. Many people did so in the 1980s as they headed for the reputed promised lands of Houston and Denver. As the booming economies in these communities went bust by the mid-1980s, many of these people experienced a new round of unemployment. The situation is likely to happen in today's reputed promised lands for the decade ahead—Seattle, Denver, Las Vegas, Cincinnati, St. Louis, Philadelphia, Boston, and Atlanta.

Don't ever take to the road until you have done your homework by researching communities, organizations, and individuals as well as created the necessary *bridges* for contacting employers in a new community. Most important, be sure you have the appropriate work-content and networking skills for finding employment appropriate for specific communities.

Target Communities

Many people are attached to their communities. Friends, relatives, churches, schools, businesses, and neighborhoods provide an important sense of identity which is difficult to leave for a community of strangers. Military and diplomatic personnel—the truly transient groups in society—may be the only ones accustomed to moving to new communities every few years.

The increased mobility of society is partly due to the nature of the job market. Many people voluntarily move to where job opportunities are most plentiful. Thus, Atlanta becomes a boom city with hundreds of additional cars entering the already congested freeways each week. The corporate structure of large businesses, with branches geographically spread throughout the national production and distribution system, requires the movement of key personnel from one location to another—much like military and diplomatic personnel.

When you begin your job search, you face two alternative community approaches. You can concentrate on a particular job, regardless of its geographic setting, or you can focus on one or two communities. The first approach, which we term follow-the-job, is widely used by migrant farm workers, cowboys, bank robbers, mercenaries, oil riggers, construction workers, newspaper reporters, college and university professors, and city managers. These people move to where the jobs are in their particular profession. Not surprising, many of these job seekers end up in boring communities which may limit their lifestyle options.

If you *follow-the-job*, you will need to link into a geographically mobile communication system for identifying job opportunities. This often means subscribing to specialized trade publications, maintaining contacts with fellow professionals in other communities, joining a nationwide electronic resume and networking bank, or creatively advertising yourself to prospective employers through newspaper ads or letter blitzes.

On the other hand, you may want to *target a community*. This may mean remaining in your present community or locating a community you find especially attractive because of job opportunities, climate, recreation, or social and cultural environments. Regardless of rumored job opportunities, many people, for instance, would not move to North Dakota—the state with the lowest unemployment rate in the country (2.5% in October 1996)—or to the "deep South" where the weather is relatively hot and humid and where the people display marked linguistic, social, and cultural differences. The same is true for Southerners who are not particularly interested in moving to what are reputed to be cold, dreary, and crime ridden northern cities. At the same time, Seattle, Madison (WI), Gainesville (FL), Philadelphia, Raleigh-Durham, Minneapolis, Austin, Boston, Baltimore, Cincinnati, Nashville, Denver, Ft. Lauderdale, Las Vegas, St. Louis, and Washington, DC are reputed to be the new promised lands for many people. Seeming oases of prosperity and centers for attractive urban lifestyles, these cities are on the community target list of many job seekers.

We recommend using this second approach of targeting specific communities. The follow-the-job approach is okay if you are young, adventuresome, or desperate; you find yourself in a geographically mobile profession; your career takes precedence over all other aspects of your life; or you have a bad case of wanderlust and thus let others arrange your travel plans. By targeting a community, your job search will be more manageable. Furthermore, moving to another community can be a liberating experience which will have a positive effect on both your professional and personal lives.

Why not find a great job in a community you really love? Fortunately you live in a very large country consisting of numerous communities that offer a terrific range of career and lifestyle opportunities. Let's identify some communities that might be a good "fit" for you as well as eliminate many which you may wish to avoid.

Know the Growing States and Communities

Frictional unemployment—the geographic separation of underemployed and unemployed individuals from high labor demand regions and communities—should present new options for you. Numerous job opportunities may be available if you are willing to relocate.

As noted in the following statistics, unemployment during the later half of the 1980s was unevenly distributed among the states.

Unemployment in the States, 1987

	1000's of Persons	Percentage
West Virginia	116	15.0
Michigan	488	11.2
Alabama	200	11.1
Mississippi	116	10.8
Louisiana	194	10.0
Alaska	25	10.0
Washington	194	9.5
Ohio	481	9.4
Oregon	125	9.4
Kentucky	160	9.3
Illinois	511	9.1
Washington, DC	290	9.1
Pennsylvania	499	9.1
Arkansas	93	8.9
Indiana	226	8.6
Tennessee	190	8.6
North Dakota	17	8.1
Nevada	39	7.8
California	972	7.8
New Mexico	47	7.5
Montana	30	7.4
Wisconsin	176	7.3
Missouri	172	7.2
Idaho	33	7.2
New York	584	7.2
South Carolina	105	7.1
Oklahoma	109	7.0
Iowa	100	7.0
North Carolina	205	6.7
Utah	47	6.5
Minnesota	141	6.3

Florida	322	6.3
Wyoming	16	6.3
New Jersey	236	6.2
Delaware	19	6.2
New Hampshire	34	6.1
Maine	34	6.1
Georgia	166	6.0
Texas	466	5.9
Colorado	96	5.6
Hawaii	27	5.6
Maryland	121	5.4
Rhode Island	26	5.3
Vermont	14	5.2
Kansas	63	5.2
Virginia	143	5.0
Arizona	71	5.0
Massachusetts	145	4.8
Connecticut	77	4.6
Nebraska	35	4.4
South Dakota	15	4.3

Unemployment was most pronounced in the states of West Virginia, Michigan, Alabama, Mississippi, and Louisiana. South Dakota, Nebraska, Connecticut, Massachusetts, and Arizona had the lowest unemployment rates.

These patterns of unemployment shifted significantly in the 1990s in response to a restructured and revitalized economy. In February 1995, for example, unemployment nationwide stood at 5.4 percent. It was differentially distributed by state and metropolitan areas as follows:

Unemployment by State and Metropolitan Areas
(October, 1996)

	Number Unemployed	Percentage
Alabama	**104,300**	**5.0**
Birmingham		5.1
Huntsville		3.3
Mobile		3.2
Montgomery		4.4
Tuscaloosa		3.5
Alaska	**22,500**	**7.2**
Anchorage		4.9
Arizona	**119,800**	**5.6**
Phoenix-Mesa		4.1
Tucson		4.1

Arkansas 69,000 **5.5**
   Fayetteville-Springdale-Rogers 3.0
   Fort Smith 4.7
   Little Rock-North Little Rock 3.5
   Pine Bluff 7.7

California 1,069,200 **6.9**
   Bakersfield 12.8
   Fresno 13.0
   Los Angeles-Long Beach 7.2
   Modesto 12.8
   Oakland 4.6
   Orange County 3.8
   Riverside-San Bernardino 7.4
   Sacramento 5.4
   Salinas 6.8
   San Diego 4.8
   San Francisco 3.6
   San Jose 3.5
   Santa Barbara-Santa Maria-Lompoc 3.5
   Santa Rose-Petaluma 3.7
   Stockton 9.6
   Vallejo-Fairfield-Napa 6.6
   Ventura 6.9

Colorado 78,900 **3.8**
   Boulder-Longmont 3.2
   Colorado Springs 3.9
   Denver 3.2

Connecticut 87,600 **5.0**
   Bridgeport 5.4
   Danbury 3.1
   Hartford 4.8
   New Haven-Meriden 4.7
   New London-Norwich 4.9
   Stamford-Norwalk 2.9
   Waterbury 5.0

Delaware 19,900 **5.2**
   Dover 4.5
   Wilmington 6.1

District of Columbia 22,400 **8.4**
   Washington (includes interstate) 6.1

Florida 359,100 **5.1**
   Daytona Beach 3.9
   Fort Lauderdale 5.0
   Fort Myers-Cape Coral 3.5
   Gainesville 2.6
   Jacksonville 3.6
   Lakeland-Winter Haven 7.3
   Melbourne-Titusville-Palm Bay 5.2

Miami-Hialeah		7.4
Orlando		3.6
Pensacola		3.5
Sarasota-Bradenton		3.4
Tallahassee		3.0
Tampa-St. Petersburg-Clearwater		3.7
West Palm Beach-Boca Raton		7.5
Georgia	**162,900**	**4.3**
Albany		6.0
Athens		2.9
Atlanta		4.0
Augusta-Aiken		6.8
Columbus		5.1
Macon		4.9
Savannah		4.6
Hawaii	**32,500**	**5.5**
Honolulu		4.6
Idaho	**30,400**	**4.8**
Boise City		3.3
Illinois	**314,000**	**4.8**
Bloomington		2.0
Champaign-Urbana		2.9
Chicago		4.6
Davenport-Moline-Rock Island		4.6
Decatur		3.5
Kankakee		5.1
Peoria-Pekin		5.1
Rockford		3.8
Springfield		4.0
Indiana	**119,800**	**3.9**
Bloomington		2.0
Elkhart-Goshen		3.5
Evansville-Henderson		3.8
Fort Wayne		2.9
Gary		4.4
Indianapolis		2.9
Kokomo		3.0
Lafayette		2.2
Muncie		3.8
South Bend		3.8
Terre Haute		5.0
Iowa	**52,800**	**3.3**
Cedar Rapids		2.1
Des Moines		2.4
Dubuque		3.6
Iowa City		3.6
Sioux City		2.9
Waterloo-Cedar Falls		3.5

Kansas	**55,700**	**4.1**
Lawrence		4.2
Topeka		5.3
Wichita		3.7
Kentucky	**90,300**	**4.4**
Lexington		2.4
Louisville		3.7
Owensboro		4.5
Louisiana	**146,400**	**7.2**
Alexandria		7.0
Baton Rouge		5.8
Houma		4.1
Lafayette		6.1
Lake Charles		7.1
Monroe		6.6
New Orleans		6.7
Shreveport-Bossier City		7.3
Maine	**33,500**	**5.0**
Lewiston-Auburn		4.9
Portland		2.4
Maryland	**129,400**	**4.6**
Baltimore		5.1
Massachusetts	**126,700**	**4.1**
Barnstable-Yarmouth		3.6
Boston		3.2
Brockton		4.4
Fitchburg-Leominster		4.4
Lawrence		5.3
Lowell		3.9
New Bedford		6.5
Pittsfield		4.4
Springfield		3.7
Worcester		3.2
Michigan	**234,500**	**4.8**
Ann Arbor		2.5
Benton Harbor		5.6
Detroit		3.9
Flint		5.9
Grand Rapids-Muskegon-Holland		3.6
Jackson		4.5
Kalamazoo-Battle Creek		3.8
Lansing-East Lansing		3.1
Saginaw-Bay City-Midland		4.0
Minnesota	**94,200**	**3.6**
Duluth-Superior		4.4
Minneapolis-St. Paul		2.9
Rochester		2.4

St. Cloud		3.9
Mississippi	**73,300**	**5.8**
Jackson		3.2
Missouri	**117,300**	**4.1**
Kansas City		3.4
St. Louis LMA		3.7
Springfield		2.7
Montana	**22,300**	**4.9**
Nebraska	**24,900**	**2.7**
Lincoln		2.4
Omaha		2.7
Nevada	**44,100**	**5.2**
Las Vegas		5.3
Reno		3.8
New Hampshire	**27,700**	**4.4**
Manchester		3.6
Nashua		4.2
Portsmouth-Rochester		3.5
New Jersey	**252,300**	**6.1**
Atlantic-Cape May		8.4
Bergen-Passaic		5.9
Jersey City		8.7
Middlesex-Somerset-Hunterdon		4.2
Monmouth-Ocean		5.1
Newark		5.7
Trenton		5.2
Vineland-Millville-Bridgeton		8.3
New Mexico	**57,300**	**7.0**
Albuquerque		4.7
Las Cruces		7.9
Santa Fe		4.3
New York	**505,300**	**5.9**
Albany-Schenectady-Troy		3.9
Binghamton		3.6
Buffalo-Niagara Falls		4.6
Dutchess County		4.0
Elmira		3.8
Glens Falls		5.0
Nassau-Suffolk		3.7
New York		7.6
New York City		8.3
Newburgh		3.9
Rochester		3.5
Syracuse		4.2
Utica-Rome		4.3

North Carolina	**158,200**	**4.2**
Asheville		2.9
Charlotte-Gastonia-Rock Hill		3.6
Greensboro-Winston-Salem-High Point		3.2
Raleigh-Durham-Chapel Hill		2.3
North Dakota	**8,700**	**2.5**
Bismarck		2.0
Fargo-Moorhead		1.5
Grand Forks		1.5
Ohio	**270,000**	**4.7**
Akron		4.1
Canton-Massillon		4.6
Cincinnati		3.7
Cleveland-Lorain-Elyria		4.8
Columbus		2.8
Dayton-Springfield		4.0
Hamilton-Middletown		3.6
Lima		5.5
Mansfield		5.3
Steubenville-Weirton		5.5
Toledo		4.1
Youngstown-Warren		5.3
Oklahoma	**64,200**	**4.0**
Enid		3.4
Lawton		4.5
Oklahoma City		3.4
Tulsa		3.4
Oregon	**90,400**	**5.2**
Eugene-Springfield		4.6
Medford-Ashland		6.2
Portland-Vancouver		4.1
Salem		4.2
Pennsylvania	**293,800**	**5.0**
Allentown-Bethlehem-Easton		4.7
Altoona		4.5
Erie		4.5
Harrisburg-Lebanon-Carlisle		2.7
Johnstown		6.9
Lancaster		2.6
Philadelphia		5.0
Pittsburgh		4.1
Reading		3.6
Scranton-Wilkes-Barre-Hazelton		6.0
Sharon		3.5
State College		2.5
Williamsport		5.2
York		3.6

Rhode Island	**21,400**	**4.3**
Providence-Fall River-Warwick		4.7
South Carolina	**113,400**	**6.1**
Charleston		5.8
Columbia		3.7
Greenville-Spartanburg-Anderson		4.2
South Dakota	**11,000**	**2.8**
Rapid City		2.5
Sioux Falls		1.6
Tennessee	**135,700**	**4.9**
Chattanooga		4.0
Johnson City-Kingsport-Bristol		4.1
Knoxville		3.4
Memphis		4.1
Nashville		3.2
Texas	**510,400**	**5.2**
Abilene		3.9
Amarillo		3.5
Austin-San Marcos		2.9
Beaumont-Port Arthur		7.9
Brazoria		5.8
Brownsville-Harlingen-San Benito		10.7
Bryan-College Station		2.0
Corpus Christi		8.0
Dallas		3.5
El Paso		10.8
Fort Worth-Arlington		3.3
Galveston-Texas City		7.2
Houston		4.6
Killeen-Temple		4.3
Laredo		10.4
Longview-Marshall		6.8
Lubbock		3.1
McAllen-Edinburg-Mission		16.1
Odessa-Midland		4.8
San Angelo		3.0
San Antonio		3.7
Sherman-Denison		4.0
Texarkana		6.7
Tyler		6.0
Victoria		4.4
Waco		3.8
Wichita Falls		3.8
Utah	**31,900**	**3.1**
Provo-Orem		2.5
Salt Lake City-Odgen		2.9
Vermont	**14,800**	**4.5**
Burlington		2.9

Virginia	**147,100**	**4.2**
Charlottesville		2.3
Danville		6.1
Lynchburg		3.2
Norfolk-Virginia Beach-Newport News		4.8
Richmond-Petersburg		3.7
Roanoke		2.8
Washington	**167,000**	**5.8**
Seattle-Bellevue-Everett		4.3
Spokane		4.8
Tacoma		5.5
West Virginia	**59,500**	**7.4**
Charleston		4.7
Huntington-Ashland		6.5
Parkersburg-Marietta		5.2
Wheeling		4.1
Wisconsin	**90,400**	**3.1**
Appleton-Oshkosh-Neenah		2.0
Eau Claire		2.3
Green Bay		2.4
Janesville-Beloit		2.9
Kenosha		2.9
La Crosse		2.0
Madison		1.2
Milwaukee-Waukesha		3.0
Racine		3.2
Sheboygan		2.2
Wausau		2.2
Wyoming	**12,100**	**4.7**
Casper		5.2
Puerto Rico	**166,000**	**12.8**
Caguas		11.8
Mayaguez		13.9
Ponce		17.6
San Juan-Bayamon		10.4

NOTE: State figures are seasonally adjusted; metropolitan area figures are not seasonally adjusted.

Throughout the coming decade we expect Colorado, Georgia, Idaho, Illinois, Indiana, Iowa, Kansas, Kentucky, Massachusetts, Michigan, Minnesota, Montana, Nebraska, New Hampshire, North Carolina, North Dakota, Oklahoma, Rhode Island, South Dakota, Tennessee, Utah, Vermont, Virginia, and Wisconsin to have above average employment rates. Numerous communities within these states, especially in the 250,000 to 500,000 population range, will offer some of the best job opportunities.

Growing regions and communities are relatively predictable for the

1990s and beyond. Several metropolitan areas that experienced high population growth rates in the 1970s continued with similar growth rates in the 1980s:

- Los Angeles-Long Beach, San Francisco-Oakland, CA
- Washington, DC
- Baltimore, MD
- Dallas-Fort Worth, TX
- Houston, TX
- Minneapolis-St. Paul, MN
- Atlanta, GA
- Anaheim-Santa Ana-Garden Grove, CA
- San Diego, CA
- Denver-Boulder, CO
- Seattle-Everett, WA
- Miami, FL
- Tampa-St. Petersburg, FL
- Riverside-San Bernardino-Ontario, CA
- Phoenix, AZ
- Portland, OR
- San Antonio, TX
- Fort Lauderdale-Hollywood, FL
- Salt Lake City-Ogden, UT

Many of these same metropolitan areas will continue to be growth areas throughout the 1990s and into the 21st century. The major exception will be California. This state has been hard hit by defense cutbacks and a large influx of unskilled immigrant labor. While most states in the mid-1990s climbed out of the recession of the early 1990s, California's economy remained mired in recession; its recovery would be slow. For the first time in decades, California was no longer a promised land for job seekers. Indeed, hundreds of individuals were leaving California each week in search of employment in other states. However, by late 1996, out-migration had slowed considerably and California may have begun its recovery.

The fastest growing metropolitan areas between 1986 and 1993 were those listed on page 290. Disproportionately found in the West, Southwest and Southeast, many of these communities, along with a few in the Northeast and Midwest, should continue with medium to high growth rates throughout the remainder of the 1990s. Depending on the extent of another energy crisis, several communities in the energy rich Rocky Mountain states may once again become boom towns. Communities with large concentrations of high-tech and service industries, supported by a strong higher education infrastructure—will continue to expand both demographically and economically. Cities with large college and university complexes, such as Boston, Minneapolis-St. Paul, Omaha, Raleigh-Durham-Chapel Hill, Oklahoma City, Salt Lake City, Madison (WI), Columbia (SC), Knoxville,

Fastest Growing Metro Areas, 1986-1993

City	1986	1993	% Gain
Punta Gorda, FL	84,100	132,055	57.0
Las Vegas, NV-AZ	661,800	983,313	48.6
Riverside-San Bernardino, CA	2,001,100	2,892,733	44.6
Yuma, AZ	86,800	124,026	42.9
Naples, FL	121,400	172,909	42.4
Fort Pierce-Port St. Lucie, FL	205,700	282,012	37.1
Fort Myers-Cape Coral, FL	279,100	381,263	36.6
Orlando, FL	1,030,900	1,388,941	34.7
Modesto, CA	316,600	416,794	31.6
West Palm Beach-Boca Raton, FL	755,600	973,630	28.9
Daytona Beach, FL	339,100	435,637	28.5
Sarasota-Bradenton, FL	424,700	542,530	27.7
Myrtle Beach, SC	130,600	164,912	26.3
Santa Rosa, CA	343,600	432,055	25.7
Ocala, FL	171,000	214,601	25.5

Atlanta, Austin (TX), Columbus (OH), San Francisco, Seattle, Honolulu, Iowa City, Ann Arbor, and Washington DC should experience steady employment growth in the decade ahead. These cities will also generate some of the best paying, high quality jobs.

We foresee major population and economic growth in and around several large cities: Seattle, Portland, Las Vegas, Salt Lake City-Ogden, Denver, Minneapolis-St. Paul, Rochester (MN), Milwaukee, Nashville, Dallas-Ft. Worth, Houston, Austin, San Antonio, Albuquerque, Phoenix, Gainesville (FL), Fort Lauderdale, Atlanta, Tampa-St. Petersburg, Raleigh-Durham, Pittsburgh, Philadelphia, Washington-Baltimore, Madison (WI), Boston, Indianapolis, Louisville, and Cleveland. We do not expect Southern California—especially the Los Angeles-San Diego corridor—to be a major growth region for population and jobs. While the California economy is slowly rebounding after a difficult recession—largely driven by its exports to newly revitalized Pacific Rim economies and Mexico—we do not expect California to transform itself into a new job mecca. Its recovery and future growth will be slow.

Even though the overall growth predictions point to the Northwest, Far West, and Southwest, these trends should not deter you from considering older cities in the Northeast and North Central regions. After all, nearly 2 million new jobs are created nationwide each year. New jobs will continue to develop in cities such as Chicago, Philadelphia, and New York; these are still the best places to pursue careers in the fields of banking, publishing, and advertising. Boston is again becoming an attractive employment center. Several communities in the Midwest—especially those with strong educational infrastructures—have rebounded as they transformed their local economies in the direction of new high-tech and service industries. Minneapolis-St. Paul, Madison, Chicago, Detroit, St. Louis, Kansas City, Indianapolis, Columbus, Cleveland, and Cincinnati in the Midwest and Philadelphia, Pittsburgh, Baltimore, Washington DC, Raleigh-Durham-Chapel Hill, and Atlanta in the central to southern Atlantic coast area will remain some of the best cities for jobs and lifestyles in the decade ahead.

Consider the Best Places to Work

If you contemplate relocating to a new community, you should consider communities that are experiencing low unemployment coupled with steady job growth as well as attractive lifestyles. A recent *Fortune Magazine* survey (November 11, 1996) identified fifteen cities as the best places to balance work and family life. These are places where you can have a good job as well as enjoy a fine lifestyle:

1. Seattle
2. Denver
3. Philadelphia
4. Minneapolis
5. Raleigh-Durham
6. St. Louis
7. Cincinnati
8. Washington, DC
9. Pittsburgh
10. Dallas-Fort Worth
11. Atlanta
12. Baltimore
13. Boston
14. Milwaukee
15. Nashville

If you are planning to go international, you might want to include these great international cities in your job search plans:

1. Toronto
2. London
3. Singapore
4. Paris
5. Hong Kong

Located outside the Sunbelt, most of the American cities are likely to experience solid growth in the decade ahead. The cities of Raleigh-Durham and Minneapolis are already star performers because of their extensive medical facilities and high-tech infrastructure as well as their attractive lifestyles. These two cities will probably continue to be great growth communities during the coming decade. They will generate a disproportionate number of high paying jobs due to the high quality nature of their jobs and workforces. They may well provide models of a new economy and workforce for the 21st century.

Find the Best Place to Live

Community growth and decline trends should be considered as part of your job and career options. If you live in a declining community with few opportunities for your skills and interests, seriously consider relocating to a growth community. Depressed communities simply do not generate enough jobs for their populations. Many communities with populations of 100,000 to 500,000 offer a nice variety of job and lifestyle options.

Except for a few people, one's work should not become one's life. After all, there are more important things in life than one's work. Different communities offer many life choices in addition to jobs. Economic development and job generation are only two of many important community choice concerns. Using nine indicators of quality living, the 1997 edition of *Places Rated Almanac* identifies what it considers to be the 50 best communities in North America (USA and Canada) in terms of their mix of cost of living, job outlook, transportation, education, health care, crime, the arts, recreation, and climate:

North America's Top 50 Metro Areas

1. Orange County, CA
2. Seattle-Bellevue-Everett, WA
3. Houston, TX
4. Washington, DC-MD-VA-WV
5. Phoenix, AZ
6. Minneapolis-St. Paul, MN-WI
7. Atlanta, GA
8. Tampa-St. Petersburg-Clearwater, FL
9. San Diego, CA
10. Philadelphia, PA-NJ
11. San Jose, CA
12. Long Island, NY
13. Riverside-San Bernardino, CA
14. Pittsburgh, PA
15. Toronto, OH
16. Portland-Vancouver, OR-WA
17. Oakland, CA

18. Denver, CO
19. Cincinnati, OH-KY-IN
20. San Francisco, CA
21. Detroit, MI
22. Dallas, TX
23. Chicago, IL
24. Miami, FL
25. Cleveland-Lorain-Elyria, OH
26. Salt Lake City-Ogden, UT
27. San Antonio, TX
28. Milwaukee-Waukesha, WI
29. Orlando, FL
30. Vancouver, BC
31. Montreal, PQ
32. Raleigh-Durham-Chapel Hill, NC
33. Fort Lauderdale, FL
34. Los Angeles-Long Beach, CA
35. New Orleans, LA
36. Indianapolis, IN
37. Nashville, TN
38. Sacramento, CA
39. Kansas City, MO-KS
40. Rochester, NY
41. Richmond-Petersburg, VA
42. Norfolk-Virginia Beach-Newport News, VA-NC
43. Syracuse, NY
44. Ventura, CA
45. Austin-San Marcos, TX
46. Oklahoma City, OK
47. Middlesex-Somerset-Hunterdon, NJ
48. Montreal, PQ
49. Boston, MA
50. Omaha, NE-IA

These 1997 rankings have already changed in other surveys; they will undoubtedly change in the coming decade. It is best to consult the latest edition of *Places Rated Almanac* to see how particular communities rank according to each and every indicator. This book is available in most libraries, bookstores, and from Impact Publications.

Money Magazine's most recent annual survey (July 1996) of the best places to live came up with a different set of conclusions on the lifestyle side of the relocation equation. They found that when considering a community move respondents most valued safety, clean water, clean air, the availability of doctors and hospitals, housing appreciation, good schools, low property taxes, low income taxes, strong state government, and recession resistance. "Recent job growth" ranked 12th and "future job growth" ranked 15th amongst their concerns. Based on such values, *Money Magazine* identified the following 50 cities as the best places to live:

America's Top 50 Cities to Live In, 1996

1. Madison (WI)	26. Brevard County (FL)
2. Punta Gorda (FL)	27. Daytona Beach (FL)
3. Rochester (MN)	28. Boulder (CA)
4. Fort Lauderdale (FL)	29. Fort Pierce (FL)
5. Ann Arbor (MI)	30. Lafayette (IN)
6. Fort Myers/Cape Coral (FL)	31. Provo/Orem (UT)
7. Gainesville (FL)	32. Charlottesville (VA)
8. Austin (TX)	33. Fort Collins (CO)
9. Seattle (WA)	34. Phoenix (AZ)
10. Lakeland (FL)	35. Houston (TX)
11. Tampa/St. Petersburg (FL)	36. Sheboygan (WI)
12. Orlando (FL)	37. Ocala (FL)
13. San Francisco (CA)	38. Monmouth (NJ)
14. Fargo (ND)	39. Dothan (AL)
15. Naples (FL)	40. Los Angeles (CA)
16. San Diego (CA)	41. McAllen (TX)
17. San Antonio (TX)	42. Nashua (NH)
18. Fort Walton Beach (FL)	43. Brownsville (TX)
19. San Jose (CA)	44. Portsmouth (NH)
20. Jacksonville (FL)	45. College Station (TX)
21. Columbia (MO)	46. Abilene (TX)
22. Miami (FL)	47. Tucson (AZ)
23. Sarasota/Bradenton (CA)	48. Portland (OR)
24. Raleigh/Durham/Chapel Hill (NC)	49. Sioux Falls (SD)
25. West Palm Beach (FL)	50. Manchester (NH)

Most of their communities had populations ranging from 250,000 to 500,000. In fact, large cities did not do well in their survey. For example, six of the cities appearing on *Fortune's* top 15 list ranked much lower on the *Money's* list: Dallas (65th), Boston (69th), Minneapolis (87th), Atlanta (115th), Washington, DC (128th), and Philadelphia (233rd). The relative importance of jobs in comparison to other relocation concerns is perhaps best exemplified by McAllen, Texas which ranked as *Money's* 41st best place to live out of 300 communities. In October 1996 this city had one of the highest unemployment rates in the country—16.1%!

Seek Out the Best Employers

You might also want to consider some of America's best employers when identifying your ideal community. According to Robert Levering and Milton Moskowitz in their newest edition (1993) of *The 100 Best Companies to Work For in America,* the companies listed on pages 295-296 are the best ones to work for in America.

100 Best Companies in America

Company	Headquarters
Acipco	Birmingham, AL
Advanced Micro Devices	Sunnyvale, CA
Alagasco	Birmingham, AL
Anheuser-Busch	St. Louis, MO
Apogee Enterprise	Minneapolis, MN
Armstrong	Lancaster, PA
Avis	Garden City, NY
Baptist Hospital of Miami	Miami, FL
BE&K	Birmingham, AL
Ben & Jerry's Homemade	Waterbury, VT
Beth Israel Hospital Boston	Boston, MA
Leo Burnett	Chicago, IL
Chaparral Steel	Midlothian, TX
Compaq Computer	Houston, TX
Cooper Tire	Findlay, OH
Corning	Corning, NY
Cray Research	Eagan, MN
Cummins Engine	Columbus, TN
Dayton Hudson	Minneapolis, MN
John Deere	Moline, IL
Delta Air Lines	Atlanta, GA
Donnelly	Holland, MI
Du Pont	Wilmington, DE
A. G. Edwards	St. Louis, MO
Erie Insurance	Erie, PA
Federal Express	Memphis, TN
Fel-Pro	Skokie, IL
First Federal Bank of California	Santa Monica, CA
H. B. Fuller	St. Paul, MN
General Mills	Minneapolis, MN
Goldman Sachs	New York, NY
W. L. Gore & Associates	Newark, DE
Great Plains Software	Fargo, ND
Hallmark Cards	Kansas City, MO
Haworth	Holland, MI
Hersey Foods	Hersey, PA
Hewitt Associates	Lincolnshire, IL
Hewlett-Packard	Palo Alto, CA
Honda of America Manufacturing	Marysville, OH
IBM	Armonk, NY
Inland Steel	Chicago, IL
Intel	Santa Clara, CA
Johnson & Johnson	New Brunswick, NJ
SC Johnson Wax	Racine, WI
Kellogg	Battle Creek, MI
Knight-Ridder	Miami, FL
Lands' End	Dodgeville, WI
Lincoln Electric	Cleveland, OH
Los Angeles Dodgers	Los Angeles, CA

Lotus Development	Cambridge, MA
Lowe's	North Wilkesboro, NC
Lyondell Petrochemical	Houston, TX
Marquette Electronics	Milwaukee, WI
Mary Kay Cosmetics	Dallas, TX
McCormick	Hunt Valley, MD
Merck	Whitehouse Station, NJ
Methodist Hospital	Houston, TX
Microsoft	Redmond, CA
Herman Miller	Zeeland, MI
3M	St. Paul, MN
Moog	East Aurora, NY
J. P. Morgan	New York, NY
Morrison & Foerster	San Francisco, CA
Motorola	Schaumburg, IL
Nissan Motor Manufacturing	Smyrna, TN
Nordstrom	Seattle, WA
Northwestern Mutual Life	Milwaukee, WI
Odetics	Anaheim, CA
Patagonia	Ventura, CA
J. C. Penney	Plano, TX
Physio-Control	Redmond, WA
Pitney Bowes	Stamford, CT
Polaroid	Cambridge, MA
Preston Trucking	Preston, MD
Procter & Gamble	Cincinnati, OH
Publix Super Markets	Lakeland, FL
Quad/Graphics	Pewaukee, WI
Reader's Digest	Pleasantville, NY
Recreational Equipment, Inc.	Seattle, WA
Rosenbluth International	Philadelphia, PA
SAS Institute	Cary, NC
J. M. Smucker	Orrville, OH
Southwest Airlines	Dallas, TX
Springfield ReManufacturing	Springfield, MO
Springs	Fort Mill, SC
Steelcase	Grand Rapids, MI
Syntex	Palo Alto, CA
Tandem	Cupertino, CA
TDIndustries	Dallas, TX
Tennant	Minneapolis, MN
UNUM	Portland, ME
USAA	San Antonio, TX
U S WEST	Eaglewood, CO
Valassis Communications	Livonia, MI
Viking Freight System	San Jose, CA
Wal-Mart	Bentonville, AR
Wegmans	Rochester, NY
Weyerhaeuser	Tacoma, WA
Worthington Industries	Columbus, OH
Xerox	Stamford, CT

While the headquarters will be the main employment centers for most of these companies, please keep in mind that many of these companies—such as Federal Express, Delta Air Lines, Avis, IBM, Lowe's, J.C. Penney, Wal-Mart, and Nordstrom—have offices, plants, and stores in other locations throughout the United States as well as abroad. If you are interested in working for one of these companies, contact the headquarters for information on their other locations as well as refer to *The 100 Best Companies to Work For in America* for more detailed information on these companies.

Look For Solid Metro Areas

Metropolitan areas exhibiting strong performance in job growth should prove to be very attractive. *Places Rated Almanac* found these metropolitan areas to be the best for overall job growth through the year 2000:

1. Atlanta, GA
2. Dallas, TX
3. Houston, TX
4. Orange County, CA
5. San Diego, CA
6. Minneapolis-St. Paul, MN-WI
7. Phoenix-Mesa, AZ
8. Orlando, FL
9. Riverside-San Bernardino, CA
10. Seattle-Bellevue-Everett, WA
10. Washington, DC-MD-VA-WV
12. Raleigh-Durham-Chapel Hill, NC
13. Fort-Worth-Arlington, TX
14. Tampa-St. Petersburg-Clearwater, FL
15. Denver, CO

Many of these areas, such as Washington, DC and Minneapolis-St. Paul, are excellent places for young people to start their careers.

A. David Silver, author of *Quantum Companies*, identifies 100 of the most exciting, cutting-edge companies that appear destined to grow and redefine business in the 21st century. A disproportionate number of these companies are located in California and Massachusetts as well as represent the hot computer and health care fields. Indeed, 37 percent of these firms specialize in computers, electronics, and communications; 27 percent represent the closely related medical and pharmaceutical industries; and 30 percent of the companies are based in California.

Acxiom Corporation	Ascend Communications
American Medical Response	Atmel Corporation
Asante Technologies	Bay Networks

Better Education
The Body Shop International PLC
Cambridge Neuroscience
Cambridge Technology Partners
Catalina Marketing Corp.
C-Cube Microsystems
Cerner Corporation
Chipcom Corporation
Cirrus Logic
Computer Network Technology
Corel Corporation
Corrections Corporation of
    America
Davidson & Associates
    Decision Quest
Digital Link Corp.
Dionex Corporation
DNX Corporation
Ecoscience Corp.
Education Alternatives
Ensys Environmental Products
Envirotest Systems Corp.
Fore Systems
Frontier Insurance Group
GTI Corporation
Harmony Brook
Hauser Chemical Research
Health Management Associates
Healthdyne Technologies
Heart Technology
Hemosol
Homecare Management
Information America
Informex Corporation
Integrated Health Services
International High Tech Marketing
Invision Systems Corporation
Just for Feet
Landstar Systems
Life Resuscitation Technologies
Medicenter
Medicus Systems Corp
Medrad
Megahertz Holding Corp.
Mitek Surgical Products
Molten Metal Technology
Mothers Work
National Health Corp.

NetFrame Systems
Neurogen Corp.
Newbridge Networks Corp.
Nextel Communications
On Assignment
Orbital Sciences Corp.
Orthogene
Parametric Technology Corp.
Parce Place Systems
Phenix Biocomposites
Pleasant Company
Progressive Corp.
Qualcomm
Quantum Health Resources
Quorum Health Group
Res-Care
Research Management Consultants
Roper Industries
Ryka
Sentinel Systems
Shaman Pharmaceuticals
SRX
Stores Automated Systems
Sunrise Medical
Swift Transportation Co.
Sybase
Synaptic Pharmaceutical
Synopsys
Systemix
Tecnol Medical Products
Tetra Tech
Thermo Electron Corp.
3Com Corp.
Three-Five Systems
Transmedia Network
Tresp Associates
Vivra
Vivus
Wall Data
Whole Foods Market
Wholesome & Hearty Foods
Work/Family Directions
Workstation Technologies
Xilinx
Xircome
Zebra Technologies Corp.
Zia Metallugical Processes

Select a Location Properly

You and your family should take into consideration several factors and questions when deciding on which communities to target your job search. Start by asking yourself these questions:

- What's most important to me/us in making a move—environment, health care, safety, education, employment, economy, taxes, culture, recreation, climate?

- Where would I/we ideally like to live for the next 5, 10, or 20 years?

- What is the relative cost of living?

- How attractive are the educational, social, recreational, and cultural opportunities?

- What are the economic and psychological costs of making a move?

- What job and career opportunities are there for me/us?

- How can I/we best conduct a job search in another community?

Many people answer these questions by remaining in their community or by targeting economically growing communities or ones offering excellent lifestyle options. The exodus from the declining industrial cities in the Northeast and North Central regions to the Sunbelt began in the 1960s, expanded in the 1970s, continued into the 1980s with the inclusion of the energy-rich Rocky Mountain states, and further expanded in the 1990s with high tech industries in the West. Several metropolitan areas in all regions, but especially in the West, will have abundant job opportunities for skilled workers in the decade ahead. Many of these communities also offer attractive lifestyles. Targeting a job search in metropolitan Seattle, San Francisco, Las Vegas, Denver, Phoenix, Dallas, St. Louis, Minneapolis, Atlanta, Raleigh-Durham, Nashville, and Boston may be a wise move. While these areas may experience numerous urban problems over the next decade, their problems are ones of growth—traffic congestion, pollution, city planning, crime, and housing shortages—not ones of decline. We believe it is better to experience the problems of growth than of decline, especially since growing economies are more likely to respond to their problems. In a situation of decline, your livelihood becomes threatened. In a situation of growth, your major problem may be fighting the traffic congestion in order to get to a job which offers a promising career.

New frontiers for renewed job and career prosperity abound throughout America if you are willing to pack your bags and move. But most such frontiers require highly skilled individuals, and there can be major financial costs in making such a move, especially if you are a homeowner. If you lack the necessary skills for industries in other communities, consider getting retrained before making a move. Unfortunately, many people making moves today do not have the necessary skills to succeed in many of today's growing communities.

Making a community move on your own involves taking risks. Many people, for example, are locked into financial obligations, such as a mortgaged house which doesn't sell well in what may be a depressed housing market. If you find yourself locked in financially, you may want to consider taking an immediate financial loss in anticipation of renewed prosperity in a community which is experiencing promising growth and prosperity. You may recoup your immediate losses within a year or two. However, you will have to pass through a transition period which can be difficult if you don't approach it in a positive, up-beat manner. The old saying, *"There is no gain without pain"* is appropriate in many situations involving community moves.

Consider Your Financial Costs

The financial costs of relocating will vary depending on your situation. They can be major, especially if you move to a community with high housing costs. Studies conducted by Runzheimer International, for example, found the average costs of relocating in 1995 to be $34,700 for homeowners and $8,938 for non-homeowners. The major costs include:

1. Search for housing—travel, child care, and associated expenses.

2. Closing costs on both the old and new homes.

3. Increases in mortgage payments or apartment rent.

4. Temporary living expenses.

5. Cost of a bridge, equity, or swing loan.

6. Costs of maintaining two residences during the relocation period—very high if the old home does not sell immediately.

7. Shipment of household goods.

8. Final moving expenses.

9. Possible increase in cost of living—property and sales taxes, food, utilities.

10. Travel and job search costs for working spouse.

11. Expenses for marketing a home or subletting an apartment.

12. Miscellaneous costs—deposits, decorating costs, fees, dues.

Housing can be a major cost if you move to a community with expensive housing. The National Association of Realtors reported the median home price for the top 25 metropolitan areas in November 1996 to be as follows:

Median Home Prices For the Top 25 Metropolitan Areas, 1996

1.	Honolulu, HI	$335,000
2.	San Francisco Bay Area, CA	$269,900
3.	Orange County, CA	$216,800
4.	Newark, NJ	$197,300
5.	Bergen/Passaic, NJ	$195,800
6.	Boston, MA	$195,300
7.	San Diego, CA	$173,600
8.	New York/Northern New Jersey-Long Island, NY-NJ-CT	$174,500
9.	Middlesex/Somerset/Hunterdon, NJ	$174,000
10.	Los Angeles Area, CA	$172,400
11.	Washington, DC/MD/VA	$164,100
12.	Seattle, WA	$163,800
13.	Nassau/Suffolk, NY	$161,800
14.	Chicago, IL	$153,400
15.	Monmouth/Ocean, NJ	$144,200
16.	Lake County, IL	$142,500
17.	Hartford, CT	$142,500
18.	Providence, RI	$139,400
19.	Reno, NV	$139,000
20.	Aurora/Elgin, IL	$138,400
21.	New Haven/Meriden, CT	$136,800
22.	Trenton, NJ	$136,500
23.	Raleigh/Durham, NC	$132,700
24.	Denver, CO	$132,300
25.	Colorado Springs, CO	$132,100

On the other hand, once you buy into these communities, your housing investment might appreciate. In the long-term, you will probably realize a return on your investment. The basic problem is initially buying into the higher priced housing, and especially if comparable housing was much less expensive in your last community.

When considering a community move, you should be aware of the relative cost of living in various communities. According to the U.S. Bureau of the Census, the following metropolitan areas exhibited the highest and lowest costs of living in 1995:

Highest Costs of Living, 1995

1. New York, NY
2. Honolulu, HI
3. San Francisco, CA
4. Marin County, CA
5. San Mateo County, CA
6. West Chester, NY
7. Boston, MA
8. Philadelphia, PA
9. Washington, DC
10. Ankorage, AK

Lowest Costs of Living, 1995

1. Ft. Smith, AR
2. Little Rock-North Little Rock, AR
3. Joplin, MO
4. Lincoln, NE
5. Johnson City-Kingsport-Bristol, TN
6. South Bend, IN
7. Tulsa, OK
8. Texarkana, TX
9. Bryan-College Station, TX
10. Clarksville-Hopkinsville, TN

Unfortunately, communities with the lowest cost of living also tend to have low rewards of living. Offering few job opportunities, many of these communities offer a disproportionate number of low paying jobs—the reason they have a low cost of living. Not surprising, communities with the highest cost of living tend to offer more job opportunities which also pay the highest wages. Our advice to people with marketable skills: consider heading for communities with a higher cost of living. You'll probably find better job opportunities and face quality lifestyle options in these places.

Do you hate commuting to a job? If you've ever driven to work in Los Angeles, Washington, DC, Chicago, or New York City, you know why many people hate commuting. They can easily spend two to three hours a day in the traffic trying to get to and from work. In 1997 Washington, DC, for example, ranked No. 1 in the country for per capita cost of wasted fuel and time: $820 a year per person.Therefore, you should consider the costs of commuting to and from work in different communities. Metropolitan areas with the longest and shortest average commutes include the following:

Longest Commute

1.	New York, NY	75.8 minutes
2.	Long Island, NY	64.6
3.	Washington, DC-MD-VA-WV	63.0
4.	Chicago, IL	61.5
5.	Riverside-San Bernardino, CA	59.3
6.	Orange County, NY	58.5
7.	Monmouth-Ocean, NJ	58.3
8.	Oakland, CA	57.5
9.	Houston, TX	56.9
10.	Vallejo-Fairfield-Napa, CA	56.8

Shortest Commute

1.	Bismarck, ND	27.1
2.	Grand Forks, ND-MN	27.4
3.	Cheyenne, WY	29.5
4.	Dubuque, IA	30.1
5.	Fargo-Moorhead, ND-MN	30.7
6.	Enid, OK	30.8
7.	Great Falls, MT	30.9
8.	Sheboygan, WI	31.5
9.	Rochester, MN	31.6
10.	Waterloo-Cedar Falls, IA	31.9

SOURCE: *Places Rated Almanac,* 1993, p. 100

Conduct a Long-Distance Job Search

How do you target your job search on a particular community? If you decide to remain in your present community, your job search is relatively manageable on a day-to-day basis. If you target another community, you will need to conduct a long-distance job search which requires more extensive use of the mail and telephone as well as carefully planned visits to the community. In fact, you will probably use your job search time more efficiently with a long-distance campaign. In both situations, you need to conduct community research prior to initiating the major communication steps in your job search.

Most of your community research can be conducted in the library or on the Internet. You need names, addresses, and phone numbers of potential employers. Use the major directories we identified in Chapter 12, such as the *Dun & Bradstreet's Middle Market Directory* and *Who's Who in Commerce and Industry*. The *Business Phone Book 1997* is an especially useful directory for anyone contemplating a long-distance job search. Search for specific communities on the Internet. Many communities maintain home pages that include a wealth of information on housing, education, and employers.

We particularly recommend starting with the latest edition of *The Sourcebook of ZIP Code Demographics* (CACI Marketing Systems). Found in the reference section of many libraries, this two-volume directory gives detailed information on population, housing, employment, education, income, and transportation in all communities throughout the United States. Organized by zip code, this directory yields a wealth of information on zip coded communities. For example, if you turn to the section containing your current zip code, you will discover how your community is structured according to population, housing, employment, language, education, income, and transportation. You can compare your current community to thousands of other zip code communities throughout the country. In some cities with five or more zip codes, you will learn average median family incomes can fluctuate from $13,000 to $65,000, depending on the particular community zip code. We recommend consulting this directory *before* committing yourself to relocating to another community.

As noted in Chapter 12, three publishers—Adams Media, Surrey Books, and NET Research—publish job bank books which identify hundreds of employers and job search services in the following cities and states: Atlanta, Boston, the Carolinas, Chicago, Dallas/Fort Worth, Denver, Detroit, Florida, Houston, Los Angeles, Minneapolis, New York City, Ohio, Philadelphia, Phoenix, Portland, San Diego, San Francisco, Seattle, St. Louis, Tennessee, and Washington, DC. Each book includes annotated descriptions of employers along with addresses and telephone numbers. While these books are available in some bookstores and public libraries, all of the books can be ordered directly from Impact Publications.

The Yellow Pages of telephone directories are especially useful sources for identifying the business and commercial structure of communities as well as for addresses and telephone numbers. The larger the community, the more specialized the businesses. For example, New York City has several businesses specializing in manufacturing manhole covers! At the same time, write to chambers of commerce for information on the community and to companies for annual reports and other organizational literature.

Numerous online resources are available for accessing information on communities, businesses, and relocation. Most libraries now have access to a variety of online resources relevant to job seekers and those interested in relocating. If you use the Internet, you can access information on numerous communities and employers throughout the country.

Homequity provides relocation counseling services. If you call their toll-free number (800/243-1033), you can receive free information on housing and schools in any community as well as spouse career counseling. You can also write to them for information: Homequity Destination Services, 40 Apple Ridge Road, Danbury, CT 06810.

United Van Lines' Relocation Services (800/325-3870) maintains a database on over 7,000 cities in the U.S. and abroad. They will send you free detailed relocation information on two cities upon request. Many banks will supply you with relocation information.

You should also examine the *Moving and Relocation Sourcebook* (Omnigraphics) which profiles the 100 largest metropolitan areas in the United States. This comprehensive volume includes information on everything from population, education, health care, arts, recreation, media, and shopping centers to government, religion, racial and ethnic groups, death rates, and per capita income. The book may be available in some major libraries. It can be purchased through Impact Publications by completing the order form at the end of this book.

Another good source for conducting a job search is Fran Bastress' comprehensive job search guide for spouses: *The New Relocating Spouse's Guide to Employment* (Impact Publications).

Part of your research may involve narrowing the number of communities you are considering. If you identify 10 alternative communities, outline the criteria by which to evaluate the 10 communities. For example, you may be particularly interested in moving to a community which has a good climate, excellent cultural facilities, unique recreational opportunities, and a sound educational infrastructure in addition to numerous job and career opportunities in your area of interest and skill. Select three communities and initiate a writing campaign for more information. If at all possible, schedule a trip to the cities to get an on-site view or feel for the relative environments. Further try to narrow your choices by rank-ordering your preferences among the three communities. Concentrate most of your job search efforts on your top priority community.

Your next step is to develop a strategy for penetrating both the advertised and hidden job markets. If you are conducting a job search outside your present community, the advertised job market will be most accessible to you. However, you need to link into the hidden job market, where most of the good jobs are located. While doing this from a distance is somewhat difficult, nonetheless it can be managed.

Penetrate the Local Job Market

The advertised job market is always the easiest to access. Buy a newspaper and read the classified ads. Contact an employment firm and they will eagerly assist you. Walk into a personnel office and they may permit you to fill out an application form.

If you target a community from a distance, begin by subscribing to a local newspaper; the Sunday edition will most likely meet your needs. This newspaper also will give you other important information on the community—housing market, economics, politics, society, culture, entertainment, and recreation. Survey the help wanted ads to get a feel for the structure of the advertised job market. Remember, these are not necessarily indicative of the true employment picture in a community—only 20 to 30 percent of the job market. Write letters to various companies and ask about job opportunities. You also may want to contact one or more professional employment agencies or job search firms—preferably fee-paid ones—for job leads. But remember our previous warnings about possible frauds and hucksters!

Efforts to penetrate the advertised job market should be geared toward uncovering the hidden job market. For example, in reading the Sunday newspaper, watch for names of important people in the society or *"Living"* section. You may want to contact some of these people by using an approach letter as outlined in Chapters 12 and 13. The employment agencies may give some indication of the general employment situation in the community—both advertised and hidden job markets. The chamber of commerce might be able to give you some job leads other than those advertised. Perhaps you can develop local contacts through membership in an alumni network, professional association, or church.

If you are conducting a long-distance job search, we recommend following the same procedures we outlined in Chapter 13 on networking. Preparation is the key to success. Do your research on potential employers, write letters, make phone calls, and schedule informational and referral interviews. The major difference in this situation is your timing. In addition, you need to give more information to your contacts. In your letter mention that you are planning to move to their community and would appreciate their advice on job opportunities for someone with your qualifications. Mention that you plan to visit the community on such and such a date and would appreciate an opportunity to discuss your job search plan at that time. In this case, enclose your resume with the letter and request a reply to your inquiry. Most people will reply and schedule an interview or refer you to someone else.

You should set aside one or two weeks—preferably more—to literally blitz the community with informational and referral interviews. This requires doing a considerable amount of advance work. For example, use your present community to practice informational and referral interviewing. Contact employers in your area who are in similar positions. Many of them may give you referrals to friends and colleagues in your targeted community.

If you have limited contacts when conducting a long-distance job search, you will probably need to use the "cold turkey" approach more frequently. You should make most of your key contacts at least four weeks before you plan to visit your targeted community. Within two weeks of your visit, you should have scheduled most of your interviews.

Try to schedule at least three interviews each day. You will probably do more because each interview will yield one or two referrals to others. Five interviews a day are manageable if you don't need to spend a lot of time traveling from one site to another. Plan to keep the sites near each other for each day. Within a two week period, you should be able to conduct 40 to 60 interviews. Use the weekends to research the community further. Contact a realtor who will be happy to show you around the community and inform you of different housing alternatives, neighborhoods, schools, taxes, public services, shopping centers, and a wealth of other community information. You should reserve the last two days for following up on referrals. Scheduling interviews with referrals will have to be made by telephone because of the time factor.

After concluding your one to two week visit, follow up your interviews with thank you letters, telephone calls, and letters indicating continuing interest and requesting referrals.

If you receive an invitation to a formal job interview in another city, be sure to clarify the financial question of who pays for the interview. Normally if the employer has requested the interview, the company pays the expense to and from the out of town interview. However, if you have invited yourself to an interview by stating that you will be "in town," expect to pay your own expenses. If you are unclear about who initiated the interview, simply ask the employer "How should we handle the travel expenses?" This question should clarify the matter so there will be no misunderstanding.

Identify Opportunity Structures

Each community has its own set of social, economic, political, and job market structures. Your job is to understand and use the particular job market structure in your targeted community. Therefore, we outline the case of Washington, DC for illustrative purposes. The principles for identifying and using the institutional and personal networks will remain the same for most communities even though the individuals, groups, and institutions differ for different communities.

The degree of structure differs for every community. However, one thing is relatively predictable: most communities lack a coherent structure for processing job information efficiently and effectively. But communities are made up of networks which enable individuals to network for job information, advice, and referrals. Each community consists of numerous individuals, groups, organizations, and institutions—many of which constitute mutually dependent networks—that are involved in pursuing their own interests in cooperation and competition with one another. The Yellow Pages of your telephone book best outline the major actors. Banks, mortgage companies, advertising firms, car dealers, schools, churches, small businesses, industries, hospitals, law firms, governments, and civic and voluntary groups do their "own thing" and have their own internal power structure. No one dominates except in small communities which also are company towns—paper mills, mining companies, universities, or steel mills. At the same time, the groups overlap with each other because of economic, political, and social needs. The bank, for example, needs to loan money to the businesses and churches. The businesses, in turn, need the educational institutions. And the educational institutions need the business-es to absorb their graduates. Therefore, individuals tend to cooperate in seeing that people playing the other games also succeed. Members of school boards, medical boards, and the boardrooms of banks and corporations will overlap and give the appearance of a "power structure" even though power is structured in the loosest sense of the term. The game players compete and cooperate with each other as well as co-op one another. The structures they create are your opportunity structures for penetrating the hidden job market. They are networks for locating job opportunities.

Examine the case of Washington, DC. The opportunity structures for your job search networks are relatively well defined in this city. While government is the major institution, other institutions are well defined in relation to the government. Within government, both the political and administrative institutions function as alternative opportunity structures in the Washington networks: congressional staffs, congressional committees, congressional subcommittees, congressional bureaucracy, executive staff, departments, independent executive agencies, and independent regulatory agencies. Outside, but clinging to, government are a variety of other groups and networks: interest groups, the media, professional associations, contractors, consultants, law firms, banks, and universities and colleges. As illustrated on page 309, these groups are linked to one another for survival and advancement. Charles Peters (*How Washington Really Works*) calls them "survival networks" which function in the "make believe world" of Washington, DC. Ripley and Franklin (*Congress, Bureaucracy, and Public Policy*) identify the key political dynamics as "subgovernments"—the interaction of interest groups, agencies, and congressional committees.

Washington is the ultimate networking community. For years Washing-ton insiders have learned how to use these "survival networks" and "subgovernments" to advance their careers. A frequent career pattern would be to work in an agency for three to four years. During that time, you would make important contacts on Capitol Hill with congressional staffs and committees as well as with private consultants, contractors, and interest groups. Your specialized knowledge on the inner workings of government is marketable to these other people. Therefore, you make a relatively easy job change from a federal agency to a congressional committee or to an interest group. After a few years here, you move to another group in the network. Perhaps you work on your law degree at the same time so that in another five years you can go into the truly growth industry in the city—law firms. The key to making these moves is the personal contact—whom you know. Particular attention is given to keeping a current SF 171 or resume, just in case an opportunity happens to come by for you. Congressional staff members usually last no more than two years; they set their sights on consulting and contracting firms, agencies, or interest groups for their next job move.

Washington Networks

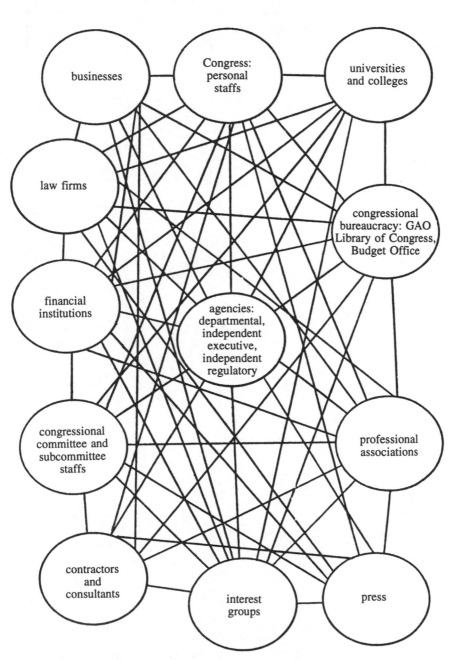

Whatever community you decide to focus your job search on, expect it to have its particular networks. Do as much research as possible to identify the structure of the networks as well as the key people who can provide access to various elements in the opportunity structures. Washington is not unique in this respect; it is just better known, and Washingtonians talk about it more because of their frequent job moves.

18

Start Your Own Business

While the previous chapters examined strategies for finding employment in other peoples' organizations, you may also be interested in working for yourself. Indeed, your self-assessment activities in Chapters 7, 8, and 9 may indicate your motivated abilities and skills (MAS) are very entrepreneurial in nature and thus you may be best suited for self-employment.

We expect the decade ahead to be another strong period for entrepreneurship in America. Millions of small businesses will develop in response to new opportunities in high-tech and service industries. Self-employment and start-up businesses will remain great frontiers for careering and re-careering in the decade ahead.

Consider Your Alternatives

Most job and career opportunities in America are found among small businesses—not large Fortune 500 corporations. Indeed, between 1979 and 1993, Fortune 500 companies eliminated 4.8 million jobs; companies employing fewer than 500 people generated more than 15 million new jobs.

We expect large corporations in the decade ahead to continue emphasizing productivity by introducing new cost-cutting technologies and management systems to improve the efficiency and effectiveness of the work place. In other words, they will continue to cut back on the fastest growing corporate expense—personnel. The advancement hierarchies of large companies will shorten and career opportunities narrow as these companies further automate as well as reduce the number of middle management personnel. Many of these displaced personnel will become entrepreneurs, starting both small and medium-sized businesses—often in competition with their former employers.

Since nearly 90 percent of all new jobs will be created by small businesses employing fewer than 500 individuals, you may wish to target your job search toward opportunities with such businesses. Finding a job with a small business will require a great deal of research because most of these businesses are not well known among job seekers.

One other alternative is to start your own business. Indeed, nearly 700,000 new businesses are started each year. In the decade ahead millions of individuals will be "pushed" or "pulled" from what were once seen as promising jobs and careers with companies to form their own businesses. As work becomes more centralized, advancement opportunities become more limited, and starting a business becomes easier, millions of individuals will opt for starting their own businesses.

While nearly 700,000 new businesses are started each year, grim business statistics also sober as well as discourage many would-be entrepreneurs; another 500,000 to 600,000 businesses fail each year; 50 percent fail within the first 38 months; and nearly 90 percent fail within 10 years. Unfortunately, starting your own business is a risky business; the statistical odds are against anyone becoming a successful entrepreneur.

Nonetheless, owning your business is a viable careering and re-careering alternative to working for someone else—if you approach business intelligently. Many people fail because they lack the necessary ingredients for success. In this chapter we outline the basics for getting started in owning your business and employing yourself.

Examine Risks and Motivations

You will find few challenges riskier than starting your own business. At the same time, you may experience your greatest professional satisfaction in running your own business.

Starting a business means taking risks. First, while you had grandiose visions of becoming an overnight success, you will probably go into debt and realize little income during the first two years of building your business. You may be under-capitalized or have overhead costs higher than anticipated. It takes time to develop a regular clientele. What profits you do realize are normally plowed back into the business in order to expand operations and guarantee larger future profits. Second, business is often a trial and error process in which it is difficult to predict or ensure outcomes. Due to unforeseen circumstances beyond your control, you may fail even though you work hard and make intelligent decisions. Third, you could go bankrupt and lose more than just your investments of time and money.

At the same time, owning your own business can be tremendously satisfying. It is the ultimate exercise of independence. Being your own boss means you are in control, and no one can fire you. You are rewarded in direct proportion to your productivity. Your salary is not limited by a boss, nor are your accomplishments credited to others. Unless you decide otherwise, you are not wedded to a 9 to 5 work routine or a two-week vacation each year. Depending on how successful your business becomes, you may be able to retire young and pursue other interests. You can turn what you truly enjoy doing, such as hobbies, into a profitable, rewarding, and fun career.

But such self-indulgence and gratification have costs which you may or may not be willing to ensure. You will probably need at least $30,000 to $50,000 of start-up capital, or perhaps as much as $350,000, depending on the type of business you enter. No one will send you a paycheck every two weeks so you can regularly pay your bills. You may work 12 and 14 hour days, seven days a week, and have no vacation during the first few years. And you may become heavily indebted, experience frequent cash flow problems, and eventually have creditors descend on you.

Why, then, start your own business? If you talk to people who have worked for others and then started their own businesses, they will tell you similar stories. They got tired of draw-ing a salary while making someone else rich. They got bored with their work and hated coming to an office everyday to engage in a 9 to 5 work routine. They wanted control over what they did. Some worked for jerks; others were victims of organizational

> **This is the old fashioned way of making money—hard work and long hours.**

politics; and others had difficulty working in an environment structured by others whom they considered less competent than themselves. Many simply couldn't work for others—they had to be in charge of their work. On a more positive note, many started businesses because they had a great idea they wanted to pursue, or they wanted the challenge of independently accom-plishing their own goals.

If you decide to go into business for yourself, be sure you know what you want to do and be willing to take risks and work hard. Don't expect to get rich overnight or sit back and watch your business grow on its own. Starting a business is usually a very sobering experience that tests your motivations, abilities, and skills. Success in a corporate or bureaucratic career may not transfer well to starting your own business which initially requires entrepreneurial skills. Be prepared to work long and hard hours, experience disappointments, and challenge yourself to the limits. You will quickly discover this is the old fashioned way of making money—hard work and long hours. But at least you can choose which 12 to 14 hours of each day you want to work!

There are few things that are more self-actualizing than running your own business. But you must have realistic expectations as well as a motivational pattern which is conducive to taking risks and being an entrepreneur. In Chapters 7, 8, and 9 you identified your motivational patterns and skills. If you like security, predictability, and stability, you probably are a candidate for a position where someone hands you a paycheck each week. If you read and believe in a get-rich-quick book, video, or seminar which tries to minimize your risks and uncertainty, you probably have been ripped-off by an enterprising individual who is getting rich writing books and producing videos and seminars for naive people!

Possess the Right Strengths For Success

How can you become self-employed and successful at the same time? No one has a magical success formula for the budding entrepreneur—only advice based on experience. We do know why many businesses fail, and we can identify some basic characteristics for success. Poor management and decision-making lie at the heart of business failures. Many people go into business without doing sufficient market research; they under-capitalize; they select a poor location; they incur extremely high and debilitating overhead costs; they lack commitment; they are unwilling to sacrifice; they can't read or count; and they lack interpersonal and salesmanship skills.

On the positive side, studies continue to identify something called "drive," or the need to achieve, as a key characteristic of successful entrepreneurs. As Kellogg (*Fast Track,* McGraw-Hill) and others have found, young achievers and successful entrepreneurs possess similar characteristics: "A high energy level, restless, a willingness to work hard and take risks, a desire to escape from insecurity."

Successful business people combine certain motivations, skills, and circumstances. Contrary to popular myths, you don't need to be rich or have an MBA or business experience to get started. If you are willing to gamble and are a self-starter, self-confident, an organizer, and you like people, you should consider this entrepreneurial alternative in your careering and re-careering decisions. These characteristics along with drive, thinking ability, human relations, communication, technical knowledge, hard work, persistence, and good luck are essential ingredients for business success.

If these are among your strengths, as identified in Chapter 9, you may be a good candidate for starting your own business with a high probability of success. If you feel you have recurring weaknesses in certain areas, you may want to consider finding a business partner who has particular complementary strengths for running a business.

Know Yourself

There are many different ways to get started in business. You can buy into a franchise which can initially cost you $20,000 to $500,000. Advertisements in the *Wall Street Journal* are a good source for hundreds of franchise opportunities from flipping hamburgers to selling animals. You can join someone else's business on a full-time or part-time basis as a partner or employee in order to get some direct business experience. You can try your hand at a direct-sales business such as Amway, Shaklee, or Avon. Hundreds of new direct-sales businesses modeled after Amway's multi-level business methods are now marketing every conceivable product —soap, computers, canoes, motor oil, and milk. You can buy someone else's business or you can start your own business from scratch.

Your decision on how to get started in business should be based upon the data you generated on your skills and goals in Chapters 7, 8, and 9. Do not go into business for negative reasons—get fired, hate your job, can't find work. Unfortunately, many people go into business with totally unrealistic expectations as well as with little understanding of their own goals, skills, and motivations. For example, while it is nice to work around pretty clothes, owning a dress shop requires handling inventory and personnel as well as paying the rent and doing bookkeeping. Getting all those pretty dresses on the rack is hard work!

> **Don't be high on motivation but low on knowledge and skills, for "thinking big" is no substitute for doing the work!**

Many people also don't understand how the business world works. It requires a great deal of interpersonal skill to develop and expand personal networks of creditors, clients, colleagues, and competitors.

Therefore, you should do two things before you decide to go into business. First, thoroughly explore your goals and motivations. The questions are familiar:

- What do you want to do?
- What do you do well?
- What do you enjoy doing?

Second, research different types of businesses in order to better understand advantages, disadvantages, procedures, processes, and possible problems. Talk to business persons about their work. Try to learn as much as possible about the reality before you invest your time and money. Surprisingly, few people do this. Many people leap into a business that they think will be great and then later learn it was neither right for them nor did they have realistic expectations of what was involved. This is precisely why so many businesses fail each year.

You should approach business opportunities the same way you approach the job market: do research, develop networks, and conduct informational and referral interviews. Most business people, including your competition, will share their experiences with you and assist you with advice and referrals. Such research is absolutely invaluable. If you fail to do it initially, you will pay later on by making the same mistakes that millions of others have made in starting their own businesses in isolation of others. Don't be high on motivation but low on knowledge and skills, for "thinking big" is no substitute for doing the work!

Look For New Opportunities

Most business people will tell you similar stories of the reality of running your own business. Do your market research, spend long hours, plan, and be persistent. They also will give you advice on what businesses to avoid and what business routines you should be prepared to handle.

Many service and high-tech businesses will be growing in the decade ahead. Given the changing demographic structure—fewer young people, more elderly, the two career family—numerous opportunities are arising for small personal service businesses to meet the needs of the elderly and career-oriented families. Businesses relating to restaurants, home maintenance, health care, housing for the elderly, and mortuaries and cemeteries should expand considerably during the next two decades.

Opportunities are also available for inventive business persons who can make more productive use of busy peoples' time—fast foods, financial planning, and mail-order shopping. The information and high-tech revolutions are taking place at the same time two career families do not have time to waste standing in lines at banks, grocery stores, and department stores. Mail-order or computer assisted home and office-based shopping should increase dramatically during the next decade.

A service business is particularly attractive. It is easy to establish, many require a small initial investment, and the bookkeeping is relatively simple. You may be able to operate from your home and thus keep your overhead down.

Knowing these trends and opportunities is important, but they should not be the only determining factors in choosing a business. You should start with yourself by again trying to identify a business that is fit for you rather than one you think you might fit into.

Prepare the Basics

You also need to consider several other factors before starting a business. Since a business requires financing, locating, planning, developing customer relationships, and meeting legal requirements, be prepared to address these questions:

1. **How can I best finance the business?** Take out a personal or business loan with a bank? Go into a partnership in order to share the risks and costs? Get a loan from the Small Business Administration?

2. **How much financing do I need?** Many businesses fail because they are under-capitalized. Others fail because of over-spending on rent, furnishings, inventory, personnel, and advertising.

3. **Where is my market?** Just in this community, region, nation-wide, or international? Mail-order businesses enable you to expand your market nationwide whereas retail and service businesses tend to be confined to particular neighborhoods or communities.

4. **Who are my suppliers?** How many must I work with? What about credit arrangements?

5. **Where is the best location for the business?** Do you need to open a store or operate out of your home? If you need a store or office, is it conveniently located for your clientele? "Location is everything" still best summarizes the success of many businesses, especially McDonald's and Wal-Mart.

6. **How should the business be legally structured?** Sole proprietorship, partnership, or corporation? Each has certain advantages and disadvantages. A corporation has several tax advantages.

7. **What licenses and permits do I need?** These consist of local business licenses and permits, federal employee identification numbers, state sales tax number, state occupational licenses, federal licenses and permits, and special state and local regulations which vary from state to state and from community to community. What type of insurance do I need? Fire, theft, liability, workers' compensation, and auto?

8. **How many employees do I need?** Can I do without personnel initially until the business expands? Should I use part-time and temporary help?

9. **What business name should I use?** If incorporated, is anyone else using the name? If a trade name, is it registered?

10. **What accounting system should I use?** Cash or accrual? Can I handle the books or do I need a part-time or full-time accountant? Who will handle the timely calculation and payment of payroll, sales, and corporate taxes as well as insurance, retirement plans, and workers compensation?

11. **Do I need a lawyer?** What type of lawyer? What legal work can I do myself?

12. **How do I develop a business plan?** A business plan should
    include a definition of the business, a marketing strategy, opera-
    tional policies, purchasing plans, financial statements, and
    capital raising plans.

Get Useful Advice

If you decide to go into business, make sure you choose the right business
for your particular skills, abilities, motivation, and interests. A good starting
point is Paul and Sarah Edwards' *Finding Your Perfect Work* (Putnam) and
Doug Gray's *Have You Got What It Takes? The Entrepreneur's Complete
Self-Assessment Guide* (Self-Counseling Press). These books provide
useful exercises for assessing your suitability for becoming an entrepreneur.
For a good overview of the many decisions you must make in establishing
a small business, see Bernard Kamaroff's *Small-Time Operator* (Bell
Springs Publishing). This book provides you with all the basic information
you need for starting your own business, including ledger sheets for setting
up your books. Several other books provide similar how-to advice for the
neophyte entrepreneur:

Bob Adams, *Adams Streetwise™ Small Business Start-Up* (Adams
Media)

National Business Employment Weekly, *NBEW's Guide to Self
Employment* (Wiley and Sons)

Gregory and Patricia Kishel, *How to Start, Run, and Stay in
Business* (Wiley and Sons)

Arnold S. Goldstein, *Starting on a Shoestring: Building a Business
Without a Bankroll* (Wiley and Sons)

James C. Gonya and Wayne M. Gonyea, *Selling on the Internet*
(McGraw-Hill)

William J. Stolze, *Start Up* (Career Press)

David E. Gumpert, *How to Really Start Your Own Business* (Inc.
Magazine)

Joseph Anthony, *Kiplinger's Working for Yourself* (Kiplinger)

LaVerne Ludden, *Franchise Opportunities Handbook* (JIST Works,
Inc.)

Paul and Sarah Edwards, *The Best Home-Based Businesses for the 90s* (Putnam)

Veltisezar B. Bautista, *How to Build a Successful One-Person Business* (Bookhaus)

Katina Jones, *Adams Businesses You Can Start Almanac* (Adams Media)

The federal government will help you with several publications available through the Small Business Administration: 1441 L Street, NW, Washington, DC 20416, Tel. 800/368-5855. SBA field offices are located in 85 cities. The Consumer Information Center publishes a free booklet entitled *More Than a Dream: Running Your Own Business:* Dept. 616J, Pueblo, CO 81009. The Internal Revenue Service sponsors several one-day tax workshops for small businesses. Your local Chamber of Commerce also can give you useful information.

If you are interested in how to get started in a particular small business, write for information from the American Entrepreneurs Association, 2392 Morse Avenue, Irving, CA 92714-6234 or use their toll-free number: 800/421-2300. This organization offers a comprehensive set of services for starting small businesses. These include a free catalog of products and services, the magazine *Entrepreneur,* and the Entrepreneur Institute. To help you get off in the right direction, this organization also publishes over 300 helpful small business start-up and operation manuals which include businesses such as energy stores, video stores, seminars, pet cemeteries, health clubs, pizza parlors, travel agencies, dating services, rent-a-hot tub, furniture stripping, pipe shop, discos, and maid services. For a six-month free subscription to *Money Making Opportunities* magazine, which lists hundreds of mail order ads, write to Money Making Opportunities, 11071 Ventura Blvd., Studio City, CA 91604. These publications will give you a sampling of alternative businesses you can establish. However, beware of hucksters who may advertise in business magazines. Many want your money for "proven success" and "get-rich-quick" formulas that don't even work for the advertisers!

Continue Your Success

The factors for operating a successful business are similar to the 20 principles we outlined in Chapter 6 for conducting a successful job search. Once your initial start-up problems are solved, you must organize, plan, implement, and manage in relation to your goals. Many people lack these abilities. Some people are good at initially starting a business, but they are unable to follow-through in managing day-to-day routines once the business is established. And others have the ability to start, manage, and expand businesses successfully.

Be careful about business success. Many business people become obsessed with their work, put in 12 and 14 hour days continuously, and spend seven day weeks to make the business successful. Unwilling to delegate, they try to do too much and thus become a prisoner to the business. The proverbial "tail wagging the dog" is a common phenomenon in small businesses. For some people, this lifestyle feeds their ego and makes them happy. For others, the 9 to 5 routine of working for someone else on salary may look very attractive only after a few months of self-employment. Therefore, you must be prepared to change your lifestyle when embarking on your own business. Your major limitation will be yourself.

So think it over carefully, do your research, and plan, organize, implement, and manage for success. Even though running your own business is risky and involves hard work, the thrill of independence and success is hard to beat!

Part IV

TAKE ACTION TO IMPLEMENT YOUR GOALS

19

Take Action to Implement Your Goals

U nderstanding without action is a waste of time. And buying a how-to book without implementing it is a waste of money. Many people read how-to books, attend how-to seminars, and do nothing other than read more books, attend more seminars, and engage in more wishful thinking. While these activities become forms of therapy for some individuals, they should lead to positive actions for you.

From the very beginning of this book we stressed the importance of understanding the job market and developing appropriate job search strategies for getting the job you want. We make no assumptions nor claim any magic is contained in this book. Rather, we have attempted to assemble useful information to help you organize an effective job search which will best communicate your qualifications to potential employers. Individual chapters examined the present and future job markets as well as outlined in how-to terms specific careering and re-careering skills for shaping your own future. We have done our part in getting you to the implementation stage. What happens next is your responsibility.

The methods we outlined in previous chapters have worked for thousands of individuals who have paid $2,000 to $12,000 to get similar information from the highly-paid professionals. While you may want to see a professional for assistance at certain steps in your job search, if you are self-motivated you can do everything on your own with a minimum expenditure of money. The major cost will be your time and effort.

But you must make the effort and take the *risk of implementing* this book. Careering and re-careering take work and are risky businesses. You try something new and place your ego on the line. You subject yourself to the possibility of being rejected several times. And this is precisely the major barrier you will encounter to effective implementation. For many people are unwilling to take more than a few rejections.

Welcome Rejections as Learning Opportunities

Planning is the easiest part of any task. Turning plans into reality is the most difficult challenge. It's relatively simple to set goals and outline a course of action divorced from the reality of actually doing it. But if you don't take action, you will not get your expected results. You must implement if you want desired results.

Once you take action, be prepared for rejections. Employers will tell you "Thank you—we'll call you," but they never do. Other employers will tell you "We have no positions available at this time for someone with your qualifications" or "You don't have the qualifications necessary for this position." Whatever the story, you may face many disappointments on the road to success.

Rejections are a normal part of the process of finding employment as well as getting ahead in life. Rejections offer an important learning experience which should help you better understand yourself, employers, and the job finding process. More important, you must be rejected before you will be accepted. Expect ten rejections or "nos" for every acceptance or "yes" you receive. If you quit after five or eight rejections, you prematurely end your job search. If you persist in collecting two to five more "nos," you will likely receive a "yes." Most people quit prematurely because their ego is not prepared for more rejections. Therefore, you should welcome rejections as you seek more and more acceptances.

> Understanding without action is a waste of time. And buying a how-to book without implementing it is a waste of money.

Get Motivated and Work Hard

Assuming you have a firm understanding of each job search step and how to relate them to your goals, what do you do next? The next steps involve *motivation and hard work.* Just how motivated are you to seek a new job or career and thus your life? Our experience is that individuals need to be sufficiently *motivated* to make the first move and do it properly. If you go about your job search half-heartedly—you just want to "test the waters" to see what's out there—don't expect to be successful. You must be committed to achieving specific goals. Make the decision to properly develop and implement your job search and be prepared to work hard in achieving your goals.

Find Time

Once you've convinced yourself to take the necessary steps to find a job or change and advance your career, you need to find the *time* to properly implement your job search. This requires setting aside specific blocks of time for identifying your motivated abilities and skills, developing your resume, writing letters, making telephone calls, and conducting the necessary research and networking required for success. This whole process takes time. If you are a busy person, like most people, you simply must make the time. As noted in our examination of your time management practices in Chapter 6 (pages 115-117), you should practice your own versions of time management or cutback management. Get better organized, give some things up, or cut back on all your activities. If, for example, you can set aside one hour each day to devote to your job search, you will spend

> **Successful job hunters are ones who routinize a job search schedule and keep at it.**

seven hours a week or 28 hours a month on your search. However, you should and can find more time than this for these activities.

Time and again we find successful job hunters are the ones who routinize a job search schedule and keep at it. They make contact after contact, conduct numerous informational interviews, submit many applications and resumes, and keep repeating these activities in spite of encountering rejections. They learn that success is just a few more "nos" and informational interviews away. They face each day with a positive attitude fit for someone desiring to change their life—I must collect my ten "nos" today because each "no" brings me closer to another "yes"!

Commit Yourself in Writing

You may find it useful to commit yourself in writing to achieving job search success. This is a very useful way to get both motivated and directed for action. Start by completing the job search contract on page 325 and keep it near you—in your briefcase or on your desk.

In addition, you should complete weekly performance reports. These reports identify what you actually accomplished rather than what your good intentions tell you to do. Make copies of the performance and planning report form on page 326 and use one each week to track your actual progress and to plan your activities for the next week.

If you fail to meet these written commitments, issue yourself a revised and updated contract. But if you do this three or more times, we strongly suggest you stop kidding yourself about your motivation and commitment to find a job. Start over again, but this time consult a professional career counselor who can assist you with your job search.

Job Search Contract

1. I'm committed to changing my life by changing my job. Today's date is _____.

2. I will manage my time so that I can successfully complete my job search and find a high quality job. I will complete my time management inventory (pages 115-117) and begin changing my time management behavior on _____.

3. I will begin my job search on _____.

4. I will involve _____ with my job search.
   (individual/group)

5. I will spend at least one week conducting library research on different jobs, employers, and organizations. I will begin this research during the week of _____.

6. I will complete my skills identification step by _____.

7. I will complete my objective statement by _____.

8. I will complete my resume by _____.

9. Each week I will:

   ▪ make _____ new job contacts.

   ▪ conduct _____ informational interviews.

   ▪ follow-up on _____ referrals.

10. My first job interview will take place during the week of _____.

11. I will begin my new job by _____.

12. I will make a habit of learning one new skill each year.

Signature: _____

Date: _____

Weekly Job Performance and Planning Report

1. The week of: _____.

2. This week I:
   - wrote ___ job search letters.
   - sent ___ resumes and ___ letters to potential employers.
   - completed ___ applications.
   - made ___ job search telephone calls.
   - completed ___ hours of job research.
   - set up ___ appointments for informational interviews.
   - conducted ___ informational interviews.
   - received ___ invitations to a job interview.
   - followed up on ___ contacts and ___ referrals.

3. Next week I will:
   - write ___ job search letters.
   - send ___ resumes and ___ letters to potential employers.
   - complete ___ applications.
   - make ___ job search telephone calls.
   - complete ___ hours of job research.
   - set up ___ appointments for informational interviews.
   - conduct ___ informational interviews.
   - follow up on ___ contacts and ___ referrals.

4. Summary of progress this week in reference to my Job Search Contract commitments:

   _____

   _____

   _____

   _____

A professional may not be cheap, but if paying for help gets you on the right track and results in the job you want, it's money well spent. Do not be "penny wise but pound foolish" with your future. If you must seek professional advice, be sure you are an informed consumer according to our "shopping" advice in Chapter 6.

Career and Re-Career For Your Future

The continuing transformation of American society will require millions of individuals to career and re-career in the years ahead. The nature of jobs and careers are changing as the work place becomes transformed due to the impact of new technology and unique events. Many career fields in demand today may well be glutted tomorrow.

Throughout this book we have emphasized the importance of *being prepared* for turbulent times. The age of the generalist armed with job search skills alone is passing. The emerging society requires a new type of *generalist-specialist* who is trained for today's technology, *flexible* enough to be retrained in tomorrow's technology, and *adaptive* to new jobs and careers that will arise today and tomorrow. In other words, the society needs more and more generalist-specialists

> **Make an effort to learn one new skill each year.**

who welcome change by being willing and able to re-career. Knowing and practicing the job search skills outlined in this book, these people also are continuously learning new work-content skills in order to better position themselves in tomorrow's job market. *They transform their careering skills into re-careering competencies.*

If you want to change your life, you should be prepared to develop and practice re-careering competencies for the decades ahead. We recommend two final re-careering actions on your part. First, make an effort to learn one new skill each year; the skill can be related to work, family, community, or a hobby such as building bookcases, operating different computer software packages, repairing appliances, or remodeling your home. If you do this, you will be better prepared for making the career transitions necessary for functioning effectively in turbulent times.

Second, develop your own five-year plan which incorporates yearly career check-ups. At the end of each year, ask yourself: To what degree have I achieved my goals? Which goals do I need to revise? What actions do I need to take to better achieve my goals?

Careers and jobs should not be viewed as life sentences. You should feel free to change jobs and careers when you want to or need to. In fact, thousands of people make successful career transitions each year. Some are more successful than others in finding the right job. If you plan your career transition according to the methods outlined in previous chapters, you should be able to successfully land the job you want.

Treat yourself right. Take the time and effort to sail into today's job market with a plan of action that links your qualifications to the needs of employers. You are first and foremost an individual with knowledge, abilities, and skills that many employers need and want. If you follow the advice of this book, you will put your best foot forward in communicating your qualifications to employers. You will find a job fit for you. Most important, you will change your life because you are able to change your job.

20

Use the Right Resources

uccessful careering and re-careering also involves knowing which
resources are the most useful for conducting a job search. While you
chose this book as one of your resources, you should also be aware
of other useful resources that can further assist you at different stages
of your job search.

Throughout this book we have mentioned several resources we feel will
assist you in assessing your motivated abilities and skills, formulating a job
objective, and identifying jobs appropriate for your particular mix of
interests, values, abilities, skills, and objectives. Let's now turn to what we
consider to be the "best of the best" resources for expanding your job search
beyond this book. Accordingly, we attempt to bring some coherence and
organization to this literature to assist you in identifying any additional
resources that might be useful in your job search. Since some of these books
cannot be found in local bookstores or libraries, you may need to order
them directly from the publishers. For your convenience, you can order
many of them through Impact Publications by completing the order form at
the end of this book or through their comprehensive catalog on the World
Wide Web: http://www. impactpublications.com.

Types of Resources

In this chapter we primarily deal with books, because they are the least
expensive and most easily accessible resources in bookstores and libraries.
However, numerous computer software and CD-ROM programs are now
available to assist you with two stages of your job search: self-assessment
and resume writing. As mentioned in previous chapters, many career
planning centers and some libraries and computer stores offer these
resources. At the same time, numerous electronic resources are available
through several commercial online services (America Online, CompuServe,
Microsoft Network) and numerous Internet sites (JobTrak, Career Mosiac,

E-Span, CareerWEB, Online Career Center). We examine these resources separately in Chapter 21. For an excellent annotated description of such online resources, be sure to see Margaret Riley, Frances Roehm, and Steve Oserman, *The Guide to Internet Job Searching* (Lincolnwood, IL: NTC Publishing, 1996). For a more process-oriented treatment of the subject— along with an examination of specific online resources—see Joyce Lain Kennedy's two books, *Hook Up, Get Hired* and *Electronic Job Search Revolution* (New York: Wiley, 1996).

Choose What's Best For You

During the past 20 years hundreds of self-help books have been written on how to find a job and advance one's career. Each year dozens of additional volumes are published to inform as well as enlighten a growing audience of individuals concerned with conducting an effective job search.

You may be initially overwhelmed with the sheer volume of the career planning and job search literature available to help individuals find jobs and change careers. Once you examine a few books, such as this one, you will quickly learn that this literature is designed to be *used*. The books are not intended to describe a subject, explain reality, develop a theory, nor predict the future.

Most career planning and job search books attempt to advance self-help *strategies* based upon the particular ideas or experiences of individual writers. They expound a *set of beliefs* —more or less logical and based on a mixture of research, experience, and faith. Like other how-to literature on positive thinking, motivation, and success, you must first *believe* in these books before you can make them work for you. Since the research base for most of these books is very thin, this literature must be primarily judged on the basis of faith and usefulness.

Given the nature of this literature, your best approach is to pick *and choose* which books are *more or less useful* for you. There is nothing magical about these books. At best, they may challenge your preconceptions; develop alternative beliefs which you may or may not find acceptable; provide you with some directions; and help motivate you to implement an effective job search. They will not get you a job.

The level of redundancy in this literature may be disturbing to many readers. More so than in many other fields, career writers tend to quote each other or rely on the perspectives of a few key writers in restating the same approaches in a different form. As a result, many individuals confuse the high level of redundancy as repeated evidence of career "facts."

What You Get

We have examined most of the career planning and job search literature with a view toward identifying the best of the lot. We've judged the literature in terms of its degree of accuracy, realism, comprehensiveness, and usefulness. In doing so, we have found three major types of books which use different approaches to getting a job:

- Books designed to teach key job search *process and strategy skills;* these books emphasize "how" questions.

- Books designed to outline various *employment fields*; these books focus on "what" and "where" questions.

- Books designed to address key career issues for *special groups;* these books enphasize "what" and "how" questions.

A growing number of comprehensive job search books attempt to apply the process and strategy skills to different employment fields and groups.

Process and Strategy Skills

The first type of career planning and job search literature concentrates primarily on developing *process and strategy skills*. Most of these books tell you *how* to develop an effective job search regardless of your particular employment field or your specialized needs. They seldom address substantive *what* and *where* questions central to finding any job. You are left to answer these questions on your own or by using other resources which focus on what jobs are available and where you can find them.

Except for several new books that examine how to find a job by using computers and the Internet, there are few surprises in this literature. Most books follow a similar pattern in approaching the subject. The major difference is that the books are more or less readable. Most of these process books are preoccupied with "getting in touch with yourself" by emphasizing the need to "know what you want to do today, tomorrow, and the rest of your life." Some of this literature is rightly referred to as "touchy-feely" because of its concern with trying to get you to know yourself—the basis for self-assessment. A mainstay of psychologists, counselors, and activity-oriented trainers, this type of positive, up-beat literature is at best designed to reorient your life around

1. identifying what is right about yourself (your strengths), and

2. setting goals based upon an understanding of your past and present in the hope you will do better in the future (your objectives).

The real strengths of this literature lie in orienting your thinking along new lines, providing you with some baseline information on your strengths and goals, and providing you with positive motivation for developing and implementing an effective job search strategy. If you're looking for specifics, such as learning *what* the jobs are and *where* you can find them, this literature may disappoint you with its vagueness.

Placed within our career planning framework in Chapter 6, much of this process and strategy literature falls into the initial two steps of our career planning process: self-assessment and objective setting. Examples of career planning literature using this approach are the popular books written by Bolles, Crystal, Sturman, Miller, Mattson, Tieger, Sher, and Krannich: *Where Do I Go From Here With My Life?*, *What Color Is Your Parachute?*, *The Three Boxes of Life*, *Career Discovery Project*, *The Truth About You*, *Do What You Are*, *I Could Do Anything If I Only Knew What It Was*, *Wishcraft*, and *Discover the Best Jobs For You!* You should read these books if you lack a clear understanding of who you are, what you want to do, and where you are going. They may help you get in touch with yourself before you get in touch with employers! If these self-discovery books don't deliver with such self-understanding, you probably need to see a professional counselor who can administer tests as well as walk you through a comprehensive self-assessment process.

Several books focus on additional steps in the career planning and job search processes, such as doing research, writing resumes and letters, networking, interviewing, and negotiating salary. While also emphasizing process and strategy, these are more comprehensive books than the others. Some books include all of the job search steps whereas others concentrate on one or two major steps. Examples of the most comprehensive such books include those by Krannich, Kennedy and Laramore, Lathrop, Jackson, Figler, Yate, Studner, and Wendleton: *Change Your Job Change Your Life*, *Joyce Lain Kennedy's Career Book*, *Who's Hiring Who*, *The Complete Job Search Handbook*, *Guerrilla Tactics in the New Job Market*, *Through the Brick Wall*, *Knock 'Em Dead*, and *Super Job Search*.

You will find hundreds of books that focus on the **research stage** of the job search. Except for Crowther's *Researching Your Way to a Good Job*, most of these books are geographic, field, or organizational directories or job banks which list names and addresses of potential employers. Examples include the Adams Media's *Job Bank Series* on 31 major cities and metropolitan areas; Surrey Book's *How to Get a Job in...* series on seven cities; Wright's *The American Almanac of Jobs and Salaries*; Schwartz's and Brechner's *The Career Finder;* Krantz's *The Jobs Rated Almanac*; *Hoover's 500*, *Hoover's Handbook of World Business*, and *Hoover's Handbook of Emerging Companies*; Lauber's *Government Job Finder*, *Professional's Private Sector Job Finder*, and *Non-Profits' and Education Job Finder*; Kennedy Publications' *Directory of Executive Recruiters*; Adams Media's *National Job Bank* and *Job Bank Guide to Employment Services*; Ferguson's *Encyclopedia of Careers and Vocational Guidance*;

Dun and Bradstreet's *The Career Guide: Dun's Employment Opportunity Directory*; and the Department of Labor's *Occupational Outlook Handbook* and *The Dictionary of Occupational Titles*. Job search approaches relating to much of this literature are in sharp contrast to approaches of the standard career planning literature. Directories, for example, should be used to gather information—names, addresses, and phone numbers—to be used in targeting one's networking activities rather than as sources for shotgunning resumes and letters.

Numerous books are written on other key job search steps—especially resume and letter writing and job interviews. The **resume and letter writing** books fall into two major categories:

- Books designed to walk you through the process of developing resumes and letters based upon a thorough understanding of each step in the job search process. Examples include Krannich's and Banis' *High Impact Resumes and Letters*, Jackson's *The New Perfect Resume*, Good's *Does Your Resume Wear Blue Jeans?*, Swanson's *The Resume Solution*, and Beatty's *The Perfect Cover Letter*.

- Books primarily presenting examples of resumes and letters. Examples of such books are numerous—most resume books you will find in libraries and bookstores fall in this category. Some of better such books include Enelow's *100 Winning Resumes For $100,000+ Jobs*, Parker's *The Resume Catalog*, Kaplan's *Resume Shortcuts* and *101 Resumes For Sure-Hire Results*, Adams Media's *The Adams Resume Almanac*, Marino's *Just Resumes*, Jacksons' *Perfect Resume Strategies*, Fournier's and Spin's *Encyclopedia of Job-Winning Resumes*, Career Presses' *Resumes Resumes Resumes*, Noble's *The Gallery of Best Resumes*, Frank's *200 Letters For Job Hunters*, Krannichs' *201 Dynamite Job Search Letters*, and Beatty's *175 High-Impact Cover Letters*.

The first type of resume and letter writing book urges the user to develop resumes and letters that represent the "unique you" in relation to specific positions and employers. They further emphasize the importance of finding a job that is right for you rather than try to adjust your experience to fit into a job that may be inappropriate for you. These books are based upon a particular approach to finding a job as outlined in several of the comprehensive career planning and job search books.

The second type of resume and letter writing book lacks a clear approach other than an implied suggestion that readers should creatively plagiarize the examples. In other words, good resumes and letters are produced by osmosis! A few resume and letter writing books, such as Parker's *The*

Damn Good Resume Guide, Schuman's and Lewis' *Revising Your Resume*, Beatty's *The Resume Kit*, Coxford's *Resume Writing Made Easy*, the Krannichs' *Dynamite Resumes* and *Dynamite Cover Letters*, Kennedy's *Resumes For Dummies*, Yates' *Resumes That Knock 'Em Dead*, and *Cover Letters That Knock 'Em Dead* fall between these two types. Several new resume books now focus on developing electronic resumes appropriate for resume databases and the Internet: Kennedy's *Electronic Resume Revolution*, Weddle's *Electronic Resumes For the New Job Market*, and Gonyea's *Electronic Resumes: Putting Your Resume On-Line*.

Several books address the issue of **networking** in the job search. A few books focus on job search networking—Krannichs' *Dynamite Networking For Dynamite Jobs*, Lowstuter and Robertson's *Network Your Way to Your Next Job*, National Business Employment Weekly's *Networking*, and Beatty's *Job Search Networking*. Boe and Youngs' *Is Your "Net" Working?* and Garnas' *How to Use People and Get What You Want—and Still Be a Nice Guy!* look at how to build contacts for career development. Baber's and Waymon's *Great Connections*, and RoAne's *How to Work a Room* and *Secrets of Savvy Networking*, Mandel's *Power Schmoozing*, and Boylan's *The Power to Get In* examine the small talk phenomenon that is the key to developing networks in career, business, and social situations. Donna and Sandy Vilas' *Power Networking* outlines 55 networking methods for achieving success.

You will also find several **job interview** books designed for both interviewees and interviewers. Most of these books examine each step in the interview process—from preparation to negotiating salary. Interview books such as the Krannichs' *Interview For Success* look at each step of the interview process within a well defined career development and job search process. Some interview books, such as DeLuca's *Best Answers to 201 Most Frequently Asked Interview Questions*, Allen's *The Complete Q & A Job Interview Book*, and Fry's *101 Great Answers to the Toughest Interview Questions*, focus primarily on questions and answers. Other interview books, such as the Krannich's *101 Dynamite Answers to Interview Questions* and Ryan's *60 Seconds and You're Hired* are more comprehensive, including interview settings, types of interviews, and nonverbal communication along with a discussion of appropriate questions and answers. Some other good interview books are written by Fein, Kennedy, Schmidt, Medley, Washington, Farr, and the National Business Employment Weekly: *101 Dynamite Questions to Ask At Your Job Interview*, *111 Dynamite Ways to Ace Your Job Interview*, *Job Interviews For Dummies*, *The 90-Minute Interview Prep Book*, *Sweaty Palms*, *Interview Power*, *The Quick Interview and Salary Negotiation Book*, and NBEW's *Interviewing*.

While most comprehensive job search and interview books include a section on **salary negotiations**, a few books have been written specifically on this subject. The Krannichs' *Dynamite Salary Negotiations: Know What You're Worth and Get It!* examines salary negotiation strategies as well as data on salary ranges. Despite its title, Chapman's *How to Make $1,000 a Minute*, examines salary negotiation strategies. Much of the general literature on negotiation tactics is relevant to this topic.

A final set of "process" books focus on **using computers and the Internet** for finding a job. Most of these books attempt to sort through the newly emerging, and extremely chaotic, electronic job market as well as examine how to use the latest electronic technology for locating job listings and transmitting electronic resumes to online bulletin boards and databases. These books represent high-tech approaches to quickly exploring classified ads and vacancy announcements, networking for information and advice, and broadcasting resumes and letters to numerous employers. Some of the best books exploring this arena include Kennedy's *Electronic Resume Revolution* and *Hook Up, Get Hired*, Dixon's and Tiersten's *Be Your Own Headhunter Online*, Glossbrenner's *Finding a Job on the Internet*, Gonyea's *The On-Line Job Search Companion*, Godin's *Point and Click Jobfinder*, Riley's *The Guide to Internet Job Searching*, Jandt's and Nemnich's *Using the Internet and the World Wide Web in Your Job Search*, and Bounds' and Karl's *How to Get Your Dream Job Using the Internet*.

Specific Employment Fields

A second type of career and job search literature focuses primarily on specific employment fields. These books come in many forms. Some are designed to give the reader a general overview of what type of work is involved in each field. Other books include educational training and job search strategies appropriate for entry into each field. And still others are annotated listings of job and career titles—the most comprehensive being the Department of Labor's *Occupational Outlook Handbook* and *The Dictionary of Occupational Titles*, Petras' *Jobs 1997*, Krantz's *Jobs Rated Almanac* and *The World Almanac Job Finder's Guide 1997*, and Wright's *The American Almanac of Jobs and Salaries '97-98*. A few books attempt to link self-assessment data on individual values, interests, and skills to specific employment fields: *Guide For Occupational Exploration, The Enhanced Guide For Occupational Exploration*, and *Exploring Careers*.

The majority of books on employment fields are designed for individuals who are considering a particular employment field rather than for individuals wishing to advance within a field. As such, most of these books are general introductions designed to answer important "what," "where," and "how" questions for high school and college students. They provide little useful information for older and more experienced professionals who need more detailed and advanced information on their specific employment field. Examples of such books include 180 volumes in NTC Publishing's *Opportunities in... Series* with such titles as *Opportunities in Architecture, Opportunities in Office Occupations, Opportunities in Public Relations*,

Opportunities in Forestry, and *Opportunities in Travel Careers*. More and more books are being produced in specific employment fields, especially for computer, business, accounting, medical, government, international, communication, media, and travel specialists.

Specialized Career Groups

A final set of career planning and job search books has emerged during the past few years. These books are designed for specific groups of job seekers who supposedly need specialized assistance not found in most general job search process and employment field books. The most common such books focus on women, minorities, the handicapped, immigrants, public employees, military personnel, educators, mobile spouses, college graduates, gays, children, and teenagers.

Many of these books represent a new type of career planning book that will most likely continue to appear in the foreseeable future. Several books deal with both **process** and **substance**. They link the substantive "what" and "where" concerns of specific employment fields to "how" processes appropriately outlined for each field.

Take, for example, the field of advertising. Several books, such as Caffrey's *So You Want to Be in Advertising*, Mogal's *Making It in the Media Professions*, and Morgan's *The Advertising Career Directory* outline the jobs available in the field of advertising (what questions); where you should look for vacancies (where questions); and the best strategies for finding a job, including resumes, letters, and interview questions appropriate for the advertising field (how questions).

These specialized career books finally identify how general job search strategies must be adapted and modified to respond to the employment needs of different types of individuals as well as to the employment cultures found in different fields. Some of the most popular such books include *The Minority Career Handbook, Job Strategies For People With Disabilities, The Complete Guide to Public Employment, The Complete Guide to International Jobs and Careers, Flying High in Travel, Educator's Guide to Alternative Jobs and Careers, The New Relocating Spouse's Guide to Employment, Summer Opportunities For Kids and Teenagers, Job Opportunities in Health Care*, and *Environmental Jobs For Scientists and Engineers*.

In the coming decade we can expect to see many more career planning books produced along these combined process, field, and specialized group lines. While general career planning books focusing only on process and strategy will continue to proliferate, the real excitement in this field will be centered around the continuing development of books which link the job search and career planning processes to specific employment fields and specialized groups. If, for example, you are in the fields of real estate or robotics, you should be able to find books outlining what the jobs are, where to find them, and how to get them. Such books will most likely be written by seasoned professionals who represent specialized groups rather than by career planning professionals who are primarily trained in process skills. Such books will meet a growing need for information from individuals who have a solid understanding of how to get a job based on familiarity with the "ins" and "outs" of each field.

The following bibliography includes some of the best career planning resources available today. Consistent with the structure of this book and our discussion of the career and job literature, we have organized the bibliography according to process, field, and group categories.

Bibliography

Job Search Strategies and Tactics

Bolles, Richard N., *What Color Is Your Parachute?* (Berkeley, CA: Ten Speed Press, annual)

Elderkin, Kenton W., *How to Get Interviews From Classified Job Ads* (Manassas Park, VA: Impact Publications, 1993)

Figler, Howard E., *The Complete Job Search Handbook* (New York: Holt, Rinehart, and Winston, 1988)

Godin, Seth, *Point & Click Job Finder* (Chicago: Dearborn, 1996)

Gonyea, James C., *The On-Line Job Search Companion* (New York: McGraw-Hill, 1995)

Jackson, Tom, *Guerrilla Tactics in the New Job Market* (New York: Bantam, 1991)

Jandt, Fred E. and Mary B. Nemnich, *Using the Internet and the World Wide Web in Your Job Search* (Indianapolis, IN: JIST Works, Inc., 1997)

Kennedy, Joyce Lain, *Hook Up, Get Hired* (New York: Wiley, 1995)

Kennedy, Joyce Lain and Darryl Laramore, *Joyce Lain Kennedy's Career Book* (Lincolnwood, IL: NTC Publishing, 1996)

Kennedy, Joyce Lain and Thomas J. Morrow, *Electronic Job Search Revolution* (New York: Wiley, 1995)

Krannich, Ronald L., *Change Your Job, Change Your Life* (Manassas Park, VA, Impact Publications, 1997)

Lathrop, Richard, *Who's Hiring Who* (Berkeley, CA: Ten Speed Press, 1989)

Lucht, John, *Rites of Passage at $100,000+* (New York: Henry Holt, 1993)

Riley, Margaret, Frances Roehm, and Steve Oserman, *The Guide to Internet Job Searching* (Lincolnwood, IL: NTC Publishing, 1996)

Siegel, Barbara and Robert Siegel, *The Five Secrets to Finding a Job* (Manassas Park, VA: Impact Publications, 1994)

Studner, Peter K., *Super Job Search* (Los Angeles, CA: Jamenair Ltd., 1996)

Wendleton, Kate, *Through the Brick Wall* (New York: Villard Books, 1992)

Skills Identification, Testing, and Self-Assessment

Bolles, Richard N., *The New Quick Job Hunting Map* (Berkeley, CA: Ten Speed Press, 1985)

Bolles, Richard N., *The Three Boxes of Life* (Berkeley, CA: Ten Speed Press, 1981)

Crystal, John C. and Richard N. Bolles, *Where Do I Go From Here With My Life?* (Berkeley, CA: Ten Speed Press, 1979)

Gale, Barry and Linda Gale, *Discover What You're Best At* (New York: Simon & Schuster, 1983)

Holland, John L., *Making Vocational Choices* (Englewood Cliffs, NJ: Prentice-Hall, 1985)

Krannich, Ronald L. and Caryl Rae, *Discover the Best Jobs For You!* (Manassas Park, VA: Impact Publications, 1993)

Miller, Arthur F. and Ralph T. Mattson, *The Truth About You: Discover What You Should Be Doing With Your Life* (Berkeley, CA: Ten Speed Press, 1989)

Sher, Barbara, *Wishcraft: How to Get What You Really Want* (New York: Ballantine, 1983)

Sturman, Gerald M., *Career Discovery Project* (New York: Bantam, 1992)

Tieger, Paul and Barbara Barron-Tieger, *Do What You Are* (New York: Little, Brown, 1995)

Research On Cities, Fields, and Organizations

Adams Media (ed.), *The Job Bank Series: Atlanta, Boston, Chicago, Dallas, Denver, Detroit, Florida, Houston, Los Angeles, Minneapolis, New York, Ohio, Philadelphia, Phoenix, San Francisco, Seattle, St. Louis, Washington, DC* (Holbrook, MA: Adams Media, 1996-1997)

Adams Media (ed.), *The National Job Bank* (Holbrook, MA: Adams Media, 1997)

Camden, Bishop, Schwartz, Greene, Fleming-Holland, *"How to Get a Job In..." Insider's City Guides: Atlanta, Chicago, New York, San Francisco, Seattle/Portland, Southern California* (Chicago, IL: Surrey, 1995-1997)

Hopke, William (ed.), *Encyclopedia of Careers and Vocational Guidance* (Chicago, IL: J. G. Ferguson, 1996)

Hoover, Gary, Alta Campbell, Patrick J. Spain, and Alan Chai (eds.), *Hoover's 500*, *Hoover's Handbook of World Business*, and *Hoover's*

Handbook of Emerging Companies (Austin, TX: Reference Press, 1996-1997)

Krantz, Les, *Jobs Rated Almanac* (New York: Wiley, 1996)

Norback, Craig T., *Careers Encyclopedia* (Lincolnwood, IL: National Textbook, 1995)

Petras, Ross and Kathryn, *Jobs 1997* (New York: Simon & Schuster, 1997)

Schwartz, Lester and Irv Brechner, *The Career Finder* (New York: Ballantine, 1990)

U.S. Department of Labor, *The Occupational Outlook Handbook* (Washington, DC: U.S. Department of Labor, 1996)

Wright, John W., *The American Almanac of Jobs and Salaries* (New York: Avon, 1996)

Resumes and Letters

Adams Media (ed.), *The Adams Resume Almanac* (Holbrook, MA: Bob Adams, Inc., 1997)

Asher, Donald, *Asher's Bible of Executive Resumes* (Berkeley, CA: Ten Speed Press, 1996)

Beatty, Richard H., *175 High-Impact Resumes* (New York: Wiley, 1996)

Beatty, Richard H., *The Perfect Cover Letter* (New York: Wiley, 1997)

Bostwich, Burdette E., *Resume Writing* (New York: Wiley, 1995)

Corbin, Bill and Shelbi Wright, *The Edge Resume Job Search Strategy* (Carmel, IN: UN Communications, 1993)

Coxford, Lola M., *Resume Writing Made Easy* (Scottsdale, AZ: Gorsuch Scarisbrik, 1994)

Enelow, Wendy S., *100 Winning Resumes For 100,000+ Jobs* (Manassas Park, VA: Impact Publications, 1997)

Fournier, Myra and Jeffrey Spin, *Encyclopedia of Job-Winning Resumes* (Richfield, CT: Round Lake Publishing, 1991)

Fry, Ronald W., *Your First Resume* (Hawthorne, NJ: Career Press, 1995)

Good, C. Edward, *Does Your Resume Wear Blue Jeans?* (Charlottesville, VA: Blue Jeans Press, 1985)

Good, C. Edward, *Resumes For Re-Entry: A Woman's Handbook* (Manassas Park, VA: Impact Publications, 1993)

Jackson, Tom, *The New Perfect Resume* (New York: Doubleday, 1996)

Jackson, Tom, *Perfect Resume Strategies* (New York: Doubleday, 1992)

Kaplan, Robbie Miller, *101 Resumes For Sure-Hire Results* (New York: AMACOM, 1994)

Kaplan, Robbie Miller, *Resume Shortcuts* (Manassas Park, VA: Impact Publications, 1996)

Kaplan, Robbie Miller, *Sure-Hire Resumes* (New York: AMACOM, 1990)

Kennedy, Joyce Lain, *Resumes For Dummies* (Forest City, CA: IDG Books Worldwide, 1996)

Kennedy, Joyce Lain and Thomas J. Morrow, *Electronic Resume Revolution* (New York: Wiley, 1995)

Krannich, Ronald L. and Caryl Rae Krannich, *Dynamite Resumes* (Manassas Park, VA: Impact Publications, 1996)

Krannich, Ronald L. and William Banis, *High Impact Resumes and Letters* (Manassas Park, VA: Impact Publications, 1995)

Montag, Bill, *Best Resumes For $75,000+ Executive Jobs* (New York: Wiley, 1992)

Noble, David F., *The Gallery of Best Resumes* (Indianapolis, IN: JIST Works, 1994)

Parker, Yana, *The Damn Good Resume Guide* (Berkeley, NY: Ten Speed Press, 1996)

Parker, Yana, *The Resume Catalog* (Berkeley, NY: Ten Speed Press, 1996)

Swanson, David, *The Resume Solution* (Indianapolis, IN: JIST Works, 1995)

Weddle, Peter, *Electronic Resumes For the New Job Market* (Manassas Park, VA: Impact Publications, 1995)

Yate, Martin, *Resumes That Knock 'Em Dead* (Holbrook, MA: Adams Media, 1995)

Cover and Job Search Letters

Beatty, Richard H., *175 High-Impact Cover Letters* (New York: Wiley, 1996)

Beatty, Richard H., *Perfect Cover Letter* (New York: Wiley, 1997)

Fein, Richard, *Cover Letters! Cover Letters! Cover Letters!* (Hawthorne, NJ: Career Press, 1996)

Frank, William S., *200 Letters For Job Hunters* (Berkeley, CA: Ten Speed Press, 1995)

Kennedy, Joyce Lain, *Cover Letters For Dummies* (Forest City, CA: IDG Books Worldwide, 1996)

Krannich, Ronald L. and Caryl Rae Krannich, *201 Dynamite Job Search Letters* (Manassas Park, VA: Impact Publications, 1997)

Krannich, Ronald L. and Caryl Rae Krannich, *Dynamite Cover Letters* (Manassas Park, VA: Impact Publications, 1997)

Yate, Martin, *Cover Letters That Knock 'Em Dead* (Holbrook, MA: Adams Media, 1995)

Networking and Small Talk

Armstrong, Howard, *High Impact Telephone Networking* (Holbrook, MA: Adams Media, 1992)

Baber, Anne and Lynne Waymon, *Great Connections* (Manassas Park, VA: Impact Publications, 1991)

Beatty, Richard, *Richard Beatty's Job Search Networking* (Holbrook, MA: Bob Adams, Inc., 1994)

Boe, Anne and Bettie B. Youngs, *Is Your "Net" Working?* (New York: Wiley, 1989)

Garnas, Les, *How to Use People and Get What You Want—and Still Be a Nice Guy!* (Princeton, NJ: Peterson's, 1994)

Krannich, Ronald L. and Caryl Rae Krannich, *Dynamite Networking for Dynamite Jobs* (Manassas, VA: Impact Publications, 1996)

Lowstuter, Clyde C. and David P. Robertson, *Network Your Way to Your Next Job* (New York: McGraw-Hill, 1994)

National Business Employment Week, *National Business Employment Weekly's Networking* (New York: Wiley, 1996)

RoAnn, Susan, *How to Work a Room* (New York: Warner Books, 1988)

RoAnn, Susan, *Secrets of Savvy Networking* (New York: Warner Books, 1992)

Vilas, Donna and Sanda, *Power Networking* (Austin, TX: Duke Publishing, 1992)

Dress, Appearance, and Image

Karpinski, Kenneth J., *Red Socks Don't Work: Messages From the Real Work About Men's Clothing* (Manassas Park, VA: Impact Publications, 1994)

Molloy, John T., *John Molloy's New Dress for Success* (New York: Warner Books, 1991)

Molloy, John T., *New Women's Dress for Success* (New York: Warner Books, 1997)

Nicholson, JoAnna, *110 Mistakes Working Women Make and How to Avoid Them: Dressing Smart for the '90s* (Manassas Park, VA: Impact Publications, 1994)

Interviews and Salary Negotiations

Fein, Richard, *101 Dynamite Questions to Ask At Your Job Interview* (Manassas Park, VA: Impact Publications, 1996)

Fein, Richard, *111 Dynamite Ways to Ace Your Job Interview* (Manassas Park, VA: Impact Publications, 1997)

Fry, Ronald W., *101 Great Answers To the Toughest Interview Questions* (Hawthorne, NJ: Career Press, 1995)

Krannich, Caryl Rae and Ronald L. Krannich, *101 Dynamite Answers to Interview Questions* (Manassas Park, VA: Impact Publications, 1997)

Krannich, Caryl Rae and Ronald L. Krannich, *Interview for Success* (Manassas Park, VA: Impact Publications, 1997)

Krannich, Ronald L. and Caryl Rae Krannich, *Dynamite Salary Negotiations* (Manassas Park, VA: Impact Publications, 1994)

Krannich, Ronald L. and Caryl Rae Krannich, *Dynamite Tele-Search* (Manassas Park, VA: Impact Publications, 1995)

Medley, H. Anthony, *Sweaty Palms* (Berkeley, CA: Ten Speed Press, 1991)

Yate, Martin, *Knock 'Em Dead* (Boston, MA: Adams Media, 1997)

Educators

Krannich, Ronald L. *Educator's Guide to Alternative Jobs and Careers* (Manassas Park, VA: Impact Publications, 1991)

Public-Oriented Careers

Damp, Dennis, *The Book of U.S. Government Jobs* (Corapolis, PA: D-Amp Publications, 1995)

Krannich, Ronald L. and Caryl Rae Krannich, *The Complete Guide to Public Employment* (Manassas Park, VA: Impact Publications, 1995)

Krannich, Ronald L. and Caryl Rae Krannich, *Directory of Federal Jobs and Employers* (Manassas Park, VA: Impact Publications, 1996)

Krannich, Ronald L. and Caryl Rae Krannich, *Find a Federal Job Fast!* (Manassas Park, VA: Impact Publications, 1997)

Krannich, Ronald L. and Caryl Rae Krannich, *Jobs and Careers With Nonprofit Organizations* (Manassas Park, VA: Impact Publications, 1995)

Lauber, Daniel, *The Government Job Finder* (River Forest, IL: Planning/Communications, 1997)

Lauber, Daniel, *The Nonprofit's and Education Job Finder* (River Forest, IL: Planning/Communication, 1997)

Smith, Russ, *Federal Applications That Get Results* (Manassas Park, VA: Impact Publications, 1996)

Smith, Russ, *Federal Jobs in Law Enforcement* (Manassas Park, VA: Impact Publications, 1996)

International and Overseas Jobs

Forbes, Moira, *Jobs in Russia and the Newly Independent States* (Manassas Park, VA: Impact Publications, 1994)

Foreign Policy Association (ed.), *Guide to Careers in World Affairs* (Manassas Park, VA: Impact Publications, 1993)

Kocher, Eric, *International Jobs* (Reading, MA: Addison-Wesley, 1993)

Krannich, Ronald L. and Caryl Rae Krannich, *Almanac of International Jobs and Careers* (Manassas Park, VA: Impact Publications, 1994)

Krannich, Ronald L. and Caryl Rae Krannich, *The Complete Guide to International Jobs and Careers* (Manassas Park, VA: Impact Publications, 1993)

Krannich, Ronald L. and Caryl Rae Krannich, *Jobs For People Who Love Travel* (Manassas Park, VA: Impact Publications, 1995)

Lay, David Caldwell and Benedict A. Leerburger, *Jobs Worldwide* (Manassas Park, VA: Impact Publications, 1996)

Sanborn, Robert, *How to Get a Job in Europe* (Chicago, IL: Surrey, 1995)

Military

Farley, Janet I., *Jobs and the Military Spouse* (Manassas Park, VA: Impact Publications, 1997)

Henderson, David G., *Job Search: Marketing Your Military Experience in the 1990s* (Harrisonburg, PA: Stackpole Books, 1995)

Jacobsen, Kenneth C., *Retiring From the Military* (Annapolis, MD: Naval Institute Press, 1994)

Savino, Carl and Ronald L. Krannich, *From Air Force Blue to Corporate Gray* (Manassas Park, VA: Impact Publications, 1996)

Savino, Carl and Ronald L. Krannich, *From Army Green to Corporate Gray* (Manassas Park, VA: Impact Publications, 1997)

Savino, Carl and Ronald L. Krannich, *From Navy Blue to Corporate Gray* (Manassas Park, VA: Impact Publications, 1995)

Savino, Carl and Ronald L. Krannich, *Resumes and Cover Letters For Transitioning Military Personnel* (Manassas Park, VA: Impact Publications, 1997)

Women and Spouses

Bastress, Fran, *The New Relocating Spouse's Guide to Employment* (Manassas Park, VA: Impact Publications, 1993)

Martin, Renee and Don, *A Survival Guide For Women* (Washington, DC: Regnery Gateway, 1991)

College Students

Bouchard, Jerry, *Graduating to the 9-5 World* (Manassas Park, VA: Impact Publications, 1991)

LaFevre, John L., *How You Really Get Hired* (New York: Simon & Schuster, 1994)

Minorities and Special Needs Groups

Johnson, Willis L. (ed.), *The Big Book of Minority Group Members* (Garrett Park, MD: Garrett Park Press, 1995)

Kastre, Michael, Alfred Edwards, and Nydia Rodriguez Kastre, *Minority Career Guide* (Princeton, NJ: Peterson's, 1993)

Kissane, Sharon F., *Career Success For People With Physical Disabilities* (Lincolnwood, IL: NTC Publishing, 1996)

Rivera, Miquela, *The Minority Career Handbook* (Holbrook, MA: Adams Media, 1990)

Witt, Melanie Astaire, *Job Strategies For People With Disabilities* (Princeton, NJ: Peterson's, 1992)

Alternative Career Fields

Basta, Nick, *Careers in High Tech* (Lincolnwood, IL: NTC Publishing, 1992)

Edelfedt, Roy A., *Careers in Education* (Lincolnwood, IL: NTC Publishing, 1993)

Hiam, Alex and Susan Angle, *Adventure Careers* (Hawthorne, NJ: Career Press, 1995)

Krannich, Ronald L. and Caryl Rae Krannich, *Jobs For People Who Love Travel* (Manassas Park, VA: Impact Publications, 1995)

Mantis, Hillary and Kathleen Brady, *Jobs For Lawyers* (Manassas Park, VA: Impact Publications, 1996)

Michael, Angie, *Best Impressions in Hospitality* (Manassas Park, VA: Impact Publications, 1995)

"Opportunities In..." Career Series (180 titles), (Lincolnwood, IL: NTC Publishing, 1990-1997)

Peterson's (ed.), *Job Opportunities in Health Care* (Princeton, NJ: Peterson's, 1997)

Rubin, K., *Flying High In Travel: A Complete Guide to Careers in the Travel Industry* (New York: Wiley, 1992)

Schaffer, William S., *Hi-Tech Jobs For Lo-Tech People* (New York: AMACOM, 1994)

Shenk, Ellen, *Outdoor Careers* (Harrisonburg, PA: Stackpole Books, 1992)

Stair, Lila B., *Careers in Computers* (Lincolnwood, IL: NTC Publishing, 1995)

Resume and Letter Production Computer Software

The Perfect Resume Computer Kit (Madison, WI: Permax Systems, Inc.)

The Right Resumes Writer I, II, and III (Vancouver, WA: The School Company)

The Resume Kit (Cambridge, MA: Spinnaker Software)

You're Hired! (Harrisburg, PA: DataTech)

Resume Videos

Does Your Resume Wear Blue Jeans? Resume Writing Workshop
(Charlottesville, VA: Blue Jeans Press)
The Miracle Resume (Indianapolis, IN: JIST Works, Inc.)
The Video Resume Writer (Vancouver, WA: The School Company)

CD-ROM Programs

Adams Job Bank CD-ROM (Holbrook, MA: Adams Media, 1996)
Electronic Enhanced Dictionary of Occupational Titles (Indianapolis, IN:
JIST Works, Inc. 1996)
The Encyclopedia of Careers and Vocational Guidance (Chicago:
Ferguson, 1997)
Interview Skills For the Future (Vancouver, WA: The School Co., 1996)
Job Search Skills For the 21st Century (Vancouver, WA: The School
Company, 1996)
Multimedia Career Center (Charleston, WV: Cambridge Career Products,
1994)
Occupational Outlook CD-ROM (Lincolnwood, IL: NTC Publishing, Co.,
1996)
The Ultimate Job Source (Orem, UT: InfoBusiness, 1995)
Win-Way Resumes 4.0 (Sacramento, CA: Win-Way, 1996)

21

Join the Electronic Revolution

Electronic resumes, optical scanners, resume databases and service bureaus, commercial online services, and the Internet are literally transforming the way individuals conduct a job search. They also are changing the methods by which employers arrive at hiring decisions. More and more employers are relying on new electronic methods for screening candidates.

New search and retrieval software programs along with Internet job sites are increasingly responsible for linking candidates to employers. Indeed, during the next decade this technology may significantly alter the nature of the job market. It is already changing the way individuals find jobs, from writing and distributing resumes to conducting research and networking for job leads. It's a revolution you need to learn to immediately ride since your next job search may well incorporate many elements of this electronic job search revolution. Much of this revolution centers on the ritual of writing and distributing resumes, especially electronic resumes.

Creating "Software Sensitive" Resumes

The electronic resume is different. As noted earlier, this type of resume requires close attention to the choice of resume language. The software literally takes keywords selected by employers and matches them with similar keywords found on resumes. If, for example, an employer is looking for a human resources manager with ten years of progressive experience in developing training programs for mining engineers, a search for candidates meeting these qualifications may result in making matches with fifteen resumes in the database. The employer receives hard copies of the electronic resumes and further sorts the batch of candidates through more traditional means such as telephone screening interviews.

The new electronic job search and hiring systems have important implications for resume writing. When writing an electronic resume, you must focus on using **proper resume language** that would be most

347

responsive for the search and retrieval software. This means knowing what keywords are best to include in such a resume. Keywords often encompass the jargon of particular fields. Traditional "dress for success" elements, such as layout, type faces, emphasis, paper texture, and color, are important at the second stage when being evaluated by the hiring official **after** the resume has been retrieved electronically. The degree to which your resume is "software sensitive" may largely determine how many employers will contact you. If your resume lacks an appropriate mix of keywords, it will be passed over as unacceptable for further consideration.

New Resume Initiatives

During the past few years numerous firms have gotten into the electronic resume business. Many use e-mail communications, online bulletin boards, and commercial online services such as America Online, CompuServe, Prodigy, and the Microsoft Network. Primarily funded by large employers, membership in these databases includes individuals, associations, and alumni, retirement, military, and other groups who are interested in linking electronic resumes to member companies. These resume services are new employer-employee networks which are redefining the job market. The marketplace is no longer confined just to the classified ads, employment firms, or executive search firms. These firms may bring together over 100,000 members into an electronic network which is constantly seeking to find "good fits" between the needs of employers and the keywords appearing on members' electronic résumés.

For individual job seekers, these electronic databases and online services enable them to quickly and conveniently conduct research on jobs and employers, acquire job information and advice, access employment data, post resumes online, and continuously target a job search toward numerous employers nationally as well as internationally. Many of the databases and services enable individuals to broadcast their resumes to thousands of potential employers who would not have been reached through more traditional job search or networking methods. These forms of electronic networking also give new meaning to the "information interview" which can be conducted with hundreds of individuals who participate in chat groups, use electronic bulletin boards, and communicate by e-mail.

The electronic job search revolution has evolved so fast, constantly changing its shape from day-to-day, that no one can say for certain where it is at present nor exactly where it is going over the next year or two or beyond. We do know the electronic job market shares one characteristic with the traditional job market—it's a truly chaotic arena. However, several new cautionary "facts of life" have emerged relevant to this new revolution:

1. **Several resume database firms that led this revolution just two or three years ago (kiNexus, Connexion, Career Place-**

Placement Registry, Job Bank USA) have either gone out of business or transformed their operations to be compatible with the latest electronic trends—the use of the Internet and e-mail. A highly competitive arena for high-tech entrepreneurs in search of content, electronic employment services have not been profitable operations for most companies venturing into this arena; most must resign themselves with the expectation that this will be a long-term investment with a few "winners" emerging in perhaps five or ten years from now. Indeed, no one has figured out how to make much money operating these databases and services, beyond charging employers for listing job vacancies and conducting candidate searches—traditional advertising and recruitment functions that used to be monopolized by newspapers and employment firms; individual job seekers have not been good paying customers. And these two ostensible profit centers (resume databases and services) may be in the process of disappearing altogether as more and more employers and job seekers use the free access of the Internet for electronic networking and services. Thus, we expect more and more electronic database and employment firms to emerge as well as go out of business within the next year or two as the Internet emerges as a major networking center for employers and job seekers. Except for those that perform highly specialized recruitment functions, we do not expect many for-profit employment database and service firms to survive beyond 1998; few will enter the 21st century. The continuing fall-out of such services and firms looks inevitable in what appears to be continuing chaos in cyberspace.

2. **Most of what you may have read about the electronic job search revolution six months ago is probably obsolete by now** because of the rapid changes taking place in this new employment arena. Even what we say here in this chapter on electronic networking and resume databases will probably be obsolete within the next few months. No one is sure where it is going, but the current chaos seems to be going anywhere but North! As one of the leading electronic job search experts, Joyce Lain Kennedy, recently observed, in the long-run job seekers are best off learning how to use the Internet and e-mail for electronic networking—electronic skills that will serve them well in the job markets of today and tomorrow. Everything else may be a short-term distraction. Indeed, right now we're seeing lots of cowboys in cyberspace trying to stake out profitable businesses that have yet to bear fruit. Most will not survive long as they continue to fall out in the face of harsh economic realities in the new electronic age.

3. **The effectiveness of new electronic networking and electronic resume databases over conventional networking and resume distribution methods has yet to be proven nor are they necessarily in competition with each other.** The hype and hoopla about electronic networking and resume databases is based on a vision or promise rather than on concrete performance. As with any self-proclaimed revolution, there is a tendency to get seduced by a vision of the future, lose perspective, and thus confuse promises with performance as well as the media with the message. It's true that some employers do recruit candidates, and some job seekers do find jobs using electronic databases, online services, and the Internet, but no one knows to what extent they do. One suspects the numbers are very low, and for good reasons. So far the technology has been primarily applied to and hyped for the least effective job search activity—broadcasting resumes to employers. This has always been the least productive job search activity anyone can engage in. It simply doesn't work in over 95 percent of the cases. Not to be dissuaded from such realities, proponents of electronic networking primarily outline the promises and mechanics of using the databases and services. The evidence of performance is largely anecdotal and most of it points in one direction—electronic networking is most effective for employers and job seekers in high-demand high-tech fields or those seeking individuals with an exotic combination of skills and experience. Ironically, the anecdotal evidence tends to reinforce what we've known all along about job listings or the advertised job market—aside from the newness of the technology, there is nothing magical nor new about this revolution in reference to job search and recruitment functions. This new electronic revolution operates similarly to classified ads and executive search firms—it lists jobs and recruits for high-demand positions. Its real advantage is that it does it faster and thus saves both employers and job seekers time and money. The result may be that less than 5 percent of all jobs will be represented through the electronic databases and services. There is little evidence that electronic networking and resume databases are very effective for individuals seeking entry-level positions outside the current high-demand high-tech fields.

4. **There's a tendency to confuse the medium with the message.** The job search message remains the same: how to best develop job leads and communicate your qualifications to potential employers. An effective job search accomplishes this by connecting with jobs that best "fit" the interests and skills of the job seeker. In the past, the main mediums for doing this have been

the mail, telephone, fax, and face-to-face meetings. The new electronic revolution now allows individuals to use computers and online services to quickly acquire job information, identify potential employers, and communicate qualifications to employers by electronic means. It's like having a typewriter connected to a telephone with the capacity to interactively communicate with a vast audience. So far there is little evidence that the new medium will substantially alter the traditional job search message—communication between employer and job seeker.

5. **Despite the hype, false starts, and current chaos, there's no question about it—the electronic job search is here to stay and in a very big way.** More and more employers will list their vacancies online and use specialized electronic recruitment services. The main casualties of this electronic revolution will probably be (1) newspapers whose classified ad sections will continue to decline in both size and revenue as more and more of their print business goes online; (2) employment firms and career counselors who do not adapt to the new technology; and (3) several employment database firms and services that failed to move to the Internet as well as failed to solve the issue of profitability on the Internet. The main beneficiaries will be both employers and job seekers who should be able to substantially cut their time and costs in navigating an increasingly competitive and chaotic job market. Our advice to job seekers is to learn how to network both interpersonally and electronically. Learn how to use both the Internet and e-mail as you develop your repertoire of electronic job search skills. You'll need to use such skills for the 21st century!

Where Is the Revolution?

What exactly is this electronic revolution in relation to the job search? During the past three years, it has taken on several forms. One of its most basic and popular forms involves linking job seekers with employers through an electronic resume. Job seekers develop an electronic resume which is capable of being scanned into a sophisticated computerized database consisting of employers who specify qualifications they seek in candidates. In its optimal form, the electronic resume is designed with keywords in mind. For a per search and/or yearly membership fee, employers request one or more of these firms to identify a specific number of candidates who meet their vacancy requirements. The requirements, in the form of keywords, are input into the resume bank.

Depending on both the size of the database and the requirements of the employer, this electronic search procedure may generate anywhere from none to 50 resumes of potentially qualified candidates. The resumes are then sent to employers who, in turn, review them and select the best ones for initial computer or telephone screening interviews which may eventually turn into a series of job interviews and the selection of one candidate.

The beauty of this electronic job search system is its speed, cost, and possible effectiveness for both employers and job seekers. While employers may normally spend $1,000 to $20,000, as well as one to three months recruiting an employee, they may accomplish the same goal within one to two weeks at the cost of $100 to $300 by using the services of an electronic resume bank. While job seekers must learn to write a new type of resume—an electronic resume peppered with keywords that are most responsive to this type of technology—the results may be extremely worthwhile and may well revolutionize the whole concept of job seeking. Whether or not they are actively seeking employment, for a yearly membership fee of $30 to $100, individuals can keep their resume in an electronic resume bank. They will be contacted by member employers if and when their resume "matches" the requirements of employers.

> Online career services enable job seekers to conduct research, join discussion groups, attend workshops, review job listings, and send resumes to employers.

Other popular forms of the electronic job search revolution involve career centers and services available through commercial online services (America Online, CompuServe, Delphi, GEnie, Prodigy, Microsoft Network) and on the Internet (World Wide Web). Here, job seekers can conduct research on jobs and employers, join discussion groups, attend workshops, acquire information and advice from career counselors and fellow job seekers, review thousands of job listings, and transmit resumes to employers. Traditional networking activities, which normally are done over the telephone or in face-to-face meetings, can be conducted through e-mail with hundreds of individuals who volunteer information and advice. Whether or not this is the same quality information and advice acquired through more traditional targeted networking activities is another story altogether. Nonetheless, it is another medium through which you can network for information, advice, and referrals.

Job Hunting That Never Stops

The revolutionary aspects of this new technology may eventually go far beyond just the electronic matching process that quickly links employers with job seekers. Given the "membership" nature of some electronic databases, they may revolutionize the way individuals make career moves. The notion that an individual stops job hunting after finding a job will likely be replaced with this concept of job hunting: you are always in the job market seeking opportunities. By paying an annual fee and regularly updating your resume for the database, your resume is always working the job market even though ostensibly you are not job hunting. You, in effect, are networking 24 hours a day, 7 days a week, 365 days a year.

The electronic job search may alter the way people think about the job hunting process. You no longer just turn it on or off when you are in need of another job. It's always turned on. Anytime of the day you can literally surf the Internet for potential job openings. On the other hand, while you may be perfectly content with your current job, as a member of XYZ Job Bank, you regularly hear from employers who are interested in your qualifications. You examine the competition and assess whether or not this is the time for you to make another career move. For you and thousands of other members of XYZ Job Bank, you are always prepared to make strategic job and career moves because you are literally wired so you can electronically network 24 hours a day. Unemployment, job dissatisfaction, and unexpected career shocks are not part of your career perspective or experience. Your continuous career health requires you to always be in the job market by way of your membership in XYZ Job Bank. In fact, you are likely to become a lifetime member of this organization. Over a 40-year worklife period, you may have found 10 of your employers through your membership in XYZ Job Bank. At the cost of $50 a year, this electronic job service was well worth the expense. Best of all, it reduced the anxiety of having to look for employment under adverse circumstances and through traditional job search methods that were extremely inefficient and ineffective.

Join an electronic job service and your job search will never end! That's if these electronic networks actually get used by employers and job seekers to the degree envisioned by proponents of these new employment networks. The performance evidence remains anecdotal at best.

Who Are the New Revolutionaries?

During the past few years numerous firms have gotten into the electronic resume and employment businesses. Many of them use electronic e-mail, online bulletin boards, and existing commercial online computer services such as America Online, CompuServe, Prodigy, and Microsoft Network. Others are accessed solely through the Internet via the World Wide Web. Primarily funded by large Fortune 1,000 corporations, membership in the electronic employment database companies includes individuals, professional associations, and alumni, retirement, military and other groups who are interested in linking electronic resumes to member companies. These electronic resume services have become new employer-employee networks which are redefining certain segments of the job market. The marketplace is no longer confined to the classified ads, employment firms, or executive search firms. It is also found in computerized databases developed by electronic resume firms. These firms may bring together over 100,000 members into an electronic network which is constantly seeking to find "good fits" between the needs of employers and the keywords appearing on members' electronic resumes.

One of the major advantages of participating in these electronic networks is that you may have access to numerous positions that are not advertised outside the network. When a vacancy occurs or new position is created, participating employers may first turn to the network for qualified candidates before advertising the position outside the electronic network. It may be to your advantage to participate in such a network because you will have access to numerous positions and employers you might not otherwise reach through other networking means.

Resume Databases

Resume databases are the most passive job search activities you can engage in. All you need to do is contact a database firm, submit a resume or complete a candidate profile form, and perhaps pay a monthly or yearly membership fee (some are free because employers pay the tariffs). The firm inputs your resume or personal profile information in the computer along with thousands of other resumes. Employers either have online access to the database or they have the firm conduct candidate searches by screening resumes on specific position criteria. Employers often pay yearly membership fees or per search fees in order to use these databases. All the individual job seeker needs to do is submit a resume or complete a profile form and in some cases pay a fee. Since the resume database firm manages the electronic networking process, all the job seeker needs to do is join the network, similar to joining other types of subscription-based organizations. The job seeker then waits to see what will transpire as the computer attempts to match individual resumes with employer needs. These new database systems are high-tech versions of the old resume broadcast method.

These are very volatile businesses still attempting to resolve the issue of profitability, especially in the face of increased competition and the role of the Internet which has quickly become the major medium for electronic networking. Indeed, several major companies that pioneered such databases have gone out of business during the past three years: kiNexus, Connexion, Career Placement Registry, Job Bank USA. More are likely to do so soon.

Some of the most popular electronic resume database firms include the following:

❑ **Career Net Graduate:** 643 W. Crosstown Parkway, Kalamazoo, MI 49008, Tel. 616-344-3017. Designed for college students and recent graduates, this service puts resumes on CD-ROM discs and distributes them to nearly 10,000 major employers. Charges less than $100 for one academic year; allows two updates.

❑ **Cors:** One Pierce Place, Suite 300 East, Itasca, IL 60143, Tel. 800-323-1352, 708-250-8677 or Fax 708-250-7362. Includes more than 1 million resumes in its database. Contracts with employers to recruit candidates from database. Charges one-time $25 fee for entering resume in database. Allows unlimited updates.

❑ **Electronic Job Matching:** 1915 N. Dale Mabry Highway, Suite 307, Tampa, FL 33607, Tel. 813-879-4100 or Fax 813-870-1883. Includes applicant resumes in database that can be accessed by employers who pay search fees. Free of charge for job seekers.

❑ **Gonyea & Associates, Inc.:** 3543 Enterprise Road East, Safety Harbor, FL 34695, Tel. 813-725-9600. Offers several types of electronic services for job seekers. Its Help-Wanted-USA database includes classified employment ads from over 50 major newspapers. The database can be accessed free of charge (less access fees) through America Online or the Internet. The company also on a weekly basis will match your goals to specific job listings or send you the database on a disk for $39.95 for six weeks.

❑ **Mainstream Job Bank USA:** 20 Signal Road, Stamford, CT 06902, Tel. 800-296-1USA or Fax 203-353-1809. Formerly operated as Job Bank USA, this newly reorganized company provides both on-line and off-line career services. You can enter your resume in their database free of charge by transmitting it by e-mail or by sending it on disk. They will scan your resume for a fee. Includes a resume review and career counseling service.

❑ **National Resume Bank:** 3637 4th Street North, No. 330, St. Petersburg, FL 33704, Tel. 813-896-3694 or Fax 813-894-1277. This online resume database includes more than 3,000 resumes for 35 job categories. Employers access the database to match job requirements with specific resumes. Job seekers pay a $40 one-time fee. Employers get free access to database.

❑ **Resume-Link:** 3972-C Brown Park Drive, Hilliard, OH 43026, Tel. 714-777-4000 or Fax 614-771-5708. Specializes in the computer and engineering fields. Includes 20,000+ resumes in its database. Free to job seekers who belong to a relevant professional society ($50 a year for nonmembers). Employers pay.

❑ **SkillSearch:** 3354 Perimeter Hill Drive, Suite 235, Nashville, TN 37211-4129, Tel. 615-834-9448 or Fax 615-834-9453. Sponsored by 60 university alumni associations, alumni associated with each sponsoring university can have their resumes included in the database for $65 the first year and $15 for each additional year. Employers pay a per-search fee to use the database.

❑ **University ProNet:** 2445 Faber Place, Box 51820, Palo Alto, CA 94303, Fax 415-845-4019 (for telephone numbers of each participating alumni group). Participation restricted to alumni of 16 member universities: California Institute of Technology, Carnegie-Mellon University, Columbia University, Cornell University, Massachusetts Institute of Technology, Ohio State University, Stanford University, University of California at Berkeley, University of California at Los Angeles, University of Chicago, University of Illinois, University of Michigan, University of Pennsylvania, University of Texas at Austin, and Yale University. Employers pay an annual subscription fee to participate in data-base. Alumni charged a one-time $35 registration fee. Operated by the alumni associations at each participating university.

❑ **V-Quest:** 5700 Fourth St. North, St. Petersburg, FL 33703, Tel. 813-528-4005 or Fax 813-528-4406. Provides resumes online to 500 major employers free of charge. Individuals pay $79.95 for the first year to have their personal profile/resume placed in the database.

Online Services

Opportunities for more active forms of electronic networking are found through e-mail, discussion groups, workshops, and career centers of online commercial services or on the Internet's World Wide Web. The major commercial online services with career segments include:

❑ **America Online:** 8619 Westwood Center Dr., Vienna, VA 22182, Tel. 800-827-6364 or Fax 703-556-3750. Today's fastest growing and most popular commercial online service claiming a membership of over 7 million users. Its popular America Online's Career Center, operated by James C. Gonyea, offers a variety of useful job search options, from career counseling and chat groups to job listings and career resources. The service also offers other opportunities to network through its chat groups (*People's Connection*), message boards (*The Exchange Message Boards*), and special interest groups and networks for educators, health professionals, lawyers, writers, seniors, and others.

❑ **CompuServe:** 5000 Arlington Centre Boulevard, P.O. Box 20212, Columbus, OH 43220, Tel. 800-848-8199 or Fax 614-457-0348. Claiming more than 3 million subscribers, this popular commercial online service is perhaps the most sophisticated of the bunch. It includes numerous forums and databases from which job seekers can explore job opportunities, exchange information and advice, and conduct research on employers. Its more than 700 forums constitute a rich resource for networking with thousands of individuals.

❑ **Delphi:** Tel. 800-695-4005. This relatively new service offers excellent opportunities to network electronically through various forums and discussion groups relevant to specific professional or career interest groups. *The Job Complex* forum, for example, includes lots of useful job search information, including job listings. Nurses should explore *The Nursing Network* for information on nursing opportunities. And if you really don't want to work for someone else, try *The Self-Employment* forum for tips on starting your own business.

❑ **Dialog:** 3460 Hillview Avenue, Palo Alto, CA 94304, Tel. 800-334-2564 or Fax 415-858-7069. This online information service functions like a big library which provides access to hundreds of newspapers, journals, magazines, and newsletters. It's especially useful for conducting research on various career fields. It includes hundreds of databases on a variety of subjects including government, law, chemistry, economics, engineering, biology, agriculture, and science and technology. You won't find career centers or discussion groups here.

❑ **GEnie:** 401 North Washington Street, Rockville, MD 20850, Tel. 800-638-9636. One of the smaller online services, GEnie includes a job bank, which is operated by E-Span, as well as the *Business Resource Directory*, the *Home Office/Small Business RoundTable,* and *Dr. Job.*

❑ **Microsoft Network:** Microsoft Corporation, 1 Microsoft Way, Redmond, WA 98052, Tel. 800-386-5550. One of the newest and most aggressive online services operated by the Microsoft Corporation and bundled in its Windows 95 software. Includes the Mainstream Career Center which offers job listings and a variety of services operated by numerous vendors who offer a combination of free and per fee services.

❑ **Prodigy:** 445 Hamilton Avenue, White Plains, NY 10601, Tel. 800-PRODIGY or 800-776-3449. Claiming more than 2 million subscribers, this service also offers several useful career information and networking opportunities through its *Careers BB* and *Classifieds* services. Prodigy is especially useful for individuals conducting a long-distance job search. It includes several major newspapers and community bulletin boards for surveying different communities and classified ads.

Most of these commercial online companies offer at least 10 free hours of connect time to sample their services. If you decide to subscribe, expect to pay about $10.00 per month, which includes 3-5 free hours of online time, plus $3.00 for each additional hour. However, in December 1996 America Online started its "unlimited use" program for $19.95 per month; other online services are likely to follow with a similar fee structure as they face intense competition from America Online and even cheaper Internet access providers. Call their toll-free numbers for information on their services. In addition to paying monthly user fees, you will need a computer, modem, and communications software to interact with these services. Each of these services can advise you on hardware requirements; they provide the software.

Once you are connected to one or more of these services, chances are you will be able to access a great deal of employment information useful to your job search. Most of these services include online classifieds, career bulletin boards, and discussion forums. Using e-mail, you can network for information, advice, and referrals. You can explore bulletin boards for job listings in your particular career field as well as participate in online discussion groups and seminars, access job search resources, and receive online counseling. While many services are free, except for the connect time, others may involve special user or service fees. You'll quickly discover your online networking opportunities are endless. All of these services also provide access to the Internet.

The Internet's World Wide Web

If you choose not to use one of the online commercial services, you can gain direct access to the Internet through an independent service provider. Within the last year, several new career-related services have appeared on the Internet's World Wide Web, and several of those which used to be accessed only through the commercial online services are now available on the World Wide Web. In fact, this is where much of the online career networking is taking place these days. Some observers predict that the future of commercial online services is now at serious risk since more and more people are gaining direct access to the multitude of new services available on the World Wide Web through independent service providers. This eliminates the need to incur the hourly charges of the commercial online services when using the Internet.

The following organizations now operate databases and career services on the Internet's World Wide Web. Most of them offer a combination of free and fee-based services and products. Some primarily operate as job listing bulletin boards (BBS):

❑ **Adams JobBank Online:** http://www.adamsonline.com. Operated by one of the major publishers of career books, this online service includes job listings, discussion forums (conferences, workshops, Q&A sessions), specialized career services, and publications.

❑ **America's Job Bank:** http://www.ajb.dni.us. Here's the ultimate "public job bank" that could eventually put some private online entrepreneurs out of business. Operated by the U.S. Department of Labor, this is the closest thing to a comprehensive nationwide computerized job bank. Linked to state employment offices, which daily post thousands of new job listings filed by employers with their offices, individuals should soon be able to explore more than a million job vacancies in both the public and private sectors at any time through this service. Since this is your government at work, this service is free. While the jobs listing cover everything from entry-level to professional and managerial positions, expect to find a disproportionate number of jobs requiring less than a college education listed in this job bank. This service is also available at state employment offices as well as at other locations (look for touch screen kiosks in shopping centers and other public places) which are set up for public use. Useful linkages.

❑ **CareerMosiac:** http://www.careermosaic.com. This job service is appropriate for college students and professionals. Includes hundreds of job listings in a large variety of fields, from high-tech to retail, with useful information on each employer and job. Includes a useful feature whereby college students can communicate directly with employers (e-mail) for information and advice—a good opportunity to do "inside" networking.

❑ **CareerWEB:** http://www.cweb.com. Operated by Landmark Communications (Norfolk, Virginia) which also publishes several newspapers and operates The Weather Channel, The Travel Channel, and InfiNet, this service is a major recruitment source for hundreds of companies nationwide. Free service for job seekers who can explore hundreds of job listings, many of which are in high-tech fields. Includes company profile pages to learn about a specific company. A quality operation. Publishes a useful newsletter called *CareerWEB Connections*.

❑ **E-Span:** http://www.espan.com. This full-service online employment resource includes hundreds of job listings in a variety of fields as well as operates a huge database of résumés. Job seekers can send their resumes (e-mail or snail mail) to be included in their database of job listings and search for appropriate job openings through the Interactive Employment Network. Also includes useful career information and resources. If you use commercial online services, E-Span can be accessed through America Online, CompuServe, and GEnie.

❑ **JobTrak:** http://www.jobtrak.com. This organization posts over 500 new job openings each day from companies seeking college students and graduates. Includes company profiles, job hunting tips, employment information, and numerous job resources compiled by Margaret Riley. Good source for entry-level positions, including both full-time and part-time positions, and for researching companies. Very popular with college students.

❑ **JobWeb:** http://www.jobweb.org. A relatively new and comprehensive online service targeted for the college scene, following the demise of kiNexus and Connexion. Operated by the National Association of

Colleges and Universities (formerly the College Placement Council), this service is designed to do everything: compiles information on employers, including salary surveys; lists job openings; provides job search assistance; and maintains a resume database.

❑ **Online Career Center:** http://www.occ.com/occ. This is the grandaddy of career centers on the Internet. It's basically a resume database and job search service. Individuals send their resume (free if transmitted electronically) which is then included in the database. Individuals also can search for appropriate job openings. Employers pay for using the service. Also available through online commercial services.

❑ **WorkLife:** http://www.worklife.com. Operated by Mainstream Access. It offers services for both job seekers and employers in four areas: career, entrepreneurship, human resources, and learning. While some services are free, many specialized services involve fees. For example, employers can use some services to conduct online psychological testing of job candidates.

Other Electronic Networks

Commercial online services and career-related World Wide Web sites on the Internet are only the tip of the iceberg when it comes to electronic networking. Numerous professional groups, from the military to health care professionals, have established, or are in the process of creating, their own World Wide Web sites and bulletin boards (BBS). Most of these groups operate discussion forums and networking groups as well as post job openings. If you are just getting started with electronic networking, the groups

> **Learn how to network online via the Internet. Put together an electronic resume and transmit it by e-mail.**

we've identified thus far should suffice in pointing you in the right direction. Starting with these resources, you should be able to quickly find useful linkages to other more specialized sites relating to employment issues.

If you know how to use e-mail and surf the Internet, a whole new job search world will unfold before your computer screen. You will discover new ways to network your way to job and career success. Indeed, as we write this material, several hundred new networking groups are in the process of developing sites on the Internet. Within the next 12 months many new employment players will be up and running online. Our best advice is this: you should learn how to operate online so you can discover as well as create your own electronic networking opportunities in the future. Learn how to put together an electronic resume as well as how to transmit your resume via e-mail. Your major challenge will be to sort through the chaos of this new electronic world to get meaningful results! This will not be as easy a task as it may initially appear. Expect to do a lot of electronic communicating that has little or no payoff for your job search.

Key Electronic Job Search Resources

Several books provide useful information on the new electronic job search era. Among some of the most useful such resources are:

Bounds, Shannon and Arthur Karl, *How to Get Your Dream Job Using the Internet* (Scottsdale, AZ: Coriolis Group Books, 1996)

Dixon, Pam and Sylvia Tiersten, *Be Your Own Headhunter: Go Online to Get the Job You Want* (New York: Random House Electronic, 1995)

Glossbrenner, Alfred and Emily, *Finding a Job on the Internet* (New York: McGraw-Hill, 1995)

Godin, Seth, *Point and Click Jobfinder* (Chicago: Dearborn, 1996)

Goodwin, Mary, Deborah Cohn, Donna Spivey, *Net Jobs: How to Use the Internet to Land Your Dream Job* (New York: Michael Wolff & Co. Publishing, 1996)

Gonyea, James C., *Electronic Resumes: Putting Your Resume On-Line* (New York: McGraw-Hill, 1996)

Gonyea, James C., *The On-Line Job Search Companion* (New York: McGraw-Hill, 1995)

Jandt, Fred E. and Mary Nemnick, *Using the Internet and the World Wide Web in Your Job Search* (Indianapolis, IN: JIST Works, Inc., 1996)

Kennedy, Joyce Lain, *Hook Up, Get Hired* (New York: Wiley & Sons, Inc., 1995)

Kennedy, Joyce Lain and Thomas J. Morrow, *Electronic Job Search Revolution* (New York: Wiley & Sons, Inc., 1996)

Kennedy, Joyce Lain and Thomas J. Morrow, *Electronic Resume Revolution* (New York: Wiley & Sons, Inc. 1996)

Riley, Margaret, Frances Roehm, and Steve Oserman, *The Guide to Internet Job Searching* (Lincolnwood, IL: NTC Publishing, 1996)

Weddle, Peter, *Electronic Resumes for the New Job Market* (Manassas Park, VA: Impact Publications, 1995)

Beware of the Lazy Way to Job Search Success

While electronic job search services may well be the wave of the future, they will by no means displace the more traditional job search methods identified in this book for finding jobs. These are proven methods used by thousands of successful job seekers. Indeed, there is a danger in thinking that the electronic revolution will offer *the* solution to the inefficiencies and ineffectiveness associated with traditional job search methods. As presently practiced, electronic networking is primarily a high-tech method for disseminating resumes to potential employers and for acquiring information on employers.

The problems with present forms of electronic networking are fourfold. First, most networks are primarily designed for and controlled by employers. Job seekers are only included in the networks for the benefit of employers. Indeed, these electronic networks are mostly funded by employers who have online access to participants' resume data. Job seekers' involvement in these networks is that of passive participant who submits an electronic resume and then waits to hear from employers who may or may not refer to their resume. Not surprising, many job seekers may never hear from employers. From the perspective of the job seeker, such a network is merely a high-tech version of the broadcast resume that is mass mailed to numerous employers—one of the most ineffective resume distribution approaches. However, when it focuses on acquiring information, advice, and referrals, electronic networking may become more useful and effective for job seekers.

Second, electronic resume services give employers limited, albeit important, information on candidates. These services are primarily efficient resume screening techniques that communicate little information about the individual beyond traditional résumé categories. Employers still need to screen candidates on other criteria, especially in face-to-face settings, which enable them to assess a candidate's personal chemistry. Such information is best communicated by networking with your resume.

Third, the major sponsors and participants—large Fortune 1000 companies—in the electronic resume banks are not the ones that do most of the hiring. These are the same companies that have been shedding jobs—nearly 5 million in the past eight years—rather than adding them to the job market. The companies that do the most hiring and thus add the most jobs to the workforce—small companies with fewer than 500 employees—are not major participants in the electronic resume banks. Therefore, you are well advised to target your job search toward the companies that generate the most jobs.

Fourth, the quality of information, advice, and referrals gained from electronic networking may be very poor or nearly useless because of the types of individuals participating in such relatively anonymous networks. You may, for example, be communicating with a kid, someone who is unemployed, people with little or no experience, or even a scam artist or a sociopath! Busy employers and employment experts—those who can really make a difference when you are engaged in quality networking—don't have the luxury of spending time online networking with strangers. If they did, they might soon be out of a job for engaging in what are ostensibly nonproductive activities.

Conduct a Dynamite Job Search

So where does this all lead in terms of your job search? We recommend that you include electronic elements in your overall repertoire of job search methods. But put these electronic elements in their proper perspective—an efficient way to broadcast your qualifications to employers through an electronic resume as well as acquire potentially useful information about jobs, employers, and job search methods through online information gathering and networking activities. Above all, avoid paying for questionable online employment services; check out an organization's performance before you send money. Don't approach electronic networking as the easy way to job search success; there's nothing magical about disseminating resumes electronically nor communicating with strangers by e-mail. Sending a $10, $20, or $50 membership fee and a resume to one of these firms ensures you nothing other than a presence in an electronic resume bank. What happens next—whether or not you are contacted by employers—depends on an unpredictable mix of factors, such as the number and quality of employer members in the system, employer hiring needs at any specific time, and the quality of your electronic resume, especially your choice of resume language. Concentrate on developing a dynamite resume that is most responsive to *both* optical scanners and human beings!

Finding a job still remains hard work. While it does take place within a chaotic arena—the job market—it does not involve a random communication process. If you explore the job market using electronic job search methods, you should be able to acquire a great deal of useful information and perhaps develop productive job leads. Best of all, you can literally conduct your job search 24 hours a day, 7 days a week, and 365 days a year by using such methods. They should further enhance what hopefully already is a dynamite job search for careering and re-careering in the decade ahead.

The Author

Ronald L. Krannich, Ph.D., is president of Development Concepts Incorporated, a training, consulting, and publishing firm. He received his Ph.D. in Political Science from Northern Illinois University where he also specialized in Southeast Asian studies. A former Peace Corps Volunteer, high school teacher, university professor, and Fulbright Scholar, he has completed numerous research, consulting, and advisory projects on local government, population planning, and rural development in Thailand during the past twenty years. He has published several articles in major professional journals.

Ron's work in the career development field began in 1980 as a result of an experimental project he initiated at Old Dominion University in Norfolk, Virginia to introduce students in the liberal arts and humanities to career planning concepts and job search techniques. He collaborated with William Banis, the director of career planning and placement at ODU, in acquiring expertise in the career field. One unexpected result of the project was the publication of his first career book, with William Banis, which also served as Ron's re-careering swan song—*Moving Out of Education*. Shortly thereafter he and his wife, Caryl, established Impact Publications, which is now a major publisher of career books and a center for all types of career resources. Ron and Caryl have conducted numerous job search workshops and seminars in the U.S. and abroad.

Ron and Caryl continue to operate in two career worlds. They have authored or co-authored more than forty books. Several of their career works are now available interactively on CD-ROM (*The Ultimate Job Source*). They continue to pursue their international interests through their innovative *"Treasures and Pleasures . . . Best of the Best"* travel series.

When not found at their home or business in Virginia, Ron and Caryl are probably somewhere in Europe, Asia, Africa, the Middle East, the South Pacific, or the Caribbean pursuing their other passion—researching and writing about quality arts and antiques.

Index

A

Abilities, 129-137
Achievements (see Accomplishments)
Acceptances, 227, 264-265
Accomplishments, 137, 151-158
Action, 1, 28, 113-114
Advancement, 47
Agreement, 262-263
Aggressiveness, 92
Agriculture, 59
Age, 56, 91
American Entrepreneurs Association, 319
America's Job Bank, 109
Appearance (see Dress)
Applications, 88
Apprenticeships, 40-41, 50, 76-77, 81
Approach letters (see Letters)
Approaches, 26-27
Armed Forces, 77
Assessment:
    centers, 112
    computerized, 137, 142
    self, 100
Assistance, 108-113
Attitudes:
    negative, 2
    success, 120
    worker, 87
Autobiography, 137
Automation, 71

B

Baby-boomers, 31, 41
Behavior:
    deterministic theory of, 135
    patterns of, 2
Benefits, 48, 50, 263-264
Business:
    behavior, 4
    failures, 312
    high-tech, 316
    questions, 316-318
    resources, 318-319
    service, 316
    starting, 46-47, 311-320
    success, 319-320
Businesses, 46-47

C

California, 46, 92
Career:
    advancement, 47, 92
    alternatives, 210-214
    changing, 48-49
    check-up, 271-272
    conferences, 112
    counselors, 4, 107-108
    defined, 99
    development, 100-103
    goals, 242
    planning, 24
    shaping, 3
    services, 108-113

Careering:
  competencies, 104-106
  process of, 3, 5, 7, 26
  successful, 24
Careers:
  declining, 87
  emerging, 65-66
  hottest, 60
  multiple, 3
  pursuing, 51
Change, 3, 30, 37-51
Cities, 291
Classified ads, 88, 192-193
Closings, 231
Cold War, 14
College placement offices, 109-110
Colleges (see Universities)
Communication:
  business, 189
  face-to-face, 223
  informal, 223
  interviews as, 240
  skills, 120, 224
  word-of-mouth, 223
Communities:
  best, 291-294
  booming, 97
  declining, 45
  growing, 45, 280-291
  researching, 218-221
  selecting, 299-300
  stagnant, 23
  structure of, 307-310
  targeting, 278-280
Community colleges, 43-44, 78
Commuting, 302-303
Companies:
  large, 47
  small, 96-97
Competition, 48, 89, 97
Computerized assessment systems, 79
Connections, 93
Contacts, 230-232
Correspondence courses (see Home Study)
Costs:
  living, 302
  relocation, 300-302

Cover letters (see Letters)
Craftspeople, 40-41
Crises, 40-41

D
Demographics (see Population)
Downsizing, 18, 47
Dress, 251-255

E
Economy:
  boom/bust, 12-15, 21, 68
  high tech, 25
  service, 25
Education:
  acquiring more, 93
  costs, 83-84
  curriculum, 43-44
  employment, 58-59
  financing, 82-83
  institutions, 4
  performance, 72-73, 84
  policies, 70
  programs, 71-84
  questions about, 241-242
  reforms, 70
  requirements, 57, 66
  system, 12
Educators, 44
Elderly, 41, 56
Electronic:
  communications, 237-238
  cottage, 36, 51
  databases, 193-194
  job search, 95-96
  resumes, 95-96, 193-194
Employers:
  benefits of, 96-97
  best, 294-298
  communicating with, 269
  hiring by, 90
  needs of, 132, 161-162
  training by, 76
Employment:
  agencies, 88, 109
  cyclical, 68
  dynamics, 15-19
  firms, 91-92, 98

forecasts, 55-60
high, 14
paradox, 16
part-time, 42-43
temporary, 42-43, 91-92, 109
white-collar, 43
Empowerment, 4-5, 7
Enthusiasm, 121
Entrepreneurship, 47-48, 311-320
Ethnic groups, 56
Executive recruiters, 110
Executive search firms, 110-111
Executives, 48
Experience, 90
Eye contact, 225-256

F
Families:
declining, 70
two-career, 42
Fields, 90-91
Firing (see Termination)
Fishing, 59
Follow-up, 94, 257
Forestry, 59
Force field analysis, 175
Forecasts, 55-60
Franchises, 314
Future:
charting, 2
image of, 3
objectives, 148
projecting into, 163-177

G
Generalists, 74-75
Goals, 11, 120, 160-161
Government:
employment, 58
programs, 5, 38-39, 69-70, 77
stimulation, 38-39
training, 69
Groups, 123-125

H
Haldane Associates, 150-153
Hard work, 93
Headhunters, 110-111

Hidden job market, 88
Hiring, 48
Home study, 77-78, 81
Honesty, 120, 229

I
Images, 181, 253-255
Immigration, 33-34, 41-42
Implementation, 6, 321-329
Individuals, 15, 20
Inflation, 14
Informational interviews (see
Interviews)
Innovation, 35
Interests, 138-149
International:
changes, 14, 21
crises, 39-40
economy, 16
Internet, 358-360
Interviews:
behavior-based, 247-249
closing, 256-257
conducting, 232-234, 239-257
face-to-face, 241
getting, 222
importance of, 239
informational, 88, 190, 222, 229,
233-234
job, 239-257
telephone, 241

J
Job:
alternatives, 210-215
banks, 96
changing, 48-49, 92-93
clubs, 123-124, 236-237
creation, 21
dissatisfaction, 87
end of, 87
fairs, 112
generation, 25
growth, 55
hopping, 3, 48-49
ideal, 169
interviews, 239-257
leads, 227-228, 234-236
lock, 12

offers, 264-265
off-shore, 50
revitalization, 275-276
satisfaction, 48
shortages, 40-41
survival, 273-274
vacancies, 98
Job-keeping, 272-274
Job market:
  competitive, 89
  concept of, 86
  decentralized, 99
  global, 50-51
  hidden, 88
  local, 305-307
  structure of, 88, 99
Job search:
  contract, 325-326
  firms, 110
  long-distance, 303-305
  skills, 3, 24-25
  steps, 102-104
  targeting, 98
Jobs:
  advertised, 88
  best, 64-65
  entry-level, 38
  finding, 88
  future, 53-67
  hot, 49, 60, 90-91
  manufacturing, 59
  new, 40

K
Key people, 230-232
Key words, 348

L
Labor:
  force, 56
  shortages, 34, 42
Lawyers, 55
Leads, 227-228
Letters:
  approach, 190, 230-231
  cover, 190
  distributing, 191
  job search, 95, 188-189

preparation, 189
resumes with, 231
sample, 201-208
thank you, 190-191, 234,
  269-270
types of, 95, 190-191
writing, 95
Lifestyles, 11
Likability, 90, 225, 240, 255-256
Listening, 121
Literacy, 31-32

M
Manufacturing, 37-38, 59
Market research, 171
Marketing services, 111
MBAs, 54-55
Microprocessors, 36
Midwest, 46
Migration, 45-46
Mining, 59
Minorities, 33, 41-42, 56
Motivated skills and abilities
  (MAS), 149-159
Motivated pattern, 149
Motivated Skills Exercise, 135,
  151-152
Motivation, 1, 313-314, 324
Myers-Briggs Type Indicator, 142
Myths, 85-97

N
Negatives, 243-247
Networks:
  community, 307-310
  developing, 225-227
  linking, 225-226
  remembering, 270
Networking:
  community, 307-310
  defined, 225
  electronic, 237-238, 356-361
  process of, 24, 222-238
  using, 93

O
Objections, 243-244
Objectives:

functional, 177
realistic, 162
stating, 160-179
work-centered, 161, 180
Occupational profiles, 53-55
Occupations:
classifying, 60
declining, 63
growing, 54-55, 57, 60-63
new, 59-60
Offers, 264-265
Online services, 356-360
Opportunities, 89
Opportunity structures, 307-310

P

Part-time, 42-43
Pensions, 12
Perceptions, 15
People Management, 150
Performance, 82, 159, 327
Persistence, 2
Personnel offices, 88, 97
Placement offices, 109-110
Planning:
action, 2
excessive, 118
traditional, 29-30
Policies, 12-13
Politics, 13, 98, 270-271
Poor, 17, 72
Population, 30-34, 45-46
Power, 1
Predictions, 21-23
Probability, 227
Production sharing, 34
Productivity, 12, 47, 266
Professional:
assistance, 107
associations, 112-113
certification, 107-108
Prospecting, 24, 222-223
Public employment services,
108-109
Public opinion, 15
Public policy:
employment, 12-13
failures,14, 23

Q

Qualifications, 89-90, 132, 158-159,
222-225
Questions:
answering, 241-249
asking, 121, 131-132, 216-218,
250
business start-up, 316-318
career goals, 242
education, 241-242
illegal, 249-250
informational interview, 232-234
personality, 242-243
salary, 259-262
work experience, 242

R

Race, 56
Re-careering, 3, 5, 7, 26
Recession, 14-15, 39
Recordkeeping, 194
Redundancy, 158
Referrals, 223
Regionalism, 46
Regions, 45-46
Rejections, 89, 122-123, 224, 228,
324
Relocation, 20, 25, 45-46, 49, 97,
277-310
Renegotiations, 264
Research:
community, 218-221
computer, 218
conducting, 88, 209-221
entrepreneurial, 315
individual, 215-216
Internet, 218-219
job, 210-214
library, 175-176
on-line, 175
organizational, 214-215
purposes of, 209-210
questions, 216-218
Resources:
best, 330-346
career, 79-82
electronic, 347-363,
job, 6-7
Results, 27-28

Resume:
  banks, 96, 348-351
  content, 184-185
  databases, 354-356
  "does", 185
  "don'ts", 184-185
  drafts, 185-186
  evaluation, 186-187
  language, 347-348
  letters, 184
  paper, 187
  production, 187-188
  reproduction, 188
  salary on, 94
  work history on, 94-95
Resumes:
  broadcasting, 97
  chronological, 183
  combination, 184
  effective, 186
  electronic, 95-96, 193-194
  functional, 184
  ineffective, 182-183
  improved chronological, 183-184
  producing, 181-208
  sample, 196-201
  software sensitive, 346-348
  traditional chronological, 183
  types of, 183-184
  using, 94
Retail trade, 58
Retirement, 33, 41
Retraining, 20, 32, 70
Rewards, 51
Risks, 1, 122-123, 312-314

S
Salaries:
  determining, 96
  executive, 49
  increase in, 49
  negotiating, 97, 258-266
Salary:
  expectations, 94
  issues, 259-260
  negotiations, 258-266
  question, 260-262
Secretaries, 230

Self-employment, 41
Service:
  industries, 37-38
  occupations, 58
  sector, 22
  society, 52
Sincerity, 229
Sitting, 255
Skills:
  exercises, 135
  functional/transferable, 130-135
  identifying, 129-137
  imbalance, 68-69
  job search, 3, 24, 88
  technical, 25
  training, 69, 74
  types of, 130-131
  work-content, 3, 24, 25, 130
Skills Map, 136, 150-151
Smiling, 256
Specialists, 74-75
Stock market, 145
Stories, 150, 249
Strangers, 225
Strengths, 131, 138, 165, 241, 314
Strong Interest Inventory, 142
Success, 86, 118-122
Support groups, 123-125, 236-237

T
Tactfulness, 121
Taxes, 13
Technical schools, 81
Technology, 34-35, 71
Telephone, 193, 234-236
Temporary jobs, 42-43
Termination, 191, 224
Testing centers, 112
Thoughtfulness, 121, 191
Time:
  finding, 325
  managing, 114-117
Trade, 39
Trade schools, 81
Training, 20, 32, 69, 75-79, 93
Trends, 37-51, 60-67
Turbulence, 29-30

U

Unemployment
    cyclical, 18, 38, 68
    insurance, 20
    international, 72
    long-term, 51
    rates of, 3, 12, 16, 21
    state/metro, 281-288
    structural, 20, 22
Unions, 44-45
Unique events, 39-40, 46
Universities, 44, 78, 82

V

Value, 132, 259
Values, 143-148, 165
Vocational:
    education, 75-76
    interests, 138-142
Voice, 256

W

Waiting, 93-94
Wardrobe (see Dress)
Washington, DC, 308-310
Weaknesses, 132
Welfare, 18
Women, 33, 42, 56-57
Women's Centers, 111
Work:
    history, 94-95
    values, 143-148
Workers:
    contingency, 43
    displaced, 19
    shortage of, 37
    unskilled, 31-32

Y

Youth, 31, 41, 56

Career Resources

C ontact Impact Publications for a free annotated listing of career resources or visit their World Wide Web site for a complete listing of career resources: http://www.impactpublications.com.

The following career resources, many of which were mentioned in previous chapters, are available directly from Impact Publications. Complete the following form or list the titles, include postage (see formula at the end), enclose payment, and send your order to:

IMPACT PUBLICATIONS
9104-N Manassas Drive
Manassas Park, VA 20111-2366
Tel. 703/361-7300 or Fax 703/335-9486
E-mail address: impactp@impactpublications.com

Orders from individuals must be prepaid by check, moneyorder, Visa, MasterCard, or American Express. We accept telephone and fax orders.

Qty.	TITLES	Price	TOTAL
____	Change Your Job, Change Your Life	$17.95	_____

Key Directories/Reference Works

Qty.	TITLES	Price	TOTAL
____	500 Largest U.S. Corporations	14.95	_____
____	American Almanac of Jobs and Salaries	20.00	_____
____	American Salaries & Wages Survey	105.00	_____
____	Big Book of Minority Opportunities	39.95	_____
____	Big Book of Opportunities For Women	39.95	_____
____	Business Phone Book USA 1997	135.00	_____
____	Careers Encyclopedia	39.95	_____
____	Complete Directory For People With Disabilities	149.95	_____
____	_Complete_ Guide For Occupational Exploration	39.95	_____
____	Consultants & Consulting Organizations Directory	545.00	_____
____	Dictionary of Occupational Titles	39.95	_____

____	Directory of Executive Recruiters 1997	44.95	____
____	Directory of Federal Jobs and Employers	21.95	____
____	Encyclopedia of Associations 1997	1,149.00	____
____	Encyclopedia of Careers/Vocational Guidance	149.95	____
____	*Enhanced* Guide For Occupational Exploration	34.95	____
____	Government Phone Book USA 1997	185.00	____
____	Guide to Internet Databases	114.00	____
____	**HOOVER'S KEY EMPLOYER DIRECTORIES**	**141.95**	____
____	▪ Hoover's 500	29.95	____
____	▪ Hoover's Emerging Companies 1996	29.95	____
____	▪ Hoover's Guide to Computer Companies	34.95	____
____	▪ Hoover's Handbook of World Business	27.95	____
____	▪ Hoover's Top 2,500 Employers	22.95	____
____	Internships 1997	24.95	____
____	**JOB FINDERS FOR 1997**	**50.95**	____
____	▪ Government Job Finder	16.95	____
____	▪ Nonprofit's and Education Job Finder	16.95	____
____	▪ Professional's Private Sector Job Finder	18.95	____
____	Job Hunter's Sourcebook	69.95	____
____	Job Hunter's Yellow Pages	35.00	____
____	Jobs Rated Almanac	16.95	____
____	Moving & Relocation Sourcebook	179.95	____
____	National Job Hotline Directory 1997	14.95	____
____	National Trade & Professional Associations	85.00	____
____	Occupational Outlook Handbook	16.95	____
____	Personnel Executives Contactbook	149.00	____
____	Professional Careers Sourcebook	99.95	____
____	Student Access Guide: The Internship Bible	25.00	____
____	Training & Development Organizations Directory	389.00	____
____	U.S. Industrial Outlook	29.95	____
____	Vocational Careers Sourcebook	84.95	____

City and State Job Banks

____	Job Bank Guide to Employment Services 1996-1997	159.95	____
____	**METROPOLITAN EMPLOYER CONTACT**		
	DIRECTORIES KIT (51 titles)	**873.95**	____
____	▪ Atlanta (Job Bank)	16.95	____
____	▪ Atlanta (How to Get a Job in)	16.95	____
____	▪ Austin/San Antonio (Job Bank)	16.95	____
____	▪ Boston (Job Bank)	16.95	____
____	▪ Boston & New England (Job Seekers)	15.95	____
____	▪ Carolina (Job Bank)	15.95	____
____	▪ Cincinnati (Job Bank)	16.95	____
____	▪ Chicago (Job Bank)	16.95	____
____	▪ Chicago (How to Get a Job in)	16.95	____
____	▪ Chicago & Illinois (Job Seekers)	15.95	____
____	▪ Chicago Area Companies (Hoover's Guide...)	24.95	____
____	▪ Cleveland (Job Bank)	16.95	____
____	▪ Dallas/Fort Worth (Job Bank)	16.95	____
____	▪ Denver (Job Bank)	15.95	____
____	▪ Detroit (Job Bank)	16.95	

____ ▪ Europe (How to Get a Job in)   17.95 _____
____ ▪ Florida (Job Bank)   16.95 _____
____ ▪ Houston (Job Bank)   16.95 _____
____ ▪ Indianapolis (Job Bank)   16.95 _____
____ ▪ Las Vegas (Job Bank)   16.95 _____
____ ▪ Los Angeles (Job Bank)   16.95 _____
____ ▪ Los Angeles & S. California (Job Seekers)   16.95 _____
____ ▪ Mid-Atlantic (Job Seekers)   15.95 _____
____ ▪ Minneapolis/St. Paul (Job Bank)   16.95 _____
____ ▪ Missouri (Job Bank)   16.95 _____
____ ▪ Mountain & Plains States (Job Seekers)   15.95 _____
____ ▪ New Mexico (Job Bank)   16.95 _____
____ ▪ New York (Job Bank)   16.95 _____
____ ▪ New York (How to Get a Job in)   16.95 _____
____ ▪ New York & New Jersey (Job Seekers)   15.95 _____
____ ▪ New York Area Companies (Hoover's Guide...)   24.95 _____
____ ▪ North New England (Job Bank)   16.95 _____
____ ▪ Ohio (Job Bank)   16.95 _____
____ ▪ Pacific Northwest (Job Seekers)   15.95 _____
____ ▪ Philadelphia (Job Bank)   16.95 _____
____ ▪ Phoenix (Job Bank)   15.95 _____
____ ▪ Pittsburgh (Job Bank)   16.95 _____
____ ▪ Portland (Job Bank)   16.95 _____
____ ▪ San Francisco (Job Bank)   16.95 _____
____ ▪ San Francisco (How to Get a Job in)   16.95 _____
____ ▪ Seattle (Job Bank)   16.95 _____
____ ▪ Seattle/Portland (How to Get a Job in)   16.95 _____
____ ▪ Southern California (How to Get a Job in)   16.95 _____
____ ▪ Southern California Area Companies (Hoover's...)   24.95 _____
____ ▪ Southern States (Job Seekers)   15.95 _____
____ ▪ Southwest (Job Seekers)   15.95 _____
____ ▪ Tennessee (Job Bank)   16.95 _____
____ ▪ Texas Area Companies (Hoover's Guide...)   24.95 _____
____ ▪ Upstate New York (Job Bank)   16.95 _____
____ ▪ Virginia (Job Bank)   16.95 _____
____ ▪ Washington, DC (Job Bank)   16.95 _____
____ National Job Bank 1997   294.95 _____

Using the Internet and Computers

____ Be Your Own Headhunter Online   16.00 _____
____ Electronic Job Search Revolution   12.95 _____
____ Electronic Resume Revolution   12.95 _____
____ Electronic Resumes: Putting Your Resume On-Line   19.95 _____
____ Electronic Resumes For the New Job Market   11.95 _____
____ Finding a Job On the Internet   16.95 _____
____ Getting On the Information Superhighway   11.95 _____
____ Guide to Internet Job Searching   14.95 _____
____ Hook Up, Get Hired   12.95 _____
____ How to Get Your Dream Job Using the Internet   29.99 _____
____ Net Jobs: How to Use the Internet   12.95 _____

____ On-Line Job Search Companion	16.95	____
____ Point and Click Jobfinder	14.95	____
____ Selling On the Internet	24.95	____
____ Three-Rs of E-Mail	12.95	____
____ Using the Internet and the WWW in Your Job Search	16.95	____
____ Using WordPerfect In Your Job Search	19.95	____

Finding Great Jobs and Careers

____ 100 Best Careers For the 21st Century	15.95	____
____ 100 Fastest Growing Companies in America	14.95	____
____ 101 Great Answers/Toughest Job Search Problems	11.99	____
____ 101 Ways to Power Up Your Job Search	12.95	____
____ 110 Biggest Mistakes Job Hunters Make	15.95	____
____ 150 Best Companies For Liberal Arts Grads	14.95	____
____ 303 Off the Wall Ways to Get a Job	12.99	____
____ Adams Jobs Almanac 1997	15.95	____
____ Adventure Careers	11.99	____
____ American Almanac of Jobs & Salaries	20.00	____
____ America's Top Jobs Book Plus CD-ROM	39.95	____
____ Best Jobs For the 1990s & Into the 21st Century	19.95	____
____ But What If I Don't Want to Go to College	10.95	____
____ Career Atlas	12.99	____
____ Career Finder	16.00	____
____ Career Planning For the 1990s	12.95	____
____ Career Success Formula	10.95	____
____ Careers For College Majors	32.95	____
____ Careers in Computers	17.95	____
____ Careers in Education	17.95	____
____ Careers in Health Care	17.95	____
____ Careers in High Tech	17.95	____
____ Careers in Multimedia	24.95	____
____ Change Your Job, Change Your Life	17.95	____
____ Complete Idiot's Guide to Getting the Job You Want	24.95	____
____ Complete Job Finder's Guide to the 90's	13.95	____
____ Complete Job Search Handbook	13.95	____
____ Crystal-Barkley Career Design Handbook	9.95	____
____ Dare to Change Your Job and Your Life	14.95	____
____ Directory of Executive Recruiters 1997	44.95	____
____ Dynamite Job Finding Skills For the 90's	69.95	____
____ End of Work	15.95	____
____ Five Secrets to Finding a Job	12.95	____
____ Free and Inexpensive Career Materials	19.95	____
____ Get a Job You Love!	19.95	____
____ Hidden Job Market 1997	18.95	____
____ Hi-Tech Jobs For Lo-Tech People	16.95	____
____ Hoover's Top 2,500 Employers	22.95	____
____ How to Get Interviews From Classified Job Ads	14.95	____
____ How to Make Use of a Useless Degree	13.00	____
____ How to Strengthen Your Winning Business Personality	11.95	____
____ How to Succeed Without a Career Path	13.95	____
____ How You Really Get Hired	11.00	

____ In Transition	12.50	____
____ Job Finding Skills For Smart Dummies	37.95	____
____ Job Hunter's Word Finder	12.95	____
____ Job Hunting For Dummies	16.99	____
____ Job Hunter's Catalog	10.95	____
____ Jobs 1997	16.00	____
____ Jobs and Careers With Nonprofit Organizations	15.95	____
____ Jobs For Lawyers	14.95	____
____ Jobs Rated Almanac	16.95	____
____ Joyce Lain Kennedy's Career Book	29.95	____
____ Knock 'Em Dead 1997	12.95	____
____ Mid-Career Job Hunting	14.00	____
____ NBEW's Job Search Books	63.75	____
____ *New* Complete Guide to Environmental Careers	15.95	____
____ *New* Relocating Spouse's Guide to Employment	14.95	____
____ Nonprofits and Education Job Finder	16.95	____
____ Outdoor Careers	16.95	____
____ Overnight Job Finder	23.95	____
____ Part-Time Jobs	32.95	____
____ Professional's Private Sector Job Finder	18.95	____
____ Quantum Companies	24.95	____
____ Rites of Passage at $100,000+	29.95	____
____ Researching Your Way to a Good Job	14.95	____
____ Resumes Don't Get Jobs	10.95	____
____ Top 10 Fears of Job Seekers	12.00	____
____ Very Quick Job Search	14.95	____
____ What Color Is Your Parachute? 1997	16.95	____
____ World Almanac Job Finder's Guide 1997	24.95	____

Cover Letters

____ 175 High-Impact Cover Letters	10.95	____
____ 200 Letters for Job Hunters	19.95	____
____ 201 Dynamite Job Search Letters	19.95	____
____ 201 Killer Cover Letters	16.95	____
____ Adams Cover Letter Almanac and Disk	19.95	____
____ Cover Letters For Dummies	12.99	____
____ Cover Letters That Knock 'Em Dead	10.95	____
____ Dynamite Cover Letters	14.95	____
____ NBEW's Cover Letters	11.95	____
____ Perfect Cover Letter	9.95	____
____ Sure-Hire Cover Letters	10.95	____

Resumes

____ 100 Winning Résumés for $100,000+ Jobs	24.95	____
____ 101 Great Résumés	9.99	____
____ 101 Résumés for Sure-Hire Results	10.95	____
____ 175 High-Impact Résumés	10.95	____
____ Adams Résumé Almanac	10.95	____
____ Asher's Bible of Executive Résumés	29.95	____

___	Best Résumés for $75,000+ Executive Jobs	14.95	___
___	Complete Idiot's Guide to Crafting the Perfect Résumé	16.95	___
___	Designing the Perfect Résumé	12.95	___
___	Dynamite Résumés	14.95	___
___	Dynamite Résumés for $100,000+ Jobs	24.95	___
___	Electronic Résumé Revolution	12.95	___
___	Electronic Résumés: Putting Your Résumé On-Line	19.95	___
___	Electronic Résumés for the New Job Market	11.95	___
___	Encyclopedia of Job-Winning Résumés	16.95	___
___	Gallery of Best Résumés	16.95	___
___	Gallery of Best Résumés for Two-Year Degree Graduates	14.95	___
___	High Impact Résumés and Letters	14.95	___
___	How to Prepare Your Curriculum Vitae	14.95	___
___	NBEW's Résumés	11.95	___
___	New Perfect Résumé	10.95	___
___	Power Résumés	12.95	___
___	Quick Résumé and Cover Letter Book	9.95	___
___	Real-Life Résumés That Work!	12.95	___
___	Résumé Catalog	15.95	___
___	Résumé Kit	9.95	___
___	Résumé Pro	24.95	___
___	Résumé Shortcuts	14.95	___
___	Résumé Solution	12.95	___
___	Résumés for Advertising Careers	9.95	___
___	Résumés for Architecture and Related Careers	9.95	___
___	Résumés for Banking and Financial Careers	9.95	___
___	Résumés for Business Management Careers	9.95	___
___	Résumés for College Students and Recent Graduates	9.95	___
___	Résumés for Communications Careers	9.95	___
___	Résumés for Dummies	12.99	___
___	Résumés for Education Careers	9.95	___
___	Résumés for Engineering Careers	9.95	___
___	Résumés for Environmental Careers	9.95	___
___	Résumés for Ex-Military Personnel	9.95	___
___	Résumés for 50+ Job Hunters	9.95	___
___	Résumés for First-Time Job Hunter	9.95	___
___	Résumés for the Healthcare Professional	12.95	___
___	Résumés for High School Graduates	9.95	___
___	Résumés for High Tech Careers	9.95	___
___	Résumés for Midcareer Job Changers	9.95	___
___	Résumés for the Over 50 Job Hunter	14.95	___
___	Résumés for Re-Entering the Job Market	9.95	___
___	Résumés for Sales and Marketing Careers	9.95	___
___	Résumés for Scientific and Technical Careers	9.95	___
___	Résumés That Knock 'Em Dead	10.95	___
___	Résumés, Résumés, Résumés	9.99	___
___	Smart Woman's Guide to Résumés & Job Hunting	9.95	___
___	Sure-Hire Résumés	14.95	___

Skills, Testing, Self-Assessment, Empowerment

___	7 Habits of Highly Effective People	14.00 ___
___	Career Satisfaction and Success	9.95 ___
___	Chicken Soup for the Soul	12.95 ___
___	Discover the Best Jobs for You	11.95 ___
___	Do What You Are	14.95 ___
___	Do What You Love, the Money Will Follow	10.95 ___
___	Love Your Work and Success Will Follow	12.95 ___
___	P.I.E. Method for Career Success	14.95 ___

Dress and Etiquette

___	110 Mistakes Working Women Make...	9.95 ___
___	Dress Casually For Success . ... . For Men	16.95 ___
___	Executive Etiquette in the New Workplace	14.95 ___
___	John Molloy's New Dress For Success (Men)	13.99 ___
___	*New* Women's Dress For Success	12.99 ___
___	Red Socks Don't Work!	14.95 ___
___	Winning Image	17.95 ___

Networking and Power Building

___	Dynamite Networking For Dynamite Jobs	15.95 ___
___	Dynamite Tele-Search	12.95 ___
___	Great Connections	19.95 ___
___	How to Work a Room	11.99 ___
___	NBEW's Networking	10.95 ___
___	Network Your Way to Success	19.95 ___
___	Network Your Way to Your Next Job	14.95 ___
___	Power Networking	14.95 ___
___	Power Schmoozing	12.95 ___
___	Power to Get In	24.95 ___
___	Secrets of Savvy Networking	12.99 ___

Interviewing

___	50 Winning Answers to Interview Questions	10.95 ___
___	60 Seconds and You're Hired	9.95 ___
___	90-Minute Interview Prep Book	15.95 ___
___	101 Dynamite Questions to Ask at Your Job Interview	14.95 ___
___	101 Great Answers/Interview Questions	9.99 ___
___	111 Dynamite Ways to Ace Your Job Interview	13.95 ___
___	Adams Job Interview Almanac	10.95 ___
___	Best Answers to 201 Most/Asked Interview Questions	10.95 ___
___	Conquer Interview Objections	10.95 ___
___	Dynamite Answers to Interview Questions	11.95 ___
___	Dynamite Salary Negotiations	13.95 ___
___	Interview For Success	15.95 ___
___	Interview Kit	10.95 ___

____	Interview Power	12.95	____
____	Job Interviews For Dummies	12.99	____
____	Killer Interviews	10.95	____
____	Naked At the Interview	10.95	____
____	NBEW's Interviewing	11.95	____
____	Perfect Follow-Up Method to Win the Job	12.95	____
____	Power Interviews	12.95	____
____	Quick Interview and Salary Negotiation Book	12.95	____
____	Sweaty Palms	8.95	____

SUBTOTAL _____

Virginia residents add 4½% sales tax _____

POSTAGE/HANDLING ($4.00 for first
title and $1.50 for each additional book) $4.00

Number of additional titles x $1.50----------------- _____

TOTAL ENCLOSED --------------------- _____

SHIP TO:

NAME _____

ADDRESS _____

_____

❑ I enclose check/moneyorder for $ _____ made payable to
IMPACT PUBLICATIONS.

❑ Please charge $ _____ to my credit card:

❑ Visa   ❑ MasterCard   ❑ American Express

Card # _____

Expiration date: _____

Signature _____

We accept official purchase orders from libraries, educational institutions, and
government offices. Please attach copy with official signature(s).

The On-Line Superstore & Warehouse
*Hundreds of Terrific Career Resources Conveniently Available
On the World Wide Web 24-Hours a Day, 365 Days a Year!*

Ever wanted to know what are the newest and best books, directories, newsletters, wall charts, training programs, videos, CD-ROMs, computer software, and kits available to help you land a job, negotiate a higher salary, or start your own business? What about finding a job in Asia or relocating to San Francisco? Are you curious about how to find a job 24-hours a day by using the Internet or what to do after you leave the military? Trying to keep up-to-date on the latest career resources but not able to find the latest catalogs, brochures, or newsletters on today's "best of the best" resources?

Welcome to the first virtual career bookstore on the Internet. Now you're only a "click" away with Impact Publication's electronic solution to the resource challenge. Impact Publications, one of the nation's leading publishers and distributors of career resources, has launched its comprehensive "Career Superstore and Warehouse" on the Internet. The bookstore is jam-packed with the latest resources focusing on several key career areas:

- Alternative jobs and careers
- Self-assessment
- Career planning and job search
- Employers
- Relocation and cities
- Resumes
- Cover Letters
- Dress, image, and etiquette
- Education
- Telephone
- Military
- Salaries
- Interviewing
- Nonprofits
- Empowerment
- Self-esteem
- Goal setting
- Executive recruiters
- Entrepreneurship
- Government
- Networking
- Electronic job search
- International jobs
- Travel
- Law
- Training and presentations
- Minorities
- Physically challenged

"This is more than just a bookstore offering lots of product," say Drs. Ron and Caryl Krannich, two of the nation's leading career experts and authors and developers of this on-line bookstore. *"We're an important resource center for libraries, corporations, government, educators, trainers, and career counselors who are constantly defining and redefining this dynamic field. Of the thousands of career resources we review each year, we only select the 'best of the best.'"*

Visit this rich site and you'll quickly discover just about everything you ever wanted to know about finding jobs, changing careers, and starting your own business—including many useful resources that are difficult to find in local bookstores and libraries. The site also includes what's new and hot, tips for job search success, and monthly specials. Impact's Web address is:

http://www.impactpublications.com